D1595962

The Mother of All Hooks

The Story of the U.S. Navy's
TAILHOOK SCANDAL

The Mother of All Hooks

William H. McMichael
WITH A FOREWORD BY CHARLES C. MOSKOS

TRANSACTION PUBLISHERS
New Brunswick (U.S.A.) and London (U.K.)

Library of Congress Catalog Number: 96-49046
ISBN: 1–56000–293-X
Printed in the United States of America

Library of Congress Cataloging-in-Publication Data

McMichael, William H.
    The mother of all hooks : the story of the U.S. Navy's Tailhook
Scandal / William H. McMichael ; with a foreword by Charles C.
Moskos.
        p.   cm.
    Includes index.
    ISBN 1-56000-293-X (cloth : alk. paper)
    1. United States. Navy—Women.   2. Sexual harrassment of women—
United States.   3. Tailhook Scandal, 1991-1993.   I. Title.
VB324.W65M38   1997
359.1'334—dc21   96-49046
                                                                        CIP

For Mom and Dad
and for Bonnie, always

Contents

Acknowledgments

The writing of a book in one's spare time is a contradiction in terms; in the course of completing the project, there is none. This book has taken much from my family, yet it is their steadfast love and support that has helped sustain me through many fits and starts.

I started thinking about writing this story on the cold Norfolk day that Capt. William T. Vest threw out the charges against the Navy's three remaining Tailhook defendants. It seemed historic, a watershed; and in the daily grind of turning out stories on what happened at this or that day's hearing, or the bigger picture of whether the Navy was ever going to right itself in terms of the treatment of women, a lot of the gray areas weren't being explored. I thought it was important that someone try to tell the whole story.

Outside my immediate family, thanks are due many individuals. Attorneys Mike Kmetz, Don Marcari, Charles Gittins, Lt. Cmdr. Jeffrey Good, Dave Beck and, especially, Robert Rae, Alan Bergstrom, and Mike Powell, spent many long hours with me discussing Tailhook in the course of interviews as well as informal chats. I thank them for the many thousands of pages of documents they shared with me, and for putting up with my sometimes-incessant (and late-night) phone calls.

I also thank the many, many dozens of active and retired Navy and Marine Corps officers who generously shared their experiences, thoughts, and insights with me over the past three years.

Also due thanks are several professional colleagues who, at various times, shared documents with me or, through general conversation, furthered my understanding of various Tailhook-related matters. These include Kerry DeRochi, on sabbatical from *The Virginian-Pilot*, Bill

Geroux of the *Richmond Times-Dispatch*, Joe Taylor of The Associated Press, Dan Weikel of the *Los Angeles Times*, and Gregory Vistica of *Newsweek* and formerly of the *San Diego Union-Tribune*. I would also like to thank my former first-line editor at the *Daily Press*, Dennis Elder, for his patience and assistance during the ten long months I was bringing him Tailhook stories back from Norfolk.

I also thank my colleague and *Daily Press* columnist Jim Spencer for editing the final chapter and the *Daily Press*, for granting me all rights to my notes on Tailhook-related matters. Special thanks go to the newspaper's librarians, all of whom put up with me and at one time or another helped me locate documents that found their way into the text as well as my articles.

A special note of thanks, also, to attorneys David Delpierre and Steve Noona of the Newport News, Va., law firm Kaufman and Canoles for their generous assistance.

I am especially indebted to Charles Moskos, who, in addition to writing the book's foreword, generously took the time to forward the original proposal to Transaction on my behalf.

My wonderful children Patrick, Evan, and Erin missed out on a lot of one-on-one time while this project was being completed. I owe them a lot. At least they now have answers to their ever-patient questions, "How thick is your book, Dad?" and "When is your book coming out, Dad?"

One's first book is usually, I suppose, a process marked by confusion, uncertainty, and insecurity. Through it all, my wife Bonnie has given me the encouragement and strength to stay focused on those weeknights and weekends when I was just plain burned out. It's hard enough being married to a journalist—cooking all the dinners and driving the kids to music lessons or baseball practice because Dad's not home yet, and not exactly living the life of Riley while doing so—without also working thirty hours a week and taking two college classes. It is the way she has given to me and believed in me that is largely responsible for the successful completion of this book.

Foreword

Charles C. Moskos

The trials and tribulations of Tailhook seemingly never end. Five years after the 1991 convention of naval aviators, the fallout continues. The debauched happenings—strippers performing public sex, men walking about with their genitalia exposed, women groped and abused in the infamous "gantlet" on the third floor of the Las Vegas Hilton—are well known.

Although the immediate events revolving around Tailhook were well covered by the media, the implications for civil-military relations have generally escaped sustained attention. This is where we are indebted to William H. McMichael, Jr. for this book. McMichael gives us not only much new information on the events at the Tailhook convention, but also an original perspective on how subsequent developments have affected civil-military relations.

The Mother of All Hooks operates at several levels. For starters, we get a striking sense of what is was like to be at the 1991 Tailhook convention and the hearings that followed. Tailhook conventions were always unique because they condoned sleazy behavior that customarily took place on liberty only in overseas ports. Tailhook conventioneers also believed that the nominal standards of behavior did not apply because they routinely performed the most dangerous work anywhere in the military—flying a fixed-wing aircraft on to a moving ship.

Second, we see these happenings from different vantage points. On the one side, we observe the intimidating procedures of the prosecutors—badgering and intimidation (promising pilots they would be left off lightly if they would report on others). On the other, we watch the stonewalling and collusion of the investigated (to keep their self-serving stories in harmony). Suffice it to say, that neither side comes off well there. This Rashomon effect does, however, give the reader some empathy for both the accusers and the accused.

Third, we have an account of how new gender roles affected the aviation community. The customary debauchery of male pilots at Tailhook conventions was heightened in 1991 by the widespread resentment of the new directives that allowed women to enter the elite flying corps. Many male pilots viewed (and continue to do so) the presence of women in combat aircraft as a social experiment with inevitable compromise of standards.

The issue of compromised standards received impetus when Lieutenant Kara Hultgreen was killed in 1994 when attempting to land her airplane on the aircraft carrier *Abraham Lincoln*. Disgruntled Navy officers leaked records that purportedly showed Hultgreen had deficiencies in flight training that would have disqualified a male pilot. The Navy denied this and insisted the cause of the accident was due to mechanical failure. To compound matters, male pilots were later placed in a "simulation" of Hultgreen's accident and none were unable to recover the aircraft. Rather than resolving matters, critics charged that the Navy constructed the simulation in such way that no pilot could recover, thus continuing the cover-up of Hultgreen's qualifications.

Nothing could be more retrograde for women's rights than a double standard in performance. And it was in the official actions following Tailhook that the double standard became most blatant. None of the women who attended Tailhook was ever subjected to investigation for improper acts. This omission is most perplexing. I had the opportunity to have a private meeting with Les Aspin shortly after his leaving the office of secretary of defense. I asked him why no female officer who had misbehaved at Tailhook was reprimanded. He replied: "I don't know. I never thought of it before."

Beyond the immediate facts of Tailhook, William McMichael leads us to yet another level of analysis. Civil-military relations in a democratic society is a two-way affair. The armed forces must be under the control of the elected civilian leadership and its appointees. At the same time, we must be wary about political intrusion into the military profession in its promotion processes (as well as in the certification of other professionals, such as lawyers, doctors, and yes, even professors.) The politicizing of promotion procedures in the military is most alarming, indeed. This danger has increased exponentially since Tailhook.

Following the 1991 Tailhook convention, pressure to produce some convictions to assuage the Administration, the Congress, and the public was intense. Internal military investigative agencies shifted their focus from crimes of commission of junior officers to crimes of omission by senior officers—their failure to stop sexual misconduct. One of McMichael's major conclusions is that the Navy is incapable of investigating itself and the Department of Defense is not much better.

The blunt truth of the matter is that those guilty of the most serious assaults got away, and that the careers of some who were innocent were ruined. On top of this, both the secretary of the Navy, H. Lawrence Garrett, and the chief of naval operations, Admiral Frank B. Kelso, had attended the convention and, most likely, witnessed some of the sexual misbehavior. Captain William T. Vest, a Navy officer for twenty-eight years and the military judge, stated he found Kelso to be unconvincing in denying that he had been present near the area where some of the worst behavior was occurring. Admiral Kelso subsequently plea-bargained his way to an early retirement. (Secretary Garrett was forced to resign shortly after Tailhook.) If there is a hero in McMichael's book, it is surely Captain Vest.

The intersect of politics and the promotion process is where McMichael's book informs us of new developments in civil-military relations. In May 1992, the Senate Armed Services Committee requested that all officers who were present at the Tailhook convention be "flagged," not just those accused of misbehavior but anyone who attended. In this way, when Navy promotions came up for consideration, the Senate would know whether or not the officers had been present at the Tailhook convention.

The case of Commander Robert Stumpf became a cause célèbre and is well covered by McMichael. In brief, Stumpf, a former Blues Angels commander who had been decorated for bravery in the Gulf War, attended a Tailhook party featuring strippers. The festivities degenerated into oral sex acts, but every witness present swears these occurred only after Stumpf had left. The Navy inadvertently failed to flag Stumpf's file and in 1994 he was promoted to captain. Upon learning of Stumpf's attendance at the Tailhook party, the Armed Services Committee sought to pull back the promotion even though Stumpf had been found innocent of any wrongdoing by a Navy Court of Inquiry. Stumpf subsequently announced he was retiring from the Navy in October of 1996 without the promotion.

The case of Admiral Stanley R. Arthur shows even more politicization of the promotion process. Arthur was a genuine war hero. He had flown hundreds of combat missions in Vietnam and was commander of Navy air in the Gulf War. With an impeccable record, Arthur was nominated to be commander of American forces in the Pacific. Arthur's nomination was quashed when Minnesota Senator David Durenberger asked on behalf of a constituent why Arthur approved a report upholding her being eliminated from flight school. The woman had asserted that her failure was due to sexual harassment. With Tailhook in mind, the new chief of naval operations, Jeremy M. Boorda, expressed fear that the confirmation process would drag the Navy through another long hearing about sexual harassment. He withdraw Arthur's nomination and Arthur retired from the Navy. Later Boorda was quoted as saying that this was "the biggest mistake of my career."

For failure to stand by Arthur, Boorda was publicly castigated by two former secretaries of the Navy: John Lehman and James Webb; They characterized the chief of naval operations, by name or innuendo, as being opportunistic or cowardly by failing to resist political pressures in the promotion process.

Boorda committed suicide on May 16, 1996. The conventional explanation of Boorda's suicide was the forthcoming exposure of his wearing combat medals that were unauthorized. Yet, it is significant that shortly after Boorda's death, Secretary of Defense William J. Perry announced that the flagging of Tailhook attendees would be stopped in the Navy's promotion process. We shall never know the full story of why Boorda took his own life, but that he felt he had lost the respect of many senior commanders because of Tailhook cannot be discounted as a contributing factor.

Another death of a career service man has some eerie parallels with that of Boorda. Coast Guard Captain Ernie Blanchard, that service's chief of public affairs, told several off-color jokes at a banquet given at the Coast Guard Academy in January 1995. The Coast Guard immediately began an investigation into whether Blanchard's remarks constituted sexual harassment. Before the investigation was complete, Blanchard, a man with no history of mental problems, killed himself. The Washington Post characterized its story as "death by political correctness."

What should have been done about Tailhook? Those that committed criminal acts should have been punished accordingly. Other than that, the Navy should have said that from this time forward, let all be forewarned that the Tailhook shenanigans that had become legend would no longer occur. Those violating the new code would know beforehand that this placed their military careers in real jeopardy.

The core error in the handling of the Tailhook affair was to have customary (albeit noncriminal, however outrageous) behavior judged by standards *ex post facto*. This facilitated the politicization of the promotion process. Most simply put, Tailhook was a case of too much ado about something.

We interject here another example of an object lesson on the political intrusion of outside influence in the officer corps—one dealing with race and ethnicity rather than gender. In 1995, the Navy announced a "12/12/5" goal which it wants to reach by the year 2000. By that date, the Navy wants to attain an officer accession composition that is at least 12 percent black, 12 percent Hispanic, and 5 percent Asian or Pacific Islander. (In time, that figure should become the standard for the total officer composition.) To reach that goal, the percentage of officers in the designated racial categories will have to triple within four years.

When queried as to where the "12/12/5" figure came, a very senior Navy official told me that this was the projected racial composition of the United States and the "Navy should look like America." It is most troubling that the goals are based on racial numbers corresponding with notions of diversity based on gross population numbers rather than new educational programs designed to expand the pool of minorities who could be raised to meet commissioning standards. The Navy could well end up with the worst of two worlds: compromising standards in officer accessions and failure to meet the "12/12/5" goals.

Although less malign than the interference in the post-Tailhook promotions, we see again how political considerations have increasingly come to affect the makeup of the officer corps. With McMichael's book as a guide, concerned citizens should also look to see if related developments are occurring in other services. Something ominous is in the works—a warping of the military profession. The erosion of proper civil-military relations may be the ultimate and pernicious consequence of Tailhook.

"Without a doubt, it was the biggest and most successful Tailhook we have ever had. We said it would be the 'Mother of all Hooks,' and it was."

—Capt. Frederic G. Ludwig, Jr.
President, Tailhook Association
October 11, 1991

1

A Day in Court

U.S. Navy Flier

It was a question of integrity. John J. LoGuidice was a commissioned naval officer. When he stood up and swore to tell the truth, nothing less than the truth was expected.

The tall, trim Navy lieutenant quickly scanned the small courtroom before him. But he couldn't avoid the cool gaze of the man he was here to testify against—his former squadron commander, forty-three-year-old Cmdr. Gregory E. Tritt, seated at a table to his right. LoGuidice broke off the eye contact, looked down, and carefully took his seat in the raised wooden witness stand. He sat up straight, squaring his shoulders against the back of the chair, resting his hands palms down atop his thighs.[1]

Wearing sharply creased khakis with a gold aviator's pin over the left breast pocket, LoGuidice looked no different than any other young, typically self-assured U.S. Navy flier. But LoGuidice didn't wear the supremely confident look that Navy pilots always seem to wear. LoGuidice wore the look of a deer caught in the headlights of a speeding truck.

The truck had a big "T" on its side. And that "T" stood for Tailhook.

It was July 7, 1993, well into the second month of the Navy's hearings at Virginia's Norfolk Naval Base on the sexual assaults that marked the abuse-laden 1991 convention of the Tailhook Association, a private booster group for naval fliers.

All the previous hearings, save one administrative session held three weeks earlier, had been nonjudicial affairs that were closed to the press. But today, the doors to the base's Naval Legal Service Office had been opened wide. And Navy prosecutors were expecting

1

LoGuidice to swear that he had seen Tritt grabbing women's rear ends in an impromptu gantlet of men on a crowded patio at the convention.[2] Reporters would dutifully record the testimony, and the following day's stories would note that the Navy seemed to be well on its way toward nailing the culprits.

LoGuidice, a naval flight officer aboard the Navy's four-man, radar-jamming EA-6B jet, was a minor player at Tailhook. His crime was streaking naked across that same pool patio on the convention's final night.[3] This, the Navy maintained, was conduct unbecoming an officer. LoGuidice had been officially chastised for his behavior. He was avoiding further prosecution by providing testimony against Tritt.[4]

A lot of naval fliers had gotten in trouble over Tailhook, an annual gathering of thousands of Navy and Marine Corps fliers from around the world who annually converged on Las Vegas, Nevada—many of them on taxpayer-funded Navy passenger jets[5]—for four days of seminars and parties.

The parties had always been wild, reflecting the devil-may-care attitude of people who made their living flying on and off aircraft carriers. But in recent years, the parties had taken on a harder edge. Alcohol abuse began to skyrocket. Inhibitions disappeared. Men became even more sexually aggressive than usual. And concurrent with the entry of female officers into the predominantly all-male ranks of naval aviation, sexual abuse of female participants began to rise.[6]

For most of the association's thirty-five years, its conventions at the Las Vegas Hilton had been one of the Navy's dirty little secrets, like its officers clubs and the X-rated after-hours action at Subic Bay, the Philippines.[7]

But when sexual assaults and harassment at the 1991 convention became public knowledge, a scandal erupted. The nation, certainly Congress, didn't expect its officers to behave this way in public—or to lie under oath. The Pentagon investigation released in April 1993 seemed to imply that many had both misbehaved and lied about it. Heads would have to roll. And Tritt's was on the chopping block.

Outside the red brick legal center, it was just another hot, humid southern Virginia day. On docks a few hundred yards distant, thousands of sailors toiling on ship and shore counted the minutes until they could take a break in the nearest air-conditioned room.

But inside the tiny third-floor courtroom, LoGuidice had barely taken his seat following the lunch break when the court reporter announced that she couldn't hear the testimony over the whoosh of the cool air pouring out of the ceiling blowers. So the windows were opened, the onlookers squirmed in their seats, and the hearing proceeded in the stuffy summer heat.

That made things doubly uncomfortable for LoGuidice. "Streak," as LoGuidice had come to be nicknamed by his fellow fliers, didn't want to be here. Hard enough, he thought, to have to sit here with the whole court watching, search his memory for events two years gone by, and remember exactly what had happened. Who was standing where? Who did what?

This was worse. LoGuidice was about to become a turncoat. By testifying against his former commander and fellow flier, LoGuidice was breaking a time-honored fliers' dictum: Take care of your wingman. Take care of your buddy. Fliers aren't supposed to rat on each other. That's why investigators had faced a nearly impossible task trying to gather evidence. In their view, wholesale lying—and even more frustrating, wholesale obfuscation—had impeded the process.[8]

Desperate to build a case, the government's solution in many cases had been to award immunity to fliers from use of their testimony—just as had been done with LoGuidice.[9] They could still be prosecuted based on additional information provided by someone else, or if they lied on the statement they gave agents after receiving the immunity grant.

Some of the worst offenders would follow LoGuidice to the witness stand in the months ahead. They'd taken part in the misconduct, but investigators felt their testimony was the key to nailing the senior officers Congress and certain Navy officials felt were responsible for letting the whole mess take place.[10]

Seated beside LoGuidice at the bench was Cmdr. Larry McCullough, a veteran Navy trial judge. McCullough wasn't here to judge Tritt's innocence or guilt. This was an Article 32 hearing, a sort of military grand jury, and it was McCullough's job to listen and decide if there was enough evidence of misconduct to recommend that Tritt be court-martialed—the military's equivalent of a felony trial—for his alleged actions at the 1991 Tailhook convention. By all accounts, McCullough was well-respected; he was said to be a fair man.

LoGuidice, now an operational test officer with the Joint Electronic Warfare Center in San Antonio, Texas, had already implicated Tritt while under oath during pretrial questioning by Pentagon investigators.[11] If he repeated that story today, his former boss stood a good chance of being court-martialed. If convicted, Tritt, commander of the Tactical Electronic Warfare Squadron 139 "Cougars," would lose his job, kiss his nineteen-year career goodbye, and possibly do time in prison.

At the defense table, across the courtroom to LoGuidice's right, Tritt, an EA-6B pilot, fixed his subordinate with a steady, impassive gaze. Seated next to Tritt was his Virginia Beach-based attorney, Robert Rae, who was poring over notes and occasionally leaning over to whisper something to Lt. Cmdr. Diane Karr, Tritt's military lawyer.

Directly in front of LoGuidice were the somber-looking government prosecutors, Lt. Cmdrs. Carole Gaasch and Mike Ritter. Against the back wall sat Tritt's pretty, diminutive wife Rosa, her brother, and a few Navy legal onlookers. On LoGuidice's far right, behind the rail, sat a handful of local newspaper and broadcast reporters, waiting.

The first of two separate Navy investigations into Tailhook had turned up twenty-five victims of sexual assault or harassment—but only three possible suspects—out of the more than 4,000 who had attended the 1991 Tailhook convention.[12] When it was learned that none of the suspects were senior officers—some of whom, it was suspected, must have known of or seen misconduct at the convention but done nothing to stop it—a third probe was launched, this one by the Department of Defense Inspector General, or DOD-IG.

The Pentagon probe turned up an alleged ninety victims—seven of them males. Pentagon investigators said that 140 officers—118 Navy, 22 Marine Corps—had exposed themselves, had groped or fondled others, or had condoned same, tacitly or openly, at the convention.[13] All this during the year following the Navy Department's official declaration that it now had a "zero tolerance" for any sort of sexual misconduct, be it harassment or assault.

The most infamous abuses at Tailhook had taken place in a third-floor hallway at the Las Vegas Hilton that ran between the party suites, where men lining the walls during the partying intermittently formed a gantlet, converging on and accosting many of the women walking past.[14]

More than half of the Navy cases were dismissed outright for lack of evidence by Vice Adm. J. Paul Reason, the Norfolk-based commander of the Atlantic Fleet Surface Force, who had been selected by the Navy to hear all of its cases.[15] Most of the officers implicated in the others—around fifty, all told—had been allowed to face the music at an "admiral's mast," a nonjudicial hearing at which a commander—normally one in the immediate chain of command—took the roles of both judge and jury. The accused officer heard the charges and pleaded his case. Reason then rendered a verdict on the spot.

The hearings were known as "office hours" in the Marine Corps, and were conducted by Lt. Gen. Charles C. Krulak. Krulak, who headed the Marine Corps Combat Development Command at Quantico, Va., similarly dismissed outright three of the twenty-two Marine cases sent his way.[16]

Most of the remaining officers, nearly all of them junior officers with the rank of lieutenant or lower, received $500 to $2,000 fines and/or letters admonishing them for their unofficerlike behavior.[17]

For some, mostly the Marines, the letters were mere slaps on the hand. But letters of a more punitive nature were inserted in the permanent personnel files of twenty-five naval officers, with predictable career-ending consequences. Some of that permanent damage, especially to the several of the guiltiest, was averted by way of grants of immunity. The Navy wanted senior officers. Like Tritt.

Tritt had never been offered admiral's mast; he was a court-martial candidate from the start.[18] Investigators felt sure he had pawed women in an impromptu gantlet formed on the third-floor pool patio in the midst of a crowd outside a party suite. They also said he had encouraged others to do the same, and that he had lied to Pentagon investigators when questioned.[19]

But something didn't quite fit. Tritt, whose call sign in flight was "Humble," seemed reserved, unassuming, the stay-at-home-with-his-wife-and-kids type. He was sociable and athletic, a man who loved skiing and snowboarding, but he wasn't known as a wild partier or hard drinker. His subordinates had taken to calling him "The Old Bald Guy." Not to his face, of course; after all, he was the squadron commander. But with his soft, blue eyes and easygoing manner, he didn't fit the mold of a hot-shot, hard-charging flier.[20]

Impressions are one thing. Witnesses are another. Their credibility would have everything to do with McCullough's recommendation.

Under questioning by Pentagon investigators months before, LoGuidice had sworn that he had seen Tritt, then his commander, grabbing women as they left suite 302 through a sliding glass door and stepped onto the third-floor pool patio on the convention's final night.[21]

Investigators were elated; they felt they had identified one of the senior officers they'd been charged with finding.

But in court, LoGuidice said he didn't remember all that much because he hadn't been aware of much on the night in question. LoGuidice drank heavily throughout the convention, and continued doing so on Saturday, September 7, 1991. The only thing he ate that day was a hot dog. His tolerance to alcohol was low because he had recently returned from six weeks at sea. By Saturday night he was, as some would term it, blitzed.

As a result, he said, he had a "static" memory of events.

At one point on Saturday evening, LoGuidice told the court, he had been standing on the patio near the sliding glass door that led into 302. It was a party reserved for the tactical electronic warfare "community," composed of fliers in his and other units that flew EA-6Bs, which all are based at Whidbey Island Naval Air Station, Washington.

At times, the patio was so crowded that partiers could only enter and exit the suite by pushing their way through a narrow path between people that snaked away from the door. At some point, said LoGuidice, that path became a "mini-gantlet," sort of a baby version of the much larger, more publicized gantlet that intermittently formed in the third floor hallway the same night. Investigators termed the path on the patio the "Cougar" gantlet after the nickname of Tritt's unit, although the suite's party was actually being thrown by VAQ-129, another Whidbey Island EA-6B outfit.

LoGuidice was fuzzy on the details. He had earlier told agents that he saw Tritt "grabbing butts." Under questioning by prosecutor Gaasch, he immediately became less certain. "We grabbed a few butts as they came out," he told Gaasch. "I believe Commander Tritt was there."

LoGuidice couldn't identify anyone else in the group, even though twenty other Cougars had attended the convention.

"The faces kind of blended in," he said. But Tritt, then second-in-command of the Cougars, stood out in LoGuidice's mind. "I have a recollection of him being there," he said. "I just remember looking to the left and seeing him there."

And what was Tritt doing? "The same thing everyone else was doing," said LoGuidice. "I seen him grabbing butts."

Asked how long he had seen Tritt, LoGuidice wavered. "The best way I can describe, and I've described it this way a number of times . . . this is more of a static memory, and not a dynamic memory," he said. "How long this happened, what time it happened, I have no details. I just remember that happening. He may have been there a minute, he may have been there five hours."

When asked to nail down the approximate time he saw Tritt, LoGuidice replied, "It was before 2 a.m., and after sunset."

These were the kind of nebulous answers Tritt's attorney wanted to hear. A tall, balding, nattily dressed lawyer with a ruddy complexion, Robert Rae had a confident look as he rose to question LoGuidice.

LoGuidice's first statement to investigators had been sworn under oath. When interviewed and tape-recorded a second time, on March 10, 1993, he admitted he had lied the first time around.

"So in essence, when you started out this taped interview, you told them what they wanted to hear, but it wasn't exactly the truth, was it?" asked Rae.

"That's correct," said LoGuidice.

"Now, prior to that you received a grant of immunity. And that grant of immunity was the reason that you provided any subsequent statements?" asked Rae.

"Exactly," said LoGuidice.

Rae held up a copy of LoGuidice's second sworn statement. "Are you concerned that if there's a variation between this transcript and your testimony today that you will be prosecuted for perjury?"

"That's a concern, but I wouldn't have adopted the statement if it wasn't true," replied LoGuidice, looking unnerved.

Asked to indicate Tritt's position in the mini-gantlet on a diagram mounted on an easel, LoGuidice pointed out his own position, a spot just outside the glass door of the suite. Tritt had been further out on the patio, two or three people to his left, he said.

Rae wanted to be sure hearing officer McCullough realized that DOD-IG agents had put those words in LoGuidice's mouth. "Is it not true, lieutenant, that in the first interview conducted by Special Agent Black, he was the one who indicated that there was evidence showing that Commander Tritt was located to your left and, in fact, you pointed to a position to your left?"

"That's correct, sir," said LoGuidice.

"Then is it fair to say that that suggestion or that information came from him during that interview?"

"That's fair to say," replied LoGuidice.

When asked if details from news stories about Tailhook had affected his memory, LoGuidice said he had been more prejudiced by "conversations with those involved." That group, he said, included investigators.

"I'm no psychologist, but I'll say the thought was put there," LoGuidice said.

Rae returned to LoGuidice's "static" memory of the event. "In that 'snapshot,' can you ever say with certainty that you saw Commander Tritt actually physically touch the woman in that line?"

"I can't say I actually saw him physically touch," said LoGuidice.

Rae asked LoGuidice where he had first heard the phrase "Cougar gantlet." LoGuidice said that other squadron fliers told him they'd heard it used by investigators during their own interviews.

Gaasch interrupted to object to McCullough. "Sir, we're talking a lot of hearsay here and there's no foundation for that . . . "

"This whole thing is hearsay," retorted Rae, cutting her off.

"Somebody else told him that somebody else said something," said Gaasch. "What use is that?"

"He's your witness," said Rae, dryly.

"Noted," said McCullough.

The DOD-IG special agent referred to by Rae, Peter T. Black, was a swarthy bear of a man who bore an uncanny resemblance to Iraqi dictator Saddam Hussein. One of the original seven Pentagon agents assigned to the Tailhook case in July 1992, Black was eventually placed in charge of all day-to-day field operations.[22]

As the formal investigation wound down, Black was one of five agents who continued trying to identify gantlet participants. Black had also remained in Norfolk for most of the Navy hearings, performing both investigative and liaison work.[23] He was a near-constant presence in the corridors of the Naval Legal Service Office.

Black was repeatedly called to testify during the hearings about the DOD-IG investigation's methods and results. His frustration with that process was readily apparent. Throughout his hours on the witness stand, Black sprinkled his replies with potshot comments about what he perceived to be the fliers' misbehavior and lack of cooperation. Black not only complained of widespread obfuscation and lying on their parts; he seemed to be carrying a grudge.[24]

Black felt that what he had perceived as lying and question-dodging stemmed from a weak code of honor substandard to that taught to officers in other service branches.[25] As a result, Black, a retired Army warrant officer, took every possible opportunity to point it out.

Taking the stand prior to LoGuidice, Black was asked by prosecutor Gaasch if he had used a set of standard questions during his interviews. Black replied affirmatively and kept right on going. "As a result of portions of our investigation, we were finding that in a number of interviews, naval or Marine aviators were being less than honest with us, or they were attempting to evade the truth," he said.

Investigators would ask a flier if he had witnessed a certain activity, Black said. The flier would say no. Subsequent information would link the flier to that activity. When re-interviewed, the flier would say, "You asked the wrong question." As a result, said Black, DOD-IG developed a standard questionnaire in an attempt to remove any ambiguity.

Gaasch's soft questions almost seemed designed to allow Black to articulate deadpan but sarcastic replies for McCullough's benefit. Asked to characterize his impression of what he had learned about the suites at Tailhook, Black replied in a chastening tone, "What essentially developed over time was that they were developing competition between various organizations to have the most interesting entertainment."

Black correctly characterized at least half of the party suites at Tailhook. The hands-down winner was the suite rented by former members of a unit that had been decommissioned the previous year: Marine Corps Tactical Reconnaissance Squadron 3, known as the "Rhinos." The unit had become legendary for annually displaying the mockup of a rhinoceros—a papier-mâché model in past years, a five-by-eight-foot mural in 1991—featuring a good-sized dildo protruding at the appropriate spot. The dildo was rigged with a plastic tube connected to a drink dispenser operated by a Marine behind the mural.[26]

The raucous cheers of the partiers encouraged women who happened by to "please the Rhino." At the appropriate time—preferably, those in the room hoped, when a woman had consented to place her mouth or hands on the dildo—the Marine behind the mural would let the liquid flow. It was an alcoholic punch called "Rhino Spunk."[27]

Black didn't mention the Rhino suite this day, touching instead on the presence of hired strippers and free leg shaves for women in certain suites. Tritt hadn't been associated with those suites.

"Objection," said Rae, standing. "This has no relevance to what the charges are before this investigating officer." McCullough, however, allowed Gaasch to continue the line of questioning to lay a "foundation."

The foundation was this: during an investigative trip to Whidbey Island, Black was told by Lt. Brian Lower, a flier in Tritt's squadron, that he had been inside the doorway of suite 302, grabbing women's rear ends as they walked outside. On the other side of the glass were six to eight others doing the same thing. DOD-IG also knew that five unclothed men who had made a mad dash down the third-floor hallway and out onto the pool patio early Sunday morning had started and finished in that same suite. One was LoGuidice. Another was Lt. Dave Musgrave, a member of Carrier Air Wing 14. Under questioning, Musgrave gave investigators the name of Lt. Daniel F. Janssen, an EA-6B pilot who formerly flew in Tritt's squadron and now belonged to VAQ-129, Whidbey Island's EA-6B training squadron.[28]

When first questioned by DOD-IG agents back in November 1992, Janssen had denied any knowledge of assaults at Tailhook. In early 1993, Janssen was questioned again. Black told him they knew he had streaked at Tailhook because one of his fellow pilots had turned him in.[29] A month later, after he was given immunity from prosecution[30] based on what he would say, Janssen started talking. According to his statement[31]—unlike most of the others, it was tape-recorded—Janssen said that sometime on Saturday evening, the "Cougar gantlet" began outside suite 302. Tritt and Cmdr. Thomas R. Miller, the unit's commander at the time, had started things up: "Let's get this going," he said they announced. "Get everybody around here."

Tritt was on one side of the line, Janssen said; Miller was farther out on the patio. But the patio was so packed, Janssen said, that he didn't actually see anyone get pinched or grabbed; instead, he heard the women trying to make their way through, exclaiming, "Oo! Ow! Knock it off!"

Janssen's recollection of Tritt and Miller exhorting their pilots to begin grabbing women became the basis for a felony charge of conduct unbecoming an officer against Tritt. Miller was charged with failing to stop what had started.

Back at Whidbey Island following the convention, Janssen said Miller and Tritt had openly belittled the subsequent investigations and had implied, during all-officer meetings, that no one in the squadron should cooperate or talk.

These were one-witness charges. LoGuidice didn't recall such exhortations, nor did anyone else in the squadron. Almost to a man, his fellow fliers said that rather than urging that they not cooperate with investigators, Tritt and Miller had repeatedly stressed that squadron members cooperate and be truthful.[32] The disparity wasn't surprising. Janssen was a particularly disingenuous character.[33]

Janssen was renowned in his own squadron as a teller of tall tales, so much so that his nickname—"Twitch"—had become synonymous in the unit with stretching the truth or outright lying.[34] Janssen had trouble getting his story right during the big February 16, 1993, interview that was the basis for his court testimony. At one point, Janssen told Black that while the mini-gantlet was in progress, a tall redhead had thrown a drink in Miller's face. Janssen said Miller told her angrily, "Fuck you, cunt. If you don't like it, go ahead and get out of here."

Ten seconds later, when asked if he had seen anyone else he knew on the patio, Janssen flip-flopped: "Just like I said, it was just that attention [paid] to Commander Tritt," he told the agents. Thereafter, whenever the thrown drink was mentioned during the interview, it was in connection with Tritt. In court five months later, Janssen had forgotten what Tritt/Miller had allegedly said.[35]

Janssen despised Miller, a no-bullshit type of commander who'd severely upbraided Janssen on several occasions for lack of ability, leadership, and veracity.[36] He had fared better under Tritt, Miller's softer-spoken successor at the squadron. He and his wife had also openly socialized with Tritt and his wife Rosa. No one could figure out why he'd be going after Tritt—unless it was to save his own skin.

Rae thought it particularly strange that although most of the officers in VAQ-139 had gone to the convention, Janssen, like LoGuidice, was hardly able to remember any of the other squadron members who'd attended.

"Janssen had been in the squadron two years," attorney Rae asked Black. "Didn't you find it hard to believe that he couldn't identify anyone else but Miller and Tritt?"

"We had a lot of people who had told us that they didn't see anybody they knew at Tailhook 1991, so it didn't surprise me," Black replied.

"When you talked to these . . . lieutenants, about what your purpose was for this investigation," asked Rae, "did you not tell them that you wanted to get higher and more senior officers, and that you believed that more senior officers were involved in this, and ask them for any information with regards to senior officers?"

"Yes sir."

"OK. So Lieutenant Janssen was aware of what you wanted?"

"Yes sir," said Black, with an air of authority.

"And he was eventually given immunity, wasn't he?" asked Rae.

"Yes, sir," replied Black.

LoGuidice also knew how Black—and the other Pentagon agents—were getting what they wanted.

"When you were interviewed by Special Agent Black," Rae asked the lieutenant, "you were told that you had to, 'Get on the train or get hit by it.' Is that correct?"

"That's . . . he told me and [Lt.] Tim Dermody."

"Now, he also told you that, 'Commander Tritt is dead in the water,' didn't he?"

"Yes, he did."

"And didn't that influence you to say, 'Well, you know, I can't hurt him. No matter what I say is not going to matter anymore.' Did you say that?"

"That was what the counsel was from my lawyer, yes," LoGuidice replied.

"Now, your testimony today is that you did not see any actual physical contact made between Commander Tritt and any woman in that line. Is that correct?"

LoGuidice's answer marked the beginning of what became a one-hour attempt by Rae and the two Navy prosecutors to get a straight answer out of the lieutenant.

"It was my conclusion but not my observation," he replied.

LoGuidice had no apparent grudges against the two officers. But he, like Janssen, couldn't get his story straight. It looked for all world as if the arms of the two lieutenants had been twisted so the government could deliver two Navy commanders to satisfy the investigation's critics.

Now, in court, LoGuidice looked a lot like a young officer fearful of blowing his Navy career who had crumbled under the pressure to provide evidence. In order to protect himself, a basically honest but scared young man and his booze-soaked recollections had been steered down the low road. It was all spilling out on the witness stand.

Prosecutor Gaasch rose to question the flier. She had asked LoGuidice prior to his testimony if he was certain he had seen Tritt grabbing women's rear ends, and LoGuidice had said yes.

"Is that your testimony today?" asked Gaasch.

"Yes," said LoGuidice.

"You're not happy about being here today, are you?" asked Gaasch.

"Not by a long shot," replied LoGuidice.

"Just as soon not be testifying," noted Gaasch. "Are you telling us the truth today?"

"Yes."

Rae stood, looking exasperated. "OK, I guess we go through this again," he said. "Your testimony as you're making it right now and as you responded to my questions is accurate and true?"

"Yes, sir."

"You stated to me earlier that you could not state that you saw Commander Tritt make any contact with any woman's buttocks."

"Right."

"And that is true. Correct?"

"That's correct."

Clearly frustrated, assistant prosecutor Ritter stood to try to salvage the Navy's witness. "Did you see him touch anybody?" Ritter asked.

"Not particularly," replied LoGuidice, weakly.

Ritter, standing ramrod-straight with his hands clasped at the small of his back, paused, searching for the right words. Earlier, he noted, LoGuidice had told Rae that today's testimony didn't "technically" agree with his DOD-IG statement. Ritter wanted to know what he meant by that.

"Well, we're getting right down to semantics," LoGuidice said. "The substance is there. Now, did I actually see him, see hand-to-butt? No, because I wasn't concentrating on what was going on. And I didn't realize that two years down the road, I'd have to sober up and remember this. So the details are going to be fuzzy."

He remained adamant that he had seen Tritt standing near him on the patio for five or ten minutes that night. But his only distinct memory was of Tritt turning and looking at him momentarily.

After Rae got LoGuidice to once again admit he hadn't actually seen Tritt touch anyone, McCullough took over.

"Was it ever suggested to you by the investigators that he was doing this?" he asked.

At this hearing and another in September, LoGuidice talked about the pressure. The first time he had met with DOD-IG, they didn't question him. But they told him they knew he had streaked. "Basically, this is an opportunity for me to get myself out of a little trouble vice, you know, being uncooperative," he said he was told.

Two days before a follow-on interview, he received a phone call at his new duty station in San Antonio, Texas, from Dermody, a former squadron mate. "They're after Commander Miller and Commander Tritt," Dermody told him.

Within a day, another flier from VAQ-139 called. "I thought I'd give you a heads-up," said Lt. Ron Bolster. "I placed you in the vicinity of this activity."

The next day, LoGuidice received a call from DOD-IG: Come to Washington. It was intimated, he said, that he leave his attorney behind. There was just a question or two to be answered, he was told.

LoGuidice didn't buy that. On March 9, 1993, he showed up in Washington with his Navy attorney, Lt. Monte Deboer. The two men sat down with Black, but Black directed most of his comments to Deboer.

"There's nothing your client can do for Commander Tritt," LoGuidice said Black told his lawyer. "He's dead in the water. There's nothing you can say to hurt him, there's nothing you can do to help him. We don't care about him. We want Commander Miller, anything you can give us."[37]

It was about this time that Black told LoGuidice to "get on the train." Black told Deboer, "We know your client was streaking. We've got your client on the streaking charge. You basically have no alternative. You can decline immunity, and go home and probably come back and face charges."[38]

Said LoGuidice, "I knew that wouldn't be true, because Lieutenant Dermody tried the same thing and was ordered to take immunity in order to testify." He talked it over with Deboer.

"It seemed that the only thing I can do is testify, to request immunity and tell them what I know," he told the court at the July hearing. He hadn't seen any males touching females, he said. He had, he said, seen females touching males.

Rae's paralegal took the stand. Luanne S. Rogers had sat in on a prehearing meeting between Rae and LoGuidice. LoGuidice had stated, she said, that he would do or say anything to avoid any prosecution for perjury.

"With respect to the typewritten statement that he provided and that was shown in court today, did he have any specific comments with respect to any variations with that transcript?" asked McCullough. It was the transcript of the March 10, 1993, interview with Black that was the basis of today's testimony.

"He had said he had lied in it," said Rogers.

LoGuidice, recalled, denied lying to DOD-IG or in court. Rae had the final word: "Lieutenant, you're saying your testimony today is true?"

"Yes, sir."

The prosecution had one more card to play: a victim. Of the three assault-related charges pending against Tritt, two involved females "whose names are unknown." There was one exception: Ensign Kim Ponikowski.

Ponikowski, a Naval Reservist assigned to Fighter Squadron 126 out of Miramar Naval Air Station in San Diego, had returned to the Hilton in search of a party suite with some familiar faces at around 9:30 p.m. Saturday.

Ponikowski stepped off the elevators at the third floor and turned toward the hallway that led to the squadron suites. It was crowded with raucous, shoulder-to-shoulder partiers, drinking, raising hell. By their haircuts, they looked to be mostly military men. She hesitated, then began walking down the hall.

She began getting pawed and grabbed. She had only gone a few feet when she spotted a friend, Lt. Sean Kelly, who agreed to escort her to her community's suite.

To avoid the rest of the hallway, they detoured through the first door on the right. It was suite 302.

The plan was to walk out onto the patio and over to Ponikowski's suite. But suite 302 was so crowded that it took them five minutes just to maneuver through to the sliding glass doors. As they edged along, Ponikowski's eyes were drawn to a man standing just outside the glass, directly in her path, "grabbing girls' buttocks as they were passing through," she testified. "I remember he was short, looked older, and was bald."

She focused all of her attention on the man, so much so that she later couldn't remember anyone else who'd grabbed her. Ponikowski had no intention of being grabbed again. As she stepped out onto the patio, the man reached for her rear end. "I grabbed his arm and said, 'No,'" she said. The man seemed surprised, she said.

Ponikowski didn't report any further assaults—although after stepping onto the patio, she had to make her way through the same area where the mini-gantlet was supposed to have taken place. Later, off by herself, she broke down and cried. Still upset following the convention, she wrote a letter of complaint to Capt. Frederic G. Ludwig, Jr., the Tailhook Association president.

When she told her story to investigators, Ponikowski seemed like she would be a solid witness. She hadn't been drinking on Saturday, and she had had a good, long look at her potential assailant. In addition, she later testified, the lighting on the patio was good. DOD-IG investigators arranged three suspect lineups for Ponikowski.

Tritt was in two of them. When the lineup he was missing from walked into view, Gaasch, standing next to Ponikowski in the viewing room, turned to her legalman and said, "Make a note that Commander Tritt is not in this lineup."[39]

In the other two, the deck was stacked. In one, two of the men were more than six feet tall. One man was distinctly overweight. One was Hispanic. One was a young man. Another had a shock of red hair. That left the shorter, balding, early-fortyish-looking Tritt.

It didn't help.

"I couldn't identify him," she told the court.

Off to the side, members of the press looked at one another in disbelief. This was the government's best case? This was what two years and millions of dollars had produced?

2

Port Call in Vegas

"Dear Tailhook Representative. . . . This year we want you to make sure everyone is aware of certain problems we've had in past year's [sic]."

The letter[1] was a preconvention reminder from Tailhook Association president Capt. Frederic G. Ludwig, Jr. to aviation squadron commanders that he didn't want the 1991 convention to bear any resemblance to get-togethers of the recent past. Ludwig hoped that the twenty-two squadron commanders who would oversee the various party suites at the 35th annual Naval Aviation Symposium would take the letter to heart.

Ludwig had reason to be concerned. Tailhook's always-rowdy parties had gotten increasingly out of hand since the early 1980s.[2] And the Navy's public image had taken a serious beating over the past six years. A string of former Navy members—Arthur James Walker in 1985, Jonathan Jay Pollard and Jerry A. Whitworth in 1986, and John A. Walker and son Michael in 1986—had been convicted of spying, as was Marine Sgt. Clayton J. Lonetree in 1987. In 1988, the USS *Vincennes* mistook an Iranian civilian airliner for a jet fighter and shot it down, killing 290. The investigation into the 1989 gun turret explosion aboard the USS *Iowa* was so mishandled that the chief of naval operations, Adm. Frank B. Kelso II, was forced in 1991 to publicly apologize to the family of the sailor mistakenly accused of causing the blast.

Although the Air Force performed the lion's share of the air combat missions during 1991's brief but violent Persian Gulf War, the

Navy had, along with the other services, basked in the outpouring of public acclaim over the decisive Allied victory.

The Gulf War helped remove some of the Navy's tarnish. A scandal over Tailhook would bring it right back.

Those unfamiliar with the ways of Tailhook would only have needed to read the first sentence of the letter's first few paragraphs to get an idea of what Tailhook was all about.

As last year, you will only be charged for damage inside your suite. . . .

In past years we have had a problem with under age [sic] participants. . . .

Also, in the past we have had a problem with "late night gang mentality." . . .

Tailhook will also have a flight surgeon on board this year.

The letter's tone abruptly shifted from cautionary to commanding in the next-to-last paragraph: "REMEMBER [his emphasis] . . . THERE ARE TO BE NO 'QUICK HIT' DRINKS served. LEWD AND LAS-CIVIOUS behavior is unacceptable. The behavior in your suite reflects on both your squadron and your commanding officer."

The finger-wagging done, Ludwig concluded: "Have a great time."

Cautionary letters to squadron commanders were first mailed in 1986 in response to the previous year's Tailhook, portions of which had crossed the line from wild party to all-out, full-tilt drinking binge and strip show.[3] Shooter-style drinks and potent punches were liberally served; in one suite, partiers earned the right to wear a souvenir bandanna after downing fifteen drinks. Even old-line Tailhookers were taken aback at the number of hangover casualties and the amount of damage to the hotel.[4]

Then there was the lewd and lascivious behavior. Party suites featured go-go dancers, some topless, on lighted platforms; X-rated videos and strip acts; even men and women having sex in some of the party suites. Sexual behavior sometimes reached new heights of raunchiness: It was said that men had stood in line for oral sex performed by women who would blow the semen out of their mouths and over the gathered crowd.[5]

For Vice Adm. Edward H. Martin, 1985 was the last straw. He called that year's Tailhook convention "a rambunctious drunken melee" in a post-convention letter to the Pacific Fleet commander demanding a change in behavior. Martin, deputy chief of naval operations for air warfare, described behavior in the hallways and suites as "grossly appalling," and wrote that "there was virtually no responsibility displayed by anyone in an attempt to restrain those who were getting out of hand."[6]

Martin made it clear that he expected individuals to be accountable for their actions, and to exercise "common sense and leadership" in an attempt to keep things under control. "We can ill-afford this type of behavior," Martin wrote. "We will not condone institutionalized indiscretions."[7]

In most organizations, leaders set the behavioral tone. Early eighties Tailhookers, a retired vice admiral told Pentagon investigators, took their cue from the guy at the top: John Lehman.

The secretary of the Navy, the admiral said, was a highly visible item at early eighties Tailhooks: slipping dollar bills into strippers' G-strings and climbing onto platforms to dance and wiggle on his knees with female dancers. In one memorable performance, the admiral said, Lehman stepped up on a platform to dance with a go-go dancer and at song's end, picked her up, threw her over his shoulder and carried her toward the door.[8]

At one point during the 1986 convention, Lehman ambled into the VFA-127 suite, where a stripper was doing her thing for the fifty or so fliers in the room. Lehman ended up in the middle of the suite, flat on his back between the completely nude stripper's legs, eating whipped cream out of her crotch. Recalled one witness, "Boy, wouldn't the press love to get ahold of this!"[9]

What's person to think? Lehman, a reserve pilot, had sent his fellow fliers an unmistakable signal: If the secretary can do it, you can.

So much for Martin's admonishment to tone things down. Still, the 1986 convention reportedly lacked some of the previous year's conspicuous consumption—despite the influence of the immensely popular movie *Top Gun*, literally a recruiting ad for naval aviation. But human nature being what it is, trouble began brewing once again. By 1990, the misbehavior had once again increased to the point that Ludwig felt compelled to make inappropriate behavior the focus of his welcome letter.

He seemed most concerned with the late-night gang mentality. Younger fliers, drinking, hobnobbing, and lining the third-floor hallway that ran between the party suites, had begun taking liberties with attractive females making their way through the passageway.

For some, it was a playful, "prankish" thing, pinching rear ends like a bunch of lecherous young Italian men in the streets of Rome. Others got carried away even more, pulling down women's tops to expose their breasts and groping their crotches as they walked past.[10]

Some of the women didn't mind. Some did.

The groping may have developed concurrently with the evolution of a practice known as zapping. Every ship and squadron keeps itself supplied with peel-off stickers that depict the unit logo, suitable for "zapping" on the nearest window or wall at every port or air base visited. It's sort of a modern-day "Kilroy was here."

At Tailhook, the practice developed into slapping the stickers on people. It didn't take much of a stretch to imagine a tipsy young flier looking for an excuse to touch a young woman to pull out a sticker and "zap" her. And eventually, one runs out of stickers.

The intermittent zapping, pinching, and grabbing became so commonplace that the hallway began acquiring a reputation. Around the mid-1980s, it acquired an informal name: The Gauntlet.

The term apparently came from a farfetched Clint Eastwood movie in which Eastwood and a female friend, trying to escape assailants while driving in a bus, are forced into an ever-narrowing avenue where they are shot at from both sides.

(A quick interjection here. The word gauntlet was used by Ludwig and others to describe two lines of people through which others had to pass. Webster's defines a gauntlet as a medieval glove. A gantlet is "a former military punishment in which the offender had to run between two rows of men who struck him with clubs as he passed." Editors around the nation wrestled with this one. Gantlet will be used in this book unless it's within a quote.)

Tailhook's gantlet was common knowledge in the naval aviation community—at least among the junior officers, or JOs.[11] And fliers say that it would be next to impossible for any senior aviators not to be aware that it took place—along with the rest of the crazy partying. Condoning the activities, they say, was no more than a form of pampering the "hard-charging JOs."

"When you come into the Navy, you're a jet pilot, you're bigger than life, taller than Godzilla. You are the man," said one young flier. "You are taught to basically eat, sleep, and breathe that kind of stuff. I mean, that's why the guys come in to fly jets, because they think it's such a macho thing. 'Hey, go low. Go fast. Drink hard.'

"I mean, drinking, boozing it up, is a big part of everything," said the flier. "Every single party is basically a huge drinking affair." Even formal parties, he said, often ended up being drunken food fights.[12]

"That's the kind of attitude that has been projected, fostered, and encouraged," he said.[13]

Some, it must be said, manage to encase the unique combination of intelligence, skill, and confidence required of pilots in a less ostentatious package. For these attendees—an impossible-to-determine percentage of the more than 4,000 guests—Tailhook was a seemingly moderate affair: a chance to take in the seminars, see old squadron mates, relax, have a few drinks, and perhaps do some serious gambling.[14]

For most of the rest, it was a license to party hard. And the tradition was so well-established that Ludwig's letter and the letters before his amounted to no more than an attempt to put a Band-Aid on a sucking chest wound.

The Tailhook Association is a private booster group for active and retired Navy and Marine Corps fliers and defense contractors. It takes its name from the metal hook that Navy planes drop and drag across carrier decks upon touching down in order to snag one of the four thick arresting cables strung across the deck. If snagged, the cable gives way but rapidly draws a plane to a dead halt.

Despite its private status, the Tailhook Association had enjoyed substantial support from the Navy for most of its thirty-five-year existence. Many convention attendees were routinely flown to the convention cost-free on Navy C-9 passenger airplanes. The office of the Navy's chief of naval operations for air warfare set up the convention program and arranged for speakers. The association enjoyed rent-free office space at Miramar Naval Air Station in San Diego, California.[15]

Associations are a big part of the military. Every unit and ship has its own historical association that collects dues from members, maintains a running history and the occasional museum, and often sponsors reunions. Other associations are more current and proactive, and generally perform a lobbying function for the services.

Many tend to be old-timers' groups. But the Tailhook Association attracts and welcomes young and old alike.

What crosses generational lines are the unique qualities shared by pilots and crews of carrier-based planes, all of whom share a love of life on the edge. Whether they fly the top-of-the-line F/A-18 fighter-bomber, the slow, reliable, box-like C-2 Greyhound transport plane or the powerful Sea Stallion helicopter, a high level of cockiness is a necessity for a Navy pilot.

Like their Air Force counterparts, they are highly skilled technicians trained to fly day and night missions at high speeds and in every type of weather.

Unlike their Air Force counterparts, they must take off from and land on aircraft carriers—moving targets that buck and roll on the high seas. In the course of a career, Navy pilots make hundreds, sometimes thousands, of carrier-based takeoffs and landings, any one of which could easily end in disaster.

Landing a helicopter on a pitching flight deck is hard enough. But the airplanes barrel in at high speed on an angle severe enough to have caused more than a few to miss low, with disastrous results.

Imagine being tightly strapped into a jet cockpit, hurtling through a squall in pitch darkness, then breaking through low clouds and angling down toward a darkened carrier deck lit with a few rows of blinking lights that don't stop moving until after they flash past as your plane strikes the deck, bounces violently, snags one of the cables and stops with a jerk.

In addition, as the jet strikes the deck, the pilot must, contrary to all natural instinct, go immediately to full power in the event the cable is missed. This allows the plane to immediately take off in case it misses, or "bolts."

The degree of danger requires a level of sacrifice above and beyond that asked of most other members of the military. It's a devil-may-care attitude that says in self-recognition, "I am an absolute professional. I put my life on the line for my country every single day. I'm just a little different than the average Joe."

Tailhook conventions brought this courageous, highly competent, life-on-the-edge community together. That's what Tailhook was all about: a fraternity bash for a unique fraternity—people crazy and cocky enough to land airplanes on aircraft carriers.

Old buddies who'd flown and sometimes fought together had a chance to catch up on old times, to find out who was serving where, what they thought of their unit or ship, or just to talk carrier aviation.

They could also catch up on what was changing, and what was new. Having trained for years on their particular aircraft, they were intensely interested in that aircraft's future. Was it getting modified? Did it have a future? It costs a lot to retrain a pilot. Often, when planes are phased out, the pilots are too.

There were lectures and briefings on tactics and technical advances. Defense contractors set up displays of equipment.

Tailhook also featured professional development seminars. An estimated 1,400 attended the Friday morning seminar that focused on naval operations during the Persian Gulf War. At least that many, if not more, attended the Saturday afternoon "flag" panel.[16]

The panel was an annual tradition, a unique, no-holds-barred opportunity for the fliers in the field to let the officers in Washington know, at the highest levels of the Navy, how they felt about those policies and regulations affecting the aviation community. Like the rest of the convention, it was a plainclothes affair. The fliers in the audience were allowed to express their ideas and concerns as freely as they wished, without regard for normal protocol.

Increasingly through the years, the comments began to border on insubordination.

But the atmosphere at the flag panel was no more than an open expression of the relaxed protocol often accepted in an aviation squadron. It is an informality unique in the U.S. military. It says a lot about why some senior officers condoned the sexual hijinks and misbehavior of junior officers at the convention.

In the air, everyone's an equal, fliers say. It's a matter of trust; you do your job, I do mine, we win, we survive. Bottom line. At times, at least, the rank disappears.

"You got 27 guys in a squadron," explained Cmdr. Thomas R. Miller, a Tailhook defendant. "You live in the same ready room, you fly the same jets . . . we don't have that rank structure so much." In mid-flight, he said, he'd sometimes find himself telling his men, 'The silver's gone; get the fuck busy with the job.'

"In the air," said Miller, "my name is Tango. I don't want Commander Miller, or sir . . . And then you live so close to people, yeah, they do become like family.

"You have to keep it a little more fluid in the air than you do as a ship driver. We're not like black shoes," he said, referring to nonaviators. "As a ship driver . . . skippers don't know their officers. Never see them. Me, there wouldn't be an officer I didn't see five, six times a day. In the ready room, at lunch, at a brief, or at planning."[17]

When a mission beckoned and his fliers were dog-tired in a ready room deep inside the carrier, Miller would sometimes become as much a cheerleader as a commander, rubbing necks and shoulders, urging rather than ordering: "Let's go! It's nighttime! Let's get the fuck out of here!," he'd say.

"And when we're in the States, every Wednesday at 1500, I'd drag 'em over to the O Club, get a couple of pitchers of beer—and some Cokes, you know, so we'd make it copacetic with the Navy—and then we'd have about a two-hour session there of what you did right, what you did wrong that week, how you flew . . .

"No rank. But that way, you'd get guys honest. And the ground rules were, it doesn't reflect in your fitrep (fitness report, or annual performance evaluation). It doesn't reflect anywhere. If you fuck up in the air, tell me about it. And tell your friends about it. I don't know if that's good or bad, but it kept the air real clean."[18]

The association's first conventions—plenty wild in their own right— were held in Mexico and San Diego. In 1963, the site shifted permanently to Las Vegas.[19] Although Navy fliers came to Tailhook from all over the country, the convention naturally drew a larger crowd from the Navy and Marine Corps air stations out west.

They weren't the only military fliers to show up in Las Vegas. Plenty of Air Force pilots attended, mostly from nearby Nellis Air Force Base. A few Army helicopter pilots also joined the party.

Part of the civilian crowd included women who regularly partied at the officers clubs on the West Coast naval bases. Many Navy clubs were wild and woolly places where happy hours and scantily clad go-go dancers were standard fare up through the early 1990s—all of it condoned by base commanders.[20] The wearing of G-strings and bikini bottoms allowed base clubs to circumvent a 1988 ban on topless and bottomless dancing at same issued by then-Chief of Naval Operations Adm. Carlisle A.H. Trost.

The Officers Club at Little Creek Naval Amphibious Base in Norfolk featured go-go dancers on mid-week afternoons, a fund-raising enterprise that was ended a year following Trost's edict. But the party continued into 1992 at Oceana Naval Air Station in Virginia Beach, Virginia.

Friday nights were go-go nights. The back bar often featured skimpily clad female entertainers, sometimes hired out for individual squadron parties. Oceana also had an "open-base policy" for women on Friday nights. They had only to show up and tell the gate guard they were headed for the club, and they were waved on through.[21]

Like the O Clubs, Tailhook was a single man's paradise. More than a few fliers later told investigators: You had to be crazy—or stupid—to bring your wife to Tailhook.

The women from the clubs weren't the only females who showed up on the third floor of the Las Vegas Hilton. Word of a good party spreads quickly, especially in Las Vegas, and women from town would also join in the festivities. Pilots arriving early distributed invitations to sororities at the University of Nevada, Las Vegas.[22]

Natural attraction wasn't the only reason women were a major topic of conversation at Tailhook '91. There'd been much talk that the Navy, in its drive to end sexual harassment and promote equal opportunity, was on the verge, with much congressional urging, of asking the Pentagon to let women join the males-only world of naval combat aviation, a notion meeting stiff resistance. Women—with a couple of test-pilot-only exceptions—didn't fly combat jets yet, although they flew nearly everything else.

As such, they wanted to be part of the crowd, to enjoy the camaraderie. And they began coming to Tailhook in increasing numbers. Some partied just as hard as the men.

Others took the concept of being officers and gentlewomen more seriously. They were there for a good time, but they weren't there to get their butts grabbed, especially by their peers. How could they expect to get respect from the men when their fellow pilots were groping them?

To many officers, even at the Navy's highest levels, what women thought didn't matter. They were totally opposed to letting women fly combat jets—a sentiment widely shared by men in other services and disciplines. At Tailhook '91's seminars, on its T-shirts and in its ordinary conversations, that opposition was expressed loud and clear.[23]

Sometimes, those sentiments went a step beyond an aversion to a larger role for women in naval aviation; they were expressed as an actual hatred for women, or as a perception that they were "property" that men could do with as they wished.[24]

Fliers also brought to Tailhook a set of wildly conflicting emotions over the Navy's participation in the Gulf War. During the war, which ended barely four months prior to Tailhook '91, Navy and Marine Corps carrier pilots were kept out of much of the action by the Air

Force-directed air campaign and an inability to communicate elec-
tronically with the Air Force. There was anger over the reduced role,
and in particular, the less-than-effective performance of the expensive
F/A-18. Despite its two air-to-air kills on the war's first day, its overall performance as a bomber was poor.[25]

On the other hand, Navy pilots produced some admirable performances in the Gulf, especially fliers of the venerable A-6 bomber.
And any way one sliced it, there still was the exhilaration at having
played a part in the overwhelming, one-sided domination of Iraqi forces,
and at being on the receiving end of the cheers at the many welcome-
home parades back home. Tailhook provided an opportunity to hear
and tell some honest-to-goodness, up-to-date war stories. For the
younger pilots, especially, it was a heady time.

To top it all off, alcohol flowed freely for four days straight. Many,
especially many younger officers, didn't give it a second thought: let's
get drunk and raise hell. For four days straight, they did.

The alcohol abuse, layered atop the raging hormones, the Desert
Storm triumph, the shared experience of life on the edge, the general
suspension of protocol, and the desire to keep women out of combat
cockpits—accentuated by the opposition expressed at the contentious
flag panel[26]—all combined to create an atmosphere that made many
fliers feel they could do just about whatever they wanted at Tailhook. It
practically guaranteed that respect for females would be left in the dust.

The sense that male fliers had such license flew in the face of a
Navy-wide message sent out eleven months earlier, in October 1990,
that affirmed the Navy's "zero tolerance" for sexual harassment.

The message was pounded home during the ensuing year in a series
of messages and new programs aimed at developing a sense that all—
not only all races, but both sexes—should enjoy equal opportunity.[27]

At Tailhook, during the late afternoons and evenings when Tailhook
partying got serious, the advice wasn't heeded.

The Navy's idea of raising hell has always been a few steps beyond
that of the other services. The other services have their own select
overseas hot spots near bases in Korea and Panama, among others. For
the Navy, though, partying has just naturally come with the territory.
Bases stay put. Ships sail the world, and make regular calls in distant
ports. There's a greater opportunity for mischief.

Until September 1992, there was one overseas port the Navy more or less owned: Subic Bay, the Philippines. Subic Bay made everything else pale in comparison.

The Air Force had its own version of Subic at Angeles City, adjacent to what used to be Clark Air Base. But for most sailors, Subic Bay was a port call, not a three-year tour. They'd spent weeks at sea before pulling into Subic for a few days. It wasn't a full-time thing like Angeles City, save for the sailors permanently stationed at Subic.

That gave a special sort of manic edge to the partying on the Navy's corner of Luzon. It began at the point where sailors walked out Subic's main gate over a bridge that crossed what sailors colorfully termed the Shit River. This was the edge of the city limits of Olongapo. One officer called it "Adult Disneyland."

This is where, even in the early 1990s, a mere $20 would buy a night's worth of beer, a bar girl to sleep with all night long, and the hotel room to boot. The girls—literally thousands of them, some working their way through college—swarmed through the hundreds of bars, sliding up to twenty-year-old sailors fresh in from three weeks at sea and horny as the day is long.

While a young sailor would watch one or more bar girls perform erotic dances on a platform in the center of the bar, another might ease up alongside him and rub her crotch up against his thigh, whispering, with a sweet, disarming smile, "I'll pop your cherry in my mouth!"

If sailors managed to resist such charms, they'd be propositioned on the way to the next bar. The girls would be on the streets, or leaning out the second floor windows. "Hey, Yankee! How ya doin?"

Then another bar. And another. Sailors got so drunk they'd stagger through the streets, amidst the noise of cars and partiers and bar music, picking their way through the broken glass and trying to straighten up for the Shore Patrol. Yaaa-hoooo! Anything went. It literally was the Wild West—without the six-guns.[28]

More than a few sailors kept a girl in town. For not much more than $100 a month, the sailor was guaranteed every time he pulled into port to have a girl, an off-base apartment, and clean clothes. She would be his girl and no one else's—at least until he went back to sea and someone else pulled in.[29]

Back on base, strippers sometimes performed in the O Club. Far from keeping it hidden, it was sanctioned and advertised.[30]

What was hidden was any mention of such activities back in the

United States. The Navy's unwritten law is time-honored: What happens on cruise stays on cruise.

The same unwritten law applied at Tailhook. It was a port call in Vegas.

3

Portrait of a Party

"Goose" Geiss was totally pumped about going to Tailhook '91. Geiss loved a good party, and Tailhook was the biggest. It was a natural match.

Lt. Gregory J. Geiss, a small-town kid from Mississippi, had made the big time: he was a Navy A-6 bomber pilot, a Persian Gulf War veteran, one of the guys Tailhook was all about. And Geiss was the life of any party. Animated, garrulous, and a great storyteller, Geiss was a very social creature.

Nearly every combat pilot is, by nature, an outgoing and extremely confident individual. But Geiss, short, barrel-chested, deep-voiced and intense, had just a little more Type A surging through his soul than most.

In addition, he was a natural leader, and that attitude bled over into everything he did. If the squadron organized a football team, Geiss was the captain. If there was a squadron party to be held, Geiss was the social chairman.

And when it was held, Geiss, who loved to drink and get loose, would be right there at the center of activity—like the times he climbed atop a table in the women's lounge at the Whidbey Island O Club for an impromptu dance and rap.[1]

Those would be in the category of milder displays. One week after the 1991 Tailhook convention, Geiss and some buddies were watching a comedienne perform at the O Club. She wasn't going over well, and Geiss decided to lead the razzing.

"Show us your tits!" Geiss shouted.

"You show me your dick," she replied.

He did. Geiss went to admiral's mast for that one.[2]

In a way, Geiss felt pressure to drink and party hard. It was one of the ways he saw other pilots in the squadron get ahead. It wasn't the kind of thing a commander would note on a fitness report, but Geiss noticed that social leaders always seemed to become leaders in the squadron.

He had seen what had happened to one of his best friends, a flier who was upstanding, a loyal husband, and a devout Christian who wouldn't normally go near a strip joint. He was only an average flier, but was the kind of hard-working man someone could count on to always do his part, who would always be there for a friend. When their squadron hit Subic Bay on a Pacific cruise, his buddy would even tag along with the bar-hopping crew.

But he didn't drink or partake of the debauchery. As such, he didn't fit in. Geiss always figured that it was one of the factors that tilted the pendulum the other way, and helped get his buddy kicked out via a field evaluation board.[4]

Geiss's evaluations—his "fitreps"—were very good. But every little bit helped, he figured.

Geiss first heard stories about Tailhook back in 1987, about a year after the start of his naval career. It was a rip-roaring, raging, drunken bachelor party, he had heard.

That was right up Geiss's alley. The following year, he managed to go.

A prior arrangement put a bit of a crimp in his 1988 weekend. A low man on the squadron totem pole, Geiss agreed to clean and re-stock the suite every morning in exchange for being allowed to sleep there without charge.

That sounded like a great deal—until Geiss realized that the parties ended at 6 a.m. and began again about four hours later. The suite was trashed. Pictures were torn off the walls. The carpet was spongy with spilled drinks. The floor was littered with plastic cups and cigarette butts.

Geiss still managed to have a good time. He made the rounds, drank a lot, and saw the gantlet in action.

For the next two years, Geiss was on overseas cruises when Tailhook took place. By the time 1991 rolled around, Geiss was in port and ready for a party.

Naturally, Geiss was placed in charge of making the arrangements for VA-196, his Whidbey Island squadron. He collected money for the suite, obtained seats on a C-9, and made room reservations in Las Vegas.[4]

At about noon on Thursday, September 5, the Whidbey Island group's C-9 touched down at Nellis Air Force Base. They were greeted by buses leased by the Tailhook Association, and piled aboard for the ride downtown to the Las Vegas Hilton.

Geiss had reserved a room at the Sahara Hotel for himself and three buddies: Lts. John Dutton, Jim Crabb, and Dan Murphy. They grabbed a cab and went to check in at the Sahara. The group then walked the half-mile back down the strip to the Hilton.

From the top, the Hilton resembles a three-armed starfish, each arm a wing of the hotel. A central bank of elevators runs up the hotel's axis. On the third floor, between the east and southwest wings, a large, plant-laden patio with tennis courts and a swimming pool abuts the main building. Both of the wings faced by the patio are lined with large suites well-suited for parties.

Only a few of the suites were set up when Geiss arrived, but he was primed to party. He and his buddies began touring the suites, sampling the free booze, strolling through the third floor pool patio, and seeing who they could see. Geiss made a point to visit the Chief of Naval Air Training or CNATRA suite, since that was his next duty assignment. It was located at the far end of the third floor's east wing, at the opposite end of the wing from the main elevator bank. The suite was a double room, laid out nicely, and Geiss would spend a lot of time there during the weekend.[5]

Geiss, ever the party guy, had made up a small card that listed "the 10 steps of drunkenness."[6] He had gotten them off one of his squadron's cruise memorial plaques displayed at the Whidbey O Club. The plaque was in the form of a large bottle of San Miguel beer, Subic Bay's finest.

The idea was to have some fun gauging his level of inebriation. Geiss knew that at a party like Tailhook, the card would be a big hit, and a great ice-breaker.

He began his day, naturally at the first step: "witty and charming." When he felt he'd had enough to rate number two's description—"rich and powerful"—he would punch out the hole on the edge of the card next to that step or, preferably, have it done by a young lady.

By number five—"fuck dinner"—Geiss wasn't feeling much pain. By step nine, he had pretty much lost any inhibitions he might have brought to Tailhook. It read: "I'm invisible. She won't notice if I reach up and grab her tits."

This became Geiss's little Tailhook *shtick*. He would walk up to an attractive female and begin a conversation. She naturally started reading the ten steps. When she would get to number nine, he'd reach up and grab her breasts for a moment. Most giggled and went along with the joke.[7]

Eventually, someone would decide Geiss had reached number ten: "Man, you're 'bulletproof,'" they'd say, punching out the number.

That didn't stop Geiss from keeping his *shtick* going through the night. After all, he was past nine.

Dan Murphy had a similar card. Geiss had also brought about thirty copies to hand out.[8] The two men, thus armed, partied nearly all night long.

Around midday Friday, after dosing a severe hangover with aspirin and water, Geiss, Crabb, and Murphy went down to sample the Sahara's buffet. By early afternoon, they were back at the Hilton.

By now, Tailhook was in full swing; all of the suites were up and running. The trio first went to the suites for the A-6 and EA-6B Prowler communities, and then on to the CNATRA suite. Geiss spent the afternoon drinking screwdrivers.

For a while, they hung out by the pool, talking and watching girls. Geiss didn't go swimming because he had a bad case of poison ivy on his legs. They also went downstairs and toured the military hardware displays in the exhibit hall, scrounging for free T-shirts, golf tees, letter openers, and other geegaws that defense contractors like to give away. All are adorned with the name of the contractor.

In the early evening, Geiss and several other junior officers from his squadron went out to dinner with the unit executive officer, Cmdr. Chris Ackerman.

Geiss didn't eat. At the restaurant, a little Mexican place, Ackerman asked Geiss if he was going to order.

"Oh, no," Geiss said with a grin. "Fuck dinner." He showed his "XO" the card, and everyone had a good laugh.[9]

Back at the Hilton, Geiss and the junior officers went to the casino, just inside the hotel's main entrance, to gamble for awhile. They were a bit noisier than the average gambler, but apparently the high rollers didn't mind them singing songs and shouting to each other with glee when they won. Generous tips kept the dealers happy.

At around 9 p.m., they went upstairs. A fresh version of his card around his neck, Geiss walked out onto the third-floor patio and slowly wandered through a mass of partiers over toward the pool. Once there, he began chatting with a group of A-6 and EA-6B fliers. Mostly they talked about women, and about Geiss's *shtick*, which was already starting to become legendary.

Their attention was drawn to a slim, attractive blonde woman standing nearby, facing slightly away from the group.

"Hey, what about her?" one flier asked Geiss mischievously.

"Yeah, why not?" replied Geiss. He walked up behind her, reached around her front side with both hands, and gave her breasts a quick squeeze.

She spun around immediately and froze Geiss with an angry glare. "What are you doing?" she demanded to know. "Uh-oh," thought Geiss. He showed her the card.

"Hey, look, I'm sorry," said Geiss, as his buddies cracked up. "I didn't mean to offend you. It's just this . . . funny little thing that we have."

"You're an asshole," she said. A couple of men who'd been standing with the woman pretty much agreed. "Hey, man, that's not cool," one said. Geiss, who felt pretty bad at this point, spent the next several minutes trying to soften her up. They sat on a bench and Geiss kept apologizing, but didn't get anywhere.

"Back off," said one of the men, finally.

"Fuck off," said the woman.[10]

Geiss shrugged his shoulders, turned, and began to make his way through the noisy crowd back into the hotel, having a drink here, doing his *shtick* with a woman there. At one of the suites, Geiss could hear shouting and raucous laughter. The catcalls told him a strip show was about to begin. His curiosity piqued, Geiss started to walk in.

"Hey, you're not from this community," said the man at the door, blocking his way. "Either pay twenty bucks or split." Geiss, who'd gotten into one of the shows in '88, turned away. "Fine. You guys just have your little show," he thought, moving on.[11]

Farther up the hallway, across from the CNATRA party, Geiss was turned away from another strip show at the VF-124 suite. Not long after, a couple of his buddies came up and corralled him. "Hey, Greg, you missed it," they said, laughing. Two women in the suite had performed a striptease, they said. When the women were done, the fliers, wanting more, passed a hat and raised a nice bundle of cash. The strippers then had sex with each other in front of the fliers.[12]

Geiss wasn't too happy he had missed it, but he moved back on down the hallway toward the central elevators.

At the next-to-last door on his left before he reached the elevators, the commotion coming from inside the suite made him turn his head. Geiss walked in. Now here was something different, he thought. On the far side of the room, in the midst of a crowd close to the large glass window by the patio, a woman wearing a shirt and panties was propped up in a chair with her legs spread open. Two men sat in front of her. One was shaving one of her legs, while the second man massaged the other leg.

Some men brought her drinks and cigarettes. Others crowded around, some sitting on their buddies' shoulders. The suite practically echoed with loud chatter.

If the shaver got too close to the woman's groin, she'd laugh and say, "Hey," and gently push his hand away. She looked to be enjoying herself immensely, Geiss thought.[13]

Then he remembered that earlier, outside, he had seen a large sign on the wall above the glass doors: Free Leg Shaves. And here it was.

After a half-hour or so, Geiss became bored with the leg-shaving and went back out on the crowded patio. One group he was chatting with began singing "Tie a Yellow Ribbon 'Round the Old Oak Tree." A few attempted tunes later, he went back into the hotel, cutting through the "Rhino" suite—the suite of the decommissioned Marine Corps Tactical Reconnaissance Squadron 3—toward the hallway. At this point, Geiss was so drunk that he thought the infamous, dildo-enhanced rhinoceros mural in the suite was a life-sized, fuzzy replica of the animal. He ambled through, went back out into the crowded hallway, and turned right.

Back down at the CNATRA suite, Geiss began chatting with a woman who worked as a waitress in town. As they talked, she read the sign. Geiss grabbed her breasts. She giggled and dashed off. Minutes later, she returned. Another tweak, more giggles, a quick exit, and minutes later, back again. Geiss wasn't really attracted to her, but he was having a great time.[14]

Geiss eventually started talking with another woman in the suite, a dark-haired Navy lieutenant whose husband, also in the Navy, wasn't at the convention. She read the card. He grabbed her breasts. She reached down and grabbed his testicles, squeezing gently. They both laughed; this was a great tease. The rest of the weekend, when they would run into each other, they'd trade tweaks, laugh, talk a bit, and move on.[15]

It ended up being another late night for Geiss. Somewhere between 3 and 5 a.m., he made it back to the Sahara and crashed.

After two straight nights of partying, Geiss was bushed. He didn't make it back over to the Hilton until mid-afternoon Saturday.

Geiss and his roommates Crabb and Murphy hit the exhibit area for free beer and snacks, once again snagging souvenirs from the contractors. They usually lost them all by the end of the night, but it was fun just getting the junk.

Then they drifted over to the flag panel. It had already started, so they ended up standing at the rear of the large hall, forming part of an impromptu peanut gallery.

Seated before them was a huge roomful of naval aviators, all facing a stage on which were seated a group of eight admirals and one Marine general. The admiral in the center of the group had a target ring printed on his polo shirt.

The target was the brainchild of the man wearing it: Vice Adm. Richard M. Dunleavy, the Navy's top aviation officer and the leader of the group on the dais. We want to know what you really think about the issues, the target said. You're junior, we're senior. Take aim and fire.[16]

The questions and comments ranged from excellent to poorly timed. When those considered to be of the latter variety were asked, such as when C-2 transport pilots and flight officers were going to receive warfare designators, the hoots and derisive laughter became deafening.[17]

Some of the answers from the flags weren't much to cheer about, either, Geiss thought. "Yeah." "I don't know." "OK." He figured most of them had downed a drink or two before mounting the stage.

A woman near the front of the room stood up at one of the microphones and asked what her chances were of gaining a seat in a combat jet. The reaction from the predominantly male crowd was immediate. Jeers. Catcalls. "Secret ballot!" someone called out.

Dunleavy, grinning, stood to take on the question. "Hoo, boy," he said in mock exasperation, drawing more laughter. But he immediately cut to the quick for the crowd.

"If Congress directs SecNav (the secretary of the Navy) to allow qualified women to fly combat aircraft, we will comply."

The Navy, of course, wouldn't have much say in the matter. But Dunleavy's answer drew about the same reaction as the woman's question. More hooting and laughter.[18]

All very entertaining, Geiss thought. When the panel ended, he and his friends headed back up the strip to the Sahara to attack the by-now-boring buffet to get fortified for the evening ahead. After dinner, they gambled some.

They'd been playing for a while when Geiss had a sudden realization. "Hey, gauntlet will happen tonight," he announced. "Let's head back over."

Geiss knew that the gantlet wouldn't start until later, so the group decided to gamble some more. At the Hilton's blackjack tables, Geiss spotted Steve Shipman, an old friend. He sat down to play cards alongside his buddy, who was sitting with a girl who Geiss figured Steve had been "doinking" all weekend.

The girl noticed the card around Geiss' neck and began to read the steps out loud, laughing as she went. When she reached nine, Geiss, true to form, reached over and grabbed her breasts.

"Hey, what are you doing?" she said, surprised.

Shipman turned and looked. "Hey Greg, you asshole," he said.

The dealer, a large black man, just started laughing. In a deep resonant voice, he said, "Goose. Goose, goose, goose," laughing some more.[19]

At around 10 p.m., Geiss and his buddies headed upstairs to the third floor. As the elevator doors slowly opened, the sounds of the party poured into the car. When they stepped out and turned right, the noise seemed to wash over them.

The first hundred feet of the hallway was crammed full of partiers, mostly young males lining the walls, laughing and drinking. Women walking into the hallway were getting their rear ends and other body parts grabbed; some, giggling, seemed to be enjoying it. The music pouring out of the suites was so loud that people had to shout to be hear each others' jokes and "sea stories." Some of the men were beating on the walls, chanting, full of themselves, raising hell.[20]

This, thought Geiss, was going to be great. He walked straight into the hallway and took a right into the first suite on the right. Inside the Prowler suite, he grabbed a drink. Then he came back out and found himself at the outer edge of the throng that stretched on down the hallway to his right, away from the elevators.

It was the gantlet, and he was at the entranceway. No "10 steps of drunkenness" cards needed here. Geiss, his mind fogged by innumerable drinks, began patting the rear ends of women he found attractive as they approached from the elevator area and began making their way down the hallway. Sometimes, he'd reach out and tweak a woman's breasts. If he felt particularly adventurous, he'd reach down and grab her crotch.[21]

Geiss recognized a couple of fliers standing nearby: Frank Truong of VA-128 and David Samples of VAQ-139, both Whidbey Island units. Lt. Truong he knew; Lt. Samples was a new acquaintance. Geiss and Samples, known to friends as "JR" or "Junior," struck up a conversation. Drinking and talking in the hallway, they'd come to an agreement, laugh, then slap their hands together in a "high-five" celebration.[22]

The gantlet wasn't organized in a formal way. But Geiss, ever the leader, quickly picked up on the going phraseology and started shouting messages down the hall. If a woman approaching from the elevators looked older, or like she wouldn't appreciate such treatment, Geiss would yell, "Wave off!" using the phrase radioed to carrier pilots if the deck wasn't clear for landing.

The words would immediately be echoed down the hall. "Wave off! Wave off!" the men in the crowd would holler. Spilling their drinks, they'd wave their arms over their heads, sort of like the landing officers on the carrier do while signaling the incoming pilots. Usually, the men would make a space down the center of the hall, and the woman would pass unimpeded.[23]

Sometimes, the older women were grabbed anyway. Some, Geiss noticed, seemed to like it; some younger women passed through repeatedly. One group of four college-age women worked and giggled their way through the thicket of men, one woman pushing the next along.[24]

Others angrily objected, but could find no one to hear their complaint or stand up for them.

When no women could be seen, Geiss and others hollered, "Mingle!" That also got repeated endlessly. When it was called out, the space down the center of the hallway disappeared. When women reappeared, Geiss or someone else turned and began pounding on the walls. Many joined in, creating a thunderous racket. The same sorts of signals were sent by another flier on the other end of the gantlet, up by the Rhino suite.[25]

One woman took exception to being grabbed by Geiss. "What do you think you're doing?" she angrily demanded. Replied Geiss, "Hey, I'm sorry. I'm sure my friends down the hall will be more polite to you."[26]

But it was a lot rougher down the hall. While some women passed through unmolested, others—some of them Navy officers—were practically getting tackled as the men pressed in on both sides. Men reached down inside the women's brassieres to grab their breasts; others had their tops pulled up or down to expose their breasts. Some women threw their drinks on the men, only to be doused in return.[27]

A woman about to enter the hallway was pulled aside by a man standing nearby. "Have you ever gone through the line before?" he asked. She said she hadn't. "Be careful," he said.

Out of nowhere, a man came up behind her, stooped, put his head between her legs and grabbed her hips. He then stood up and plowed into the hallway. As he jostled through the throng, she was grabbed and groped; she crossed her arms in front of her to protect her chest. A hand swinging through the air struck her in the mouth. At the end of the gantlet, the man dumped her off his shoulders onto the floor.[28]

A woman in the midst of the gantlet was lifted off the ground by two men who pulled the skirt of her cocktail dress over her waist and tried to get their hands inside her panties.[29]

Some of the women being groped began kicking or taking swings at the men. One woman who felt her crotch being grabbed hard outside suite 307 turned to see a man grinning at her. "Did you grab me?" she demanded. "Yep," he replied with a smile. She punched him in the face, knocking him over. The other men booed loudly, and her rear end was continually grabbed as she kept walking down the hall.[30]

A few fliers lured women into the gantlet by striking up a conversation and suggesting a visit to one of the party suites. En route—through the third floor hallway—Geiss saw the men walk past and fade into the crowd of gropers, leaving the women to fend for themselves.[31]

For some of the men, it was a sort of primal scream, a free license to be sexually assaultive. For others, it was just a hell of a party.

Geiss was having a blast. He turned from the gantlet back toward the elevators when a woman jumped into him, wrapping her arms and legs around him, and knocked him down. They landed on the carpet, with the woman on top.

"Hello," she said, and Geiss returned the greeting, as the fliers nearby roared with laughter. They laid there for a moment, laughing, and briefly chatted. She rolled off, Geiss got to his feet and helped her up, and she went on her way.[32]

At the other end of the gantlet, one woman had just finished being pushed and pulled through the hallway—an ordeal that included one man reaching up her dress to grab at her crotch—when she realized she had lost the pager she wore at her waist. She complained to a man standing nearby. He stood back and nobly shouted down the hall, "Hey, she's lost her beeper!"

The loss of the beeper seemed to provoke a sudden jolt of conscientiousness from the gropers and grabbers. In a truly comic moment, everyone stopped accosting women and began an intense search for the woman's pager. It was finally found and passed down to the woman, who went undisturbed on her way.[33]

The gantlet then resumed.

As Geiss and his friends frolicked in the hall, Anne Merritt was ordering a beer in one of the adjacent third-floor suites, where one of Tailhook's typically loud, raucous parties was in full swing.

The twenty-three-year-old Merritt, a short, pretty woman, was accustomed to the military life. Her mother was a civilian who worked at McClellan Air Force Base in Sacramento, California; her father was an Army sergeant major. As such, she felt comfortable around military men, even though she had been shocked at the behavior at the previous year's Tailhook.

She had made a pass through the 1990 gantlet, but her feet had never touched the ground as she was "herded" toward the crowded hallway. She remembered being grabbed as she traveled through—bigger men were closest, and smaller men reached around from behind to grope her. She remembered men banging their fists on the walls and chanting, "She's a player! She's a player!"

She also remembered it as being "scarier than shit."

Merritt also remembered peeking into the Rhino suite that year. It seemed dark, strange, mysterious. Still, she could make out the papier-mâché Rhino and men wearing costume-like rhinoceros horns on their heads. She saw women, but couldn't tell what they were doing. The

"Rhinos" beckoned her to come in, but the stench coming from the room repulsed her. This year, Merritt was keeping the Rhino suite at arm's length.

Merritt was in a great mood; she had just finished turning $50 into $500 during a two-hour stint at a $25 blackjack table. She had then come upstairs with the polite Marine officer who'd kept her company while gambling. But once they arrived on the third floor, he wandered off.

Merritt hadn't had a drink while gambling, and she was ready to celebrate. Suddenly, as the bartender fetched her beer, a hulking man approached and grabbed Merritt, pinning her arms to her sides so hard that when he picked her up, it knocked the wind out of her.

She knew the man, a Marine captain. She knew him well enough to know that when he got drunk, he became violent. He had asked her out before, but, much to his chagrin, she wasn't interested.

The deafening music drowned out Merritt's screams and curses as she kicked the Marine captain repeatedly in the shins. He responded by twirling her around in the air, to the amusement of others standing nearby. She became frantic, cursing more loudly. Said the captain, "I love it when you talk dirty to me."

This was a nightmare.

The Marine dragged Merritt out of the suite onto the pool patio and stopped outside what looked to be an empty suite. Still holding her tightly, he sat down in a plastic chair and pulled her down into his lap, wrapping his legs around her to keep her from wriggling free. Then he pulled up her baby blue T-shirt to expose her breasts, cupped in a bikini bathing suit top, and, while holding her arms down, began roughly kissing her breasts, neck, and face.

It seemed like hours, but the assault lasted less than ten minutes. The captain then abruptly got up and told the shocked Merritt to wait around while he went to the bathroom. When she was free, she ran away, crying and shaking. Sickened, she felt like she had to throw up. In the bathroom of a party suite, she could only dry heave.

When she left the suite's bathroom, she told a Marine lieutenant colonel in the suite about the assault. The colonel, angry, told Merritt that he would "break the man's knees" in retribution, but Merritt, for reasons unknown, refused to reveal her attacker's identity.[34]

Back in the hallway, Geiss had been at it for at least an hour when several helicopter pilots stepped out of suite 315, near where he was standing, carrying a large, long-haired young woman who was very drunk. They carried her by her arms and legs, her body sagging low, like hunters might carry a limp deer. Sitting her down unceremoniously in a heap on the floor, they spun around, re-entered the suite, and shut the door behind them.[35]

Julia Rodgers, eighteen, was extremely drunk and barely conscious. Geiss was about ten feet away. Out of the blue, Geiss, Truong, Samples[36] and at several other men spontaneously decided to pick her up. But not to help.

As the men in the hallway laughed and beat on the walls, Geiss and the others lifted the overweight young woman and carried her down the hall. It was fun, passing her through the throng like a wild crowd at a football game might do. Somehow, her pants and panties came off and were thrown through the air.[37]

Someone yelled, "Security guard's comin'!" Bare naked from the waist down, Rodgers was half-set down, half-dropped on the floor.[38]

Suddenly, the inebriated group realized what it had done. "Holy shit!" said Geiss. Everyone scattered. Geiss dashed into 304.[39]

Two security guards who had been watching rushed down the hall, followed by a swarm of curious partiers. As they stared, the guards help Rodgers to her feet. Geiss peeked out the door and saw them walk her down the hall.[40]

Gradually, men started filtering back into the hall, and the gantlet started up again. Geiss remained inside 304; it was too damn hot in the hallway, anyway. About a half-hour after the Rodgers incident, an agitated Truong came in the suite to complain to Geiss that "there's two stupid ensigns out near the elevators warning women away from the hallway, screwing things up. How about straightening them out?"

Geiss walked up to the young officers and asked them what the hell they thought they were doing. The ensigns said they didn't like the way women were being abused. It's been going on for decades, Geiss responded. It's OK. It's tradition.

"If you don't like it and it bothers you that much, why don't you just go out to the patio or something?" Geiss said.

It got a bit more heated, but they kept talking for several minutes. The ensigns made some headway. Geiss felt a bit of a twinge.

"Hey, you know, you guys are probably right," Geiss said. "I'm out of line." He apologized, and they shook hands. Geiss stepped out of the hallway.[41]

At the other end of the hallway, a Navy civilian named James T. Kelly stepped out of the CNATRA suite and surveyed the hallway. Kelly, a pilot in the Naval Reserve, was now a civilian employee at the Naval Air Test Center at Naval Air Station Patuxent River in southern Maryland. This was his first Tailhook.

Kelly had come up to the third floor at around 10 p.m. and had promptly begun wandering in and out of various party suites. While standing on the end of the hallway closest to the elevators, he had seen Julia Rodgers get carried off.

After the guards carried Rodgers away, Kelly walked up to the other end of the hallway to see what was going on up there. At about 11:30, he left the CNATRA suite and headed back down toward the elevators. It was once again very crowded, and the going was slow.

Halfway down, near the Rhino suite, he heard shouts of, "Clear deck!" and "Make a hole!" He moved to his left and plastered his back up against the wall. Suddenly, to his right, a long-haired civilian male began manhandling a woman.

He turned and looked in the direction of the elevators. At the far end of the hall, he spotted Lt. Paula Coughlin, a CH-53E helicopter pilot who he knew from Patuxent River as the flagaide (basically, an executive assistant) to the prestigious test center's commander, Rear Adm. Jack Snyder.[42] They'd arrived at the convention on Thursday.

Coughlin had attended the Secretary of the Navy banquet that evening. Then she went back to her room at the Paddle Wheel Hotel to change, and returned. She had had a few drinks that evening, but nothing excessive. Like everyone else at the convention, she was in civilian clothes. A slender, athletic woman with fairly short reddish-brown hair, Coughlin was wearing a sleeveless black tank top, a medium-length denim skirt and cowboy boot-like shoes.

After hanging around the patio for awhile, Coughlin came back inside to look through the suites for a friend, Lt. Michael "Trusty" Steed. Just past the main elevators, she looked down the hall, hesitating, looking for a familiar face. The hall stunk, like a locker room full of spilled beer. Up ahead, about 30 feet away, a large group of large men wearing short military-style "whitewall" haircuts stood around. Coughlin began walking forward.[43]

Kelly, watching, saw the same man he had earlier seen lifting women into the gantlet grab her upper right arm with his left hand. Coughlin was unconcerned. As cocky as any other pilot, she just kept walking forward into the crowded hallway.

Kelly turned his head to see what was going on to his right. The woman had fallen down. Livid, her eyes were riveted on the man's face. Kelly's head, as if on a swivel, turned back towards the elevators.[44]

Coughlin had squeezed in between two men standing with their backs to the center of the hall. The man on Coughlin's left threw his hip into hers, bumping her. "Excuse me," she turned and said.

At that moment, the man on her right loudly exclaimed, "Admiral's aide!" Others down the hall began to join in, repeating the phrase.[45]

The shout could have been a warning. Earlier in the evening, the men in hall would have heeded it, knowing to keep their hands off someone so highly connected.

This time, it didn't seem to matter. Or else, it was said derisively. No one remembers clearly.

As she was turned toward the man who'd shouted, the man who had bumped her did so again, grabbing her rear end, lifting her off the ground and propelling her forward. As she touched back down, the 5'4" Coughlin spun around to her left and looked up at a man she later remembered as a tall, well-built man, either a deeply tanned white or lighter-colored black.

"What the fuck do you think you're doing?" Coughlin screamed. As she did, a second man standing behind her grabbed her rear end and lifted her up. "Admiral's aide" was still being chanted.

Coughlin, furious, spun around and got up in his face. "What the fuck do you think YOU'RE doing?" she screamed.

The first man moved in behind her again, forcing her down the hall with his body. He then reached over her shoulders, forced his hands under her tank top, and grabbed her breasts.[46]

Kelly saw Coughlin being grabbed from behind in a bear hug. Her assailant, holding on tightly, backed up against the wall, pulling Coughlin with him. Kelly saw them slide to the floor.[47]

Coughlin crouched, trying to throw off her assailant. But he was holding on too tightly. She leaned over and bit down hard on his left forearm, forcing him to let go with that hand. She quickly turned and bit his right hand, and broke free.

At that moment, someone reached up between her knees and pulled on the crotch of her underwear. Coughlin recoiled and fell back. Frightened, she launched herself forward, got to her feet, and tried to enter a suite on the right. But two men standing nearby suddenly moved together and blocked it. She turned and kept going.[48]

Kelly didn't want to be spotted by Coughlin. He didn't like her, and didn't much care that she was in dire straits. Nor did he want to be accused of taking part in the gantlet. "This is no place for me," he thought. Kelly turned right and scooted out of the hallway through the fire exit on the other side of the Rhino suite.[49]

Coughlin, by now afraid she was about to be raped, fought her way forward and broke free from the gropers. She continued forward, working her way for a few feet between other partiers who left her alone. A few feet ahead, through a break in the crowd, she saw an opened door. On the way, Coughlin, half-stumbling, reached out and tapped a man on the hip, hoping he'd help her. He looked a little older than the others; maybe he'd get her out of this.

"Help me!" she implored. "Would you please let me get in front of you?"

The man turned around, raised both his hands, and placed them on her breasts.

Coughlin broke away, hugging the wall on the right, and found an open doorway. She practically dove inside.

It was practically empty; only a few people sipped drinks down by the sliding glass doors. The room was full of empty cups and kegs. She sat down and cried.

A few minutes later, Lt. Matt Snell walked in from the hallway. She knew him from Patuxent River.

"Do you know what they're doing out there?" she said, angry.

"You didn't go down the hallway, did you?" he asked.

"What the hell is going on out there?" she demanded. "What is that?"

"Someone should have warned you," said Snell. "That's the gauntlet."

They talked for a couple of minutes. Snell left. Coughlin, angry, upset and alone, sat down in a chair, crying.

Close to ten minutes passed. Coughlin gathered herself, walked down toward the glass doors and stepped out onto the patio. The first person she recognized was Lt. Cmdr. John Thorough, a familiar face from Patuxent River. Trying to explain what had just happened, the tears began to well up again. He asked if she was OK. She said she was, then turned to leave the hotel. She made it to the lobby before deciding she wanted to talk to Steed.

Steed was out on the patio. Coughlin, still angry, told him the story. "I can't believe what just happened to me," she said, bitterly. "Those guys are a bunch of fucking animals, man."

They sat down and smoked a cigarette. Coughlin wanted a drink, so they grabbed a margarita in one of the suites. Coughlin, angry, confronted some F-14 pilots she recognized, demanding to know if they knew what had been going on out in the hall. They didn't. She and Steed then decided to leave the hotel.

Back inside, just past the elevators, they spotted Lt. Cmdr. George Dom, Vice Adm. Dunleavy's aide. Steed and Dom were good friends. They whispered to each other for a moment, Steed pointed to Coughlin. Steed and Coughlin then walked on down the hallway. Coughlin hoped she could spot her attackers.

The hallway was nearly empty. The only person she recognized was another Patuxent River officer, Lt. Donald Sheehan. As she and Steed walked past, he mouthed the words, "Are you OK?" That made Coughlin think he had been watching.

"No," she responded.

At the end of the hallway, they turned around to walk through again. They left the hotel for breakfast, came back to the Hilton's casinos to play slots for an hour, and then called it a night.[50]

Anne Merritt's night had a similarly subdued conclusion. After her conversation with the Marine lieutenant colonel, she went back out onto the pool patio. Near the pool, she saw another large Marine officer—not the man who'd assaulted her—and asked if she could sit with him.

She told him about the assault. He made her feel safe, and she stayed in the chair until 5:30 a.m. Still shocked that it had taken place, she didn't get up once, not even to relieve herself. She chatted with officers who happened by; occasionally, one of them brought her a beer. As she sat, she began to notice an amazing phenomenon: large numbers of officers still partying on the patio were "ballwalking"— hundreds, it seemed to her, walking around with their pants unzipped and their genitals hanging out.[51]

While an odd custom, ballwalking didn't cause anyone physical harm. But another post-midnight incident could have had tragic results. James Kelly heard the glass shatter shortly after he had made his way out onto the patio following Coughlin's assault. At close to 12:30 a.m., someone up on the eighth floor had pushed his or her rear end up against the window glass in order to create an image known as a "pressed ham." But the person pushed too hard, and the plate glass fell five floors and shattered on the patio.[52]

A female University of Nevada at Las Vegas student, Kimberly Colton, was struck by a piece of glass and treated for a concussion. But incredibly, no one on the crowded patio was badly cut or critically injured.[53]

Geiss walked out onto the patio a few moments later. He heard people talking excitedly.

"Boy, we were sure lucky," he heard someone say. Lucky about what, he wondered out loud. Someone pointed out the glass shards scattered on the patio near the building. Hoo boy, Geiss thought.[54]

A couple of hours later, Geiss had had enough. The next morning, the party over, he caught a C-9 back to Whidbey Island.

4

All Hell Breaks Loose

The cold desert sun peeked over the hills and began its usual rapid ascent, rousing and blinding those hung-over partiers with east-facing rooms foolish enough to have left the curtains open the night before. Others, lying in darkness, suffered in various states of disrepair, spending their first waking hours groaning at the ceiling or clinging to the commode.

This was the human debris floating in Tailhook's wake throughout Las Vegas on Sunday morning, September 8, 1991. Most of it was strewn throughout the Las Vegas Hilton.

It didn't include Lt. Paula Coughlin, who had already showered, dressed, and had arrived from her nearby hotel to join her boss, Rear Adm. Jack Snyder, for an early breakfast before jetting back east to Patuxent River Naval Air Station. Coughlin had brought along Lt. Scott Wilson, another flag aide and a close friend.[1]

Snyder, a deeply religious and conscientious man, was a brand-new admiral; this was the first big event he'd attended in that role. The intense Coughlin was a hard-knuckled woman who wasn't shy about using rough language.

Snyder had never had an aide. He had inherited Coughlin. They hadn't exactly bonded.[2]

Snyder may have had something specific he wanted to talk about. But if he did, Coughlin beat him to it.

"I was almost gang-banged last night by a bunch of fucking F-18 pilots," she told him.

Snyder, preoccupied, nodded. But it didn't click. "Paula, you need to stop hanging around with those guys," he said.[3]

Coughlin aroused conflicting emotions in people. Some described her as "earthy," a way of saying she exuded a natural sexuality. Hard-edged, yet poised and articulate, she was a typically outgoing Navy flier, a highly social woman who loved to party.

Some whispered, perhaps vindictively, that she had been freely drinking and carousing on the third floor, and had boldly decided to walk through the very hallway that many women had avoided like the plague just to prove that she could. She'd had her legs shaved, said the lieutenant who'd shaved dozens of other women's legs during the convention.[4] She was no less a party animal, said some, than the men that she claimed had assaulted her.

Was she an innocent victim? Or had she invited the pawing by carousing with and teasing a bunch of drunk young men who figured they could carouse with and tease her right back?

In Coughlin's favor lay a fact that would play well in the press and in court: from the outset and for the next two years, the story of her Saturday night assault, as told to investigators, remained remarkably consistent in all its details.

Weeks later, Snyder agreed that they had had breakfast. But he didn't remember talking about the assault.[5] Neither did James T. Kelly, the Patuxent River civilian who'd watched the previous night's assault on Coughlin and, curiously, walked up and asked to join them for breakfast. No one objected, but Kelly didn't join in the conversation during his thirty minutes at the table.[6]

Snyder said he first heard about the incident two weeks later through the grapevine back at Patuxent; Coughlin told one of his close friends on the test center's staff, who told Snyder's chief of staff, who told Snyder.

It clicked.[7]

"That got through the chain of command to me," Snyder later said. He called Coughlin into his office. "I got the story, and was absolutely shocked and appalled," he said. "We basically right there came up with a plan of action."

Snyder said that he hand-delivered his own letter and a letter from Coughlin to Vice Adm. Richard Dunleavy, the highest-ranking naval aviator and his direct superior.[8]

For Coughlin, it was too late.

Coughlin recalled telling Snyder all the gritty details at the Sunday morning breakfast. She said he told her he would call Tailhook president Capt. Frederic Ludwig to complain, and that he'd be writing a letter about Coughlin's allegations to Dunleavy.[9]

Then, trusting that her commander would continue to stand up for her, for his own aide, she stepped back and waited for a response like a proper lieutenant should. After a week or so went by, while at Snyder's house one evening, Coughlin said she raised the subject again.[10]

After a couple of weeks had passed, she learned the letter hadn't been sent. She decided he had blown her off.

Snyder hadn't. But he also hadn't gotten the message.[11] On September 29, 1991, Coughlin, frustrated, sent her own letter to Dunleavy.[12]

When Vice Chief of Naval Operations Adm. Jerry Johnson read Paula Coughlin's letter, he didn't need a soothsayer to predict the possible consequences. Johnson, the senior naval aviator on active duty, known as the "Gray Eagle," quickly called Rear Adm. Duvall M. "Mac" Williams, Jr., commander of the Naval Investigative Service and one of the Navy's highest-ranking attorneys. Williams worked not in the Pentagon, but in an office at the Navy Yard, located in a gritty section of Washington, D.C.'s southeast side at the edge of the Anacostia River.

Johnson wanted to know who assaulted Coughlin, and who took part in the gantlet. It was to be a criminal investigation, pure and simple, he told Williams.[13]

Williams, hardly a big fan of women in the military, was less than thrilled over the assignment. He also immediately grasped his agency's dilemma. If he didn't find the perpetrator, criticism would rain down on the Navy. And to find that one person, he was going to have to burn a lot of bridges in the close-knit aviation community.

"Admiral, this is lose-lose for NIS," Williams said.[14]

The same day NIS began its probe—October 11, 1992—Tailhook president Capt. Frederic Ludwig coincidentally sent a post-convention letter to the Tailhook suite commanders. It was at once congratulatory and admonishing.

Dear Skipper,
    As President of the Tailhook Association, I wanted to take this opportunity to give you a debrief of the "goods" and "others" of this year's annual symposium at the Las Vegas Hilton while it is still fresh in your mind. Without a doubt, it was the biggest and most successful Tailhook we have ever had. We said it would be the "Mother of all Hooks," and it was. . . .

After trumpeting the large turnout, the flag panel participation, and the attendance by the secretary of the Navy and the chief of naval operations, Ludwig downshifted.

> This year our total damage bill was $23,000. . . . We narrowly avoided a disaster when a "pressed ham" [a bared rear end pressed against a window] pushed out an eighth-floor window which subsequently fell on the crowd below.
>
> Finally, and most serious, was "the Gauntlet" on the third floor. I have five separate reports of young ladies, several of whom had nothing to do with Tailhook, who were verbally abused, had drinks thrown on them, were physically abused and were sexually molested. Most distressing was the fact an underage young lady was severely intoxicated and had her clothing removed by members of the Gauntlet.[15]

No one really remembers much reaction out in the fleet to Ludwig's letter, or whether it was posted in squadron ready rooms for the "hardcharging JOs (junior officers)" noted by Ludwig to read and think about.

There was plenty of reaction the afternoon of October 28, 1991—at least in the Pentagon offices of H. Lawrence Garrett III, secretary of the Navy. That was when reporter Gregory Vistica of the *San Diego Union* faxed Garrett a copy of Ludwig's letter, along with a couple of questions.[16]

Garrett was shocked. He hadn't seen Ludwig's letter. He hadn't even known about the ongoing NIS investigation, much less about women being groped at the annual convention of his hot-shot fliers. But the cautious Garrett chose to sleep on it before making a move.

Given the current social climate, that was a big mistake. Sexual harassment was a hot topic in the fall of 1991. At the contentious confirmation hearings for Supreme Court nominee Clarence Thomas, University of Oklahoma law professor Anita Hill accused Thomas, her former boss, of gross sexual harassment, sparking a national debate on the subject.

On October 15, the Senate confirmed Thomas by the narrow margin of 52-48. Two weeks later, Congress and the nation learned the ugly truth about sexual harassment at Tailhook. Vistica's story made the national wires, even though the conservative *Union* tucked the story on its inside pages.[17] But in Navy-rich San Diego and elsewhere, the sensational October 29 headline couldn't be ignored:

Women reportedly abused by Navy pilots at seminar
Investigation is under way of 5 separate reports of physical and verbal assault

That afternoon, former Navy flier Sen. John McCain, a member of the powerful Armed Services Committee, lashed out at the Navy on the Senate floor. He called for an immediate high-level investigation, and for the Navy to end its support of the Tailhook Association.[18]

McCain got the Navy's attention. After meeting with Chief of Naval operations Adm. Frank B. Kelso, Garrett quickly decided to cut the Navy's ties with the fliers' group.

He also fired off a letter to Ludwig that same day.

"I am writing to you, and through you to your organization, to express my absolute outrage over the conduct reported to have taken place at the Tailhook Association symposium in September ...

No man who holds a commission in this Navy will ever subject a woman to the kind of abuse in evidence at Tailhook '91 with impunity.

In a separate memo, Garrett instructed Undersecretary Howard to direct Rear Adm. George Davis, the Naval Inspector General, to begin an investigation of noncriminal abuses at Tailhook. Howard sent a memo to Davis to investigate the Navy's support for and relationship with the Tailhook Association, the use of Navy resources in support of the organization, and violations of regulations and policies on alcohol abuse and sexual harassment.

But Howard also told Davis to limit the inquiry to the Navy's "business relationship" with the Tailhook Association. Davis decided that meant to look into the use of Navy aircraft to fly participants to Las Vegas and the group's use of free office space at Miramar Naval Air Station in California.[19]

In the first few weeks of the investigation, NIS commander Williams and Inspector General Davis each reported separately on the status of their investigations to Undersecretary of the Navy Dan Howard. By late October, Howard had decided to combine the biweekly meetings into one weekly briefing.[20]

Five senior Navy leaders took part: Howard; Williams; Davis; Rear Adm. John E. "Ted" Gordon, the Navy Judge Advocate General; Cmdr. Pete Fagan, Garrett's personal lawyer; and Barbara Spyridon Pope, who was completing her second year as the assistant secretary of the Navy for manpower and reserve affairs.[21]

A slender, attractive, intense and energetic woman, Pope was the senior female naval official. As a policymaker, she was appalled at what she'd heard had happened at Tailhook '91; it flew in the face of everything the Navy had been trying to do for the past two years. Garrett had sent out three separate memos on the subject in implementing a policy mandating a "zero tolerance" for sexual harassment and misconduct. As a woman, she was furious.

But when it came to determining how to prosecute the Navy's investigations, Pope found herself bucking the narrow scope of the investigations ordered by Howard.

At the briefings, Pope couldn't believe what she was hearing. The individual misconduct was reprehensible. But the failure of Navy commanders to step in and stop the misconduct, she thought, indicated a distinct failure of leadership.

Inspector General Davis later tried to broaden his inquiry.[22] About three weeks after receiving the initial memo from Howard, Davis told him the Navy needed to do an "all-up investigation" of Tailhook. He told Howard he wanted to form a large investigative team to examine whether the Navy had a "cultural problem" that led to the Tailhook assaults; whether the chain of command had acted appropriately when informed about assaults; and whether there were noncriminal violations that should be referred to the separate chains of command around the world for administrative punishment.

It never happened. Instead, said Davis, Howard limited the IG further, telling him the Navy didn't have the funds for an "all-up investigation." He was also afraid that an all-encompassing investigation could turn into a witchhunt. Let NIS take the lead, he told Davis, and follow up as necessary.

Howard denied having the conversation.[23]

Ted Gordon came to the meetings for personal reasons. He very much liked being an "insider," and wanted to know everything that was going on. On the other hand, he was the type of man who didn't want to be held accountable should things turn sour.[24]

One indication of Gordon's character was an incident at the end of the Persian Gulf War, when the 7th Fleet commander, Vice Adm. Stanley R. Arthur, sent in a request to award the Combat Action Ribbon to all who had sailed within a certain geographic area where ships had been exposed to mines. The uniformed leadership supported the idea. Gordon was opposed, arguing that approval would water down the award's significance. He'd put down those thoughts in an unsigned memo he was carrying, but after hearing out Vice Chief Johnson, announced that he would tear it up.

Within forty-eight hours, Barbara Pope approached Johnson with the same unsigned memo in hand. "Ted's giving me this memo, but doesn't want to sign it," Pope said. "What do you think?"

Johnson, a straight arrow, had distrusted Gordon ever since.[25]

It seemed to the others that the Navy's top uniformed lawyer was present to give Howard legal advice on how to avoid prejudicing the investigation, and to follow up on any leads pointing at criminal activity. Howard didn't seem to think so. Questioned later by Pentagon investigators, Howard said, "The purpose of having Admiral Gordon present? God, I don't know."[26]

A common purpose seemed to be lacking. The Naval Investigative Service wasn't cooperating with the Inspector General; IG investigators had to request permission from the NIS to conduct specific interviews.[27]

The investigation faced an even greater barrier from within; from the very beginning, Mac Williams tried to limit its scope. An out-and-out sexist, he did not like women in his Navy. And Williams didn't think the Tailhook problem was serious enough to expend his agency's effort. When the topic was raised during a chat at his Navy Yard office, he told his guests, perhaps hopefully, "Something else will pop up in the press; next week, it'll be gone."[28]

Garrett's letter wasn't three weeks old before Mac Williams began voicing doubts about his own investigation's chances. He told Beth Iorio, the top NIS agent on the case, that the agency didn't have "a fart's chance in a whirlwind" of finding Tailhook culprits.[29] By late November, he was saying as much during the briefings. Nobody saw anything. Nobody was talking. And no one, to Pope's dismay, had been asking senior officers and commanders about failures of leadership at the convention, or had even taken any of them to task for such failures[30]—with one exception. On November 10, Kelso, although he had attended the Tailhook convention and would later be questioned by Pentagon investigators, relieved Snyder of his command, saying he'd lost confidence in his ability to lead.

Johnson, the vice chief, fought hard for Snyder; he felt Snyder's "filters" were up when Coughlin first told him of the assault, and felt that, in a way, both officers were telling the truth. Kelso agreed somewhat—he didn't take Snyder's star—but felt that Snyder still should have reacted more quickly to Coughlin's complaint.[31]

Snyder was the exception and became the first sacrificial lamb the

Navy served up to placate McCain and Congress. Like many junior officers to come, Snyder, his misconduct a huge question mark, took the fall for his senior leaders.

As the weeks passed, Williams and Davis kept saying they weren't getting anywhere. No one saw anything; no one did anything, reported Williams. At a late December meeting, Pope exploded.

"Wait a minute," she said, angry. "We had 5,000 people there. Nobody saw anything?"[32]

Williams and Davis admitted that they knew the fliers were "closing ranks"; in at least some of the squadrons, they said, a conspiracy of silence existed. Said Pope, "You've got to go back to senior officers and figure a way to get people to cooperate."

Pope went to Dunleavy, the Navy's senior aviator, to ask him to send out some sort of message condemning the abuses at Tailhook and stressing the need to cooperate with the investigators and come clean. The fliers aren't cooperating, she said; they're not even listening to Kelso, the Navy's top officer. Early on, Kelso had put out a message stressing the need to cooperate.

But Dunleavy said he'd been told by Gordon, the lawyer, to lay off until the investigation was complete. A letter to the men under investigation could later be construed as undue command influence, Gordon had told him. That could get cases thrown out of court. "Be patient," Dunleavy and others told her. "The investigation's not finished."

Pope wasn't in the mood. She wanted agents to talk to senior officers. It was a question of abdicating responsibility, she thought.[33]

Mac Williams wanted no part of it. One morning in early 1992, he and Pope got into it during a Pentagon meeting with Undersecretary Howard at which the subject of women's right to serve in the military came up. Pope viewed it as inalienable, no different than the right of men to serve.

Williams begged to differ. "What you don't understand, Barbara," he said, "is that men in the Navy don't want women in the Navy."

Pope's eyes lit up, but Howard, wanting to cool things down, jumped in first. "That's bullshit, Mac," he said, emphatically. Pope softened her reply.

"Mac, you don't get it," she said. "Yes, some men don't want women in the Navy. It's a fact of life. Things *were* easier when women weren't there. But if men can't accept women and integrate women into the military, then they shouldn't be here."

Replied Williams, "Well, you know, a lot of female pilots are top-less dancers and hookers."

It was an unbelievable comment, a gross exaggeration, and it was being made by the Navy's top investigator on a case that centered around harassment of women. Pope was furious.

"Bullshit!" she snapped at Williams. "You're crazy. You give me the name of one female aviator who is dancing topless after hours, and I will personally see that they are brought up on conduct unbecoming charges."

Williams apologized to Pope. They left the meeting together. At the receptionist's desk, they began again, and Howard stepped between them. "You're out of line, Mac," he said. Pope and Williams left the office and started what turned into a half-hour screaming match down the long halls of the Pentagon.

"You can't understand," insisted Williams. "Men's hormones are different, and as a female, you can't understand. Men look at women as sex objects."

"Sure, men and women are attracted to each other," exclaimed Pope. "It's a fact of life. But you learn to control those desires and feelings."

The next day, Williams apologized, and the two spent two hours talking it out. At least he was being honest, she thought. But his views remained unchanged.[34]

On another occasion, Williams was being briefed by agent Iorio on Coughlin's statement, in which she recalled she'd screamed at an assail-ant that Saturday night, "What the fuck do you think you're doing?"

That, thought Williams, was a clear indication of Coughlin's char-acter. He told Iorio, "Any woman that would use the 'F' word on a regular basis would welcome this type of activity."[35]

Despite Williams's obvious bias, he knew he had to identify Coughlin's assailant. By January, agents felt they had found a possible suspect. But Williams knew that unless the case was locked down tight, her assailant would escape prosecution and the Navy would have another public relations disaster on its hands. That had to be avoided at all costs.[36]

He made a call to Norfolk.

On Friday afternoon, January 24, Navy lawyer Lt. Cmdr. Hank Sonday was trying to wrap things up a little early to get a head start on Super Bowl weekend. The Washington Redskins were playing the Buffalo Bills, and Sonday was a pretty big football fan.

Hank Sonday was a seasoned courtroom litigator, a fifteen-year veteran of military legal work who had spent most of his career arguing cases as either a prosecutor or defense counsel. He was regarded as one of the Navy's best litigators, a fair man who was unflappable under pressure. At one point in his career, during a tour in Philadelphia, he served as a special court-martial judge.

For the past two years, Sonday had served as senior trial counsel at the Norfolk Naval Base's Naval Legal Service Office, or NLSO. As such, he'd prosecuted every Navy national security case that had been assigned to Norfolk.[37]

He was about to leave when Capt. Ed Ellis, the NLSO commander, poked his head through the door and said to come by his office.

"I just got a call from Admirals Gordon, Schachte, and Williams," Ellis told Sonday. "There's an investigation going on, and you need to be involved."

One possibility came to mind immediately. Sonday and Ellis had been talking a lot recently about a fairly consequential case in which some classified information had been compromised.

Wrong case. Mac Williams, Gordon, the Navy's top lawyer, and Rear Adm. William Schachte, Gordon's deputy, wanted Sonday to get involved in the Tailhook investigation.

Sonday had heard about the convention, and knew an admiral had been fired over it. That was about the extent of his knowledge.

"There was an admiral's aide who was assaulted out there," Ellis said. "She identified someone out of a photo lineup. The NIS has asked to have a trial counsel assigned to the investigation."

NIS agents were gathering evidence on Coughlin's assailant and others, he said, but Mac Williams wanted to make sure they were gathering the right kind—the kind that wins cases. A trial lawyer, he figured, could best determine the strength of the evidence, and whether more was needed in a particular instance to win a conviction, just as an assistant U.S. attorney would do in a federal case. Mac Williams, Gordon, and Schachte wanted Sonday to oversee the process. If any made it to trial, he would be the lead counsel.

Sonday tried to picture the three admirals together in the same room. It was a pretty weird picture.[38]

Schachte, Gordon's deputy, commanded all the NLSOs in the Navy; both he and Gordon had previously served as NIS commander before moving up the ladder. Schachte was an old professional associate of Mac Williams's.

But Gordon harbored an intense dislike for Schachte, an enmity grounded in pure jealousy. Schachte was a proven and decorated leader who as a young officer had commanded patrol boats in riverine combat operations during the Vietnam War. An unpretentious man, he had risen to become a highly respected attorney in the Navy community, and had developed a reputation as an expert on international law.

Gordon, on the other hand, made admiral ten years after becoming a Navy lawyer more for his political connections than his ability. He had never been a staff judge advocate to an operational commander, never been to sea or stationed overseas, and had spent virtually his entire career in Washington, D.C. He had a reputation for being quick to take credit for the work of others, and being just as quick to pass the blame to subordinates.

In addition to being close to Gordon, Mac Williams was very well connected in the Pentagon. He'd been the top lawyer for four secretaries of the Navy: William Ball III, John Lehman, James Webb, and Larry Garrett. He had his first star, and like any rear admiral, he was ready to get another.

If Gordon had his way, he would extend for a year to make it a total of three years as the Judge Advocate General, or JAG. At the same time, he would somehow force Schachte out and bring Williams up to the number two spot.

One of Gordon's strategies was to keep Schachte out of the Tailhook loop. Once what he imagined as a successful investigation was concluded, Gordon figured that Williams's rising star would enable him to jump past Schachte.

It was a pure and simple grab for power. The Persian Gulf War had George Bush riding high with the American public, no one had yet heard of Bill Clinton, and it looked for all the world like another four years for Bush. That would mean another four years for Larry Garrett, and extra time in grade before retirement for a couple of legal beagles hanging on his coattails.

Williams and Garrett, a former Navy lawyer, were best friends since their days serving together in Hawaii. Garrett and Gordon had also known each other in uniform, and had remained friends. Gordon had served under Lehman; they were old poker-playing buddies. With the exception of Gordon and Schachte, it was a tight little circle. And Williams was fiercely loyal to his friends.[39]

Ellis understood the political picture. He also knew that NIS, an agency of civilian investigators, was run by a military attorney. A lot of agents didn't like that. Both situations, he knew, could keep Sonday from getting a clear, untainted picture of things. To get the story's other side, he told Sonday, be sure to talk to Charlie Lannom. Lannom was the agency's deputy director and its number one civilian.

"By the way," Ellis said, "you probably need to go up tomorrow." Damn, Sonday thought. So much for the Super Bowl. But after a follow-up call to Washington, it was decided that Sonday didn't need to fly up until Monday morning. Sonday stayed home and watched the Redskins wallop the Bills, 37–24.

Sonday figured he'd been chosen because he had a good reputation in the JAG Corps. He'd worked on some high-profile cases, including serving as the investigating officer who oversaw the administrative hearing of acknowledged homosexual Lt. Tracy Thorne.

Sonday was also a known quantity because Williams was once his boss. When Sonday arrived in Norfolk back in May 1990, his commander had been a Capt. Mac Williams. A few months later, Williams was selected for admiral and was transferred to Washington to become NIS commander.

After landing at National Airport Monday morning, Sonday took a cab to NIS Headquarters in the Forge Building at the dilapidated Washington Navy Yard. There, he met with Lannom.

Lannom got right to the point: The focus of the investigation, he told Sonday, was to be extremely narrow. Williams, he said, wanted only to explore "clearly assaultive criminal activity," and Lannom agreed with those limits.

The Navy needed results. After the expenditure of roughly 12,000 to 13,000 man-hours, only two suspects had been turned up: a Royal Australian Air Force officer named Jim Ibbottson, and Capt. Gregory Bonam, an F/A-18 Marine instructor pilot out of Meridian, Mississippi.

Ibbottson was suspected of "sharking": of crouching down, sneaking up behind women and biting them on their rears. One of his targets was Lt. Kara Hultgreen, an A-6 bomber pilot who would later become one of the Navy's first female F-14 pilots.

Hultgreen's method of dealing with sexual assault was more direct than the official Navy's; when Ibbottson struck, she turned and drove him into the floor with a crushing blow. Hultgreen told DOD-IG that she didn't consider herself a victim.

U.S. authorities notified Ibbottson's superiors in Australia. He later committed suicide. But even if he'd been an American, his case would have paled next to Bonam's.[40]

Bonam was the prize suspect: Paula Coughlin had identified him as her assailant. But she'd only seen him in a photo. It would be Sonday's job to find out if she was positive enough to bring Bonam up on charges.[41]

Before Sonday had arrived, Coughlin and NIS agents had reviewed thousands of photos of naval fliers. It had been slow going. One NIS agent, Laney S. Spigener, ended up being suspended without pay for three days later in the year after Coughlin accused him of pressuring her for dates.[42]

On November 26, 1991, Coughlin thought she'd discovered her attacker.

"That looks exactly like him," she told Iorio, the assistant resident agent-in-charge at Patuxent River. "If it's not him, it's his brother."[43]

But it wasn't. About a month later, according to agent Beth Iorio, Coughlin called and said, "I hear I picked the wrong guy."[44] She'd heard it through the grapevine, she said. It later turned out that her selection, a black Marine, was a lance corporal from Quantico who hadn't even gone to Tailhook.

They had nearly given up finding the mysterious light-skinned black an artist had rendered in a composite sketch when Iorio spotted Bonam's photo on the wall in Marine Corps Headquarters, at the Naval Annex to the Pentagon.

"Hey, that looks just like the composite!" she said to herself. NIS obtained the photo and showed it to Coughlin. Bingo.

Lannom wanted Sonday to put together a live lineup that included Bonam. The immediate concern was assembling a group that didn't appear stacked against Bonam, whose appearance was distinctive. He was a light-skinned black man, tall, muscular, and handsome.

Sonday simultaneously began planning the lineup and familiarizing himself with the investigation, working in Washington Monday through Friday and driving back home to Norfolk on weekends. He set up shop with lead agent Iorio and agent Tim Dannahey in the regional NIS headquarters office in Crystal City, across the Potomac River from the

Navy Yard in Virginia and just a stone's throw from the Pentagon. John D'Avanzo was agent-in-charge of the office and head of the NIS National Capitol Region; Iorio had been working with Coughlin from the outset.

The next day, Sonday met with Mac Williams. He soon learned that Lannom's narrow definition of the probe's scope was too broad for the admiral.

"This needs to be done with quickly," Williams told Sonday. "If we get involved with trying to figure out everything, we'll never get out of this."

The bottom line: Forget trying to find every assailant. Find out who assaulted Paula Coughlin. Period.

To emphasize the point, Williams told Sonday that when Garrett first ordered the investigation, Williams hadn't wanted NIS to get involved at all because he realized that a disproportionate amount of his limited assets would end up tied up in the case. Besides, he said, NIS doesn't do misdemeanors like streaking and leg shaving.

The pragmatic Sonday agreed that some limits would be a good thing. For instance, the Navy should avoid trying to prosecute fliers on the charge of conduct unbecoming an officer. It can be a very nebulous offense, he told Williams, and it's wide open to interpretation. Worse, he imagined the opposing defense counsel in court saying, "OK, then let's look at the type of conduct the Navy is willing to tolerate from its officers; let's look at all of the conduct at Tailhook."

But Sonday argued that it was important to look at any other clearly felonious assaults, as well as at people agents believed had lied during the investigation.

To his surprise, Williams agreed.

As the investigation proceeded during the next two months, Sonday gave Williams or Lannom a weekly briefing on how things were going. He later learned that that the two were subsequently briefing Kelso, Howard, or another Navy official on the investigation's status.

During the course of Sonday's research, he learned of the incorrect identification Coughlin had made of her assailant back in November. This was a major source of concern. Once a witness has done that, Sonday thought, it's an uphill battle for any subsequent identification. And in court, the witness becomes much easier to impeach.

He also read complaints in letters to the independent newspaper *Navy Times* from readers complaining that NIS wasn't having any luck identifying Coughlin's attacker and that the agency was singling out minorities.

That implication was especially troublesome. In the vast, overwhelmingly white world of naval aviation, Sonday thought, the only U.S. citizen they had identified was a black Marine in Mississippi. That wouldn't go over too well with the general public. If Bonam was the guy who did it, he thought, they would need to find that out.

About a week went by before Sonday told Lannom he wanted to hold two six-person lineups at Camp Lejeune, N.C., where Bonam could be brought for a few days without arousing undue suspicion back at his home base. The anonymity would protect his reputation. Even if he was the man, he still had the right to a trial. And at Lejeune, light-skinned blacks and Hispanics from the base's large Marine population could be found to flesh out the lineups.

The two-lineup approach would also be harder for the defense to challenge. With one lineup, there's no doubt that the suspect is somewhere in that lineup. Using two would prevent Coughlin from making that assumption and provide for a more objective review.[45]

To find visually similar candidates for the lineups, NIS agents drove around Lejeune the week prior to the lineup looking for Marines with some of Bonam's features. If someone was spotted, the car would screech to a halt, the Marine would be called over, and his ID card would be checked. If he fit the bill up close, he was requisitioned for the lineup.[46]

Sonday met Coughlin for the first time on the way to National Airport the day of their flight to Lejeune. She told him of her efforts at contacting members of Congress and other government officials. She also seemed to Sonday to be putting on airs, to be a bit pretentious. Sonday was less than impressed.

"You have to realize a couple of things here, Lieutenant Coughlin," he said. "You need to remember that in the grand scheme of things, you're not dead, you weren't raped, you have no missing body parts. So it's an assault with battery."

But, he added, there was no denying the sensational nature of the case: "This does push just about every political button you could push in the Navy," he told her.

Coughlin just looked at Sonday with a cold stare.

At Lejeune, Bonam was placed in one of the two lineups. Coughlin picked him out of the second one. She said she was sure.[47]

Afterward, she admitted she wasn't. "What is bothering me," she told Iorio and Sonday, "is I'm afraid I have this minor shadow of a doubt. . . . I remember him being larger. He weighed more."[48]

Sonday had Bonam weighed. He came up about a pound short of the figure on his ID card, an imperceptible difference. Sonday figured it was nerves. In March, he learned Bonam had malignant spinal cancer. Bonam later testified that he hadn't lost any weight because of the cancer.

Back in Washington, Sonday continued his review of the NIS probe. It was, he thought, kind of disorganized. Thorough, but unfocused. A lot of interviews had been conducted, but agents were just collecting information in a broad-brush manner. There had been scant review of the information, nor had there been an attempt to collate the files. Some of the case files were missing. These later turned up out on the West Coast.

Sonday also discovered the IG probe. But the effort to examine violations of the Navy's Standards of Conduct suffered from two major problems. For one, manpower was in short supply. Sonday found only one IG attorney, Cmdr. Paul McPartlin, who was working on the investigation. In addition, there was no effective liaison between the two groups, even though an NIS agent was listed as such at the IG office. This despite the fact that both commands were co-located at the Navy Yard.

Sonday felt the IG probe was important. He also saw it as a potential resource. If the two agencies built a liaison, he reasoned, they could both trade information and eliminate duplication of effort.

Sonday called McPartlin over to his office at Crystal City to talk. Afterward, they went to look at what IG had collected. Sonday was shocked. After months of trying, the IG had next to nothing. McPartlin had interviewed a few senior officers; that was about the extent of it.

Williams learned that Sonday had met with the IG, and he wasn't pleased. The word quickly filtered back down to Sonday: Do not provide any information to the IG without going up through the chain of command.

It was crazy. If Sonday wanted to look at any of the IG's material, all he had to do was go to McPartlin's office.

The limitations and shortcomings were becoming frustrating. "It's the investigation from hell," Sonday thought.

Pettiness abounded. For instance, the West Coast office of the NIS felt early on that it should be taking the lead on the inquiry since most of the naval aviators at the convention had hailed from West Coast bases. Williams wanted it in Washington, closer to the Navy leadership.

Naturally, Williams won. But the West Coast NIS became very slow in responding to Sonday's requests for the statements it had collected. At first, they wanted to send only summaries of statements because of the volume of paper involved. Sonday, however, wanted it all; there might be a piece to the puzzle hidden in a statement that a summary might not reflect.

Eventually, the West Coast NIS relented. But sometimes, as much as a month would pass before Sonday received statements he'd requested.

One West Coast statement was worth the wait. Lt.j.g. James Carson Reynolds of North Island Naval Air Station, California, had told an agent back in November that fliers were systematically lying. They were actually conspiring to withhold information, he said.

According to the agent's notes, Reynolds said that members of his unit, VS-41, "have a grapevine system where they discussed what was said/not said and what information they should provide in the future."

Reynolds also told the agent he'd learned how to avoid answering questions at survival, evasion, escape, and rescue, or SEER, school, where students are taught how to act if downed and possibly captured behind enemy lines.

This was explosive stuff. When Sonday gave Lannom the news during the weekly briefing, the deputy NIS chief turned beet red. "When the Under sees this, he's going to hit the fucking roof," he exclaimed. "This is exactly what he was afraid was going on."

Said Sonday, "There it is."

Lannom wanted an immediate reinterview. "Let's start pinning him down," Sonday told an agent at the North Island, California, office. "Who did he talk to? Who was saying, 'Let's provide misinformation to the NIS?' Was the commander aware of this?"

But when the agent went back, the flier's story changed. There was no collusion among the fliers. He denied he'd made any of his previous comments. "I've been completely misunderstood," he told the agent. "I never meant to indicate that they were conspiring to provide misinformation."

Sonday was livid. He knew that the opportunity to catch the fliers in a conspiracy to deceive investigators had been lost. And now that they knew what he was looking for, he knew he'd get the same story from all of them.

The second Reynolds interview was more typical of the initial interview with other Navy fliers. "They were bending like reeds in the wind, so you could never break them," said Sonday. "They were more adept in the art of obfuscation. They would say, 'Could have happened. Might have happened. Saw some hands go out and grab somebody. Didn't see any faces, though.'"

Marines were easier to question, Sonday later told Pentagon investigators—in a way. As a group, he said, they take "sort of the direct, straight-ahead, 'I see the hill, I take the hill,' approach to things. You know, 'Nothing inappropriate happened. I saw nothing. Nobody was there. No Marines attended Tailhook.' You know, that kind of approach, clearly wrong.

"But when they take that sort of rigid, straight approach, you can break them like a stick over your knee when you've got somebody else that doesn't take that rigid approach," he said.

That worked fine when the Marines agreed to talk. At El Toro Marine Corps Air Station, home of the "Rhino" squadron before it was disbanded prior to Tailhook '91 in a downsizing move, they weren't much in a mood to do so.

There was bad blood between the NIS and the El Toro Marines, many of whom had attended Tailhook and were mighty angry about being interrogated. The NIS agents there literally couldn't get any cooperation; many of the officers just weren't answering questions. They knew they didn't have to since, just as in civilian life, they could avoid incriminating themselves by taking the 5th Amendment.

The situation at El Toro eventually deteriorated to the point where the Marine commands stopped cooperating with NIS on investigations that had nothing to do with Tailhook. NIS agent Tom Clark was brought from the Marine base of Twentynine Palms, California, to perform the questioning so the agents at El Toro could get some cooperation on future investigations.

The stonewalling had been a major hindrance to making a case against Bonam. Sonday had a fairly solid ID on the flier. But at this point, it was Coughlin's word against his. Bonam had admitted he had been at the convention, and had even been on the third floor at the approximate time of her assault. But during questioning on January 21, he had denied doing it.

During that same interview, Bonam had let on that at one point, he'd recently run into Lt. Col. Michael S. "Wizard" Fagan, his former commander in the Rhinos, "at the exchange." Investigators later determined that Bonam, stationed in Mississippi, had visited El Toro while out west on one leg of a cross-country training flight. Fagan, Bonam let on, had told him, "Listen, I've been approached by NIS, and I told them that you weren't at Tailhook."

Said Bonam, "I hope I'm not getting him in trouble by saying this."

Fagan, the popular and final commander of the defunct Rhinos and now executive officer of all El Toro fliers, had been first interviewed over the phone in December 1991, when Bonam first surfaced as a suspect. Fagan was asked if there were any mulatto-skinned officers in his squadron back in 1991, or if he had seen any at Tailhook. When he asked who the agent was talking about, Fagan was sent a copy of the police sketch that had been done based on Coughlin's description.

Asked again if any of his officers looked like that, Fagan replied that he used to have a mulatto guy in his squadron named Bonam, but that the sketch "doesn't resemble him at all. And, anyway, Bonam was never at Tailhook. I didn't see him there; nobody I talked to saw him there."

The agents had taken his word for it. The report of interview sat in a file cabinet, unread. Fagan's name didn't surface again until the January 21 interview.

During a briefing in Vice Chief Johnson's conference room, Sonday was reeling off the names of suspects for Capt. Don Guter and Cmdr. Ron Swanson, the lawyers for Kelso and Johnson, respectively. When Sonday read off the name of Lt. Col. Michael Fagan, it rang a bell with Swanson, who knew Pete Fagan had a brother in the Marine Corps.

"Is that Colonel Fagan Commander Fagan's brother?" he asked. Sonday didn't know. "Find out," Swanson said.

Sonday did. It was.

Pete Fagan, the lawyers realized, had an obvious conflict of interest with the case. His brother was a suspect; Sonday wanted to nail him for obstruction of justice. If Pete Fagan found out what was going on, how could he be expected not to tell his brother Mike?[49]

Plus, it was Garrett's—his boss's—investigation. Pete Fagan not only had no business sitting in on the weekly Tailhook meetings of senior Navy leaders, he had no business knowing anything about the probe. Swanson told Johnson, Guter told Gordon, and both lawyers told Williams.

To the lawyers, it was clear that Gordon and Williams already knew. Williams's response: "It's not a problem. Pete's not that close to his brother."

Actually, Fagan was too valuable to the two senior lawyers to lose. Pete Fagan was Williams's and Gordon's spy in Garrett's office, telling them everything he heard relative to the investigation.[50]

In addition, the three men were closely connected. Williams and Fagan were good friends. Garrett's lawyer was also Williams's protégé, and Williams, of course, was Gordon's. It was no secret in the JAG Corps that Williams was grooming Fagan for admiral. He had even told Fagan he was planning to move Ed Ellis out of Norfolk a year early to free that slot for him.

The Norfolk NLSO command was considered a key launching pad to make admiral in the JAG Corps. But Ellis, never shy about speaking his mind, wasn't exactly politically connected. He had a habit of saying what needed to be said, which was not a popular habit.

Gordon, especially, held a grudge against Ellis for a comment made a couple of years earlier, when Ellis was the top lawyer for U.S. Atlantic Command and Kelso, its commander at the time. A colleague had asked Ellis what he thought of Gordon being tapped as the Navy's judge advocate general. Ellis, citing Gordon's background, said Gordon was "uniquely unqualified to lead the JAG Corps."

The comment got back to Gordon, and Ellis learned of his displeasure. A few days later, Ellis went to meet with Gordon and apologize for upsetting him—not for what he said—but Gordon never forgave him.[51]

Fagan's power base was a substantial roadblock for Sonday. Still, he had to somehow press ahead with the Bonam issue. Sonday needed corroboration of Coughlin's identification. He was still one witness away from a court-martial.

The third week in February, he thought he'd found him in the person of Marine Capt. Ray Allen.

Like Bonam, Allen had also been a Rhino, and had been Bonam's roommate at Tailhook. Coughlin had said she'd bitten one of her assailants hard enough to draw blood. Maybe Allen had noticed a wound on Bonam?

To get a positive ID on Bonam and to put the lie to Fagan, Sonday knew that Allen had to be questioned. He called Clark.

"Ask Allen where Bonam went," Sonday told Clark. "Don't give him any names. Ask if he saw any senior officers in the room at that time." Sonday didn't want to force-feed the pilots; he wanted them to come up with the names on their own. He also didn't want to alert Fagan that he had become a target.

As soon as it was over, Clark called Sonday back.

Allen had appeared very nervous, said Clark. On top of that, he added, Allen said he had the flu, and had repeatedly interrupted the interview to go in the bathroom and vomit.

"What did he tell us?" asked Sonday.

"He said he saw Bonam and Fagan in the room at the same time," Clark reported. "And you're not gonna believe this. As I was asking him what senior officers he saw in the Rhino Room, he said he'd seen Larry Garrett."

"Oh, shit!" Sonday replied. "You've got to be kidding." Unbelievable. They talked some more. Before closing, Sonday wanted to be sure Navy Secretary Garrett's presence in the suite was placed on the record. "Make sure you put that in the report," Sonday told Clark. "Make sure all of that stuff is in there."

Just being in the suite wasn't a crime, to be sure, but it wasn't going to look good for the Navy's leader, a man who had publicly expressed his "absolute outrage over the conduct" that took place at Tailhook, to have been in the same room where drunk Marines—his very own U.S. Marines—were urging women to perform oral "sex" on a plastic dildo protruding from a mural of a rhinoceros.

"That's not the type of activity you'd want the secretary witnessing," Sonday later testified. "The political implications of that were pretty clear-cut."

Sonday went to tell D'Avanzo, director of the Washington NIS office. D'Avanzo agreed they should go over to NIS to tell Williams. He wasn't in, so he and D'Avanzo went into the office of Lannom, the NIS deputy, to give him the news.

"We have got a statement that says the secretary of the Navy was in the Rhino room," said Sonday.

Lannom, sitting at his desk, rolled his eyes and laughed in a resigned sort of way. "Oh, shit!" he said.

"Listen, it's not a crime to be in the Rhino room," said Sonday, trying to be helpful.

"Does Admiral Williams know about this?" asked Lannom.

"No," said Sonday.

Sonday then asked for an interview with Garrett.

"Oh, God!" said Lannom.

"What's the matter?" asked Sonday.

"This just hasn't been a good day for the secretary," said Lannom. "His son is apparently in a little trouble out in San Diego with regard to some marijuana."

H. Lawrence Garrett IV, a Navy sailor, maintained a room in the basement of his father's West Coast home. The home would have to be searched. The son was also to be interrogated and given a lie detector test.

Sonday said Lannom gave him the OK for an interview with Secretary Garrett. Lannom later denied the conversation took place.

The Garrett interview was a long shot, but to Sonday's thinking, it could bear fruit. Bonam had been with Michael Fagan, ex-commander of the Rhinos. Fagan might have approached Garrett in the suite and used his brother's name as an ice-breaker to start a conversation with his brother's boss. And Garrett might remember this light-skinned black who'd been standing with Mike Fagan.

Mac Williams was on a business trip to Naples, Italy. About a week later—on February 20—he returned. With Lannom and D'Avanzo present, along with NIS investigators Bob Powers and Bill Hudson, Sonday told the NIS commander about the potentially explosive Allen interview and Garrett's presence in the Rhino suite.

Powers tried to be encouraging: "There's nothing wrong with being in that room." Replied Sonday, "I hope to God he was drinking beer and not making the Rhino happy." Even if he hadn't been, said Sonday, "there's a lot better places he could have been than the Rhino room."

Ultimately, the consensus was that Garrett hadn't committed a crime by simply being in the party suite. Sonday assumed that Williams would tell Garrett about the statement. After all, they were old friends.

But shortly after the briefing, Sonday received a witness statement from another Marine captain who placed Fagan and Bonam in the same room at the same time. He decided to call off the interview with Garrett the day before it was scheduled to occur. He had the information he wanted. He didn't want it to appear as though he was doing the interview just to say he could do it.

That decision, he later realized, was a big mistake.

February was drawing to a close when D'Avanzo gave Sonday the news: he had to be finished with the probe by the end of March. It was understood that the order came directly from Williams, who wanted out of the Tailhook investigation. The order put the pressure on agents Iorio and Dannahey. It meant their agents in the field had to finish exploring all major leads and send in their reports—even if they weren't complete.

On March 27, Sunday was done with it, and drove back to Norfolk to take up his new position as chief of the NLSO's legal claims department. It was left to the agents and officials of NIS to assemble the final report over the next few weeks.[52]

Back in Washington, Barbara Pope told Mac Williams and Inspector General Davis that they shouldn't just dump the report in Garrett's lap. He ought to have the benefit of their recommendations at the same time. That was agreed to, and these were also prepared.

On April 28, Garrett was briefed. Pope was scheduled to give a speech at the Naval Academy in Annapolis, but she changed the time of the speech so she could be present.[53] Garrett heard them out. The actual NIS report would be complete in a few days, Williams told him; Davis had to review the finished investigation for Standards of Conduct violations, which would take a few more weeks.

But Garrett was leaving the next day on a two-week trip to Australia. Before he left, he twice told Undersecretary Howard to wait until he returned before releasing the finished report.[54]

"I do not want this report released prematurely, like the *Iowa*," he told Howard, referring to the botched inquiry into the 1989 explosion on the battleship. "I do not want another *Iowa*."[55] But even as Garrett left, portions of the report were being leaked to the press.

The next day, Howard, concerned over the public relations damage a less-than-complete version of the report could do, and angry and embarrassed over the report's findings—he later vowed to service officials to end the "hard-drinking, skirt-chasing, anything-goes philosophy" that led to Tailhook's abuses—decided to release everything.

All the time and effort had turned up three American suspects: Bonam, Michael Fagan, and Mike Clancy, a pilot out of a Jacksonville-based S-3 Viking antisubmarine squadron. Bonam, for assault; Fagan, for obstruction of justice and making false official statements, and Clancy, for trying to encourage certain partiers to keep partypoopers from interfering with the gantlet.

The number three had a resoundingly low sound to it. Only three suspects? The public outcry was immediate. Mac Williams, at lawyer Gordon's request, went back through the reports of interview to develop a better-sounding number. Every time the word gantlet or gauntlet or activity consistent with those words was mentioned in a report, Williams counted the person being interviewed as a suspect. He came up with the number 65, which was released to the press.

That, thought Sonday when he later heard it, is completely bogus. Besides, ROIs are statements by agents, not interviewees.[56]

When the enraged Garrett returned from his trip, Pope rushed to see him—but not about the report's early release. Instead, she complained that the reports were inadequate. None of the twenty-six squadron commanders who had been in charge of the Tailhook suites were interviewed. This whole spin doctor approach, she said, is a mistake.

When she had interviewed for the job two years before, Garrett had told Pope that he placed a premium on loyalty. Pope promised she'd be loyal, adding, "if I ever come to a point where I feel I can't support you, I'll leave."

Now, she was at that point. "I made you a promise," she said. "I'm at the point where . . . these reports are not up to Navy standards."

Some heads should roll, she said. If he wouldn't take some sort of action against those commanders, she'd resign.

"People are lying," she said. "People have lied to IG and NIS, and we can't accept this report." Garrett turned to Davis and Williams, now in the office, and said, "Is that true?" Yes, they replied. They told Garrett that many fliers had refused to incriminate themselves.

"There is a major difference between taking the Fifth Amendment and lying to investigators," said Pope. "You can't go forward with this report. I will not go to the 'Hill' and present this report."

Pope and Garrett talked about the importance of due process. But Pope, who oversaw standards of conduct and separations, said Garrett had the power to relieve the commanders for lack of confidence. No hearing required. Garrett, nodding, didn't reply.[57]

Practically lost in the shuffle were George Davis's IG reports on personal conduct and the Navy's relationship with the Tailhook Association, released the same day as the NIS report. Although it didn't name any names and didn't include input from senior officers who'd attended Tailhook, the report was much more well-received. It concluded that the Navy should cut off all support for the Tailhook Association, although it left the door open for revisiting the idea. And it found "a marked absence of moral courage and personal integrity" on the part of officers interviewed for their failure to accept responsibility for their actions, an attitude among fliers interviewed that the way women were treated at Tailhook "was what women should have expected and accepted," and that there was "a long-standing, continued abuse and glamorization of alcohol" within the aviation community.

It also noted that of the 1,730 passengers carried to Las Vegas on Navy and Marine Corps support aircraft, only 100 were traveling on funded orders, a requirement for space-available travel, and recommended stricter adherence to policy.[58]

In order to placate Pope and help alleviate her very real concerns about congressional reaction, especially on the Senate side, Garrett ordered Gordon to prepare a briefing on what sort of actions he could take with regard to individuals and squadron commanders who saw inappropriate activity and failed to take action, and on possible obstruction of justice charges.

It was May 14; he wanted the briefing within a week.

Sonday was brought up north to help draft the memo, along with Capt. Tom Kahn, Capt. David Guy, Lt. Cmdr. Don Risher, and Cmdr. Frank Prochazka. The visit marked the first time Sonday had seen the completed report. He also learned that a 55–page supplemental report containing follow-up witness interviews had been generated after the main report was completed.

But he didn't get a copy, didn't pay it much mind, and never looked through it. It was never released to the press.

On the 18th, Mac Williams briefed the group before meeting with Gordon. That night, Williams called Sonday to his office to get his opinion on how he had performed. He was concerned that he would have to brief Congress on the NIS report later in the summer. Was there any way the report could be improved? Was it thorough enough?

Sonday assured him that it was factual as it stood. But after they talked for a while, he got on his soapbox. He told Williams the group was probably going to recommend to Gordon that Garrett expand the investigation. Williams said he didn't think it would fly.

"Hank, you just don't seem to understand," he told Sonday. "Our job is to make this thing narrower, not wider."

Sonday said he couldn't believe that, in light of what Garrett had done, he was considering pursuing action against the squadron commanders.

"How in the world does this man feel he has the moral authority to hold commanders accountable for what they'd done in not stopping inappropriate conduct they'd witnessed when he himself was in the Rhino room?" Sonday demanded.

Williams just shrugged his shoulders, Sonday said.[59]

On May 20, the group met with Gordon, the JAG. There has been a real failure of leadership, they told Gordon. The Navy has been turning a blind eye to Tailhook for a long time. Neither of these investigations examines the responsibility of flag officers or higher for what occurred.

They strongly recommended that the Navy IG investigation be re-opened to look into the accountability issue, adding that individual misconduct may be indicative of a failure of leadership. The NIS investigation should focus on that misconduct, they said.

Garrett, said the group, had no business castigating the suite commanders. Said Kahn, "You've got to remember that Secretary Garrett was in the Rhino Room. How can the secretary hold them accountable when he himself was in there?"

This kind of talk was not destined to become the party line, a sentiment reflected in the glare of Marine Col. Rich Vogel, chief of military justice for the Navy and a reknown company man. If looks could kill, Risher thought.[60]

Gordon just smiled. "Even if he was there, it doesn't matter," he said. "Your job is not to tell the secretary to re-open the investigation. Your job is tell the secretary his options for holding responsible the COs (commanders) of the hospitality suites."

Gordon's reply caused the group grave concern. What Gordon was saying bordered on unethical and conspiratorial behavior.[61]

On the 22nd, Gordon advised Garrett that further investigation by the Navy "is unlikely to be productive," and that the cases indicated by the investigations as possibly warranting further study be sent back to the officers' units for their chain of command to handle.

That wasn't good enough for Pope, who wanted the Navy to take a tougher stance. She was also feeling the congressional pressure from representatives like Barbara Boxer and Pat Schroeder. The recommendation also fell short of the expectations of Craig King, Navy general counsel—the Navy's top civilian lawyer. King told Garrett that Gordon's plan wouldn't go far enough to placate Congress. At a meeting attended by King, Garrett, Dan Howard, and Pope, the Gordon plan was rejected. King, a four-star equivalent, wanted a shot at coming up with a plan — one that would save Garrett's skin.

King wanted to recommend that the Navy's commanders-in-chief convene boards of inquiry, bring in the squadron commanders, read them their rights, and essentially force them to cooperate.

King's plan was opposed by Gordon, who also considered it a blatant invasion of the JAG Corps' turf. Gordon lobbied to maintain a uniformed legal presence in the effort to nail those guilty of misconduct. Risher was asked to draw up a memo on the constitutionality of King's involvement.

All the angst was for naught. Within days, the two proposals evolved into a plan to re-examine the Navy inquiries. Lawyers would collate the two reports. As they did, they would attempt to come up with some more suspects, as well as everything the Navy had on the squadron commanders. These briefing packages would then be forwarded to the chain of command of each suspect for action.[62]

Tailhook had preoccupied Congress since the day the story broke. In addition to his speech to the Senate, McCain had written to both Gen. Colin Powell, the Joint Chiefs of Staff chairman, and Secretary of Defense Dick Cheney, requesting that an independent commission investigate Tailhook. The suggestion was rejected. But congressional interest in Tailhook was far from diminished.

On May 27, Pope was scheduled to testify before the Senate Armed Services Manpower Subcommittee in a hearing on personnel issues. Before she went, Garrett was assured there wouldn't be any questions about Tailhook. But that morning, when Pope looked up and saw the face of Sen. Sam Nunn, the Georgia Democrat who, as chairman of the powerful Senate Armed Services Committee, rarely attended subcommittee hearings, she knew she was in for it. For the next hour, Pope was peppered with a barrage of tough questions on the Navy's investigation from senators like Nunn and Sen. John Glenn, D-Ohio.

She was also given two letters addressed to the Defense Department. One called for disciplining irresponsible squadron commanders. The second froze all Navy and Marine Corps officer promotions—4,500 were pending—until the committee members, the final arbiters of officers' fitness for promotion, were given a list of every officer who had misbehaved at Tailhook.[63]

This was no more than the standard notification that an officer's file contained adverse information, but it went well beyond the standard in the required detail. A letter signed by an assistant secretary of defense was to be attached to each promotion packet stating that a particular nominee had or had not been questioned about or "identified as potentially implicated in the Tailhook incident or in any cover-up, failure to cooperate, or interference with the Tailhook investigation" or subsequently identified as such. If they were, the SASC wanted everything the Navy Department could provide on that officer's case.

The freeze shattered officer morale fleet-wide. This didn't affect just those who'd attended Tailhook. This affected *everyone*. For the first time, even those who hadn't attended Tailhook began to fear a witchhunt.

After Gordon's meeting with the lawyers who drafted the accountability memo for Garrett, it had become clear that the plan was to hold individuals accountable — not the institution. On June 2, Garrett notified his Navy and Marine service chiefs that he was ordering the chief of the Naval Reserve, the chief of Naval Education and Training, and the Atlantic and Pacific Fleet commanders to assist the Office of the General Counsel of the Navy, or OGC, in the questioning of Tailhook suspects.

That same day, King tasked Don Risher and Cmdr. Richard Ozmun, King's JAG aide, to reread the Navy's investigations over the next three weeks and develop case files on the squadron commanders, anyone else who might have been overlooked, and to develop plans for holding them accountable. Cloistered in a cypher-locked Pentagon room with the reports and files from the investigations of the Naval Investigative Service and the Naval Inspector General, Risher and Ozmun began a fresh page-by-page review, compiling lists of victims, potential suspects, classifying the whole gamut of wrongdoing. The two lawyers came up with the names of thirty-three officers—seventeen squadron commanders and sixteen other officers—who they felt might warrant a second look.

The four admirals affected by Garrett's decree weren't pleased at his decision; they didn't want King or his civilian lawyers coming around and questioning their fliers. The decree was lacking in details; it seemed to them like a "Washington" idea that might have sounded good in Garrett's Pentagon office but would be difficult to implement. To ease their concerns, King, under the pretext of showing them how to implement the plan, asked the four officers to send their lawyers to Washington to meet with officials.

The visiting lawyers met with Risher, Ozmun, King and Joe Lynch, an OGC lawyer. The visitors expressed the concern that any assistance rendered by their bosses might later lead to charges of undue command influence. Still, Garrett ultimately forwarded to the major commands the names of the thirty-three officers OGC investigators wanted to question.

During the course of the OGC review, Risher, when he had run across references to the reports of interviews conducted by Navy agents, had made a point of turning to the actual reports to cross-check the information. Gradually, he began to notice he was coming up short by four or five reports, and called NIS to ask where they were. He waited, but they never materialized. Instead of telling King, Risher mentioned the shortfall to Swanson, the vice chief's lawyer, an old and trusted friend from their days together in Norfolk.

In early June, both Garrett and Kelso received media queries from *The New York Times* asking whether either had been in Tailhook's party suites. Cmdr. Debra Ann Burnette, Kelso's public affairs officer, didn't think her boss had, but asked Guter if he knew anything she didn't. Guter did not, but decided to go downstairs and call on Swanson, who had a copy of the NIS investigation.

They gave it another quick once-over. Nothing was found, but the two lawyers decided to make a couple of calls, just to make sure. Guter called the Naval Inspector General's office, and Swanson called Ed Ellis. It was June 8.[64]

Swanson made small talk for a few minutes before getting to the point: had Sonday turned up anything about Secretary Garrett during his investigation?

The question took Ellis by surprise. He told Swanson that Sonday had told him on a number of occasions that Garrett was up in the party suites on the third floor of the Hilton. According to Sonday, he said, it was all there in the Allen statement.

At Ellis's behest, Sonday called Swanson and said that not only was Garrett's presence in the Rhino suite an established fact; he'd also been told by IG attorney McPartlin that Garrett had also been in the HS-1 suite, four doors down and across the hall from the Rhino suite, that same night.

That wasn't all, Sonday said. At one point that night, an extremely drunk eighteen-year-old Julie Rodgers had been booted out of the HS-1 suite, 315, into the gantlet. And the gantlet, investigators knew, had taken place intermittently throughout the latter part of the evening—between HS-1 and the Rhino suite.

It was possible, of course, that Garrett could have left HS-1, crossed the hall into another suite, gone out onto the patio, and then entered the Rhino suite from the outside, he reasoned. But it could also mean that Garrett was going down the hallway at about the time the gantlet was in progress.

Sonday had also learned from McPartlin that Garrett had been preceded through the suites he visited by Vice Adm. John H. Fetterman, Jr., the chief of naval education and training, presumably to clear out any kind of inappropriate activity so Garrett wouldn't see it.

Swanson hung up and went back up to Guter's office to pull the Allen statement. When he and Guter couldn't find it, they started to get anxious, and called Sonday back. "Where is it?" they asked. "I've got it here in front of me," Sonday said. Send it on up, they said. He put it on the fax machine and dialed up Guter's office.

As he did, Sonday asked why such a sudden fuss had been raised about Secretary Garrett's activities. After all, he said, they had been common knowledge.

Swanson replied, "Well, the secretary has made a statement, a public statement, that he wasn't there."

"You get out of here," said Sonday. "You've got to be kidding. How can he possibly have come forward and made a public statement that he wasn't in the Rhino room?"

"Well, he has," said Swanson.

"Oh, man!" said Sonday.

Guter was looking at Allen's statement as they spoke. "Hank, this is big shit," he said. He knew the press was going to have a field day. He could see the headline now: "Navy secretary visited Tailhook's bawdiest suite; Incident omitted from final investigative report."

Then Guter asked, "Hank, is this statement in the NIS report?" Sure, said Sonday.

"Where?" asked Guter. He hadn't seen it; he wanted to know why Sonday was so sure.

"Well, I told Beth Iorio to put it in there," he said, explaining the Allen statement's relationship to the Bonam case.

Sonday told them he would look at his own copy of the 750–page document and find the statement. He hung up and looked. No dice.

Sonday couldn't believe it.[65] Neither could Adm. Frank Kelso. Just before Garrett had gone public, Chief of Naval Operations Kelso had called up Mac Williams and asked, "Is there anything in your report that is going to contradict him, and is going to implicate the secretary with regard to Tailhook?"

Williams replied, "I have taken the pulse of all the agents that are involved, and no, there is nothing out there."[66]

Sonday shook his head at hearing the story. Williams hadn't taken *his* pulse lately. Besides, he'd told him on two separate occasions that Garrett had been in the suite.

Swanson and Guter also wanted to know what Gordon knew. Had he known about Garrett's activities? Sure, said Sonday.

Sonday said they ought to take a moment and consider the content of their conversation. "What we are implying is that the director of the Naval Investigative Service, the judge advocate general of the Navy and the secretary of the Navy entered into a conspiracy to remove a document from an official investigation which was politically embarrassing to the secretary," he said.

After Johnson saw the statement, he called Williams. "Do you have a statement from a guy named Allen?" Williams said he didn't, but added, "Let me check, I'll get back to you."

At midday on June 10, Sonday was heading out to lunch with Ray Jackson, an assistant U.S. attorney (and soon to become a federal judge) in Norfolk, when he was called by Capt. Ellis's secretary. "Get over to the office now," she said. "You need to go up to Washington."

He returned and called Swanson. The vice chief, Swanson said, wants you up here now. Travel discreetly, and wear civilian clothes, Swanson told him.

This was getting crazy, Sonday thought. On the plane, two people behind him were talking about Tailhook. He landed at around 2 p.m.

At the Pentagon, Swanson ushered Sonday into his office. When briefing the vice chief, he told Sonday, "tell him exactly what you've told me." But for now, Swanson said, stay put.

Swanson and Guter were concerned. They knew they were playing with fire, and didn't want Williams's crowd to catch sight of Sonday; Pete Fagan, in particular, was always roaming the Pentagon halls.

As Sonday sat, a Navy attorney in the room tossed in some advice for his meeting with Johnson: "Don't swear. He doesn't like that."

And as a by the way, Swanson added that Sonday might have to brief Admiral Kelso.

Sonday felt like he was in a grade-B movie, or a bit like the double agent dashing through the Pentagon's corridors portrayed by actor Kevin Costner in the movie *No Way Out*. Here he was, hiding in civilian clothes, trying to avoid fellow officers he had known for fifteen years.

Sonday sat there for an hour.

At about 3:30 p.m., Sonday was ushered into Johnson's office and took a seat around a large coffee table with Johnson and Swanson. Sonday had brought a copy of Ray Allen's statement. He gave it to Johnson, and told the long story about obtaining the information about Garrett's presence in the Rhino suite. During the course of the account, Sonday mentioned Allen's constant vomiting during the interview by Clark.

Johnson's eyes flashed. What had he said?

In May, Sonday said, he had learned that shortly after his February 20 meeting with Mac Williams, the NIS commander had briefed Johnson about the existence of a witness's statement as it related to the hunt for Bonam. As a humorous aside, Sonday had learned, Williams had told Johnson that the interview had been repeatedly interrupted to let the witness throw up.[67]

That jogged Johnson's memory. He remembered the story. But what he now realized was that Williams had never told him the part about Allen seeing Garrett in the Rhino suite.

Johnson gritted his teeth, his cheeks becoming flushed. He was livid. "Lieutenant Commander Sonday, I want you to go to Captain Guter's office," he said when the briefing was completed. "I have to talk to someone right now. I'll be done in a minute."

The group walked into hallway together. A few steps later, Johnson turned toward a side door. It led into the office of Kelso, chief of naval operations. Sonday and Swanson kept going.[68]

At around 6:30, Swanson called down to Guter's office. Sonday wouldn't be briefing Kelso, and he was free to go. Sonday figured that could change, so he elected to spend the night nearby, just in case. Guter took him to a nearby hotel.

The next morning, he called NIS agent Beth Iorio. He wanted to know why Allen's statement hadn't made it into the report.

"What's going on?" he asked. "What's the story about the report?"

"I just wasn't sure it should be in there," she told Sonday. "It just didn't seem to be very relevant."

"I told you I wanted you to include it," said the frustrated Sonday. He couldn't believe it. He and Iorio had worked together for months, and she had never failed him. Every time he'd given her a tasking, he said, it had been done.

"I know, I know," Iorio said. "I didn't think it was pertinent. I tried to get ahold of you."

Sonday said he never received a message—at home or at his Norfolk office—that she had called.

If she hadn't removed it at the direction of Mac Williams, Sonday thought, Williams knew it was missing and didn't include it. He was too sharp.

When Sonday had first arrived in Washington, the NIS had developed a quick index to access the investigation files by name. They had come up with it because Williams was asking so many specific questions about the investigation. During the May briefing to the memo group, Williams recounted the NIS investigation to date without notes and with complete accuracy, including names and squadron designations. Mac Williams was no dummy.[69]

The morning after Sonday's briefing, an angry Johnson called Mac Williams into his office to talk about Ray Allen's statement. Johnson wasn't in the mood for a discussion.

Johnson, a war hero who had flown numerous combat missions during the Vietnam War, was straight as a pin, a very religious man of unquestioned integrity. He tended to take subordinates at their word, expecting no less than the utter truth from a fellow naval officer. He simply could not believe that he had an admiral who was lying to him. He was also deeply concerned about how news of a heretofore unknown supplemental report would play before Congress.

He read Williams the riot act.

Williams strongly denied knowing about the Allen interview, as well as the existence of any report of interview that claimed that Garrett had been in any party suite.

Johnson pulled out the Allen statement. "Then what's this?"

Williams looked at it. "I've never seen this before," he said, vehemently. "Where'd you get this?"

"It doesn't matter how I got it," said the angry Johnson. "What matters is that I didn't get it from you."

Williams just stood there. He had nothing to say. The angry Johnson dismissed him. He stomped across the hall into Swanson's office.[70]

When Swanson walked in, Williams, seething, cornered him. Williams had a legendary temper, and when he "got a burn against somebody," one senior officer recalled, "he'd take 'em out."[71]

"Ron, I want to know where that statement came from," said Williams, his eyes flashing.

"Admiral Johnson didn't tell you, sir," Swanson said, summoning inner calm. "I'm not in a position where I can tell you. Sir, I can't tell you."

"Ron, this is a loyalty check," said Williams. "I want to know who gave him that document."

Swanson stood firm. "Sir, I can't tell you."

Frustrated, the admiral spun around and stalked away.

That same day, Kelso decided to fire Williams. He called him into his office, but Garrett interceded on behalf of his friend, and convinced Kelso not to do it.[72]

That afternoon, Garrett released a carefully worded second statement saying that he'd learned about the statement in the supplemental NIS report only "yesterday." He had gone to a party suite at Tailhook, he said, but he'd only stuck his hand in to grab a beer. The choice of drink kept him on the fringe of the action; the Rhino itself, a few observers quickly noted, dispensed only mixed drinks.

On the 12th, Garrett went to Defense Secretary Cheney and offered his resignation. Cheney refused to accept it.

Congress was getting tired of hearing about the Navy's failure to deal with Tailhook; both the House and Senate were threatening to hold independent hearings. The Navy realized it had to turn the matter over to an outside agency. The DOD-IG was already looking into the missing Allen statement; the Navy hoped it would be friendly or at least sympathetic to a fellow member of DOD. On the 18th, at Garrett's request, the agency took over the investigation.

Five days later, Risher and Ozmun were briefing acting DOD Inspector General Derek Vander Schaaf on the Navy probes. To Risher, Vander Schaaf seemed like what the Navy hoped he'd be: sympathetic. "We're here to help you" seemed to be his attitude.[73]

As far as Paula Coughlin was concerned, this was all going nowhere. It had been ten months since she'd been assaulted, and she'd gotten zero satisfaction from the Navy.

On June 25, Coughlin went public. Before a nationwide television audience on ABC news, she told the sordid story of her assault in the third-floor hallway of the Las Vegas Hilton during the 1991 Tailhook convention. One of the viewers was President George Bush.

Late the next afternoon, Paul Beech, Pentagon general counsel, knocked on Secretary Garrett's door. Cheney had changed his mind.

Garrett took responsibility for the entire affair, but only as a commanding officer takes responsibility for his ship, he wrote to Bush. He told the president he would also ask the DOD-IG to review the Navy's investigation.

Bush's statement, issued that evening, omitted the usual presidential note of thanks customarily accorded a high official.

The day before Garrett resigned, Risher was assigned to Gordon's office to handle media and congressional queries on Tailhook, as well as to prepare congressional testimony for Assistant Secretary of Defense for Manpower and Readiness Christopher Jehn. On the 29th, he found himself working for Barbara Pope.

Pope was deeply concerned about those she viewed as the innocents being dragged down with Tailhook's guilty by way of the Senate's frozen promotion list. Of particular concern were new assignments for two four-star officers: Marine Gen. P.X. Kelly and Adm. Paul D. Miller. Risher, with the assistance of Navy and Marine personnel officers, reviewed every page of the investigations over the July 4 weekend and assembled for Pope a database indexed with the names of everyone mentioned in the Navy investigations. Armed with such a list, Pope could persuade the Senate to at least approve most of the promotions that were pending. The rest could be sorted out later.

Risher's group also received a query from the Air Force, asking whether the investigations identified any of their officers as suspects. There were none, although several Air Force officers serving in "exchange" tours with the Navy had given statements to investigators. Risher's group also had statements from French, British, Australian and Canadian officers who'd attended Tailhook.[74]

For the Navy, though, the hits just kept on coming. On July 1, Kelso had relieved two senior officers of their commands as the result of a lewd skit performed by F-14 pilots at Miramar Naval Air Station that featured a poster or banner that made references to Rep. Pat Schroeder, D-Colo., and oral sex. Schroeder, a thorn in the Pentagon's side on funding and personnel issues, had come down hard on the Navy for the Tailhook scandal. The officers, Vice Adm. Edwin R. Kohn, Jr., commander of the Pacific Fleet Naval Air Force, and Capt.

Richard F. "Skip" Braden, chief of staff of the Pacific Fleet Early Warning Wing, would both resurface later in the Navy's 1993 Tailhook hearings.

On July 2, the House hit the Navy in the pocketbook, eliminating funds for roughly 10,000 administrative personnel from the fiscal year 1993 defense appropriations bill in protest over the Tailhook scandal. On July 7, Cheney named thirty-six-year-old Sean O'Keefe, a close associate of Cheney's serving as Pentagon comptroller, as acting Navy secretary. Dan Howard remained as undersecretary.

There would be no 1992 Tailhook convention. The Tailhook Association announced on July 16 that it was cancelling its next get-together, scheduled for later in the year at San Diego. But before Hilton Hotels could announce in August that the group was no longer welcome in Las Vegas, ending a twenty-year association, the city of Virginia Beach offered itself up for the 1993 convention—an announcement greeted with much derision, given the city's ongoing attempts to sell itself as a family resort in the wake of racially charged riots in 1989.

DOD-IG agents fanned out all over the world. They interviewed thousands of Navy and Marine Corps officers on U.S. bases, in off-base hotel rooms, aboard aircraft carriers at sea. One particular point of focus: the squadron commanders given short shrift by the Navy investigation.

The Pentagon agents were well aware of the Navy probe's short-comings, and had been given marching orders to do whatever it took to avoid a repeat. Everything was fair game: indecent assaults, indecent exposure, conduct unbecoming an officer, dereliction of duty, false statements.[75]

DOD-IG by and large investigates improprieties within government departments, and white collar crime such as contract fraud; most of its agents are auditors. The reins of the Tailhook investigation, however, were handed over to the agency's Defense Criminal Investigative Service or DCIS, a group more suited to the task.

But the investigation's scope, the outside pressures, the agents' aggressive approach and their failure to tape-record most interviews were a catastrophic combination. These factors combined to produce a highly problematic report that ultimately produced little of value in court. Navy and Marine officers alike complained bitterly about tactics they viewed as confrontational and verbally assaultive.

"The investigating techniques used by the investigators range from cordial to barbaric," wrote Marine Capt. M.E. Marek in a letter dated August 1992, "The standard techniques used by the investigators include lying, hearsay, harassment, intimidation, trickery, badgering, innuendo and accusation. The investigators freely bring an officer's relationship with his wife into the interrogation. This is demeaning, insulting, humiliating and only results in raising the ire of the officer being interrogated."

Agents convinced fliers to meet them without an attorney present; badgered and browbeat the fliers during interviews; and handed out promises of immunity. Worst of all for the Navy and Marine trial counsels who would later attempt to press the charges, the agents were sometimes dispensing with reading those being interviewed their rights before questioning, a requirement in military criminal investigations.

"No congressman, senator, or military officer would condone what happened to Navy Lt. Paula Coughlin and other women," Marek wrote. "It stands to reason that no congressman or senator would stand for what's happening to thousands of Navy and Marine Corps officers either. The Defense Criminal Investigative Service is treating *everyone* as a *suspect* and a *criminal* [his emphasis]. Those who have sworn to give their life for this country are being treated as though common criminals off the streets.

"Actually, common criminals have more rights," Marek concluded.

The agency's tactics weren't pure bludgeonry. The approach depended upon whether agents had a solid lead on the flier, or whether they were trolling the waters. Mike Bryan had the opportunity to see both.

1991 marked the second Tailhook for Lt. Bryan, an A-6 Intruder bomber pilot and member of Air Test and Evaluation Squadron 5, or VX-5 for short. The squadron's party room, on the opposite end of the third floor from the Rhino room, stood in stark contrast to most of Tailhook's parties—milquetoast, others called it. The DOD-IG report contained nothing derogatory about the VX-5 party, one of only two units, other than Pacific Fleet Strike Fighter Wing, to earn such a distinction.

Bryan came upstairs at around 9 p.m. Saturday, looking for a hot dog and his first beer of the day. Bryan came out of the elevator, looked to his right, and saw the crowd in the narrow hallway, drinking and milling about, shouting, and pounding the walls. Bryan stepped into the edge of the crowd and leaned his back up against the wall on the right.

A couple of minutes later, Bryan was looking back at the elevators when he saw two women standing, looking down the hallway, sizing up the crowd. All at once, everyone began pounding on the walls, a mass, macho steam-letting, and Bryan joined in. Then Bryan realized that the pounding was a signal to those farther down the hall that some women were about to enter the hallway.

He had heard about the gantlet during his last Tailhook, in 1988, about women being grabbed and passed down the third-floor hallway. No one was getting grabbed or abused yet, but he had the feeling they were about to.

Instead, the women turned and walked out onto the patio. The men in the hall quit pounding on the walls, and so did Bryan. Bryan reconsidered cutting through the hall to get a hot dog, but trying to get through looked entirely too difficult. He turned and walked away from the gantlet, past the elevators, and down toward the VX-5 suite.

A year later, Bryan was summoned to meet with DOD-IG agents in a Navy facility at Point Mugu (California) Naval Air Station. The agent, he recalled, took the "big tough guy approach" as he opened Bryan's file. Just as quickly, he looked back up. "Oh, you're a 'random,'" the agent said, visibly brightening.

In other words, Bryan wasn't suspected of assault. But he had attended Tailhook, and was being questioned in hopes of developing a fresh lead.

The agent closed the file and asked Bryan to recount his third floor experience at Tailhook. Bryan did so, and was cordially sent on his way.

On December 16, 1992, Bryan was told to come to the beachfront Mandalay Beach Resort Hotel in Oxnard, California, to meet DOD-IG agents for a second interview because, he was told upon arrival, "My story didn't wash." Bryan was one of a small group of three officers and a government worker who had been summoned. The civilian was a female government who worked at China Lake. She'd been pinched at Tailhook, slapped the person who pinched her, and didn't consider herself a "victim."

Bryan didn't bring a lawyer. He'd never been told, he said, that he was a suspect. But the group was met in the lobby by several military defense attorneys from Long Beach Naval Air Station. The agents had

said that no attorneys would be allowed in the room during questioning, but that those being questioned could call one in if the agents
decided to press charges.

When Bryan was behind the suite's closed doors, agent Pete Black
opened with a long, confrontational diatribe, reeling off examples of
what he thought constituted "lying, cheating bastards." The agents
then began the good guy-bad guy routine.

Black would rise after a few minutes of questioning, turn and stroll
to the window, shake his head and say, "This just isn't going to wash."
Agent Mike Parker would then take Black's seat and, with eyebrows
raised, softly warn, "You'd better come clean." Then Black would
jump back in: "Your career is over if you don't cooperate with us,"
Black would say. "We'll make sure you go to admiral's mast."

"The fact that they saw my initial testimony to be damaging was a
complete shock to me," Bryan said later. He figured he was being
called back on a case of mistaken identity, that perhaps the agents had
a picture of someone who he resembled.

Not so, he was told. "Your initial statement appeared damaging to
your career," Black said. "This is your second chance to come clean."

During questioning, after Bryan said he hadn't recognized any of
the five or ten people standing near the entrance to the hallway that
Saturday night, Parker asked, "In your opinion, do you consider that
point in time when you were banging on the wall as you being a part
of the so-called Gauntlet from what you knew the Gauntlet was?"
Parker, who hadn't grabbed or groped anyone, replied, "Yes." In his
mind, it didn't constitute an offense.

But the agents seemed convinced since Bryan had been "in the
gantlet," he must have witnessed sexual misconduct. "It doesn't match
up," he was told.

After repeated denials by Bryan, Black exploded.

"Naval aviators are no better than street winos!" he exclaimed.
"When this report comes out, people will be spitting on you in air-
ports! If we find out you were lying and were an active part of the
gauntlet, we're going to make you pay."

After a couple of hours, Bryan was running out of ways to say he
hadn't been involved. "Look," he told the agents, "we're going to stay
here as long as it takes, until you believe that everything I've told you
is the truth."

"Are you willing to raise your right hand and make a sworn statement to that effect?" the agents asked. Bryan said he was and did so, repeating his earlier version of events into a tape recorder.

The agents told him he was cleared. And what, they politely wondered, can we now do for you?

Bryan asked that they call his commander and tell him that he was cleared. The agents did so on the spot. Mike Bryan, they told his commander, was not a suspect, was completely cleared, and his case was closed.

Bryan ended up on the list of 140 original suspects.[77]

Bryan was one of the few junior officers who was recorded; the agency's standard procedure was for agents to take notes, reporter-style, and later type up a report of interview not intended to be verbatim. In addition, faced with the possibility of recording thousands of hours of interviews, officials decided that the cost of transcription would be too prohibitive.[78]

The practice certainly saved money, but in the long run, it provided defense attorneys with an extremely useful tool. During judicial hearings, witnesses would be asked if they thought there were any errors in their statements.

Many were rife with mistakes; one witness at a hearing in Norfolk pointed out eighteen. Without a tape recording or transcript, there was no way to check who was telling the truth. It was the witness's word against the agent's.

There were further complications. A year had passed. Memories were becoming hazy. Many of the fliers had been so drunk that the entire night was no more than a blur.

Many officers also flat-out lied; others "had trouble with the details." In court a year later, DOD-IG Agent Matthew Walinski reflected back on the agents' frustration.

"We had been out for nine months doing interviews," he said, "where hundreds of naval aviators had said to us, 'I was standing next to my friend.' 'What's your friend's name?' 'I can't remember.'"[79]

"I found that sort of behavior astonishing," Sonday said later. "Not only that kind of cowardice, but that so many people, not just the [lieutenant] j.g.s, but the captains and the admirals, were willing to lie at the drop of a hat to save their butts. The absolute lack of honor and integrity was incredible.

"But they were just following the example set by Secretary Garrett," Sonday said.[80]

Many, however, felt obligated to protect their buddies, an attitude ingrained since flight school. They were angry at what appeared to be a politically driven investigation into what they regarded as consensual playfulness between adults at a private, out-of-uniform party. They felt like they'd been hung out to dry by their own leaders, many of whom had condoned the atmosphere at Tailhook but none of whom had stood up to say so and take some responsibility for same. They sensed a witchhunt, they felt railroaded, and many saw no recourse but to lie.

All this was buzzing through the West Coast aviation community as DOD-IG agents traveled from base to base. One group, the Marines at El Toro, soon found they had more to fear than just the prospect of a hot-box interrogation. Many, it turned out, would be left to their own devices.

DOD-IG had just finished questioning fliers at Miramar Naval Air Station in San Diego, and El Toro was next on their list. In late August 1992, close to 100 Marine officers gathered at the base for a briefing by members of the Marine Corps Defense Service. The officers came to hear what to expect from the Pentagon agents, and what to expect in the way of help from their own lawyers.

The answer: Not much. El Toro's legal services office had a grand total of two defense attorneys. And their supervisor, Lt. Col. Pete Solecki, the Corps' top West Coast defender, had come to discourage their use.

First, Solecki told the fliers that if they'd taken part in assaults, "you better keep your mouth shut, because they're going to get you," but to do so "in a very cooperative and unevasive way" so fliers couldn't be labeled as uncooperative. "If you get tagged for being uncooperative, then you're dead," Solecki said.

"Your career is probably going to be over if you fail to talk," Solecki said.

He also said the fliers "may or may not be given a rights warning," and that DOD-IG agents would likely employ lies, "good guy-bad guy tactics," and the questioning of their wives in order to get the fliers to talk.

But, Solecki told the fliers, although they had the right to have an attorney present during questioning, "You don't want us in there," because agents might label a represented officer as uncooperative. Besides, he said, the lines between consensual and nonconsensual conduct, and public versus private conduct, were too fuzzy even for his lawyers to give out proper advice on.

And, Solecki added, "I don't want my lawyers sitting in on 130 interviews."

Asked one flier, "Where's the due process in all this?"

Said Solecki, "Hey, no one gives a shit about due process at this point. No one cares."

"Everyone in this room cares," said the officer, loudly.

"Hey, by the time you get due process, you're already dead meat," Solecki replied. "Forget about that now. It doesn't make any difference. Don't start crying about your rights."

He told the fliers they could talk to one of his lawyers, but said he had told the latter "to do everything they can to discourage you from doing that because I don't want my attorneys going in there with you."

The top West Coast Marine aviation attorney, Col. Jim Schwenk, stepped up and told the fliers that when they reported for their interviews, he'd have a couple of Navy lawyers downstairs. "They will not be defense counsels," Schwenk said. "They will be there to give you general advice." If the agents read a flier his rights and the flier decided he wanted counsel, Schwenk said they could leave and drive over to visit a defense attorney.

"He won't be your attorney," Schwenk said, "but he will talk to you and you can get one-on-one advice from the guy."

One angry Marine rose to ask Solecki, "So the legal advice that we're getting here is, that the investigators are not looking out for our rights, and don't care for our rights. And we shouldn't be getting a lawyer to look after our rights, and . . . "

"The advice I'm giving you is for you all to look out for your own rights," Solecki responded. "You ought to exercise some. What do you want me to say? Life's tough. What do you want me to say to you? I didn't make up the rules.

"You're getting screwed! I can't help you!" Solecki said.[81]

Solecki later explained that he only wanted to bring home to the fliers the harsh reality of the situation.

"There was a national spotlight on this, and there was tremendous political pressure," Solecki told the *Los Angeles Times*. "Things are going to happen. People are going to get screwed. That's the way it is. That and a quarter, two bucks today, will get you a cup of coffee in this thing."[82]

The lack of representation may have contributed to an ugly confrontation that shortly followed the meeting. Marine Capt. Scott Bolcik, initially a suspect in both the Coughlin and Merritt cases, was being questioned by two DOD-IG agents in a hotel room near El Toro. Bolcik denied any wrongdoing, saying he didn't understand why he was being questioned. He agreed to tell the agents everything he had seen, including details about activities in the Rhino suite. But, he said, "I'm not telling you about my private life, or what I did in my hotel room."

After two hours, tempers became frayed. One of the agents got up into Bolcik's face, nose-to-nose, and grabbed the flier's shirt with both hands.

Bolcik, a large man built like an Olympic weightlifter, shoved the agent back across the room, slamming him into the wall. The agent's knees buckled, and he fell to the floor. Bolcik turned to look at the other agent, who had placed his right hand inside his sport coat, as if reaching for a pistol.

Bolcik figured he had screwed up.

Instead, other agents ran into the room, and Bolcik was read the riot act. Amidst the shouting, Solecki, who had been in the lobby, rushed inside to defuse the confrontation. Once he heard both versions, he turned to the agents and said, "You're wrong. You hit him first. He's leaving with me. Any objections?"

There weren't.[83]

Three months after Garrett resigned as Navy secretary, on Sept. 24, acting DOD Inspector General Derek Vander Schaaf released the first part of his report. It focused on the Navy's investigations, and called for the ouster of Williams and Gordon. At a press conference that same day, Navy Secretary Sean O'Keefe fired both but declined to punish them, allowing both to retire at their current ranks. He also booted Inspector General Davis, moving him to another job, placed NIS under civilian leadership, and blasted Undersecretary Howard for his "failure to provide effective leadership" and "abrogation of responsibility."

Gordon, the JAG, later denied ever being told that he knew there was a statement by a Marine captain that Garrett was in the Rhino room. In their rebuttals to the DOD-IG report filed months later, both said Hank Sonday had lied when he'd said they knew early on about Garrett's presence in the Rhino suite.

A few weeks before the firings, Kelso had confronted Gordon on that very topic. Did Gordon know about Garrett being in the suites? Gordon said he didn't. When Gordon left, Kelso turned to Don Guter, his top lawyer, and said, "He just lied to me."[84]

Vander Schaaf's report also revealed that three other witnesses, including a retired Navy captain who had known Garrett for twenty years, had corroborated Allen's statement or had placed Garrett in another suite.

Still to come was the second part of the report, which Vander Schaaf promised would focus on the actual misconduct at the convention.[85]

That was still being compiled by Vander Schaaf's agents.

By October 1992, it was becoming clear to Sonday that some sort of trials would have to be held. The Navy, he thought, was sitting around with its thumb up its butt. Tailhook was on the cover of a national newsmagazine. A national election was three weeks away, but Tailhook was still making news. This wasn't going to die out.

Sonday figured he'd be getting involved again. He decided to draft a memo.

The scope is potentially so big, he wrote, that the Navy needed to ensure that the cases are handled uniformly. It had to avoid sending Lt.j.g. X in California to captain's mast for a certain offense, for instance, while Lt.j.g. Y on the East Coast went to general court-martial for the same thing.

Sonday also recommended a unified convening authority who would oversee the hearings, with one exception: Give the Marines their own top man. The leathernecks would never let the Navy hold court for Marines, he wrote.

And since Tailhook courts-martial were likely to generate a lot of publicity, Sonday wrote, the Navy's military justice system was going to be on trial as much as the officers themselves. The Navy, he said, needed to *look* fair and impartial, as well as *being* fair and impartial, especially since Navy defense lawyers and trial counsel, unlike those in the other services, both work for the same commander.

That meant, he wrote, that the Navy needed experienced trial counsel, even if that meant flying in Navy attorneys from all around the country.

The Navy, Sonday wrote, also needed to immediately begin making contact with the DOD-IG. Once their report was released, the Navy was going to feel a lot of pressure to take immediate action. The Navy, he wrote, needed access to that report as soon as possible.

Ellis, the Norfolk NLSO commander, sent a copy up to Schachte, now the acting JAG and his immediate superior. Schachte agreed. Ultimately, separate consolidated disposition authorities for Navy and Marines were recommended. All that remained was to organize the two groups and receive the DOD-IG investigation. If everything fell into place, the Navy could quickly put this affair to rest.[86]

That wasn't going to happen. Like Brer Rabbit in Walt Disney's movie *Song of the South*—the Navy was about to wrap its big paws around the Tarbaby.

5

Little Creek

"Hello. I'm Capt. Jeffry Williams. And my hair's on fire."

That's not exactly how Jeff Williams introduced himself to colleagues. But as far as many were concerned, he might as well have.[1]

As 1992 gave way to the new year, Williams, a tall, lanky, graying man of legendary intensity, was the staff judge advocate, or principle lawyer, for Vice Adm. J. Paul Reason. Reason commanded the Atlantic Fleet Surface Force, or SurfLant; as such, he, like other commanders, was entitled to his own attorney. When he needed legal advice on any Navy matter—be it charges against a commander who had run his ship aground or a potential conflict of interest, Reason turned to Williams for advice.

With the imminent release of part two of the Tailhook report by the DOD-IG, Reason, a Vietnam veteran, a formal naval aide to President Jimmy Carter, and the Navy's highest-ranking black officer, had learned that he was one of three East Coast commanders in line to oversee the Navy hearings that would follow.[2]

A large, tall, imposing figure with close-cropped hair, a wide mustache and a ready smile, Reason trusted Williams completely. If Reason got the nod, the direction and tenor of the Navy hearings would be his alone to decide; he would take the heat for the ultimate success or failure of the Navy's effort. But it would be his adviser who would, more than any other officer, end up exerting the greatest influence on the results.

Despite his intensity, Williams was generally well-regarded. But when he confronted an issue, Williams tended to put his blinders on. A rigid, Type A personality, Williams dealt in blacks and whites, not grays.[3]

For all his Navy legal experience, Williams also had a reputation for having problems dealing with pressure. And he had never had pressure like 1993 might bring. If his boss was selected to lead the hearings, Williams would be responsible for advising Reason on how to proceed in the cases of what could turn out to be more than 100 officers charged with misconduct at the 1991 Tailhook convention. The potential caseload was overwhelming. In addition, Tailhook had the attention of the press, and the disposition of the cases would be widely reported.[4]

The combination had all the makings of a recipe for a time bomb.

The decision to place all of the Tailhook cases under what were termed consolidated disposition authorities, one each for the Navy and the Marine Corps, rather than handle them through each officer's local chain of command, had been made by Navy Secretary Sean O'Keefe, who took Garrett's place when the latter was forced to resign.

"We want to make sure that the actions we take are consistent from individual to individual," explained Adm. Frank B. Kelso when making the Navy's choices public on April 23, 1993. "This will also ensure that no convening authority would face any potential conflict of interest for having attended the Tailhook convention."

Defense attorneys argued that the decision to form CDAs took fliers away from their own "chain of command," where disciplinary problems are normally handled or forwarded from. Those commanders are more competent to hear cases involving their people, they said. And by centralizing the hearings, travel expenses would prevent some defendants from bringing their own defense attorneys with them—particularly, as it turned out, West Coast fliers.

Attorney Mike Powell, who represented both Navy and Marine fliers in Tailhook cases, complained in a June letter to the Senate Judiciary Committee that the CDA process "is untested in court and is a Draconian way to handle the Tailhook cases. Without a doubt, it is a large-scale violation of the Marine Corps and Navy chain of command, which heretofore has been the bedrock of the military justice system."[5]

To date, the Navy had royally screwed up the Tailhook investigation. One Navy secretary and three admirals had gone down in flames, and its nine-month, multimillion dollar investigation had produced all of three suspects.

Now, with the Pentagon's subsequent inquiry nearly complete, the

Navy Department had an opportunity to right itself, to use this new Pentagon probe to seek justice for the women who had been assaulted at the convention it had so wholeheartedly supported, to prove it could police its own ranks, and to prove it was serious about wiping out sexual harassment.

Doing so was important, and not simply because Congress and the American public expected as much from the Navy. Since the previous summer, the pressure had been building to repeal the combat exclusion law and give women a direct role in the military's combat missions, especially on combat ships and combat aircraft. Properly clearing the air was critical to proving that women would receive a fair and open opportunity to compete for and serve in such positions.

That pressure was exacerbated by the new Clinton administration's proposal to lift the military's ban on service by homosexuals—if they agreed to serve "discreetly." And as if those issues weren't enough to deal with, the military, its ranks shrinking in the wake of the Cold War, faced in the coming months yet another round of congressionally mandated base closures. 1993 was going to be a tumultuous year.

During the first week of January, Reason had been bringing up the rear of a short list of three East Coast admirals being considered by O'Keefe and Kelso as the Navy's CDA for Tailhook: Adm. Jerry Johnson, the vice chief of naval operations; Adm. Henry H. Mauz, Jr., commander of Atlantic Fleet and Reason's boss, and Reason.[6]

Johnson was powerful, but he didn't have the staff to pull off the task logistically. Mauz did, but during January, his name popped up during an investigation into senior officer misuse of recreational Navy facilities on the island of Bermuda.[7] Mauz kept his job, but fell from consideration as CDA.

There were other possibilities. Two other major commands besides SurfLant fell under Mauz, both commanded by vice admirals. But asking the Atlantic Fleet Naval Air Force commander to serve as the CDA was out of the question; no one would buy the results of an investigation into misconduct by Navy fliers that had been conducted by the officer who commanded every flier in Atlantic Fleet. The commander of the much smaller Submarine Force, like Johnson, just didn't have the staff to handle an investigation.[8]

That left Reason as the Navy's odd man in.

Reason's command was significant. Operating from Norfolk Naval Base, he was the temporary owner of 120 ships—more than a quarter of the Navy's total. Only the Atlantic Fleet's aircraft carriers weren't his—a key consideration, since, if selected as the CDA, he'd be deciding the merits of cases against Navy fliers.

But the final decision was still dangling when Bill Clinton was sworn into office on January 20. O'Keefe, along with Barbara Pope and thousands of other political appointees, cleaned out his office.

Kelso became acting secretary of the Navy. The decision on who to choose, as well as the entire investigation itself, was now in his hands. Although he had attended Tailhook '91, he pushed ahead.

At 7 a.m. on Saturday, Jan. 30, Reason got the call he had been expecting: Kelso told him that he was now the Navy's consolidated disposition authority for Tailhook. Reason would have jurisdiction over every Tailhook case, Navy-wide—the first time such all-encompassing authority had ever been granted. It went without saying that Reason would still have to perform his everyday command responsibilities, which were substantial.[9]

It was an overwhelming task. And to Reason, it sounded like a no-win situation. And he had been around long enough to know that the normal enmity between the regular fleet, the "black shoe Navy," and the "brown shoes" who made up the naval air force would only be worsened with his being selected to stand in judgment of its fliers. There is an old saying: the air Navy protects its young; the surface Navy eats its young. Fliers sometimes viewed the black shoes with a jaundiced eye.

"You know," Reason told Kelso, "this could go either way. As far as a career marker, it could be a positive step or a negative step."

Replied Kelso, "Well, you have your orders."

Kelso added that the investigative files from the DOD-IG would be coming down as soon as the agency completed the second part of its investigative report.

Kelso hung up. The ball was in Reason's court.[10]

Reason was determined to do this right. But he also wanted it done as quickly and expeditiously as possible.

With an unknown but potentially overwhelming number of cases coming his way, the mission was daunting. The first thing Reason needed was legal advice. He turned to Williams, his top lawyer.

By Monday, Feb. 1, the two had settled on an initial plan. They would appoint a group of legal advisers who would brief a group of senior captains who weren't lawyers. This "executive panel" would in turn advise Reason on the appropriate handling of each case. The thinking was that the legal input, combined with the experience of the line captains, would lead to measured, appropriate decisions.

The team of legal advisers included three attorneys out of Washington: Capt. Robert McLeran and Cmdrs. Ron Boro and Gene Irvin. Irvin was the former executive officer of the Norfolk Naval Legal Service Office, or NLSO. Others were now-Cmdr. Don Risher, from the NLSO at Mayport, Florida, Lt. Cmdr. William Sweeney from the Naval Justice School in Newport, Rhode Island, Lt. Cmdr. Alicia Nemec, out of Groton, Connecticut, and Lt. Cmdr. Hank Sonday of the Norfolk NLSO, who had already done so much work on the Navy's first investigation. With such a background, Sonday was an obvious choice as one of the lead prosecutors.

Reason had specifically requested Irvin to ensure that the board had a black officer on board; Nemec gave the board female representation.[11]

The Tailhook team would work out of nearby Little Creek Naval Amphibious Base, Williams decided. Home to about twenty amphibious ships and three of the Navy's teams of Sea-Air-Land or SEAL commandos, Little Creek was situated on the watery boundary between Norfolk and Virginia Beach, roughly twenty minutes east of the huge Norfolk Naval Base. The location also provided a bit of a buffer zone between the team and the naval base, where the hearings would be held.

Insiders thought a couple of the choices to advise Reason and Williams were questionable. Boro was a solid attorney, but was just about to receive orders to come to Norfolk to become the staff judge advocate for the Atlantic Fleet Naval Air Force. That, many felt, put him in an untenable position. And Sweeney, prior to the tour at the justice school, had been the aide to the now-fired Ted Gordon.[12]

On Wednesday, Sonday briefed Capt. Ed Ellis, the Norfolk NLSO commander, on the Boro situation. Ellis said he would try to get the makeup of the legal advisory group changed.

But Ellis had other concerns, as well. During the hearings, he stood to be commander of both the prosecutors and defense attorneys, standard Navy practice. But this was much bigger than the standard Navy prosecution. In addition, Ellis thought, there were too many people getting involved in the decision-making process.

Ellis, agitated, called his boss, Rear Adm. William Schachte, who had replaced Ted Gordon as the Navy's top lawyer.

Schachte had already talked with Williams about the plan. But Schachte wasn't in to take Ellis's call; Ellis instead reached Capt. John Dombrowski, Schachte's assistant. Sonday knew Dombrowski well, and the three began talking over the speaker phone along with Cmdr. Rand Pixa, Ellis's top assistant at Norfolk. On his end, Dombrowski brought Capt. McLeran into the conversation.

Ellis settled down and went through the potential problems presented by the Williams plan. Everyone agreed that Boro had to go. They also openly worried about dealing with the high-strung Williams and his top assistant at SurfLant, Cmdr. Robert Monahan.[13]

Everyone knew Williams's reputation. Monahan was nearly as excitable as his boss. Around the Norfolk NLSO, they were known as Lotta Torque, and Little Rudder. Williams was also sometimes referred to euphemistically by the phrase, "Ready, fire, aim."

The two were famous for, as Sonday liked to put it, "running around with their hair on fire all the time." When Pixa had first taken the job as the NLSO's executive officer, Sonday had welcomed him with a can of lighter fluid and a pack of matches.

"When SurfLant calls," he told Pixa, "pour this in your hair and light it, and you'll be in the same condition they are."

There was a method to some of Williams's apparent madness. Sometimes he would propose an outrageous solution to a problem just to gauge the reaction. "He throws trial balloons up to see what people do with them," Risher later recalled.

Williams and Monahan were regarded individually as bright, knowledgable lawyers. But teaming *two* Type A personalities on such a high-profile case was a critical mistake. Some later suggested that the Navy's hearings might have been lot less bloody if one or the other had been paired with a cooler head to balance things out.

The group came to the conclusion that to keep the pair in check, the level-headed McLeran was going to have to exert his seniority.[14]

That same afternoon, Sonday visited Jeffry Williams at his SurfLant office. While there, McLeran called from Washington to say that he had spoken with Don Mancuso, director of the DOD-IG's investigation. Mancuso wanted Reason to issue a testimonial grant of immunity to Lt. Dan Janssen, the lieutenant from Whidbey Island, Wash., who was a prime witness against the present and previous commanders of his squadron, Gregory Tritt and Thomas Miller.

Good grief, Williams thought. These guys don't quit. It had only taken a half-hour after he had been told that Reason was CDA before he had gotten a call from DOD-IG lawyer Ann Kanamine requesting the same thing.

The three attorneys agreed this was putting the cart before the horse. They hadn't seen any of the DOD-IG report. They didn't even know what Janssen had done.

Williams then told Sonday and McLeran that Reason had decided that if accused officers refused to submit to an administrative hearing before him—an admiral's mast—Reason planned to take them to special courts-martial.

Sonday questioned the choice. Officers, he said, can get more punishment at an admiral's mast than at a special court-martial. And once suspects saw that special courts-martial were the result of refusing mast, Sonday and McLeran argued, none of them would take admiral's mast. The officers would opt for a general court-martial—a jury trial, where they'd be entitled to an attorney, and to a jury of peers from whom they could possibly win sympathy.

That would broaden the process exponentially, they argued. And the longer all this takes, the worse it will be.

If you want to take an officer refusing mast to trial, Sonday said, send him to an Article 32 pretrial hearing, the precursor to a higher-level general court-martial. There, if the evidence warranted a trial, the accused officer could be dismissed from the Navy, face a prison sentence, or be dropped lower on the service-wide promotion list—three punishments not available at a special court-martial.

If Reason opted for Article 32s, Sonday and McLeran recommended holding the pretrial hearings at the officers' home bases. It would streamline the process, they said. And suspects could more easily call character witnesses, an Article 32 entitlement if the witnesses live within a 100–mile area. Coming to Norfolk, most couldn't do that.

Williams agreed with their line of thinking. But Williams said he had to support his boss, who didn't.

Ultimately, Reason changed his mind on the special courts-martial idea. But he was adamant on holding both the masts and the Article 32 pretrial hearings in Norfolk. In fact, Williams later told Sonday, Reason wants all of the 32s to start at the same time. Reason, he said, "thinks we can have everything done by April."[15]

Williams also remarked that Kelso had told Reason that if the Tailhook workload became too great, judges and prosecutors would be brought in from the Air Force and Army. That, Williams said, would be like admitting that the Navy can't do the job.[16]

At about the same time the three men were talking, Reason was getting similar pressure in Janssen's case. During a duty trip to Newport, R.I., Reason was called by acting Inspector General Derek Vander Schaaf, who wanted Reason to reconsider immunity for Janssen. Reason rejected the request. He wanted more information on the flier. And he didn't want to wait until the agency was done with its investigation before getting the files. He wanted what they had *now*. The rest could come later.

Within two days, Williams had drafted a follow-up letter to Vander Schaaf, signed by Reason, that made it clear: no files, no immunity.[17]

On February 4, the Navy lawyers learned that Quantico, Va., less than a three-hour drive to the north, would be the home of the Marine CDA. Lt. Gen. Charles C. Krulak would lead the effort, assisted by his personal lawyer, Col. Dave Hague, and Lt. Col. Joseph Poirier, the deputy staff judge advocate and Jeffry Williams's counterpart at Quantico. Maj. Phil Seymour would lead the prosecution effort, assisted by Capts. Michael Blessing and Steven Lyons. The chief defense counsel at Quantico was Maj. Dave Neesen.

Krulak, commander of the Marine Corps Combat Development Command at Quantico, was fairly new to the job. Born in Quantico, he was an infantry officer who'd commanded a platoon and two rifle companies in Vietnam, earning a Silver Star and two Purple Hearts in the process.

The infantry background concerned Gen. Carl E. Mundy Jr., the USMC Commandant. "This is going to look horrible having a ground-pounder judge all these aviators," he told aides. And Krulak was said to harbor a general dislike for the aviation community.

But Krulak was an unusual general officer. Known as a screamer who "loves to chew people out," he was also deeply religious. Krulak kept a Bible on his Quantico desktop, and needlepointed, framed Biblical quotations adorned his desk and walls. He had a reputation for being a fair man.[18]

In Norfolk early the next morning, Ellis told Sonday to get ready to go to the DOD-IG offices in Washington that afternoon to look at the files—and possibly deal with a grant of immunity request. But just after lunch, Sonday learned that instead of making the trip, Mancuso would be coming down to Norfolk—*sans* files.

The group met in Reason's office: Mancuso, Williams, Monahan, Sonday, and Kanamine. If Reason refused to grant immunity for Janssen, Mancuso said, he would go to Defense Secretary Les Aspin and complain he wasn't getting any cooperation from the Navy. For an hour, they argued about the grant of immunity.

They were wasting their time, someone said: Without seeing the evidence they had nothing to justify such a grant. Mancuso relented. It was all back up in Washington, and the Norfolk group could go up to D.C. the next day to take a look at it.

At 4 p.m., as the meeting was breaking up, Mancuso mentioned that in the previous week, he had gotten the commander of Naval District Washington to issue a grant of testimonial immunity to Lt. Greg Geiss.

The news didn't surprise Sonday. Two weeks before, he had been called by Capt. John Dombrowski, Schachte's assistant, who had wanted to know if Sonday knew anything about Geiss.

Sonday had told Dombrowski that Geiss was stationed with VT-7 in Meridian, Miss., and that Sonday had spoken on several occasions with his commander. And, he said, Geiss, one of the sixteen officers former Navy secretary Garrett had targeted for further disciplinary action following release of the NIS investigation, had been taken to flag mast and awarded a nonpunitive letter of reprimand for trying to keep two guys from breaking up the gantlet.

Dombrowski had said he had been approached about the question of granting immunity to Geiss. Sonday said that, as with Janssen, it was way too early to start immunizing anybody. They might need to hand them out later on, but not now, he reasoned; Geiss might be somebody they really needed to go after.

"What can I tell them to put them off?" Dombrowski had asked. He and Sonday went through the Judge Advocate General manual over the phone and came up with the idea of telling DOD-IG that the request has to go through trial counsel and that it should be issued by the convening authority.

That argument apparently didn't fly.

"This is really like making a pact with the devil," Sonday thought, when Mancuso gave him the news. "We may have immunized the wrong guy."[19]

On Saturday, February 6, Sonday, Williams, and Monahan went up to Mancuso's office in Washington. For the first time, they learned that DOD-IG claimed to have found evidence of more than eighty assaults. And although it wasn't news to Sonday, Williams and Monahan learned that participants from Garrett on down had witnessed all manner of consensual and nonconsensual misconduct and done nothing about it.

Monahan also gave Sonday a written order, issued by Reason, ordering him not to discuss Tailhook with anybody other than SurfLant attorneys working on the case. More than preventing him from talking to the press, the secrecy oath was aimed at keeping Sonday from talking Tailhook legal strategy with Norfolk NLSO commander Ellis, whom Jeffry Williams absolutely couldn't stand. By month's end, all of the CDA attorneys then on board had signed a similar form.

The three began an overview of the DOD-IG's probe in order to see what had been gathered and how it was stored, files and photos alike. Strangely, while they worked, a call was received from a CBS News producer wanting to know if any Navy lawyers were there being briefed on Tailhook.

The group began talking with Mancuso about immunity for Janssen. Jeffry Williams seemed to be assuming that the immunity would be granted, although he still hadn't seen any evidence to justify such a grant.

Perhaps he realized that at this point, the wheels had turned too far, and he was simply resigned to the move. But the discussion was more about what they would do after the immunity would be approved than about whether it was necessary. Williams also wanted Monahan to arrange a Sunday meeting with Schachte asking for more resources, especially in terms of people, but the admiral couldn't be raised.

Williams commented that Schachte didn't understand the depth of the problem and couldn't grasp what was going on with the investigation. He also opined that the Navy JAG Corps couldn't handle a criminal investigation of this size.

"I think you're selling Admiral Schachte short," said Sonday. "We can handle this." Williams disagreed, saying the system had other shortcomings, as well. For example, he opined, good judges in the Navy were a rare commodity.

Williams also told Sonday and Mancuso that he and Monahan would be entirely responsible for the legal advice Reason would receive. So much for McLeran, Sonday thought.

When they finished for the day, Sonday said he wanted to stay up in Washington and look at some of the case files more closely to start

getting a handle on the investigation. All told, the DOD-IG had created 300 case files, 160 of which weren't deemed worthy of prosecution. Of the 140 remaining, 118 were Navy officers, and 22 were
Marines. Another 35 files were compiled on the admirals and generals
who had attended.[20]

On Monday the 8th, Sonday began his review, and the first file he
looked at was Janssen's. Janssen, investigators said, had streaked naked across the pool patio after midnight on the convention's last night.
Not exactly the crime of the century, thought Sonday. In exchange for
immunity, Janssen said he could identify two commanders he claimed
saw the gantlet. For that kind of trade-off, he would recommend approval, Sonday thought.

On the 10th, Janssen was granted immunity. On the 11th, Sonday
was back at Little Creek in what the Tailhook group began calling
"The Bunker," the old Marine Expeditionary Brigade building on the
west side of the base where they were based. He got an early call from
Janssen's attorney, Pat Padgett.

Padgett, a Navy lawyer from Whidbey Island, was steamed. Janssen,
he said, had been told by DOD-IG agent Pete Black that the agency
would trade information for *transactional* immunity, meaning that
Janssen would be absolutely immune from prosecution, even if additional evidence of misconduct later surfaced. Black had insisted DOD-
IG had that authority, and Padgett had produced a proffer of expected
testimony.

DOD-IG did not have such authority. Now, said Padgett, he and
Janssen felt like they'd been lied to because the immunity issued was
testimonial, meaning that although Janssen couldn't be prosecuted for
anything he told investigators, he could be charged based on information provided by someone else. This was the first time that Sonday had
heard that DOD-IG was making promises about immunity.

"As long as he complies with the order to testify, Reason's going to
have to consider that," Sonday told Padgett. "But the grant's not going
to get changed." But afterward, Sonday called Jeffry Williams. "If
they're doing this to Janssen for streaking, what are they telling other
people?" he wondered.[21]

On Tuesday, February 16th, the legal adviser group reported to the
Bunker—with the exception of Boro, who never showed up. His father had become ill. He ended up submitting his retirement papers.

The first order of business: sizing things up. Without the cases, that would be difficult. But Risher, as the executive officer of the NLSO at Mayport, Fla., had first-hand knowledge of the manner in which the cases had been investigated; up until now, he had been appointing defense counsel for accused officers.

Risher recited the list of problems with the DOD-IG's interview tactics: the promises of immunity, isolating fliers from their counsel during interviews, heavy-handed pressure to cooperate, and browbeating fliers during interviews. "If you don't cooperate, we're going to report you to Admiral Kelso," was a typical harassing tactic. This, the attorneys knew, was going to present problems with admissibility of witness statements.[22]

But the agents' inexperience had produced a greater obstacle for the prosecution: the agents weren't reading officers their rights prior to questioning, as required by the UCMJ.

In the civilian world, the reading of the Miranda warning that informs a suspect he or she has the right to remain silent and to consult an attorney isn't required until the suspect is being arrested. Under Article 31 of the Uniform Code of Military Justice, a suspect must have his or rights read to him prior to *questioning*.

Early on, the DOD-IG agents were reading legal rights to officers being questioned. The agency made a conscious decision to halt the practice. The rationale was that it put people "on edge." Rights were read in certain instances; it was each agent's call.[23]

The Norfolk group, however, faced a more immediate problem: the files still hadn't arrived in Norfolk. The group had to rely on Sunday, who was briefing them from the notes he had taken up in D.C.

The DOD-IG wanted the Navy to take the files off its hands—especially the "flag files"—the case files on the 35 active-duty admirals and generals who'd attended Tailhook '91. But it was hesitant to hand them over for two reasons. The Pentagon investigators were afraid that if the files on the 140 junior officers were given to the Navy before the report was publicly released, there could be premature leaks to the press. After all, the agents reasoned, someone in the Navy had sabotaged the service's own probes by leaking enough to convince acting Navy Secretary Dan Howard to release them prematurely.[24]

The agency also didn't want to hand over those files before the flag files could be reviewed by the new Navy secretary. "How the heck are you going to take action against an ensign without knowing what some of these admirals had done?" Mancuso later said. And neither

Navy General Counsel Craig King nor Capt. Don Guter, Kelso's top attorney, wanted Kelso to receive the files, since one of them had his name on it.

"Nobody wanted these damn things," Mancuso said.

The CDAs couldn't accept the flag files, since, Navy officials determined, Reason and Krulak couldn't punish officers of equal or higher rank. The Navy proposed that all 300 case files be given to Kelso, but to hand the flag files directly to Defense Secretary Les Aspin, who was already feeling congressional pressure to produce his inspector general's investigation. Either way, Mancuso told the Navy lawyers, his agency would soon be washing its hands of Tailhook. "Once we turn this report over to you, we want out of it," he said. "We don't want to do any follow-up investigation. Use NIS agents."

Whoa, came the reply. The DOD-IG did this investigation, not the NIS. Besides, the new NIS director, a civilian, said he didn't want to get involved with Tailhook again. No surprise there. Ultimately, Reason convinced DOD-IG to stay with the investigation.

After much haggling, the DOD-IG agreed to unofficially release the files of the 140 prime suspects to the Navy and thus to Reason and Krulak, the CDAs, so that attorneys could begin to prepare their prosecutions. The agency held onto the other 160 junior officer files. In an agreement hammered out between DOD-IG and King, all of the 140 prime suspect files, as well as those of the 35 flag officers, would be officially turned over to the Navy Secretariat—literally, to the office, not to Kelso, the acting secretary—once the report was officially released. But the potentially explosive flag files would be physically held for the Navy by the Office of the Secretary of Defense—Aspin's people.

In a strictly technical sense, then, they were apparently acting Secretary Kelso's files, although it couldn't be determined whether Kelso had the actual legal authority to order their transfer to Norfolk and Quantico for the purposes of his investigation. What's more certain is that Reason and Krulak never saw them before or during the process of deciding which junior officers to punish, even though Kelso later testified that the two three-star officers had the authority to at least handle the cases of flags with one or two stars. Reason and Krulak proceeded without them.[25]

On February 16, the first charges were preferred against a Tailhook defendant: Janssen, for streaking. Although he was immune from use of his own testimony, the charges were brought based on the statements of others. The legal adviser's group still hadn't seen Janssen's statements.

A week later, on February 23, they arrived—along with 117 other files and the computerized "ZY" investigation database, brought down from Washington by agents Tom Bonnar and Jennifer Wallace. Another twenty-two went to the Marines. The Navy wouldn't see the other 160 or so files, Bonnar told the group; they hadn't been deemed worthy of pursuing.

Bonnar also told the lawyers that while traveling to various posts during the investigation, Mancuso had been telling commanders that the DOD-IG was going to have a hard time recommending punishment for acts that the Navy had condoned for a long time. Wonderful, the lawyers thought.

The next day, on Feb. 24, the Navy's Tailhook review began in earnest. The initial task was to screen the files and reduce what seemed like miles of reports into something more manageable they could use to prepare briefings for the panel.

Sonday, Sweeney, Nemec, Risher, and Irvin divided up the cases. Mornings were devoted to reading, early afternoons to discussion of the cases, late afternoons to more reading, followed by an even later meeting.

McLeran's participation was sporadic. His wife Judy had become seriously ill, and he rarely came down from Washington.

Williams, who lived at Little Creek, decided to fill the gap. In February and March, except for a couple of days when he was sick, Williams was at the Bunker nearly every day. Observers said nothing was done without his advice and consent.

Sometimes tempers flared. "He and Alicia got into it," Risher recalled. "She had the feeling that her opinions weren't being regarded as highly as they should be." Nemec, Risher said, felt Williams gave her opinions the short shrift because she was a woman.[26]

Williams knew he was crossing the line. At one point, McLeran called him aside and asked, "If you're going to make these kinds of recommendations to the lawyers, you know, then why do you bother to have us here?" Williams agreed.[27] And in late February, while waiting at Little Creek to meet with Bonnar and Wallace, he told Sonday, "I'm going to back off. From now on, all I'm going to know is what you tell me."[28]

Perhaps McLeran's wife's illness changed that—or, perhaps, Williams couldn't help himself. Several months down the road, Williams would testify that in his mind, the secretary of the Navy and two admirals had lost their jobs "because they hadn't handled Tailhook at all, and now it was being given to my admiral. Someone had to be responsible for it." That person, he told the court, was himself.[29]

As the lawyers read the files, they found many instances where punishment had been recommended for nonassaultive conduct. Ballwalking, in which a man exposes his genitals while walking in public, was one such charge. This wasn't generally the stuff courts-martial were made of.

The lawyers also quickly determined that the number of fliers DOD-IG said were guilty of misconduct had been grossly inflated. Twelve such cases were dropped almost immediately, bringing the number of working files down to 106.

When the attorneys started going through the files, they found nearly fifty cases in which agents had recommended that fliers be punished for failure to cooperate. This included fliers who asserted their constitutional right to remain silent. Fliers couldn't be prosecuted for exercising their constitutional rights, the lawyers knew.[30]

But flimsy cases were the biggest problem. "A lot of the cases were very lacking as far as the DOD [Department of Defense] evidence was concerned," one prosecutor said.[31] The Tailhook team knew it had an uphill battle, and would be lucky to obtain any convictions.

Williams plowed forward. If nothing else, he was heard to say, the defendants's attorney fees will serve as form of punishment, and the publicity will ruin their careers.[32]

By early March, Williams was choosing his first trial counsel. Sonday would work as lead prosecutor, along with Cmdr. Thomas Devins, Lt. Cmdr. Carole Gaasch from San Diego, and Lt. Cmdr. Wayne L. "Mike" Ritter, out of Treasure Island, Califonia. All began to assist with the file review.

The prosecutors were assigned to SurfLant instead of to the NLSO. It was a trial counsel department parallel to Ellis's own, which handled the everyday caseload at the Norfolk NLSO. This wasn't the normal setup. Prosecutors and defense attorneys in the Navy legal system normally worked for the same commander; Ellis, then, would oversee the prosecution team as well as the defense. As Ellis noted at a meeting held early in the process with Williams, Pixa, Sonday, and

McPherson, it won't look real good for Tailhook prosecutors to be working, in essence, for Reason.

At that same meeting, Ellis gave Williams a number of other suggestions: give the defense counsel full and immediate access to all of the Tailhook files as part of the "discovery" process; get the flag files and let the defense counsel see them; don't get so involved that you lose your objectivity and your role as staff judge advocate; treat everyone fairly because the military justice system will be on trial. The last two items went without saying. And timely discovery, Ellis thought, was the only fair way to do it.

Williams didn't like being given advice. This was his show. The flag files stayed in Washington. Timely discovery remained an issue through most of the hearing process. And although the trial counsel came back to Ellis, Williams kept effectual control of them.[33]

As Ellis later testified, "I think it would have made significant ripples if I had tried to intervene in any way with the assignment of prosecution personnel to Tailhook."[34]

In late March, additional prosecutors were brought on board to help handle the caseload. Lt. Damien J. "D.J." Hansen, a reservist, had been assigned to the NLSO from the Special Warfare community at Little Creek, and was scheduled to be released from active duty in September. But Ellis asked him to extend to assist in the Tailhook prosecutions, and he agreed.

Lt. Cmdr. Christopher Morin, just completing postgraduate work, was scheduled to be senior defense counsel, but Ellis wanted to give him prosecutorial experience. To fill the defense counsel slot, Ellis brought in Lt. Cmdr. Charles "Chip" Meade from Oceana Naval Air Station. Meade already had a Tailhook client.[35]

Most of the prosecutors weren't thrilled to be part of the Tailhook hunt. None had volunteered.[36]

One of Jeffry Williams's concerns was the relative youth of the prosecutors. NLSO commander Ellis assured him that these were the best he had available. The best alternative to Hansen, said Ellis, was his own Cmdr. James McPherson. But McPherson was heavily involved in a capital murder case at Camp Lejeune, N.C., and Ellis wasn't pulling him off of it.[37]

When McPherson finally arrive, he was asked, like the others, to sign the secrecy oath. He refused, saying it was an insult to his integrity. His ethical standards, he said, should be good enough to satisfy anyone.

Imposition of the secrecy oaths had a doubly negative effect on the prosecutors. For one, they reinforced a bunker mentality amongst the prosecutors, working in their isolated offices at Little Creek. That separation, in turn, effectively cut these relatively young prosecutors off from their more experienced colleagues elsewhere in the JAG Corps, for whom they could have turned for advice.[38]

As the files were sorted, the big question for the legal team was how to handle the disciplinary actions. Normally, military discipline is meted out by an offender's chain of command; the Navy had never taken such authority out of its individual commanders' hands and given it all to one admiral, as it was doing with Reason.

How could the consolidated disposition authority handle the dozens of cases with maximum efficiency and fairness? And how could the Navy, at the same time, get more evidence on offenders, especially the senior officers Congress and Barbara Pope had wanted held accountable?

DOD-IG had a plan. They would look at the cases, investigation director Mancuso told Williams, and separate them into two groups. One should include serious allegations—those suspected of sexual assault—and lesser misconduct. The other group would include cases where the advisers decided not to take action.

After the latter files were weeded out, he said, the officers suspected of misconduct could be brought to Norfolk and, one by one, go before Reason in an administrative admiral's mast hearing.[39]

Admiral's mast has no civilian equivalent, as it is nonjudicial in nature; the closest example would be a behind-closed-doors heart-to-heart with one's boss. But in a military unit, the commanding officer can hear misdemeanor charges against subordinates and mete out punishment. The subordinate can have a "representative" speak on his or her behalf, and the commander can allow that representative to be a lawyer.

If the subordinate is deemed guilty, the punishment can range from verbal counseling to fines to written letters of admonition to, for enlisted subordinates, reduction in rank.

For officers, the letters are the most worrisome outcome. The nonpunitive variety, such as letters of caution, are official reminders that certain behavior is expected to be modified. But these are personal in nature; no one else ever sees them. They are a wake-up call.

Punitive letters, however, have a devastating impact, especially on officers, who in today's military are basically expected to lead mistake-free careers.[40] The letters are inserted into permanent personnel files, where members of promotion selection boards can see them. In a shrinking military where competition for higher ranks is keen, a punitive letter makes it easy to decide who not to advance. When an officer has been considered twice for promotion and passed over, his or her career is finished.

After Reason made his rulings, Mancuso suggested, the officer in question would be advised of his post-mast rights, given a grant of immunity from use of his testimony and an order to testify, and then immediately interviewed by DOD-IG agents with the hope of obtaining more evidence to use against others.[41]

Said agent Matthew Walinski, "It was their opportunity to come in, tell us the truth, tell us everything that they knew that went on there, and then have the ability to walk away from it and know that they could go on with their naval career and not have Tailhook . . . hanging over them for any length of time."[42]

It was up to Reason to choose who would be go to admiral's mast, who would be court-martialed, and which cases to drop altogether. But he would rely heavily on the recommendations of Williams. Williams, in turn, would rely both on his own judgment and that of the five officers he and Reason had selected to make up the executive panel. They were McLeran; Capt. Lorry M. Hardt, the SurfLant inspector general; Capt. Pete Tzomes, from the Charleston, S.C., Naval Base; and two female captains: Capt. Carolyn Deal, from Atlantic Command, and Capt. Bonnie Potter, about to become executive officer of Portsmouth Naval Hospital.

Reason was insistent that the panel contain female and minority representation. As Williams later testified, "they might regard . . . a rather innocuous comment or gesture . . . from a very different perspective."[43]

The executive panel would be briefed by the legal adviser group that was poring through the DOD-IG files. Four of the five captains they would be briefing had absolutely no legal experience. It was a deliberate decision. Reason wanted the perspective of officers of the line, experienced leaders who could give him a read on how the disposition of these cases might be regarded by the Navy community at large.[44]

Deliberations began on March 8th. But from the outset, the panel floundered around, unsure of how to proceed, and what of the nonassaultive behavior merited punishment. It was, to be sure, confusing.

The panel was faced with 106 cases that ran the gamut from no action required to felonious assaults. It was a lot to ask of anyone, even with legal assistance. More confusing was the question of how to punish officers for behavior that had been institutionally condoned—if only tacitly—for as long as anyone could remember.

Deal and Potter, the two female officers, wanted to put the hammer down on commanders who allowed strippers in party suites. The lawyers countered that at the time Tailhook took place, the commanders of Little Creek and nearby Oceana Naval Air Station were still allowing strippers in their officers clubs one night a week. The practice had been officially encouraged in order to increase revenue at the clubs.

Deal and Potter also wanted to punish those who had touched strippers. Said the lawyers, if you're a stripper, being touched kind of goes along with the job, the whole five dollar bills-in-G-strings routine.

On the other hand, the male line officers wanted to pursue the officers who hadn't cooperated with the investigation. The lawyers argued that people can't be prosecuted for exercising their constitutional rights.[45]

As with the legal advisers, Williams, Reason's personal lawyer, was supposed to keep his hands off the executive panel. His role was to enter the process at the end of the review to provide the admiral with impartial legal advice on the executive panel's recommendations.

Officially, said Tailhook spokesman Cmdr. John Tull, Williams had been "tasked to advise the Commander, Naval Surface Force, U.S. Atlantic Fleet, regarding legal matters. That necessarily includes advice to the Tailhook investigation. He, however, is not involved in the prosecution of courts-martial cases or the assignment (or relief) of trial counsel."

But Williams was playing both sides of the field. Even as he continued to advise Reason, Williams was taking an active part in the review, helping to determine which cases merited punishment.[46]

The procedure itself was fairly standard. The briefing officer would make a presentation and conclude with a recommendation for disposition. The panel members would then debate each case.

Assault allegations corroborated by photos, witnesses, or statements were referred to Article 32 hearings for possible court-martial. Lesser transgressions could be referred for nonjudicial punishment, or nothing at all.

There was one other option. If the briefers felt there was a hole in a particular case, they would tell the panel. If the panel members agreed the case was circumstantially strong but was lacking real proof, Sonday or another trial counsel would call Bonnar, the DOD-IG liaison in Washington, with a request: We need you to send an agent back out to gather more evidence.[47]

One such case involved Lt.j.g. Elizabeth J. Warnick, a Florida-based officer. She was one of only three females included in the original 140 suspects; the other two were leg-shaving cases. Lt. Melanie Castleberry, reportedly a gantlet victim, was charged with allowing her legs to be shaved at Tailhook but neglecting to tell investigators; Lt.j.g. Kelly L. Jones admitted having her legs shaved, but agents hadn't read her rights to her before or after her admission.

Both cases were eventually dropped; none of the women who had their legs shaved, a group that, insisted the officer doing the shaving, included Coughlin, were brought to Norfolk to face Reason.[48] This later angered male officers charged with conduct unbecoming an officer, who contended the women were being held to a different standard.[49]

Warnick was a different case. She had her legs shaved and had done "belly shots"—liquor poured into a prone person's drawn-in belly and slurped up—at both the 1990 and 1991 Tailhook conventions. But in a statement to DOD-IG, she claimed that she had been raped at the 1990 convention by Lt. Cole V. Cowden, an officer with whom she had had consensual sex at 1991's gathering.[50]

The lawyers felt that her accounts of what had occurred were inconsistent, and the Navy had no way to reconcile them. But if the legal team took no action, she took her case public as Coughlin had, and the consolidated disposition authority then announced that it had taken no action because her story lacked veracity, the Navy would get creamed in the press. In addition, the lawyers were also worried about smearing Cowden's name all over the country on the basis of a weak case.

The lawyers decided to offer Cowden admiral's mast on a separate charge; he had been captured on a party photo licking a woman's chest above the dress line, and the executive panel thought this warranted a charge of conduct unbecoming an officer.

But the group also wanted more information on the rape allegation.

In late April, Sonday, not an agent, would be sent to Florida to interview Warnick.[51] Reason denied such activity took place. "This board did not go out and collect evidence," he later testified.[52]

In mid-March, a large chunk of evidence was nearly destroyed. The Tailhook team learned that Mancuso had decided to burn all the files containing nonreferral cases. Sonday hurriedly called Mancuso. The NIS, he told him, left one statement out of its final report, and two admirals got fired. Did they really want to destroy 160 files?

Mancuso wasn't convinced. But Sonday wanted the files. The statements could provide some leads, he said. In addition, all of the agents' notes were in the files. Mancuso apparently didn't know that under military law, the notes were discoverable by the defense. The agency had also in some instances completely missed offenses that people had committed, such as dereliction of duty.

On March 11, McLeran faxed a letter to Bonnar asking that the agency not destroy the files. If they did, he warned, it would jeopardize the trials. Bonnar agreed, and apparently persuaded Mancuso to change his mind.

During a follow-up call, Bonnar confided to McLeran that all of the files had been sitting in burn bags awaiting destruction by the time Sonday first called. Someone had to go down to the agency's incinerator to retrieve them.

In the end, the agent statements in the bags contributed mightily to the defense effort after lawyers found discrepancies in what had been written down versus what was typed in the formal reports of interview. The prosecution would have been better off letting them burn.

The files finally showed up at Little Creek in early May—just before the masts began.

The analysis of the files continued through late spring. The executive panel's recommendations were assembled by the legal advisers and other attorneys into a briefing book—the contents of which were approved by Williams—to present to Reason for use as a background reference so he could become more familiar with the cases.[53]

On Friday, April 23, Les Aspin sent the DOD-IG report to the Navy, and the Navy released the DOD-IG report at a packed Pentagon press conference. The media had a field day with the half-inch-thick book, chock-full of lurid stories that detailed assaults on eighty-three women and, surprisingly, seven men. It said twenty-three officers had taken part in assaults, another twenty-three had indecently exposed themselves, and fifty-one officers had lied to investigators. Reporters wrote of beer- and vomit-soaked hallways and drunk fliers who groped passing females. Kelso, announcing that "we had an institutional problem in how we treated women," called the report "a valuable teaching tool" that he would pass to commanders to help them re-educate their charges.[54]

On April 27th, Sonday went to Pensacola to interview Warnick. The Tailhook team didn't want to send a DOD-IG agent, the thinking went, because the masts and hearings were fast approaching, and the team wanted someone who could evaluate Warnick's credibility and determine what kind of a witness she would make. While there, Sonday also interviewed the agents who had conducted her previous interviews.

When he was done, Sonday called back to Norfolk. She was not going to make a real great witness and was very impeachable, he told Williams. But Williams wanted to send Cowden to an Article 32, the pretrial preface to a court-martial. Well, OK, Sonday thought, if Cowden goes to a 32, his name will make the papers. But the case will die right there. He'll be represented by a lawyer, Warnick will be able to testify under oath, and if Cowden wants to take the stand, he can. And no one can come back and say, "Woman alleges rape in the Navy and nothing happens."[55]

Cowden was later offered mast. He refused, and Williams had his wish.

Sonday didn't get his: a promotion, and a chance to retire as a commander. By the time he left for Florida, he had already decided to call it quits.

In the spring of 1992, Sonday had been passed over for promotion to commander. While one of the best litigators in the Navy, he had a key disadvantage in relation to his peers: lack of sea time due to an ongoing illness in his family.

Perhaps more significantly, Rear Adm. Mac Williams was the senior member of the board, and Cmdr. Pete Fagan was also a member. At the time, Sonday had been running the NIS investigation. He was going after Fagan's brother, who he suspected had lied about the whereabouts of Marine Capt. Greg Bonam, Paula Coughlin's alleged attacker.

Pete Fagan was well aware that Sonday was after his brother. His inclusion on the board seemed, like his attendance at the weekly senior leaders' meetings on the Tailhook investigations, to be an obvious conflict of interest.

Afterward, Sonday requested a special selection board, which was approved by O'Keefe. That board met in January 1993, and the results were reported out in March.[56]

Sonday wasn't selected. Nor was there an early retirement program in place that he could take advantage of. But back in February, before he had rejoined the Tailhook inquiry, Ellis had promised to reward Sonday for what he regarded as more than fifteen quality years of service with a special assignment at the U.S. Attorney's office in Norfolk. "If you go down in May, you'll have three years to go and you can serve out your 20 years there," Ellis told him.

When Sonday got the bad news in March, he told Ellis he'd take the offer. The job sounded good. Plus, it had become glaringly apparent that most of the government's cases were unbelievably weak, and Sonday wanted no part of them. Ellis agreed to grant the transfer, even though Sonday had orders to work on the Tailhook team.

Reason wasn't pleased with the decision. But Ellis, Kelso's top lawyer when the Navy secretary and chief commanded both the Navy's Atlantic Fleet and, later, the joint-service Atlantic Command, had a lot of credibility and sway. Sonday moved on, and Chris Morin was named chief trial counsel.[57]

Ellis agreed wholeheartedly with Sonday's assessment of the Tailhook cases. On April 28, he sent a memo to Schachte in which he criticized the quality of the evidence being used to prosecute fliers, especially those headed for court-martial. "Given the information I have received regarding the state of the evidence in the DOD-IG report, it will probably be necessary to substantially re-investigate the cases," Ellis later warned.[58]

May 1 was Sonday's last day. On the 3rd, he began working at the U.S. Attorney's office as a Navy adjunct attorney. But he returned to Little Creek May 10-11 to take part in what were known as the "murder boards" at which Reason would decide which officers to prosecute.

Over the course of those two days, Reason listened to briefings on the 106 cases that remained of the Navy's original 118. When the process was complete, Reason decided that about fifty lacked enough evidence to prosecute, even under the uncertain umbrella of conduct unbecoming an officer. That left him with roughly seventy fliers to deal with.

Convincing Reason to drop nearly half of the cases, the Navy attorneys felt, was one of their major accomplishments at Little Creek.[59]

In mid-May 1993, the rush to Norfolk began. Attorneys requesting information on their clients' cases prior to meeting with Reason were given folders containing the bare essentials—what Williams and Monahan considered to be "relevant" to each case. Things happened quickly. Suspects would arrive in Norfolk, meet with Williams, go before Reason the following day, and be gone.[60]

All told, forty-two fliers went to admiral's mast. The charges ranged from indecent exposure—"ballwalking," to be precise—conduct unbecoming an officer, providing a false official statement, and lying under oath.[61]

On May 20, Reason handed down his first verdicts. Three officers stood separately before him and admitted they had ballwalked on the convention's final night. All three were hammered with punitive letters of admonition and $1,000 fines. The letters had a permanent status: they automatically were placed in the officers' personnel files. This essentially ended their careers by ending any hopes of future promotions.

Like the first three, most of the officers who came to face Reason were immediately contrite: they admitted their poor judgment, they pled guilty, they threw themselves on Reason's mercy. Many brought along their commanders or other witnesses to testify as to their career achievements, true character, and potential for future service.[62]

Jack Marshall wanted justice, not mercy. A lieutenant commander then assigned to the staff of the Pacific Fleet Naval Air Force, Marshall was apologetic and respectful during his May 26 admiral's mast, but he argued at length on his own behalf and pled not guilty to the two charges against him: assault, and conduct unbecoming an officer. To Marshall, the charges seemed ridiculous. He had been flown across the country so he could be punished for a September 6, 1991, dance with a stripper behind the closed doors of a crowded hotel suite at which, the Navy charged, he had touched her rear end and breasts and "painted" same with the opened end of a fluorescent "day-glo" stick.

Marshall claimed that he never touched her private parts. As proof, he said, she hadn't objected. The only one of the some 100 people in the VS-41 suite who had, Marshall said, was a flier who'd been angered that his view of the strip act was blocked—and that Marshall had turned and pulled rank to shut him up. Marshall also argued that it was so crowded and dark in the suite that night that his primary accuser couldn't possibly have seen much of anything.

As Marshall made his case during his May 26 admiral's mast, he gave voice to feelings shared by many naval fliers, whether they went to Tailhook or not:

"I attended a private party, in a private room, in civilian clothes. Historically, these types of actions have not only been condoned, but expected by senior leadership in the naval aviation community. I don't feel that it is right to judge behavior that was acceptable in the Navy beginning in 1991 by 1993 standards. What I did at the time, I did not consider inappropriate."

Marshall's military attorney pointed out a parallel sea change in Navy social behavior by noting the phasing out of the physical abuse associated with the initiation of chief petty officers.

"No one took notice that these activities were inappropriate until the senior leadership said so," his attorney said. "It wasn't applied as an *ex post facto* matter, or [sic] was it retroactive." Reason acknowledged the point, but added, "You must understand that by the time a person has two-and-a-half stripes on his shoulder . . . he must have within himself the ability to differentiate between right and wrong conduct as an officer." Reason cleared Marshall of the assault charge, but fined him $500 and handed down a letter of admonition—the career-killer.[63]

One option for fliers was to refuse mast. The thinking was that if the Navy didn't have much to go on, it wasn't likely to invest the time, trouble and money a court-martial would take up. On June 7, attorney Mike Powell and a Navy flier charged with ballwalking met with Jeffry Williams at the SurfLant offices to hear the charge and discuss options. The next day, they sat down again, and Powell's client refused nonjudicial punishment—NJP, in military shorthand.

Williams, sitting across the table, handed over the document so the flier could sign and formally register his refusal. As he did, the lanky Williams stood and leaned across the table, his eyes boring in on the accused officer.

"Lieutenant, if you sign that document and go to an Article 32 investigation," Williams warned, "don't think I'm going to take it back to NJP when you realize you're going down in flames."

Powell sent his client out of the room—and exploded. "You do not talk to my client like that in my presence!" he exclaimed. "That's the kind of stuff that's going to get you in trouble down the road!"

"What are you talking about?" Williams said, raising his own voice. "I'm the SJA (staff judge advocate) here. I can say anything I want to these guys."

Both men were now yelling. "That is unethical," Powell said. "You cannot get between a lawyer and his client. If you do that again, I'm going to file a complaint against you."

"There's nothing wrong with what I did," Williams exclaimed.

In this case, refusing mast worked; the Navy wasn't going to hold a felony trial for an officer accused of exposing his genitals. The charges were later dropped.[64]

Within a month, the Navy masts were basically completed. Few of the cases involved assaults on women; more than half of the officers had been charged with ballwalking. Of the forty-two fliers, two were exonerated. Twelve received nonpunitive letters or verbal counseling, neither of which would be noted in a permanent record. Twenty-seven were disciplined stiffly, forfeiting between $500 and $2,000; twenty-four received punitive letters of admonition or reprimand.

Little did any of the 140 original suspects know that, two years later, the mere fact that they were on the DOD-IG's list would be short-circuiting many of their careers.

The Tailhook hearings in Quantico got going a couple of weeks after those in Norfolk. Like their Navy counterparts, Marine prosecutors spent the spring assessing the cases they'd been handed. Three of the twenty-two cases were dropped outright; of the nineteen that remained, only two looked serious enough to warrant Article 32 hearings and possible courts-martial.

The third week of June, the Marine hearings began at Quantico's Lejeune Hall.

The first officer seen by Krulak, the Marines' consolidated disposition authority, was 1st Lt. Kenneth C. Cooper of Cherry Point (N.C.) Marine Corps Air Station. Cooper was accused of groping women's rear ends, and he was the only Marine who admitted being in the gantlet. But he was also the son of a general who participants assumed was a friend of Krulak's. The association didn't hurt him: Cooper was found guilty, but given a nonpunitive letter. His file remained clean.

Next to face Krulak was Maj. Phil Gabriel of Yuma (Ariz.) Marine Corps Air Station. Gabriel was charged with propositioning a woman at Tailhook and touching her, acts he readily admitted to DOD-IG agents. The woman had never come forward.

The night before his June 18 hearing, Gabriel had met with his attorney, Capt. Evan Roberts, in the basement law offices in Lejeune Hall. While the two discussed strategy and how to handle Gabriel's defense, Gabriel told Roberts that he trusted Krulak, that he believed the general would give him a fair shake. Therefore, he told Roberts, he would opt for office hours rather than demand a court-martial.

The hearing was uncontentious. DOD-IG agent Patricia Call even testified about how cooperative Gabriel had been during questioning, something she made a point of doing in other cases, as well.

At this point, Krulak's prosecutors stopped the proceeding and advised Krulak that a nonpunitive letter was in order. Gabriel decided to throw himself on Krulak's mercy.

He was sorry he did. Krulak threw the book at him, and inadvertently broke the rules in the process.

Under Article 15 of the Uniform Code of Military Justice, the section that governs nonjudicial punishment, the officer doing the judging is supposed to pause after pronouncing guilt or innocence before awarding the punishment unless all parties agree beforehand to different ground rules; in Norfolk, the Navy didn't allow for the pause. But when agreed upon, it allows the accused one last chance to refuse nonjudicial punishment and possibly to take his or her chances at a court-martial.

Everyone connected with the Quantico hearings had agreed on the pause. But no one apparently had told Krulak. If they had, he hadn't remembered. He had also forgotten to pause during a few recent hearings that didn't involve Tailhook offenses.

"I find the offense is warranted by the evidence," he told Gabriel, adding, without skipping a beat, "I award you a letter of reprimand and a $1,000 forfeiture." Roberts, who'd been told to sit in the back of the room, was too far away to intervene.

When Gabriel walked out of Krulak's office, Roberts couldn't look his client in the eye. Gabriel was shattered. Outside, Seymour apologized profusely to Gabriel, trying to explain the snafu. Mike Powell, waiting nearby with a client, asked Gabriel what had happened. Gabriel said he was waiting for the pause, was being respectful, and didn't interrupt. "He didn't give me a chance," he said.

Powell turned to Roberts. "The general just snookered you," he said.

Speculation for the stiff punishment was that Gabriel was married, and Krulak expected more from field grade officers. But Gabriel, it turned out, would later gain a reprieve, thanks to the presence of a court reporter in Krulak's office who documented the nonpause.[65]

Tony Eaton, a Powell client next in line to see Krulak, didn't like what he was hearing. Nor did Powell. They walked out.[66]

A lieutenant could legally get away with such a move, but having a civilian attorney alongside sure made it easier to help deflect negative repercussions. Any show of disrespect, especially before Krulak, would produce a disastrous result.

Respect was a big topic in a confidential Marine Corps legal memo that originated in late August 1992 out of the legal defense office at Quantico—by way of Camp Pendleton, California

Seymour and one of his assistants, Capt. Michael Blessing, had prepared a five-page summary of the nineteen Marine Tailhook cases for Krulak and Col. Dave Hague, his top lawyer. Seymour agreed to share the information with Lt. Col. Geoffrey Lyon, the lawyer who succeeded Pete Solecki as West Coast regional defense counsel, as long as Lyon agreed not to release it to defense counsel. It was faxed to Lyon at Camp Pendleton.

There, an enlisted paralegal who got wind of the memo decided that Lyon wasn't keeping the proper distance from Seymour, and told a defense counsel who didn't have a Tailhook case, and who apparently agreed with the Marine. The lawyer, a captain, began listening in on phone conversations between Seymour and Lyon and taping them. The captain then prepared his own summation of the cases, and released it to the *Los Angeles Times*—an act for which he was later relieved.

The captain's version of the memo warned of dire consequences for any demonstration of disrespect, noting that "if the accused does not show the proper repentance, contriteness and martial spirit, he is likely to be punished more severely." The memo also stated that in most cases, Krulak, whom the captain characterized in the memo as a "Bible-thumping redneck," would award nonpunitive letters of caution, with stiffer letters of admonition and $1,000 fines for more serious cases. Field grade officers (major/lieutenant commander or higher) punished at office hours, the memo said, were expected to retire.[67]

The day after the Gabriel debacle, Eaton and Powell returned to Lejeune Hall for a meeting with Krulak's staff. When they arrived, Hague assured them that Krulak had been informed that he must pause before announcing the punishment during office hours hearings.

DOD-IG agents felt that Eaton was the man in an infamous photograph taken at Tailhook '91 who was lying on the floor and looking up at a naked stripper gyrating over top of him. It had been taken in the suite of Marine All Weather Fighter Attack Squadron 242 out of El Toro and published in the second DOD-IG report.

During a meeting with Lt. Col. Joe Poirier, Krulak's deputy staff judge advocate, Eaton announced that he wanted nothing to do with meeting Krulak, and would demand a court-martial.

"The CDA is illegal," Eaton told Poirier. "It's command-influenced. I don't think I'm getting a fair shake."

Poirier produced the famous picture and pointed at the figure on the floor. "Do you know who this is?" he asked.

Powell intervened. "You may think you do, but you can't prove it," he told Poirier. "To do that, you have to tell me who took the picture."

Poirier, however, had promised not to, and refused.

Powell was undeterred. "I'll get it through discovery," he said. Eaton then told Poirier that he was going to refuse the administrative hearing with Krulak, and would ask that he would take his chances with his own commanding general out in California.

Under military law, Eaton wasn't required to explain his refusal. But that didn't stop Krulak from calling Eaton into his office for a chat.

Powell had no intention of allowing Eaton to stand alone before Krulak, as Gabriel had previously. Before they went in, he said to Roberts, also representing Eaton, "Do you know what a flanking movement is?" Powell told Roberts they would walk with Eaton, one on each side, right up to Krulak's desk, no matter what anyone said to them.

As they entered, Powell was told, "Mr. Powell, we have a seat for you."

"No thanks," he replied, continuing. Someone else repeated the offer, but Powell declined again.

Krulak looked up from his desk. "Tony, I understand you do not want to stand NJP (nonjudicial punishment) with me."

"Sir, I don't think I'll get a fair shake with you," Eaton said, adding that he wanted a hearing in front of his own general.

"That's impossible," Krulak said. "I am the only one who's holding hearings for Marines involved with Tailhook."

Eaton wasn't buying it. Krulak persisted. "I can be very lenient to you," he said. Still, Eaton refused.

"I think your civilian attorney gave you some bad advice," Krulak said. "You go back to California."

Once he was out of the room, Krulak told his lawyers, "We'll deal with him last." Eaton wasn't seen again until September.[68]

Service members facing administrative hearings have the right to a "spokesperson" who can testify on their behalf. That spokesperson can be a lawyer, but since the conduct of the hearing is up to the commander, it is the commander who sets the ground rules. At first, Krulak mandated that there be no civilian attorneys at all, either during office hours or one-on-one discussions. One such encounter tested Krulak's mandate early on.

While Krulak heard another case, DOD-IG agents Pete Black and Patricia Call had been trying to question another one of Powell's clients. They had given the flier immunity, hoping to get information on another case. But after his office hours hearing, Krulak's legal advisers never reminded Krulak to sign the required order to testify.

Therefore, Powell's client didn't have to talk. Krulak was in a bad mood that day, and Poirier and Hague, Krulak's personal lawyer, didn't want to go back in and admit their mistake so they could get the order signed. Poirier, instead, asked him to "do it for the good of the Marines." He declined.

Hague then ordered the flier to go downstairs and talk to the agents. Powell figured the order didn't exclude him from accompanying his client, and said so.

"You can't be there," Poirier said. "We have taken the position that once NJP is completed, and you've been exonerated, you have no right to an attorney."

Powell said he would take his chances. Powell, a military lawyer, and their client headed down to the first floor.

Black and Call were waiting. Powell took a seat. Majors Phil Seymour and Ron Rodgers, the military justice officer for Quantico, came right in behind the group.

Rodgers ordered the military attorney to leave. He did. Powell then asked Black, "What does that mean?" Replied Black, "I think it means that you have to leave."

Black, a big man, didn't intimidate the tall, broad-shouldered Powell, who had flown helicopters in Vietnam before going to law school and spending the rest of his Marine career as a military lawyer. Powell refused to move. Seymour, an ex-Marine grunt and Vietnam combat vet, and Rodgers then both approached Powell, reached down, and nearly grabbed Powell's arms when he gave in, saying, "All right, all right, I'll go."

Powell then stood and stalked next door into Rodgers's office, approaching a clerk, "Where do I file the complaint?" he asked, loudly. "You all have just interfered with my right to give my client legal services."

The next day, Powell sent a written complaint to the commandant and assistant commandant of the Marine Corps. Ten days later, he returned to Quantico to represent another client.

"They just treated me as nice as pie," Powell later said.[69]

Corps commandant Carl Mundy had a far more direct impact on the Tailhook case involving the highest-ranking Marine of the twenty-two referred.

While the DOD-IG was making its West Coast tour of naval bases in the summer of 1992, Mundy and his top lawyer, Brig. Gen. Gerald Miller, paid a visit to El Toro, a few weeks prior to the agency's visit there and just before the famous Solecki speech to its assembled fliers.

Mundy was operating on the assumption that the DOD-IG's mandate was narrow; he wasn't clued in to the wide range of offenses they were chasing down. That explained, during a meeting with a group of officers, his throwaway comment that evoked the bacchanalian atmosphere around U.S. bases in the Philippines: "Hey, we've all been to Olongapo before."

More importantly, Mundy told the group, "As long as you didn't put your hand on a woman at Tailhook, don't worry about it."

During his visit, Mundy met with Col. Donald A. Beaufait. Already selected for brigadier general, Beaufait had gone to Tailhook and was the senior officer present in the VMFA-242 suite. He was worried that Tailhook's taint would cheat him out of his promotion, even if he was cleared. Mundy, however, told Beaufait that, "If you go to Quantico and you're found not guilty, you will be promoted to brigadier general."

At 8 a.m. on July 20, 1993, Beaufait, having been charged with walking through the Rhino suite and the VMFA-242 strip show and doing nothing to stop either, met one-on-one with Krulak. He told Krulak what he was told at by Mundy at El Toro, and reeled off the names of the commanders who were there at the meeting with Mundy.

Krulak was taken aback, and sent Beaufait out of his office. Krulak called Washington. Mundy confirmed the speech, and the conversation.

Beaufait went back in without an attorney, and Krulak found him not guilty on both charges. But Beaufait, he said, would receive a letter of caution. And, he added, "I'm going to recommend to General Mundy that you not be promoted to brigadier general."

Beaufait wasn't too concerned. Although Krulak had no business trying to influence the promotion process, it didn't matter, Beaufait thought. After all, he reasoned, I've got Mundy's word. He accepted Krulak's verdict.

Beaufait wasn't promoted. Mundy later told him, "I had to change my mind."[70]

Beaufait just wasn't well enough connected. But as the Cooper case had demonstrated, it didn't hurt to have a Krulak connection. Lt. Col. Daniel Driscoll, the executive officer of Marine Air Group 11 during Tailhook '91, had been a student of Krulak's at the Naval Academy back in the early 1970s. Both also were members of the Navigators, a popular Christian organization with a substantial Annapolis chapter.

Although Beaufait was the senior officer present in the VMFA-242 suite, the site of some hot and heavy Tailhook action, it was Driscoll's responsibility. Driscoll was charged with being less than forthright about what he saw and knew.

On July 22, Driscoll went to office hours. For two hours, he and Krulak talked. At one point, Driscoll, desperate, got down on his knees and admitted his guilt, and Krulak came out from behind the desk to listen. When Driscoll was done, Krulak declared: "I forgive you."

Krulak found him guilty, but didn't hand out any punishment.

Driscoll came out into the waiting room and fell down on his knees. He then clasped his hands together and announced to the lawyers and defendants gathered there, "God bless the Marine Corps, and God bless General Krulak."[71]

Krulak's office must have seemed at times more like a sanctuary than a commander's chamber to the fliers ushered into its confines. During at least the first couple of hearings, a Bible remained prominently displayed on his desktop.

During Eaton's first meeting with Krulak, he and Powell noticed on the desktop a small, square pad of paper, like a stand-up desk calendar, labeled "Scripture of the Day." But it faced away from Krulak and toward those facing him. The inscription read:

"I am your confessor."[72]

During an early August meeting with five company-grade officers—among them Capts. David S. "Skippy" Prudhomme, Scott Bolcik, and Jerry Doyle—called to Quantico for "discussions" about Tailhook, Krulak, as he had with Driscoll, again played the role of confessor.

"I know you guys didn't do anything wrong," he told the officers. "But I'm worried about your souls."[73]

Few of the nineteen Marines were offered immunity in return for testimony. Marine prosecutors seemed more interested in disposing of their cases and putting it all behind them than did the Navy, which made liberal use of the prosecutorial tool. Of the forty Navy officers who received some form of punishment at admiral's mast, thirty received grants of immunity from further prosecution based on what they'd told investigators, Dan Janssen and Greg Geiss included.[74]

All told, fifty-one Navy officers,[75] not all of them listed among the original 118, were granted some form of immunity. It was part of a conscious strategy to obtain information that could be used to prosecute others—especially senior officers.

There were five of these—two captains, three commanders—that Reason didn't know quite what to do with. The evidence was either poorly substantiated or circumstantial, but Reason was convinced there'd been wrongdoing. All five were temporarily shelved.

Four Navy officers refused mast outright. This surprised the Navy's Tailhook team, which hadn't expected anyone to refuse. Refusal meant one of two things: move the case to court-martial via a grand jury-style Article 32 hearing, with its witnesses, cross-examination, and deliberations, or drop the case.

For two officers, mast wasn't an option. Cmdrs. Thomas Miller and Gregory Tritt had from the beginning been prime targets for courts-martial. The Navy felt it had enough evidence to make short work of each case. Prosecutors would soon find they had grossly overestimated the strength of each case, and underestimated the tenacity of the defense.[76]

Williams wanted to rush these cases to trial; he told each of the officers when charges were preferred that their Article 32 hearings would commence in five days, in what amounted to a sort of judicial shotgun start. Five days didn't give defense counsel much time to prepare, especially since, as with the officers sent to admiral's mast, Williams offered defense counsel only the bare essentials of their clients' cases. Defense attorneys countered by talking to the media, and asking for continuances. Williams backed off from his five-day decree, but continued the pressure.[77]

Reason had thought Tailhook would be past him by the end of April. But April had come and gone, and the Tailhook proceedings still hung like a pall over the Navy.

6

Junior, the Little Squirrel, and Gandhi

Junior Samples was a worried man, and with good reason. The 28–year-old Navy lieutenant had lied to investigators about what he had seen at Tailhook '91, and had paid the price with a letter of admonishment and a stiff fine levied by Vice Adm. J. Paul Reason, the admiral overseeing the Tailhook cases. Now, he thought, Tailhook was behind him.

But two days after he'd stood before Reason, a buddy told investigators he'd seen Samples take part in a Tailhook assault. Suddenly, Samples, out of the frying pan, had jumped into the fire. Now, he was facing prison, and the possible loss of his naval commission.[1]

Fines, punitive letters, and prison sentences were the prospects facing Samples and dozens of other officers—ensigns, lieutenants, commanders, even a lone captain—who had begun descending upon Norfolk in droves beginning in mid-May, flying in from stateside bases and ships at sea to stand at Reason's desk at Atlantic Fleet Surface Force, or SurfLant, and face up to their conduct at the Tailhook convention.

Less than two years before, they had taken part in one of the biggest parties on the continent. Now they were taking part in one of the biggest sets of hearings in the Navy's history.

Some were angry at charges that seemed downright frivolous, being brought for behavior far milder than they had seen exhibited and condoned on a typical overseas port call. And it seemed odd that although the Navy had, year after year, condoned this wild party in Las Vegas, it was now planning to admonish or prosecute officers for taking part in it—for running naked across a patio during the party, exposing their genitals, and for being captured in a party photo licking a woman's chest.

One flier was being accused of disobeying a direct order, a very serious offense—except that the alleged order was to refrain from shaving women's legs above the mid-thigh, in all likelihood a first in naval, if not military, history.

In stark contrast to such tomfoolery were the gantlet-related charges against officers like Samples. These were the fliers who were the focus of the lurid report issued in April by the DOD-IG, fliers who were being charged with lying to investigators, obstructing justice, and sexual assault.

Nearly as serious were the crimes of *omission*. These were brought against the higher-ranking officers, including at least half of the suite commanders at Tailhook, who investigators said had let the drinking and debauchery get out of hand. By doing so, they had committed crimes the Navy now regarded—officially, anyway—as seriously as the assaults.

Not one admiral was among them.

Barbara Pope had wanted to see the suite commanders punished for allowing an atmosphere of debauchery and drunkenness to flourish. But to members of the public, Tailhook was still synonymous with assaults on females. They had heard the news reports. They knew the name Paula Coughlin. And for the time being, they expected the Navy to nail officers for groping females, not for looking the other way.

There were two assaults that demanded redress: Coughlin's, in which the Marine Bonam was a suspect, and the public undressing of a young woman named Julia Rodgers.

Rodgers, eighteen, had driven to the Hilton with a couple of friends on Saturday night, September 7, 1991. She visited several third-floor parties, but for the most part hung around suite 315, the weekend home of Helicopter Anti-submarine Squadron 1 out of Jacksonville, Florida. The teenager stayed, drinking and dancing, for several hours. She wouldn't last the night.[2]

One of the fliers squeezing through the crazy, crowded, beer-soaked hallway outside the suite while Rodgers was finishing what was probably her last drink at Tailhook '91 was Lt. Frank Truong. He was attending his first Tailhook convention and, as he later admitted to investigators, he'd been having a pretty good time drinking, joking with friends, and groping unsuspecting women. For most of the evening, he'd been up at the far end of the hallway, in the suite operated by the chief of naval aviation training, or CNATRA. At around 10:30 p.m., he later testified, he decided to leave the suite to go exploring.

Halfway toward the main elevators at the central intersection of the hotel's wings, he passed a fire exit that led out onto the patio to his left. But Truong decided to stay inside where the action was. Strolling past the suite operated by Marine Corps Tactical Reconnaissance Squadron 3, the "Rhinos," he stopped outside the next suite on the left, suite 307, which had been rented by his unit, Attack Squadron 128 out of Whidbey Island, Washington. About five feet away, he spotted the gregarious Greg "Goose" Geiss, another Whidbey Island flier whom he had met at the convention. Truong hung around to shoot the breeze. So far, he had knocked back six or seven beers.[3]

"JR!" someone called out. Truong spotted a man who seemed to acknowledge the greeting. It looked like Lt. David "Junior" Samples, another Whidbey Island flier.[4]

Samples, a short, handsome flier with an easy smile, was a mocha-complected black man who was easy to spot at the nearly all-white convention. He was assigned to VAQ-139, an EA-6B Prowler squadron commanded by Thomas R. Miller.

As the fliers milled about in the hallway, Rodgers, still in suite 315, was losing it—literally falling-down drunk. As she lay on the floor, one officer reached down to help the heavy-set woman up. Giggling, she resisted, then passed out. It was around 11 p.m.

The other Florida helo jockeys standing nearby saw their party taking an undesirable turn. Several of the pilots picked her up by the hands and feet, carried her out of the suite, and dumped her unceremoniously on the floor against the wall on the hallway's opposite side. They then did a quick about-face, went back to their party, and shut the door behind them.

Three doors down, Truong heard a commotion. He squeezed through to see what was going on. There, on the floor of the hallway, they saw Rodgers, slumped against the hallway wall, hunched over. Truong later remembered noticing JR nearby.

Suddenly, without speaking and as if by prior agreement, about seven of the men standing in the hall decided to pick Rodgers up and have some fun. They leaned over to grab her, hoisted her into the air, and began carrying her down the hallway, face up. Truong held her head, and Geiss held her legs. Samples, said Truong, was in the middle. No one could identify any of the others.

The incident didn't last long; Rodgers was difficult to carry. As they lifted her back toward the Rhino suite, someone managed to undo her shirt and bra. Truong remembered her pants being pulled off, and said Geiss also grabbed her crotch, a charge he later denied. Either way, Rodgers, passed out and limp, didn't resist.

Truong said she was carried twenty feet; Geiss said it was five feet before the group began to lose its grip.

Rodgers ended up in a heap on the floor, naked from the waist down. For a moment, the slightly spent and mostly drunk fliers stood around her, eyes fixed on the half-naked young woman, not sure what to do next.

Someone yelled, "Security guard's comin'!"

The hallway emptied. The officers scattered into the nearby suites. Two security guards arrived, helped Rodgers to her feet, and half-dragged her down the hall to the second floor security office, where, wrapped in blankets, she threw up in a trash basket. Just past midnight, her mother arrived to take her home.

That's the way Truong remembered things. Geiss didn't recall either Truong or Samples touching Rodgers. Samples denied taking part at all.[5]

DOD-IG agents thought Samples was lying about not having seen sexual misconduct, and also suspected that he may have been involved with the Rodgers assault. That bought Samples a ticket to Norfolk to face Reason.[6]

After arriving from Whidbey Island on June 1, Samples went straight to the offices of SurfLant. There, he ended up in a conference room with six or seven other officers. He was given a file folder containing a summary of the charges against him, and assorted statements made by himself and others that pertained to his case.

Almost immediately, Samples was taken aside by Capt. Jeffry Williams, Reason's top lawyer, who told him in an aside, "Your case is a bit different from everyone else's." Williams told Samples that a panel of senior officers appointed by Reason to review cases had unanimously decided to send his case to court-martial, not admiral's mast, but that Samples could still make the decision to accept mast.

He asked Samples if he had a lawyer. Samples said no. Williams gave him directions to the Norfolk Naval Base Naval Legal Service

Office. At the NLSO, a staff lawyer told him he would be represented by Lt. Timothy Keck. Samples met with Keck to discuss his case, and called it a day.

The next morning, Samples arrived at SurfLant and again met with Williams; Williams met everyone scheduled to go before Reason. Samples told Williams that his file contained some misstatements, and that he would like to review the taped statement he had made to DOD-IG agents in February. Williams replied that the file in his hands and the Navy's file on him were identical. Samples then said he thought his file didn't exactly present both sides of the story, saying that "any reasonable, rational person" reading the file would immediately think him guilty. Williams told Samples that Reason would be fair, and also that if he elected mast, he would have the opportunity to tell his side of the story—something he might not be able to do at a court-martial.

Samples tried to get ahold of Keck, but failed; Keck was working on a different case at the time. But Samples had already decided to take mast, and chose to press ahead. Williams took back Samples' file and walked off to brief Reason. In the meantime, Samples sat down and typed up a statement to be added to his file. Shortly thereafter, Samples was standing before Reason, with Williams and a recordist present.

Samples denied being involved in the assault on Rodgers. Reason dismissed that charge. But Reason decided Samples had made a false official statement in telling investigators he hadn't seen any sexual misconduct at Tailhook, and levied a $2,000 fine and a letter of admonition.

Then, as did the other officers who went before Reason, Samples proceeded directly to a post-mast briefing with Williams. Williams was convinced that Samples had lied to Reason, and decided to tell him so.

"I think you got off because in my personal opinion, I think you assaulted Julia Rodgers and many other women," Williams told him. "But I've got to go with what the admiral found. He's the boss; he's the three-star. So I'm going to live with that." Williams advised Samples of his post-mast rights, and sent him down the hall.[7]

Samples then went before Cmdr. Robert Monahan, Williams's top assistant. Monahan, after a lengthy explanation, gave Samples a grant of immunity "from the use of your testimony." Monahan also handed Samples an Order to Testify, which directed him to submit to questioning by DOD-IG agents.

But the wording of the order seemed to contradict the language of the immunity grant. It implied that he was completely immune:

" . . . no testimony or other information given by Lieutenant David Samples or any information directly or indirectly derived from such testimony *or other information* can be used against him in any criminal case, except a prosecution for perjury, giving a false statement, or otherwise failing to comply with this order." In effect, his lawyers later argued, this amounted to *transactional* immunity—in other words, that he'd been made completely immune from further prosecution, even if someone else testified against him.

Monahan concluded by telling Samples that if he would tell investigators everything about that Saturday night, he wouldn't be prosecuted. Samples signed the paperwork.[8]

Monahan then walked Samples into a separate office for the requisite follow-up interview with a DOD-IG agent. Matthew Walinski began with his standard spiel. The order to testify, he told Samples, was necessary to put everyone on a "level playing field." Walinski then told Samples that if he'd tell the truth, tell everything he knew about everything he'd seen or done at Tailhook, his case would become a "wash-out"—he'd be "done with Tailhook." Walinski then noted that Samples was unrepresented, and told the flier that if he had any questions, or wanted legal advice, Walinski wouldn't start.

Samples, said Walinski, said no on both counts.

The interview lasted two hours. For the first time, Samples admitted he'd seen the tail end of the undressing of Julia Rodgers. He'd been leaning up against the hall not far from the service elevators, he said, when he saw two security guards dash past him; one exclaimed, "Oh my God!"

To his left, five to ten feet away, he had seen Rodgers on the floor, partially disrobed. But he denied that he had taken part. He'd been facing the opposite way, he said, and hadn't heard anything until the guard ran past.

Walinski suspected that Samples was still lying. How could he have been so close and not heard anything until it was all over? At the same time, Walinski wasn't much concerned about whether he was or not. He knew that Samples had immunity. Walinski figured he had "washed out" as a suspect.

Walinski wanted names. But Samples provided nothing new.

The next morning, Navy prosecutors Mike Ritter and Tom Devins interviewed Samples. They weren't interested in the Julia Rodgers incident. They wanted information they could use in the prosecution of Cmdrs. Thomas Miller and Gregory Tritt. Ritter told Samples that if he would tell the truth, he didn't have to worry about being prosecuted or disciplined. Samples didn't provide anything useful.[9]

The same day Samples had met with Williams and Reason, Lt. Frank Truong had arrived in Norfolk for the standard "disposition of Tailhook-related matters." On the 3rd, Truong agreed to go to admiral's mast. The next day, Reason gave him a letter of admonition and a $2,000 fine for lying about not having seen any sexual misconduct at Tailhook.

No one knew about Truong's role in the assault on Rodgers. He had lied during the interview with the Naval Investigative Service and two more times to DOD-IG agents.

Following mast, Truong was given testimonial immunity. Now, Monahan told him, was his chance to come clean. He agreed to talk, and two DOD-IG agents began the post-mast interview. A couple of hours into it, they took a break. Outside the interview room, one of the agents ran into Walinski.

"Didn't you interview Lieutenant Samples yesterday?" the agent asked. When Walinski said yes, the agent replied, "Then we think you should hear what Lieutenant Truong is telling us about Lieutenant Samples."

After listening for ten minutes, Walinski decided Samples had once again become a suspect. Over the weekend, he drove up to D.C. to retrieve some photo lineups to show Truong.

On Monday, June 7, Truong pointed out Geiss—and Samples. Both men, Truong said, had helped him pick up Rodgers, and Samples, standing right next to him, had helped remove her pants.

Samples, who the government maintained could still be prosecuted if implicated by others, was charged with indecent assault and lying under oath.[10]

One of the officers called to face Reason didn't have far to travel. Thirty-two-year-old Naval Reserve Lt. Cole Cowden was stationed a stone's throw away, at Norfolk Naval Air Station, where he was assigned to Carrier Airborne Early Warning Squadron 78.

Cole Cowden was born to be the life of the party. A short, bright-eyed man with a distinctively deep, raspy voice, a rapid manner of speech, an easy smile, and a good memory for jokes, he was exceptionally outgoing. It was easy to picture him at a party, chatting with the men and charming the women.

But the Navy had in its files a photograph snapped at Tailhook which captured Cowden in a position the Navy regarded as more outrageous than outgoing—and hardly what it considered proper social behavior for a Navy officer.

On the evening of Friday, June 6, 1991, Cowden, then stationed in San Diego, and some friends were hanging out in the VAW-110 suite, the Tailhook home of the Navy's E-2C Hawkeye community. Across the room, the infamous leg-shaving booth of Lts. Rolando Diaz and Andy Jones was open for business, and the line of women waiting to get their legs massaged and shaved snaked out the sliding glass doors onto the patio. The party was in full swing.

Cowden was sitting and talking with two women: Lisa Mattiello, a civilian nurse from Las Vegas, and a friend of hers named Mary Ann Gabel. Both were attractive, outgoing women; both seemed to be having a great time at Tailhook. Mattiello, said Cowden, was "kind of a social butterfly, a real nice person, very intelligent. And she was a lot of fun, extremely witty." Many, Cowden included, thought her name was Helen. Mattiello wore a nametag on her sundress that read, "Helen Bed."

From out of nowhere, a wad of paper soaked in beer sailed through the air toward Mattiello, curving in for a landing smack inside the bodice of her strapless sun dress. Perfect shot, someone thought. Mattiello reached up and pulled her top away from her chest slightly, trying to shake out the wad. Cowden offered his services.

"Here, let me help you with that," he said. "No thanks," said Mattiello, standing to better shake out the wad. Cowden also stood, reached toward Mattiello, and crooked his finger into the top edge of the dress. Pulling it back, he leaned over.

Gabel laughed, reaching down for her point-and-shoot camera. "Wait! Let me get a picture of that," she said. Cowden obliged: he leaned into Mattiello's chest and stuck out his tongue. As he licked her at the spot where her left breast began sloping outward, he looked sideways to his left. Gabel snapped the shutter.

"Yech," Mattiello thought, sort of squirming and laughing at the same time. Cowden lifted his head. Mattiello walked away. Cowden laughed and kept on partying.[11]

Investigators got a copy of the photo. And there was Cowden, plain as day, his tongue licking the top of a woman's breast. Her hand was on the back of his neck, and didn't appear to be forcing him away.

Mattiello later told an investigator that she had been to the past four Tailhook conventions and that "nothing offensive has ever happened to her."[12] Nor was she listed as one of the eighty-three female victims of sexual misconduct the DOD-IG listed in its final report. The Navy, however, decided Cowden was guilty of conduct unbecoming an officer.[13]

But the government had yet another more serious charge to levy against Cowden. It had its roots in an incident that took place at the previous year's Tailhook involving then-Ensign Elizabeth J. Warnick.

For a period of sixteen months that included both conventions, Warnick, a Naval Academy graduate and prospective helicopter pilot, had worked at the Pentagon office of Vice Adm. Richard Dunleavy, the chief of naval aviation. Officially, she was an aide; unofficially, she was a "stash ensign," tucked away in the Pentagon while waiting for orders to report for her initial flight training at Naval Air Station Pensacola.

Warnick was no social wallflower. In court, she characterized herself as a "player" at Tailhooks '90 and '91. One of the ways she played at both conventions was to let men perform belly shots on her in various areas of the Las Vegas Hilton. To give a belly shot, a person would lay back while another poured some tequila onto their exposed bellybutton, with the stomach sucked in a bit to form a bit of a hollow. A person would then bend over and suck out the tequila.

Warnick was also listed as Victim Number 10 in the final DOD-IG report; at one point, while in the Rhino suite, a male flier pushed her head up to the dildo/drink dispenser on the Rhino so she could "please" it, and she ended up getting squirted with the drink mixture.

Warnick had consensual sex at both conventions with Cowden. She also had consensual sex at Tailhook '91 with a married officer, Lt. Cmdr. Michael French. At the time, Warnick was engaged to another man. She also had her legs publicly shaved at both conventions, which some thought to be behavior no more inappropriate than the act of shaving women's legs in public.[14]

On October 15 and 28, 1992, Warnick, twenty-four and now a lieutenant junior grade, was interviewed by DOD-IG investigators Lindy Billings and Colleen Nichols. At the time, she was enrolled in a helicopter flight training course at Whiting Field Naval Air Station in Florida.

In the first interview, she didn't mention having sex with French, but did say that French, whom she termed a "sleaze" and a "snake," kept following her around at the convention. She didn't mention Cowden at all. She admitted doing the belly shots and having her legs shaved. But Warnick also told the agents that she'd been sexually assaulted at the previous year's convention.

It was a Friday afternoon, she said. She had met three Navy lieutenants on the Hilton's third-floor patio; they had asked her to dinner. After dressing for the evening, she went to meet the men at a room in the Hilton. Entering the darkened room, she was grabbed by three men and blindfolded. They held her face down on a bed and tried to pull off her clothes. She fought them off, kicking one so hard he flew back into a dresser. Panicked, she ran out the door, leaving some of her clothes and her purse behind.

On the 28th, the story changed. Warnick had met Cowden and two of his friends on the patio. They chatted, and within an hour or so, she and Cowden were upstairs having sex. Later, back downstairs in one of the suites, Cowden asked her to join him and some friends for dinner. After changing, she went to a Hilton hotel room rented by his squadron (Cowden was staying elsewhere) at about 6:30 p.m. to meet the three men.

The door opened, but she couldn't see anyone in the darkened room. Despite that, she walked in. She was jumped by what she estimated to be two or three people, who blindfolded her and forced her onto the bed. As in the previous version, she fought the men off and escaped. But this time, she told the agents that one of the men's voices might have been Cowden's.

Asked how she could have fought off the three men, Warnick told Billings, "I certainly was not going to be the victim of another incident like that." Prompted, she said she had been raped in her dorm room in 1986 while a freshman at the Naval Academy. She said she told three officers in her chain of command; they all later denied it. Her medical record, according to Billings's in-court testimony, noted that she came in to the doctor's office with bruises on her neck, shoulders, and arms. There was no mention of a rape.[15]

On December 4, 1992, Warnick told local Navy investigators that she had been getting a series of late-night phone calls that had begun on November 2, shortly after the second of her two DOD-IG interviews. The caller told her that by talking to investigators, she was hurting a lot of careers, including her own. Warnick told the investigators it might have been Cowden.

She also said that on November 25, she had received six withered red roses delivered in a vase by U.P.S. It contained a death threat, she said. The note, she told Navy Special Agent Ken Coyle, said something to the effect of, "These flowers may be your death flowers if you don't stop talking." She had thrown out the note, she said. She also told Coyle that her car tires had been slashed, and that she'd told two off-duty police officers who lived in her complex about the incident. The screen door of her apartment had also been slashed, she said.[16]

On December 16, Warnick was interviewed again by DOD-IG, and the suspicious Billings was in no mood for niceties. United Parcel Service, said Billings, does not deliver flowers. Warnick admitted that she had found the bunch of flowers by her front door, without any note attached. Billings also told her there was no record of Warnick reporting any vandalism. Told the two off-duty officers were being questioned, Warnick admitted that her tires hadn't been slashed; one had been flattened, probably by a nail. She also admitted that the slash on her screen was a small rip that the neighborhood kids might have done.

Billings also didn't believe that Warnick could have broken away from three men intent on raping her. She questioned Warnick about it for hours, and the interview became especially intense. But Warnick stuck to her story the rest of the day. Billings told her she knew there was more to it, but Warnick wasn't giving in. Exhausted from the all-day ordeal, they called it quits late in the afternoon.

The next morning, they met again. Warnick told her she had thought things over, and wanted to give a statement. Now, it was Cowden who opened the door of the darkened room. She and Cowden made small talk on the bed. He kissed her, and they lay back. While Cowden was caressing her, she said, she became aware of a change in the way she was being touched, and said she realized another man was behind her. She kicked Cowden away. The other man, she said, told Cowden, "Let her go, it's not going to happen." The other man let go, and she ran away from the room.

When questioned why she had lied, Warnick told the agents, "I only want someone to take care of me."[17]

Despite the holes in her story, the DOD-IG thought there might be something to the harassing phone calls. Cowden's then-commander in San Diego was told that the DOD-IG wanted to reinterview

Cowden—in Jacksonville, Florida. His attorney, Roger Keithly, and his commander contacted a local DOD-IG agent and asked, "Could you do this in San Diego?" Absolutely not, said the agent. Cowden's commander demanded something in writing. He received a list of forty people to be reinterviewed in Jacksonville in the first week of January. In a margin, someone had scrawled, "talked to Diaz, Cowden and Warnick on the same day."

Keithly asked Cowden if he knew the people named. He did. Keithly advised Cowden to call Warnick to see if she knew why he was being called to Jacksonville. Cowden called and left a message.[18]

On December 22, Warnick called back. DOD-IG agents were also on the line, and the tape was rolling.

With the agents coaching, Warnick asked why he had called, and Cowden said his attorney had advised calling her because her name was on the message his commander had received, and she might have an idea why Cowden was being summoned to Jacksonville. He had hired one, he said, because the DOD-IG had been questioning him about a buddy who had exposed himself at Tailhook '91. When agents told him, "you're going to be in big trouble," he decided he had better hire a lawyer.

"You don't think you did anything wrong?" she asked.

"No. Why?" he said.

"Do you think I did anything wrong?" she asked.

"No. Why? he replied.

"Well, I'm just a little concerned. I mean, you call me out of the blue . . . "

He assured her it was strictly about the message. He also said her name had come up in an interview, and he'd told agents he'd had consensual sex with her. She said she wouldn't have a problem talking about it, and Cowden agreed that "there was absolutely nothing wrong with it."

"No, no," replied Warnick. "What about later that night?"

"What happened later that night?" said Cowden.

"You tell me," said Warnick. "That's what I'm worried about."

"I . . . you know, I don't think I was around. I mean, honest Beth, 100 percent, I don't remember."

"You were around. You were right there," said Warnick.

"For what?"

"You were part of the whole thing," said Warnick.

"For what?" said Cowden. "I don't know what you're talking about."

"I know you remember it," said Warnick, pressing him.

The subject shifted, but Warnick steered it back. "Well then, what about what you guys tried up in that room? Nobody has mentioned that."

"No one has mentioned that to me, either," said Cowden.

"OK. Well, then what are you going to say if someone asks you about that?"

"I'm taking the Fifth," said Cowden.[19]

In an unsworn statement made the following summer, Cowden said he invoked the Fifth Amendment on Keithly's advice, and that he was referring not to a sexual assault in 1990, but to any kind of conduct he might be accused of at Tailhook conventions. In the summer of '92, Cowden told Keithly he was concerned that, "conduct unbecoming an officer, it seems to me that it's . . . a different standard for anybody with Tailhook than it's been for the past 10 years I've been in the Navy."[20]

Cowden later testified that Keithly replied, "We're not really sure what's going on. We're not sure if this thing's all politically motivated. We're not sure what conduct unbecoming is right now. . . . If you're not sure, you don't have to answer any questions. . . . You're allowed to take the Fifth Amendment. No one can make you incriminate yourself."[21]

Cowden's version of he and Warnick's relationship was less complicated than Warnick's. At the 1990 convention, he and Warnick had met at a dinner party and started chatting. They had sex the next day. The following year, they did so again, on a Friday afternoon.

Afterwards, Cowden and Warnick were on the third floor patio, chatting with other partiers. When Warnick stepped away for a moment, Cowden remarked that he and Warnick had just had sex. "I checked that block two years in a row," he told Lt. Walter Adelmann, boasting. The sex he'd had with Warnick, said Cowden, was "completely consensual."[22]

The Navy liked Warnick's third version better. Although DOD-IG investigators had caught Warnick in lie after lie, their sole recommended charge against Warnick was conduct unbecoming an officer—for getting her legs shaved and doing "belly shots." The Navy decided to charge Cowden with conduct unbecoming and sexual assault.[23]

On May 25, Cowden, now stationed in Norfolk, and his Navy attorney, Lt. Ronald Hocevar, went to Jeffry Williams office in the SurfLant compound to review the charges.

Williams read them off. He showed them the picture, which he termed "indecent." Then he explained Cowden's rights. He said that the lieutenant had the right to refuse admiral's mast but added, "considering that we have this indecent photo, why would you want to do that?"

Cowden rolled his eyes. "That's not indecent," he replied.

Williams got hot. "Well, I don't know if you pose for indecent photos like this every weekend," he said angrily.

Cowden took the cue and shut up. Williams then brought up the alleged rape of Warnick in 1990. Williams said the charges "were very serious, and would probably be referred to an Article 32 [pretrial] investigation."

"Those are ugly allegations," said Cowden.

"Yes, they are very ugly allegations," replied Williams.

Cowden wanted to know what Reason would have in front of him if Cowden accepted admiral's mast. The same information, Williams told him.

Does Admiral Reason know about Warnick's accusation?

"Yes, the admiral is aware of that."

Williams gave Cowden and Hocevar two days to decide whether to accept mast.

Cowden and Hocevar went back to Hocevar's office on the second floor of the Naval Legal Service Office, several miles away on the sprawling Norfolk base. Hocevar told Cowden that if he continued to represent him, there might be a possible conflict of interest because Hocevar was also representing Rolando Diaz, the leg-shaver.[24]

Cowden's new attorney was a Coast Guard lawyer on loan to the Navy for six months as part of a legal exchange program. Tall, wide-shouldered and easygoing, Lt. Jeffrey Good had a confident manner that belied the fact that he was only a year out of law school. He had spent his first seven years on active duty as a line officer aboard Navy and Coast Guard ships.

On May 27, Cowden and Good returned to SurfLant with Cowden's decision. They arrived at 11:30 a.m. Twenty minutes later, they were shown into Williams's office.

Williams asked if Cowden would accept nonjudicial punishment.

Cowden replied emphatically, practically yelling at an officer four grades his senior: "Absolutely not."

Williams was stunned, flabbergasted. He could not believe that, faced with the photograph, Cowden would refuse mast. But there wasn't much Williams could do; it was Cowden's right. Good showed Cowden where to sign the paperwork to indicate his refusal.

Williams told them to wait in the SurfLant legal offices because Reason would want to talk with them. Other Tailhook suspects were in the room with their lawyers; people were constantly coming and going. It was hectic. Cowden and Good wondered, "are all these people going to be seeing Vice Admiral Reason?"

They were. One of them was Diaz, sitting with Hocevar. Diaz had also refused mast. Eventually, Monahan came in and told Cowden, Diaz, and their attorneys to wait in the second-floor conference room.

Throughout the day, Reason conducted admiral's masts, tending to his everyday business in between the hearings. At one point, Reason had to leave the office to take care of some things. Cowden, Diaz and their attorneys waited for 6 1/2 hours.

Late in the day, Williams went in to see Reason and told him that Cowden and Diaz had refused mast. Reason pursed his lips, saying nothing.

Then he looked up at Williams. "Do you think I should see them?"

"No, sir," Williams replied. "I'll see them."

Williams returned to the conference room. "The admiral has decided not to see you," he told them. "Frankly, the admiral is surprised at your decision. He thought that these two cases would not be mast refusals."

Reason hadn't indicated any such thing. But in Williams's mind, Cowden and Diaz had just earned tickets to a court-martial—even though one of his own prosecutors would advise against it.[25]

On June 14, the charges were filed. Reason told investigating officer Cmdr. Larry A. McCullough that he wanted a report in twenty days, so McCullough set Cowden's Article 32 pretrial hearing for June 30. To Good, it was a preposterous schedule: two weeks to prepare a defense? On the 15th, he asked Reason for a continuance. Although routinely granted for Article 32s, Reason denied it.

Good got the news the next day at a pretrial session held to iron out administrative details. It was the first Tailhook hearing in Norfolk opened to the press. Good asked McCullough to grant a continuance, but under the consolidated disposition authority setup, McCullough didn't have the authority.

Good wanted the time. And he figured that the Navy wanted to at least give the appearance of holding fair hearings. The only way he could bring pressure on the Navy, he realized, was to go public.

Following the hearing, Good and Cowden met with reporters on the steps of the Naval Legal Service Office and explained the dilemma. Cowden called the DOD-IG agents "Nazis," and termed the investigation a "witchhunt." Good tossed off a comment guaranteed to make the local news, saying that the "Navy is not interested in justice, but a body count."[26]

An angry Jeffry Williams complained to NLSO commander Ed Ellis that the aggressive tack being taken by Good and other military defense counsel was improper and unethical. He also asked Ellis, who supervised the defense counsel, to "rein in" his defenders—specifically Good, who Williams was especially upset with. Williams even threatened to go to the Coast Guard with his complaints.

Ellis refused to rein in his defenders; he told Williams that he thought they were doing a fine job.

After the hearing, Ellis fired off yet another memo to Schachte that focused on the continuance issue. "I think the denial was a mistake," he wrote. Ellis told Schachte that Good's complaint was valid because "the Navy had nearly two years and teams of investigators and lawyers working on the case" and that Good was given less than two weeks to prepare.

Ellis also said that he had warned prosecutors that they and "the military justice system . . . were going to be under the gun to demonstrate that these cases could be handled fairly and appropriately."

Added Ellis, "I'm beginning to get very concerned that we're not passing the test."

Copies of this memo and the one Ellis previously sent to Schachte were obtained by a Navy defense attorney with a West Coast client. They ended up in the hands of a *Los Angeles Times* reporter. On June 19, Ellis's memos went nationwide.

Williams, furious, could do nothing.[27]

Good's tactic and the Times story apparently had an effect. On June 22, Reason granted McCullough twenty more days to produce his report, giving Good another two weeks to prepare.

At Cowden's Article 32 hearing on July 15, DOD-IG special agent Peter Black testified that Lisa Mattiello didn't consider herself a victim, and that she didn't want to see Cowden punished for the chest-licking incident. He said she told him, "It just happened."

Six days earlier in Las Vegas, Mattiello had sworn out a statement refuting some of what Black had written down in his report of interview. He had asked if she had consented to Cowden's act. She told Black "it happened so quickly that there was no opportunity for consent." Black then told her, she said, "that this constituted an assault," and that he defined an assault as any nonconsensual touching. Mattiello told Black she didn't consider herself a victim and didn't see how the government could call it an assault if she said it wasn't.

He replied, "That's the way the law sees it."

She also said she hadn't been offended by Cowden. "While I would have been offended had this happened under different circumstances (e.g., church social)," she wrote, "in the context of the Tailhook convention this was simply no big deal to me. Everyone was joking, laughing, and having a good time. There was a great deal of horseplay going on and his actions were not out of line." She'd been to the previous four Tailhooks, and said she had had a "wonderful time" at each.

"The idea of using my name for criminally prosecuting Cole for this is absurd, and I resent my name being used to do it," she wrote.

On the witness stand, Black maintained his report was "correct and accurate."

Asked Good, promoted July 1 to lieutenant commander, "If the statement is correct and accurate, why didn't you put in the statement that she said she did not consider herself to be assaulted?"

Black replied, "I have no answer to that."

When Warnick took the stand following Black, she repeated the third version of the rape story.

Good asked Warnick why she'd lied to the DOD-IG investigators. "Why didn't you just stand up and do what was right from the beginning?"

"Because I was scared," said Warnick.

"Scared of what?"

"Like I said, scared of what everybody would think, scared because my career hasn't even started, scared because I didn't tell anybody any of this until two years after it happened."

"None of that explains why you came up with a story about being accosted by three unknown men and held face down on a bed," said Good. " . . . If what you said today was the truth, why didn't you just stand up at the very beginning and tell that story?"

"I don't know, sir," replied Warnick.

Good asked Warnick about the belly shots. "It was sometime after the attack, right?"

"Yes, sir," said Warnick.

"Did you have your legs shaved, too?"

"Yes sir, I did."

Good asked her which nights she had had them shaved, noting that witnesses say she'd had it done Friday and Saturday nights.

"Sir, I only recall Thursday or Friday," she said.

"Well, is it safe to say, then, that this assault didn't ruin your weekend?"

"Objection," said prosecutor Lt. D.J. Hansen.

"Noted," said McCullough, from his seat on the bench.

Asked Good, "Did you ever moonlight as a stripper in Washington, D.C., while you were on Admiral Dunleavy's staff?"

"Objection," said Hansen. "What is the relevance . . . ?"

McCullough interrupted. "Does it go to credibility or motive?"

"I've got three witnesses who say she told them she moonlighted as a stripper while in Washington, D.C.," said Good. "Now, it goes to motive because Lieutenant Cowden repeated that to a number of other people."

McCullough allowed the question. Warnick denied it.

Warnick had also told DOD-IG agent Billings that Lt. Cmdr. Michael French had followed her around and pestered her for sex at Tailhook, but initially neglected to say they had actually had sex. "He was making unwanted sexual advances on you at Tailhook '91?"

"Yes, sir, he was."

"Yet you had sex with him?"

"Yes, sir, I did."

"How many times?"

"Just once." French had told investigators they had had sex three times.

Later, she explained her decision. "If I had sex with him, maybe he would have just left me alone," she said.

"Are you aware that having sex with him also constituted adultery?"

"Yes, sir."

"Are you aware that he was married?"

"He showed me pictures of his family," she replied.

Good also wanted to talk about her "training time-out." Two weeks before the first DOD-IG interview in 1992, Warnick had requested a break from training. It was a standard procedure implemented when students felt that personal problems might interfere with their ability to fly.

Good believed that Warnick had been having difficulties in flight school all along, and had made up the assault to explain her problems and deflect attention from her performance. But the Navy had turned down his request for Warnick's flight training record, saying it "wasn't relevant to the pretrial investigation."

In court, he established that she hadn't flown since September 28, 1992—the first DOD-IG interview had taken place on October 15—except for a brief "warm-up" flight on November 14. She was practicing auto-rotation, a powerless glide practiced by helicopter pilots to learn how to attempt to control free fall in the event the engine fails. While descending, she lost control of the helicopter. An instructor had to take over to keep from crashing.

"Isn't it after that that you made some allegations . . . further allegations of harassment?" asked Good.

"Yes, sir."

"Let's go back over some of your testimony," said Good, winding down. "Now, you indicated already that you lied on your initial account of having been assaulted?"

"Yes, sir."

"You also indicated that you lied about having sex with Lieutenant Commander French. Correct?"

"Yes sir, I did."

"Initially, you denied having consensual sex with Lieutenant Cowden at Tailhook '90?"

"Yes, I did."

"You lied about having your tires slashed?"

"Yes, sir."

"Is that a fair summary of your testimony?"

"Yes, sir."

"Thank you."

Under questioning by investigating officer McCullough, Warnick continued to maintain that Cowden and another man had tried to sexually assault her in the darkened room at Tailhook '90.[28]

On July 19, after hearing several days of testimony, McCullough recommended dismissing both charges against Cowden. Finding "exceptionally significant issues of credibility" in Warnick's testimony "which are supported by the record" and are "well documented" in the testimony and exhibits, he advised Reason to drop the sexual assault charge altogether and to handle the conduct unbecoming charge through counseling and a nonpunitive, nonpermanent letter of caution.[29]

Although the decision wouldn't be announced for four days, the Tailhook prosecutors quickly learned which way McCullough had decided to lean. Capt. Robert McLeran, the leader of Reason's executive panel and assigned to lead the prosecution effort out at Little Creek, wanted a prosecutorial analysis prepared listing the pros and cons of proceeding against Cowden. With Cmdr. Thomas Devins, the lead trial counsel, out of town, McLeran turned to Hansen, actually the assistant prosecutor on the Cowden case, to prepare it.

At Little Creek, Hansen and the junior prosecutors working on the cases had informally agreed that the case should not go to court-martial. But the others didn't have to put their names on the "blame line."

On the 23rd, Williams summoned Hansen to his SurfLant office for a briefing on the Cowden case.

"I told him what I was going to put in the memo, that there were a number of reasons this case shouldn't go forward," said Hansen. For one, he noted, McCullough had recommended against it. For another, Hansen said, it would be a frivolous prosecution on both counts.

"This was a trivial case to bring to court-martial," said Hansen. "We had a very unwilling victim [Mattiello], a number of differing statements, the picture was the only evidence . . . and the instructions were horrendous for the government. We would have to go a long way to prove this was conduct unbecoming an officer. I didn't believe there was enough evidence to win a trial."

The latter argument was an ethical consideration, and he and Williams had a long discussion about recommending court-martial in the face of a dearth of evidence. Cowden also told Williams that even if he could convince Mattiello to come and testify, she would be a hostile witness because she didn't think Cowden had done anything wrong. And he noted that since reporters had obtained copies of McCullough's report, media interest in the case would continue to be especially intense.

Hansen didn't refuse to prosecute the case. But, he told Williams,

"We're pushing the envelope. It's not worth it. It's a waste of government time and money."

Williams told Hansen to draft the memo, and he would review it.

On July 23, Cmdr. Rand Pixa, the executive officer of the Norfolk NLSO, got a call from McLeran. The Tailhook team needs fewer prosecutors on its staff, he said. Pixa could take back D.J., and Lt. Cmdr. Chris Morin could pick up the slack. Besides, he told Pixa, Hansen is "lackluster" on Cowden.

"His heart's not in it," he said. And the advice prepared by Hansen for Williams put the case "in the worst possible light."

Pixa then spoke with Williams, who told Pixa the Tailhook workload was such that it didn't warrant Hansen's continued involvement. Hansen "wants out" of the Cowden case, he told Pixa. Hansen was saying it would be "unethical" to go forward.

Pixa hadn't gotten any previous indications that Hansen was an excess presence on the prosecution team. But the clear implication, Pixa later testified, was, "I'm sending him back to you."

A few days later, Hansen and Morin were meeting in the NLSO with Pixa; both lawyers were assigned on paper to the NLSO. Hansen told Pixa that the Tailhook prosecution "was boiling down to five cases, I was involved in three, and I felt I was seriously underemployed." The normal caseload for a Navy trial counsel is ten to twenty cases; Hansen wanted some additional Tailhook work.

After lunch, Pixa told Hansen not to worry about Tailhook. He was coming back to the NLSO.

Hansen wasn't being fired, Pixa and Williams later insisted. As Pixa termed it, "all the NLSO did was take back one of its own."[30]

Meanwhile, Cowden was getting good press coverage. It was due in part to his magnetic personality, but mostly to the government's pursuit of what seemed to be a paper-thin case. Good had scored big points in court. And from the beginning, Good, like his civilian counterparts, had met willingly with the media.

The Tailhook team began going after Good. During a July 26 phone conversation with Capt. Patrick Kelly, who worked on the Navy Judge Advocate General's staff, Williams commented that Good "seems to have begun a media campaign to impugn the motives and integrity of Vice Admiral Reason." Monahan, Williams's deputy, told Pixa that Good was "cultivating the media." Williams began refusing to accept Good's calls.[31]

Good didn't seem to mind the treatment. Being a Coast Guardsman, he said, was a bit of an advantage.

"It's perfect," he said following one hearing. "I'm outside of the process a little bit. It gives me some additional insulation."

Good also had the advantage of being officially insulated from Williams. The defense counsel fell under Ellis, the NLSO commander. Ellis, not Williams, wrote their performance reports.

On August 13, after reviewing McCullough's legal conclusions, Williams submitted to Reason his formal advice on Cowden's case. Williams agreed that the assault charge should be dropped, saying that Warnick "has little credibility based on her apparent habit of making false or misleading statements, which she admitted under oath."

Not so with the charge of conduct unbecoming an officer. Williams advised Reason to press it, and to use the same incident to bring a second charge of "conduct of a nature to bring discredit upon the armed forces."

McCullough had argued that conduct unbecoming must be "morally unfitting and unworthy rather than merely inappropriate or unsuitable." It must also, he argued, be considered "under the circumstances" that existed at the time. And the statements of Mattiello and Special Agent Black, he said, made it clear that the paper wad incident was consensual.

Inappropriate or unsuitable, yes, concluded McCullough. Criminal in nature, no.

Williams disagreed. "The consent of the victim in a prosecution for indecent acts is not a defense," he wrote.[32]

To an outsider, it seemed amazing. The Navy wanted to try Cowden at a general court-martial, the equivalent of a civilian felony trial, for posing in a randy gag photo at a wild, out-of-uniform party.

That afternoon, Cowden and Good were summoned to Reason's SurfLant office. Knowing McCullough's recommendations, they thought Cowden was about to be cleared of all charges. Instead, the admiral told Cowden he was to be court-martialed.

Minutes later, they ended up in Monahan's office to hear the particulars of the amended charges. In the midst of Monahan's explanation, Cowden interrupted.

"When is Warnick going to be charged?" he asked.

"We're here to discuss your case," Monahan replied.

"Well, I just want to know . . . "

Monahan blew up. "Goddamn it lieutenant, you won't be insubordinate in my office. Now just shut up!"[33]

After the session in his office, Monahan later remarked to Pixa that he'd had to "dress the little squirrel down."[34]

Lieutenant Rolando Diaz freely admitted he'd shaved women's legs at Tailhook '91. He just didn't think he'd done anything wrong.

But Diaz, the Navy said, was guilty of behaving in a manner unbefitting a naval officer—by official standards, anyway. And, far more seriously, he had ignored the command of an officer senior in rank.

Both congressional mandate and long-standing tradition allow officers to give orders to subordinates, as long as the orders relate specifically to military duty. The only exception would be orders to commit illegal acts; an extreme example would entail ordering a subordinate to summarily execute a prisoner of war.

The authority is twofold: command authority gives officers dominion over those they actually command; general military authority covers those outside their units—or services. A Navy commander, in a given situation, can give a lawful order to a Navy lieutenant on a different ship. Or to an Army sergeant, for that matter.

The key word in Diaz's case was the word *lawful*, but only if one bought the prosecution's assertion that such an order was given.

Diaz said it wasn't.

Christopher Remshak said it was.

Remshak was commander of San Diego, Calif.'s VAW-110 when he went to Tailhook '91. His squadron was to host a suite that represented the entire community of VAW, or radar surveillance, fliers. This consisted of the crewmen assigned to E-2C Hawkeyes and, for the Tailhook convention, also included the Navy's C-2 carrier onboard delivery planes. Community members contributed $20 each to foot the bill for the room and the liquor.

During the preconvention planning back at the squadron, Remshak heard that an officer known as "Gandhi" had shaved women's legs in the community's suite at Tailhook '90. But these were no ordinary shaves; they were elaborate rituals in which a woman's legs were wrapped with hot towels, shaved, and rubbed with warm oil.

The leg shaves attracted lots of onlookers—voyeurs, in essence—and that was the idea. It was a *schtick* to get people inside, an assurance of a successful Tailhook party.

He asked his fliers if Gandhi would be attending this year, but no one knew. Diaz was assigned to an East Coast squadron.

Remshak arrived at Las Vegas on the afternoon of Thursday, September 5, 1991. Once on the Hilton's third floor, he stepped off the elevator and headed up the same hallway where the gantlet would take place on the convention's final night. He stopped at 303, the second suite on the right, and opened the door.

Inside, Remshak saw about a dozen people standing around, but he didn't recognize anyone. Over on the left, against the wall adjacent to the large glass windows and sliding door, was an overstuffed chair, where Rolando Diaz was arranging shaving implements in a wooden box. Remshak walked over and introduced himself.

"You must be Gandhi," he said. "I've heard a lot about you."

They chatted a bit. "I guess you're going to do leg-shaving," Remshak said. Diaz said he was. As Remshak later testified, he gave Diaz three ground rules for the shaving booth:

- No coercion;
- No underage women;
- No shaving above mid-thigh.

Remshak said Diaz replied, "Are you serious, skipper?"

Said Remshak, "I'm absolutely serious." Asked in court if he considered this an order, Remshak replied, "Yes I did."[35]

Diaz heard it differently. He'd told DOD-IG special agent Patricia Call that Remshak hadn't given him any instructions about the leg-shaving booth. Diaz's partner—Lt. Andy Jones, a member of Remshak's squadron—had said in a sworn statement that he never received any guidance from Remshak, either.

At that first meeting, Remshak asked for a demonstration. Later that evening, with about twenty others crowded around, a woman with shoulder-length hair, wearing white shorts and a blue top, received the treatment. Jones performed the "leg preparation." He wrapped the first leg with hot towels to soften the hair. Diaz then applied the shaving cream, and did the actual shaving. Jones then cleaned the excess shaving cream off the leg, applied a cold towel, rubbed baby oil into the leg and gave the woman a foot massage. They then repeated the process on the other leg. The whole process took thirty to forty-five minutes.[36]

"It looked perfectly above board and tasteful," Remshak testified at

Diaz's pretrial hearing. He told Diaz, "If that's the way we're going to do this, it's all right with me."[37]

On Friday night at 7:30, as the party swirled around them, Diaz and Jones opened for business. There was no charge, as promised on the fifteen-foot-long, one-foot-high, computer-generated sign on the well-lit outside wall over the glass doors that read: FREE LEG SHAVES. Diaz had learned the ritual in the Philippines, and he'd apparently learned it well. Women were lined up for shaves all weekend long. Some were only shaved to the knee. Most wanted their thighs shaved as well.

Things were going just swimmingly until it was Stormy's turn.

Stormy, unbeknownst to Diaz and Jones, was a local stripper. She'd been hired by fliers from another suite as a prank. Stormy wanted a "bikini" cut, a trim that would keep her pubic hair out of sight while wearing a skimpy swimsuit, but initially didn't mention that to Diaz.

Some of the lookers-on in the suite knew she was a stripper. As Diaz and Jones proceeded, the men watching decided they wanted to see some flesh. "Show your tits!" sounded out, and others joined in. Stormy "flashed" the group by quickly pulling up her top and pulling it down. Finally, she took it off entirely. That had the immediate effect of increasing the crowd's size.

As Diaz and Jones continued to work, Stormy loudly informed the crowd that if they wanted to see more, they'd better pay up. When she'd collected almost $40, she stood up in the chair and pulled off her pants. She was completely naked.

She then told Diaz she wanted the bikini cut. She sat down and Diaz proceeded to shave her as requested, keeping his hands on the outer fringes of her pubic area.[38]

Remshak was chatting with Lt. Kirby Miller out on the patio when someone walked up and said, "Someone's getting their pubic hair shaved in the suite."

"Oh, shit!" said Remshak, dashing to the suite. But when he arrived, a large crowd was blocking the sliding glass doors. Frustrated, he turned around and left, knowing it was the only way in. The door leading inside from the hallway had been locked on his orders because vandals had marked up the walls the previous night.[39]

Despite the ruckus over Stormy, other women continued to queue up for shaves. And on Saturday night at 7, the booth opened again. According to Jones, no one said a word about Stormy's Friday night shave. Investigators said one other woman received a bikini cut, remaining clothed but pulling back her shorts to allow Diaz to work.

"At no time did I receive any complaints from anyone, either senior, equal or junior to myself in rank, prior to or after the 'bikini' cut that this was improper and would not be tolerated," Jones said in a sworn statement.[40]

And Remshak said he didn't know for sure that Diaz had performed the bikini cut until a year later, when Remshak was talking with the E-2C "detailer," the officer at the Bureau of Naval Personnel who determined future assignments.

The detailer told Remshak that Diaz's promotion to lieutenant commander had been held up because of Tailhook. "Oh, by the way, skipper," he added, "your file is also flagged."[41]

"Flagging" an officer's records temporarily halts any new assignments or promotions.

When Remshak testified at Diaz's Article 32 pretrial hearing, he looked alternately bemused and agitated. As Diaz attorney Robert Rae rose to question him, Remshak raised his left hand to the side of his head and, out of the sight of Cmdr. Steven Seaton, the investigating officer seated at the bench to his right, he grinned slightly, looked straight at Rae, and crooked his middle finger to his head in an obvious "fuck you" gesture. Rae didn't see it, but others did.[42]

Despite Remshak's animosity, he admitted to Rae that there had been discrepancies between his testimony and the report of his interview by the DOD-IG.

"It makes things come out of context," Remshak told Rae. "There are elements in here that are true. There are some that are all wrong. They took notes when they felt like it."

"Many of the things you said were left out of that report?" asked Rae.

"Absolutely," said Remshak.

"Taken out of context?"

"Yes."

Remshak said that more than a few senior officers had known about leg shaving. He said he'd chatted about it with then-Vice Adm. Richard Dunleavy, assistant chief of naval operations for air warfare. Dunleavy told Remshak he personally didn't have a problem with it.

The commander of the Pacific Naval Air Force, Vice Adm. Edwin R. Kohn, Jr., had also dropped by the booth. "So that's leg-shaving?" Remshak said Kohn had remarked.[43]

The Diaz case didn't require as much detective work on the government's part; he'd readily admitted to Call that he'd shaved women's legs at both conventions. So who was lying? Diaz, or Remshak? And if Remshak had given the order, was it legally binding, in the military sense? Didn't an order need to be specifically related to military duty?

And, as Rae rhetorically phrased it for reporters after the Article 32 hearing for Diaz, "What is conduct unbecoming an officer in Las Vegas?"[44]

While the answer may have been that there was no such conduct short of assaultive behavior, a bitter irony hung over what had taken place in suite 303. The leg-shaving booth, a soft-core voyeur's delight, was operated in the suite of the only fixed-wing carrier community—a temporary integration, at that, since the C-2s had been thrown in with the E-2Cs—in which female fliers were welcome. It was a not-so-subtle demonstration of how far they still had to stoop—and how accepting they had to be of such attitudes—to be "one of the boys."

7

Bigger Fish

When Tom Miller was born and the doctor smacked him on the rear end, Miller probably turned with a smirk and cracked, "Is that your best shot?" Broad-chested and square-jawed, Cmdr. Thomas R. Miller was a merry prankster, a man with a twinkle in his eyes and a quip for every comment.

He had been to Tailhook '91. And as far as investigators were concerned, he was the stereotypical attendee: a smart-assed, cocksure Navy pilot, the kind who thought the rules were different for fliers, the kind who had condoned sexual assaults at Tailhook.

True, the government was anxious to nail younger fliers like Cole Cowden, Rolando, Diaz and Junior Samples. But the bottom line was that Cowden and Diaz were just guppies in the pond—pests who were being pursued because they'd had the audacity to refuse admiral's masts. Of the three lieutenants, only Samples, charged with assault, was a legitimate target.

What the government really wanted were some bigger fish: the commanders and senior officers (but not admirals) who Barbara Pope wanted to nail for letting things get out of hand. And Thomas R. Miller, a Navy commander, was just the right size.

So was Gregory E. Tritt, then Miller's executive officer, or "XO." But Tritt certainly didn't look the part. He was a soft-spoken family man, a quiet type who seemed more like he would be at home in the subdued intellectual atmosphere of a submarine than in the cockpit of an EA-6B Prowler screaming off a carrier deck.

The Navy wasn't buying it. The prosecution had a witness who said the mild-mannered Tritt had been grabbing women's rear ends on the

Hilton's third-floor patio on the final night of the convention. He had also failed to stop others from doing likewise. And he had lied about it to investigators.[1]

Miller hadn't been grabbing butts, investigators said; he had stood back and let it all happen, even encouraged it, and then told everyone else to lie about it, they said.[2]

A former Marine sergeant who served in Vietnam, Miller did everything hard. When it was time to work, he worked; at the end of the duty day, he loved to party.

He also cared deeply about his "kids," as he called his fliers. When it came time to critique fliers' aerial abilities, he said what was on his mind, and expected the same from his men. Every Wednesday afternoon, Miller gathered his fliers at the Whidbey Island O Club where they could, over a beer, lay out their problems or concerns—and, most important to Miller, any mistakes they had made while flying—without fear of undue criticism. The idea was to get the problems out in the open, and deal with them.[3]

Miller wasn't one to mince words. You always knew exactly where you stood with him. That's why it was easy to believe the story told by one flier, a married man who didn't bring his wife to Tailhook: When he walked up to Miller at the party, a strange woman hanging onto his arm, Miller had offered Janssen his room key and told him, "Take her up to the room and fuck her." That was Miller at Tailhook, as told by Lt. Daniel F. Janssen.[4]

Miller faced a total of nine charges: six counts of conduct unbecoming an officer, two counts of obstruction of justice, and one count of dereliction of duty. The conduct charges centered around the room key incident, and Miller's allegedly telling his fliers not to cooperate with Tailhook investigators. The obstruction charges were another way, under military law, of charging him for the same alleged exhortations. Investigators also said Miller was derelict in duty by failing to stop sexual misconduct at Tailhook. It was the longest charge sheet of any Tailhook defendant.[5]

In at least six of the nine charges, Janssen was the prime witness.

In the fall of 1991, Miller was commanding Tactical Electronic Warfare Squadron 139. Greg Tritt was his executive officer, and was next in line for command of the unit. "Twitch" Janssen was one of the unit's eighteen pilots.

Janssen was a controversial character in the squadron. He had some

talent as a flier, but also drank heavily. Hardly unusual. But co-work-
ers said he had a character flaw that set him apart from the crowd:
Janssen was one of those people who always feels compelled to em-
bellish his stories in order to elevate himself in the eyes of others.

Some embellishment is to be expected. Pilots are like fishermen.
They like to exaggerate a little, especially in front of unfamiliar
listeners. Naturally, the farther from home, the grander the stories
become.

Janssen, though, told his "sea stories" in front of his own incredulous squadron mates, who would listen in amazement at tales of glory
they knew simply weren't true. These weren't just generous exaggera-
tions or tall tales constructed for laughs; at least, they didn't come off
that way. Most thought he really believed the tales. He became such a
renown yarn spinner that fellow pilots, aboard the USS *Independence*
in the Persian Gulf during Operation Desert Shield, the run-up to the
1991 war, began to apply a "twitch factor" to grade a storyteller's
level of credibility. Someone would tell a story, and one of the unit's
pilots might respond with, "I'd say that's got a twitch factor of 8.5."[6]

Janssen also had an ingratiating manner that eventually drove Miller
crazy. When Miller first came to the unit as executive officer, his
commander was Jack Flanagan. "I watched Dan Janssen and his wife
basically kiss the Flanagans's ass," said Miller. "I watched that for a
year-and-a-half."

When Miller took Flanagan's place, he said he called Janssen into
his office. "Kissing my ass, if anything, is going to get you a worse
fitness report," he told Janssen, "because it shows me that you can't
compete on a level playing field." Janssen, said Miller, quit his whee-
dling. Miller began to be more impressed with the flier.[7]

It showed. Janssen's first "fitrep" fairly glowed with praise. "Has
my strongest personal recommendation for early promotion," Miller
wrote. "Consummate naval aviator"; "Top choice for combat"; "Exceptional knowledge of aircraft systems and operation"; "Role
model."[8]

But while Janssen initially performed well for Miller, he had also
found a new target for his fawning: Tritt and his wife Rosa.

"He rolled in hot on Rosa and Greg," said Miller, later. "And that's
something that poor Rosa and Greg still don't understand—or maybe
they do now."[9]

The Tritts took Janssen under their wing. They went skiing and snowboarding together, invited him and his wife over for Thanksgiving and Christmas dinner. It was more than a mentoring relationship. They were friends.[10]

To some extent, Tritt's leadership style invited Janssen's advances. The rapport Miller established with his "kids" was more old-school, built on male bonding, performance, and trust—but not much on personality. Tritt had been a hard-charging XO, but once he made commander, he developed a more relaxed and personal style than Miller's. Not every junior officer had been comfortable with it, but Janssen acted like he was.

That, Miller maintained, was because he had to. The younger pilots were quickly passing him. "Dan knew he couldn't compete," said Miller.

Tritt learned of the superficiality of the relationship only later—when Janssen gave agents a story about Tritt's activities at Tailhook that Tritt said simply wasn't true. He later told Miller, "I can't believe he was nice to us for only that reason. I thought we'd developed a relationship, the wives and stuff." Replied Miller, "Greg, what'd I tell you before I left?"

Janssen's stock with Miller had began to plummet not long after that first fitrep. Perhaps Janssen had put himself on his best behavior after Miller had chewed him out, and found he couldn't maintain same. But Miller began to feel that he had overrated Janssen. More and more, Miller found Janssen to be a mediocre pilot and poor leader, and found himself regularly chewing out the young flier for transgressions big and small.

He was "one of those guys who was always on the edge of stupidity," Miller recalled.[11]

Eventually, a powerful enmity developed between the two. One night at a squadron officers' dinner party at a hotel in Seattle, Janssen, attending with his wife, had gotten too drunk. He became loud and obnoxious, and started bragging to everyone within earshot. Miller walked over and shut him up, dressing him down publicly in the process for making a fool of himself. The confrontation silenced the other partiers.

Tritt and his wife, standing nearby, separated the two men; Tritt pulled Miller to the side, while Rosa and Janssen's wife took Janssen back to his hotel room and tried to calm him down. Janssen, angry and embarrassed, stomped about the room, hurling objects against the wall. He told Rosa Tritt, "I'm gonna fuck him in the heart."[12]

That was also a signal to the Tritts that they needed to put a little distance between themselves and the Janssens. Still, Tritt wanted to cut the young flier some slack. Maybe he can learn from this, he thought.

Meanwhile, the edge on Miller's natural ebullience was slowly being dulled by marital problems. On March 19, 1992, during a training flight over the Olympic Peninsula, it vanished altogether.

Miller was riding in one of the two back seats of an EA-6B Prowler performing what one unit flier called acrobatic maneuvers.

Suddenly, the plane began spinning out of control. The pilot, Lt. James P. Hogan, didn't have his internal mike turned on when he yelled, "Eject! Eject! Eject!" and pulled the command ejection handle.

All four men were shot out of the aircraft in their ejection seats. Miller and the other rear-seat occupant, a lieutenant named Becker, were only banged up slightly. But Lt. V.M. Verges, the co-pilot, had been leaning forward. As he was propelled out of the cockpit, his left hand was torn off.[13]

It tore Miller up. "He was kind of a loud, happy kind of person," recalled Lt. Sean Cassidy during a June pretrial hearing for Miller in Norfolk," and that basically went away after the mishap."[14]

In the summer of 1992, not long after the shortcomings of the Navy's first Tailhook investigation had been splashed all over the papers, Paula Coughlin had gone national, and the DOD-IG had begun its investigation, Janssen, Miller, and a few other pilots were sitting in the squadron ready room at Whidbey Island shooting the breeze. Janssen was reading a newspaper article that criticized the Navy investigation for its failure to question Navy commanders who had attended Tailhook as well as the younger officers who might have committed assaults.

"Hey skipper," Janssen announced. "If a junior officer was in trouble, all he had have to do is blame you, and you'd be fucked."

Miller just shook his head. "Dan, no matter how screwed up the non-operational Navy is, nobody in their right mind would ever believe a buffoon like you."[15]

As Miller was about to transfer in the fall of 1992 and leave the squadron in Greg Tritt's hands, he was, like all commanders, required to write a final fitrep on each of his officers. He didn't like Janssen, but he wanted to give him a fair shot. That was Miller's style. As he did when writing fitreps for the squadron's other officers, he sought performance input from his division chiefs, as well as his senior enlisted man. To double-check his final evaluation, he had Tritt review the fitrep and comment.

When the document was complete, Miller summoned Janssen to his office and walked him through the evaluation. To the untrained eye—and without comparison with any other—the fitrep would have looked positive, even exceptional. But to a Navy detailer in Washington, the subtle changes in verbiage from the previous fitrep were written in a code that sent a clear message: This is a mediocre officer, or at least, one whose stock has fallen far.

"Strongest recommendation for early promotion" had become "strongly recommended." "Consummate naval aviator" turned into "superior" naval aviator. "Top choice in combat" downshifted to "will excel in combat." The reference to Janssen being a "role model" was gone.

Worst of all, Miller had dropped him in the squadron rankings. Janssen had been ranked tenth out of eighteen on the previous fitrep; now, eight months later, he had fallen to fourteenth. It was a "vanilla" fitrep.

"This is like you really weren't here for a year," Miller said.

As he concluded the meeting, Miller tried to soften the blow and let Janssen know, despite his dislike for the flier, that this wasn't necessarily the end of his career.

"I haven't killed you on this fitrep, but I haven't helped you," he said. "What you do is, if you bust your ass for Greg Tritt, you can show an improvement, and it's all fixed. I could be wrong."

On the way out of the office, Janssen turned and said, "Skipper, you really don't like me, do you?"

Miller, his eyes opened wide, lost his temper. "Get back in my fucking office and sit the fuck down!" he screamed. Miller read him the riot act on his behavior, his character, and on embarrassing the command.

"You want to be fucking ranked? I'll rank you," Miller told him. "I'll rank you 19th out of 18. That's where you fall out."[16]

Miller left in August 1992 for an assignment aboard the Japan-based carrier USS *Independence*. Janssen didn't forget his former commander.

More than twenty members of Janssen's squadron had attended Tailhook, and the "129" suite was their home base for the party. Miller and Tritt, the squadron's top two officers, were part of the group. It was Miller's second Tailhook, Tritt's fourth.

On the convention's final day, Tritt spent his time wandering around the exhibit hall and attending the highly informal flag panel discussion. Miller spent most of the afternoon beside the pool out on the far end of the patio, reading and sipping cocktails, soaking up the sun, and watching women walk by.

"There were a few girls with their tops off, which is always nice," Miller later recalled. "I mean, I'm a guy. I'm sorry. If they're going to take their tops off, I'll probably sit in my chair and watch."[17]

Miller and Tritt attended the Secretary of the Navy banquet together Saturday evening. Afterwards, both left to change into casual clothes. Back down on the third floor, Miller spotted Tritt inside the crowded VAQ-129 suite. They hung out for about a half-hour, talking with others and occasionally with each other. The two were close professionally but not personally; they were cut from different cloth.

Later, Miller found himself back out on the patio, roaming around the general vicinity of a planter a few dozen feet from the VAQ-129 suite, on the edge of the sea of people outside the suites and not far from the revolving doors that led to the central elevators. He had already been introduced to Secretary of the Navy Lawrence Garrett, who had flown out from Washington to deliver the keynote address at the banquet.

The fringe was where the senior officers generally congregated, away from the much younger "JOs" who dominated the inner part of the patio, the noisy, raucous suites and the inside hallway. The seniors knew it was foolish to even try to deal with that junior officer craziness. "Why run up and down there [in the hallway], with a bunch of kids throwing beer on you and shit?" Miller later said.

At one point, Miller was talking with another commander alongside a palm tree in a planter when a young, well-built woman, probably a student at the University of Nevada, Las Vegas, walked up, lifted up her sweater, and asked both of us if we had any stickers. The woman's ample breasts were covered with "zappers," stickers that depict squadron logos.

The two men looked incredulously at each other, and then began laughing hysterically. The young woman walked off. Miller said to the commander, "Boy, I wish I was a fucking fleet lieutenant."

Miller later said that any temptation to "zap" the woman was tempered by the company he was keeping. "I'm going to sit there and do something wrong in front of every admiral and every senior captain that I know? I don't think so. Did I have zappers? Did my skipper friend? Yeah, we had zappers. But there's no way in hell I was going to put a zapper on a woman in front of God and country.

"If I was a lieutenant, I probably would've, if I was asked. And would it be considered wrong, or was it wrong in the old days? No, it wasn't."[18]

Janssen didn't attend the banquet. He and his buddies had been sightseeing, drinking, and gambling most of the afternoon, and arrived at the Hilton around dusk. They proceeded to the VAQ-129 suite—the first door on the right off the elevators on the third floor.

Janssen walked through and ambled out onto the patio. There, he struck up a conversation with the wife of a Las Vegas police officer. During the course of their chat, she was "zapped" with squadron stickers four or five times on her rear end and breasts. It didn't seem to bother her, Janssen recalled; she thought it was kind of fun. At one point, someone bit her on the rear end. She turned and, laughing, bit the man back on his rear end.

She and Janssen began getting chummy, and Janssen put his arm around her. At one point, they embraced and kissed. Janssen, who was married, then introduced her to Tritt, and the three chatted briefly; it was the only time Tritt remembered seeing Janssen all evening. Tritt thought Janssen looked drunk.

Miller was standing nearby, and Janssen walked the girl over to meet him. Miller, Janssen said, tossed him his room keys and said, "Take her up to the room and fuck her."

Janssen and the woman giggled and declined. Janssen later testified that he felt it was said mostly in a sarcastic sense, an attempt to embarrass Janssen, as opposed to a serious offer to go commit adultery. Miller repeated the offer twice more, Janssen said, adding that he finally pocketed the keys to end Miller's insistence.[19]

There was a big problem with Janssen's story. Guests at the Las Vegas Hilton didn't use keys to unlock their rooms. Since 1989, guests at the Hilton have used coded cards to enter their rooms. To unlock the door, a guest slides the card in and out of a slot above the door handle.[20]

A plastic card is tough to toss back and forth. If Miller was throwing keys, they weren't hotel keys.

Saturday night partiers out on the patio who wanted a fresh drink had a problem: they had to wade through the huge crowds outside the suites in order to reach the bars and kegs set up inside. What gradually developed were impromptu pathways that snaked from the glass doors of the suites through the crowds and out onto the patio so people could get in and out.

Sometime around 10 p.m., according to Janssen, Tritt began rallying the troops. "Hey, Cougars! Let's get this going," Janssen told investigators he heard Tritt announce. "Get everybody around here." Miller, said Janssen, was standing next to Tritt.

In court, all Janssen could remember was Tritt calling out, "Hey, Cougs!" Or something like that, he said.

Janssen said that a distinct pathway came to be formed through the crowd up to the sliding glass doors, with men standing on either side, facing in. As Janssen described the action, Miller was at the tail end of this "mini-gantlet," out by the planter. Tritt, he said, was in the midst of it—on the side of the mini-gantlet closest to the pool, opposite from where LoGuidice had placed him during his later testimony.[21]

LoGuidice wasn't known for stretching the truth. But he was known for his drinking. And at this point, he was one drunk flier. He had been drinking all day and had recently returned from time at sea, so his tolerance to alcohol was low. And the last thing he had eaten was a hot dog, early that afternoon.

LoGuidice was up by the door at the head of the line, as he recalled. He didn't recognize anyone else in this mini-gantlet, save for a nebulous "snapshot memory" of Tritt swinging his arm in a "cupping" motion.

Janssen didn't remember seeing LoGuidice or anyone else in the mini-gantlet—including Tritt—even though he said he went into the suite and back out again twice, once with his female companion.

The pinching and groping continued for twenty to forty minutes, the two lieutenants said. Janssen thought he had heard women exclaiming as though they had been pinched, but he hadn't actually seen anything. LoGuidice admitted he had touched women's rear ends, and had seen others doing it as well. But he couldn't identify them. And he couldn't say with certainty that he had seen Tritt touch anybody.[22]

Miller and Tritt didn't remember any of this. Both said flatly that an organized mini-gantlet didn't take place.

During his taped DOD-IG interview, Janssen told Black that while he was inside the suite and about to return to the patio, he saw a tall redhead out on the patio throw a drink in Miller's face and exclaim,

"Knock it off." Janssen said Miller told her angrily, "Fuck you, cunt. If you don't like it, go ahead and get out of here." Within moments of that response, Janssen substituted Tritt for Miller.[23]

In court, Janssen testified that the drink was thrown at Tritt, and that Tritt had chewed the woman out. Asked why he had changed his story, he said it was "due to the fact of later on, somebody mentioning some words that may have been said, and then I associated them with that incident."[24]

Given the number of people present in the suite and on the patio and the noise such partiers were generating, it was hard to believe that Janssen, standing at the doorway of the suite, could have heard anything spoken, even exclaimed, thirty to forty feet away on the outside.[25]

On the witness stand nearly two years after the incident, Tritt acknowledged that he and a woman had bumped into each other. The woman took exception to being bumped and began to get angry with Tritt. He backed off, telling her it was an accident, he said.[26]

After the alleged mini-gantlet dissipated, Janssen decided to cross the hallway and look for a friend in the Fighter Squadron 1 suite. When he left that suite and reentered the hallway, he spotted Cmdr. Robert C. Yakeley, the chief staff officer for Carrier Air Wing 14. Janssen's unit belonged to the wing, and Janssen knew Yakeley. The night before, he had watched as a woman out by the pool who had been teasing fliers and flashing her breasts had pulled Yakeley's pants down.

When the two men made eye contact, Janssen rushed towards Yakeley, arm raised, to give him a "high five" hand slap. Instead, he struck Yakeley's arm and slammed his head into the wall. Yakeley hit the deck, out cold.

Janssen leaned down and tried to wake him up, slapping his face a few times. No luck. He stood back up, and noticed LoGuidice standing next to him. "I think I killed a commander," he said solemnly to LoGuidice. Then he turned to leave.[27]

Onlookers who recognized Yakeley said, "Hey, you can't just leave him there. He's a commander." Janssen just laughed and said, "Well, I'm out of here." He walked back into the VAQ-129 suite.[28]

Sometime after midnight, five lieutenants—Janssen, LoGuidice, Dave Musgrave, Andy Monson, and Jack Healey decided to "streak" naked through the Tailhook party.

They disrobed in the bathroom of suite 302, home of VAQ-129. Wearing only their shoes, they left the bathroom, ran into the hallway, turned right, and dashed down the nearly empty third-floor hallway toward the far end of the hotel wing. Halfway down the hallway, just past the "Rhino" suite, they made a hard right at the fire exit, dashed onto the patio, and danced amidst the partiers on their way back to the suite.

When they ran back inside, they headed straight for the bathroom. Their clothes were missing.

Someone said the clothes were out by the pool. So the inebriated LoGuidice walked over to a couch, grabbed pillows to cover his front and rear end, and went back out onto the patio to retrieve the clothes.

He didn't make it. Security guards spotted him and began giving chase. LoGuidice turned about and dashed towards suite 302. Partiers cheered him on and formed impromptu pickets to block the guards. He joined the others in the bathroom, slamming the door behind him.

A couple of minutes later, LoGuidice peeked out the bathroom door.[29]

The first face he saw was Miller's. "You fucking idiots," he said. "Get your fucking clothes on and get the hell out of here."[30]

LoGuidice looked sheepishly at Miller. "Skipper, the girls stole my clothes." Miller shook his head in disbelief. Someone nearby offered to go try to find them. Fine, he said.[31]

Miller shut the bathroom door, then turned back and stood against the door, not allowing anyone in. That didn't surprise LoGuidice. "His nature is to watch out for his men," he later said.[32]

The two security guards finally made their way through the crowd and into the unit's party suite, known as an "administrative" suite in Navy parlance, sort of a home away from the squadron. "Open the door," one shouted.

Miller shooed them away. "Get out," he said. "Get out of my admin. Leave these guys alone." They left.[33]

At one point, DOD-IG and the Navy considered this grounds for an obstruction of justice charge.

After the guards left, Capt. Frederic Ludwig, the Tailhook president, arrived, and asked what was going on. Ludwig, like every other officer at Tailhook, was wearing civilian clothes. Miller, who didn't know Ludwig, gave him a curt reply. "Look, we're trying to get this calmed down," he said.

An older man standing with Ludwig took exception to Miller's tone. "You know who this is?" he said. "He's Mr. Tailhook."

Miller laughed. Mr. Who? Then he realized what the man meant. Immediately deferential, he gave Ludwig a detailed explanation.[34]

The clothes were returned. A wallet and watch were missing. Janssen and Musgrave went down to security to file reports. The other fliers left the party. Janssen went to his room and fell asleep.[35]

Prior to the first Tailhook interviews at the squadron, conducted by the Naval Investigative Service, Miller called an all-officers meeting. The pilots, LoGuidice later recalled for DOD-IG agents, regarded the upcoming questioning as a joke. What made this Tailhook any different than others before it?

But at the meeting, Miller, LoGuidice said, told his fliers that this was serious business, that this was going to be regarded differently than any other Tailhook. Miller, said LoGuidice, said that "we were not to lie to these people, but we were not to volunteer anything."

Asked by DOD-IG agent Peter Black during a taped interview what that meant, LoGuidice chose his words carefully. "Allegations can be dangerous," he said. "They will be taken very serious, and could lead to a lot of problems for the person making the statements." If someone said they knew something but couldn't identify a face, that could be interpreted as lying, LoGuidice explained.[36]

Black and his fellow agents had come to Whidbey Island in October 1992, less than a year after the Navy's first stab at nailing down the case. It was the final stop on an investigative tour of West Coast naval bases that had begun outside San Diego at Miramar Naval Air Station.

When they arrived, the word had already flashed up the coast about what was going down, even to the extent of which agents were using which techniques to ask certain questions.[37]

Miller claimed he would have none of it. He was angry that so much ado was being made about what he regarded as nothing—except for the Coughlin and Rodgers cases—but he wasn't going to be part of a conspiracy to cover up wrongdoing.

At another all-officers meeting, Miller reiterated his first stance.

"I didn't see anything," Janssen quoted Miller as saying. "And I don't know what you guys are going to do. You guys do what you have to do, whatever you feel is right, you go ahead and do it. But, as I said before, I didn't see anything." This, Janssen later claimed, amounted to asking officers not to cooperate with investigators.[38]

By the time a charge sheet had been issued by the Navy, the alleged quote had been strengthened in favor of the government's case. "This is bullshit," the charge sheet reads. "I can't believe they're wasting money on this investigation. I didn't see anything inappropriate. You do what you have to do, but I didn't see shit. I'm not telling them anything."

Janssen later said Miller had suggested "not telling them anything" repeatedly over a nearly one-year period.[39]

When DOD-IG arrived at Whidbey, Miller was already gone. Janssen soon discovered he was a prime target; he had been identified by Lt. Dave Musgrave during an earlier interview. But what the agents really wanted, he learned, was information about commanders who had attended Tailhook—Miller and Tritt, in particular. And Janssen, as well as LoGuidice, the agents soon found, were willing to supply what they wanted.

Janssen showed up for the January 20, 1993, interview with his attorney, Lt. Patrick Padgett.

When they walked in the door, Black cut loose. "You're hosed!" he told Janssen. "You're going to jail with your buddy Geiss!" Padgett shot back that Janssen wouldn't be talking to anyone. Black advised Janssen of his rights and charged him with indecent exposure, conduct unbecoming an officer, making a false official statement, and hindering a federal investigation.

Padgett grabbed Janssen and headed out the door. "Unless you're arresting my client, we're leaving," he said. Black told Janssen that the government knew he had done more than just run naked across the patio, that they knew he more to tell, and that they were prepared to offer immunity to learn more about what had gone on earlier in suite 302.

At Padgett's office, the attorney strongly recommended taking the immunity.[40]

The following month, the now-immune Janssen was interviewed at length at DOD-IG headquarters in Washington, D.C. He told agents his version of events, and the rush was on to get Miller and Tritt.

Ten days later, when Miller was interviewed for the first time by DOD-IG's Black, the bearish agent launched into a ten-minute soliloquy that turned into a screaming, melodramatic fit.

"When I was a young boy, I always wanted to fly naval jets off aircraft carriers," it began. "I thought you guys were the bravest of the brave . . . .

"And then after interviewing 1,500 of you, I've found that you're all liars!," Black exclaimed. "You started the gauntlet. You knocked down women. You ripped their blouses off."

He also accused Miller of sending one of his pilots to a field evaluation board for review of the flier's flight qualifications. The pilot ended up losing his flight certification. That, Black maintained, allowed Miller to keep the pilot "hidden" from investigators.

"I'm not used to being talked to like that," Miller later said. "And it's not the rank."

Black finally gave Miller three choices: refuse to talk and get prosecuted; conduct the interview and face possible prosecution, depending on what he said; or testify against Tritt, and receive immunity.

The last thing Miller would have done was to testify against Tritt, his former executive officer. After talking it over with a lawyer, Miller decided not to talk at all.[41]

That same day in Washington, D.C., Tritt also invoked his rights and declined to be interviewed. Back in November, he had told agents at Whidbey that he had left the banquet, changed, and spent most of the next two hours on the patio, although he also visited the CNATRA suite. At about 11 p.m., he said, he went back to his room, took a nap, then got up and went to another casino to gamble. He hadn't seen any misconduct, he had said.[42]

Despite their denials, Tritt and Miller were prime targets—due almost exclusively to the statements of LoGuidice and Janssen, the latter of whom the fliers back at VAQ-139 had started calling "Snitch" instead of "Twitch." It wasn't until summer was well underway that both admitted they'd been coached as to what to say.

At the tail end of his testimony at Tritt's first pretrial hearing in July, the investigating officer, Cmdr. Larry McCullough, asked Janssen about his statement to DOD-IG investigators in which he had affirmed that Tritt had lied to agents when he had sworn he hadn't seen a gantlet or any women being assaulted.

"Now that's . . . is that still in your sworn statement?" asked McCullough.

It is, Janssen replied, "but that's just based duly (sic) on the fact that he was in the same spot, or in the same general vicinity, that I was in and it was, you know," and here, Janssen began scrambling, "you could tell people were, you came, like I said, being . . . from the best of my knowledge, being pinched. So, that's the reason I said that in my statement, because it's like, you know . . . "

McCullough cut him off. "Well, did he lie to them, or did he not? Or do . . . you don't know?"

"I . . . in my sworn statement, I said, 'Yes.'"

"But under oath here, you're saying you don't know," said McCullough. "You can't say?"

"I can't say, because I don't know what people say or what they heard or what they did," Janssen replied. "I just based on where he was, and that's what was placed on me from this investigator . . . but under oath, did I say . . . no, I'd have to say no."[43]

During the September 17, 1993, hearing for Tritt, his attorney, Robert Rae, questioned Janssen about that same interview with DOD-IG.

"Would it be fair to say that before the . . . actual taping was done, you had a prolonged period of time in a preliminary interview discussing what was going to be asked and what was going to be answered with in that transcript? Would it be fair to say that many of the pieces of information were provided to you from DOD-IG Special Agent Black?"

"Towards the end of the interview," said Janssen, "you can see where that is, yeah."

When Lt. Cmdr. Diane Karr, Tritt's military attorney, asked Janssen if it was true that he didn't have any basis for concluding that Tritt's calling over the Cougars was aimed at starting up a gantlet for sexual assaults, he agreed.

"OK," she said. "Now, isn't it true that based on all the information you've been provided through the press, through the investigators, through the prosecutors, that now you look back and say, 'Well, it was a short period of time after that and so, golly, it must be true that he was calling us to form a gauntlet.' Is that what your testimony is today? That's the basis of your conclusion?"

"Some of it, yes," said Janssen. When asked if he had been influenced by suggestions of investigators or prosecutors, he replied, "Not really."[44]

LoGuidice was also coached. During the first Tritt hearing, in July 1993, LoGuidice had told Rae that it was Black's suggestion that led him to state that Tritt had been standing to his left in the mini-gantlet. When he was recalled in September, he reaffirmed that statement during questioning by Rae.

"Well, they even told you what they did," said Rae, referring to the Pentagon agents. "When they told you they had statements putting Commander Tritt right next to you, they in fact told you what he did before you even offered it to them."

"Well," said LoGuidice, "that's correct."

"And the same goes for Commander Miller, is that correct?"

"That's correct," LoGuidice replied.[45]

What officers considered coaching, investigators considered a questioning technique. When Black was questioned by Rae at a September 1993 hearing for two other officers being investigated, he confirmed the coaching.

"Would it be proper to say that there is no proper investigative technique that includes suggesting the answers to witnesses?" Rae asked.

"No, I would disagree with that, sir," Black replied.

"OK," said Rae. "So, sometimes you do suggest answers to witnesses?"

"Yes, sir," said Black.[46]

The case against Tritt seemed exceedingly weak. LoGuidice, drunk for the second straight night, had only a "snapshot memory' of his commander standing nearby, moving his arms. In addition, Ensign Kim Ponikowski, Tritt's alleged victim, couldn't identify him. Even if Tritt was where LoGuidice had claimed he was—to LoGuidice's left, with several people between himself and the sliding glass door—it would place the short, balding Tritt well away from where Ponikowski had said she had held off the approaching hand of an "old bald guy."

The case against Miller, at least the part relating to the third-floor patio, seemed similarly flawed. The key story didn't wash. No one could clearly remember him trying to organize the squadron into a mini-gantlet. No one could say for certain that Miller, out on the edge of the patio, had seen any groping when people five feet away from sexual misconduct couldn't see anything.

All that seemed clear. The mystery lay in why the two lieutenants had tacitly agreed to serve the likeable Tritt up on a platter to the Navy. While Janssen clearly disliked Miller, he had actually socialized with Tritt. There was no apparent ax to grind. Tritt himself didn't have a clue.

Nor could anyone account for the testimony of LoGuidice, who bore no apparent grudge against either man.

"He's a complete mystery," Miller later said. "Janssen, at least I can understand why he did what he did"—at least as far as Miller was concerned, anyway. But why try to hurt Tritt? Perhaps, Miller said, Janssen, trying to use Tritt as a springboard to success, saw his tactic was failing and turned on him, as well.[47]

The holes in the cases were apparent to Navy prosecutors, who were relying exclusively on the DOD-IG investigation. But the government wanted Miller badly—so much so that Janssen's recollections of the squadron's trip home from the Persian Gulf War, seven months prior to Tailhook, became the basis of additional charges against his former commander.

Miller, Janssen told investigators after he had gone to mast and received immunity, had "ballwalked" on rooftops and golf courses in Singapore, Honolulu, and San Diego during the USS *Independence*'s port calls that had taken place the year prior to Tailhook.[48]

"Ballwalking," wrote investigating officer Cmdr. Steven Seaton in his findings following Miller's July 14 pretrial hearing, "is understood, apparently, to be some peculiar sort of preposterous buffoonery not uncommon within the aviation community."

Ballwalking was the male Navy's off-duty version of letting it all hang out. It wasn't too complicated an act; participants simply undid their trouser fly, pulled out their genitals, and continued about their business.

There had been a lot of ballwalkers at Tailhook, both on the pool patio and outside the hotel, on the streets of Las Vegas. Miller hadn't joined them. But he had ballwalked before. Once, he unzipped himself and pulled out his genitals while walking at night along the golf course at North Island Naval Air Station in San Diego with some fellow male pilots, who joined in.

The Honolulu penthouse, atop the Waikiki Outrigger Hotel, had been rented by VAQ-139 officers while on a Hawaii port call. One afternoon, Miller strolled out onto the sunny balcony *sans* pants.

Janssen also said he had seen Miller sitting in a hotel room in Singapore, naked from the waist down, a tie wrapped around his head, swigging from a bottle of whiskey.[49]

All told, Seaton decided that Miller had only ballwalked or walked around "admin" suites partially nude in the presence of other squadron members. This was no more indecent exposure than would be represented by naked men in a football locker room, he said. Seaton recommended handling the charge at an admiral's mast, or dropping it altogether.

But Seaton found enough credibility in the testimony of Janssen, LoGuidice, and DOD-IG agent Peter Black to recommend that Miller be court-martialed on charges of failing to stop subordinates from engaging in offensive behavior, for offering his "room keys" to Janssen, and for telling his men to withhold information from investigators.[50]

The night before Tritt's initial Article 32 pretrial hearing, Rae called Robert Monahan, the number two lawyer at SurfLant to Jeffry Williams. Monahan was an old friend of Rae's; they'd been classmates at the Naval Academy, and Rae was only a year out of the Navy JAG Corps. Rae figured they could talk.

"Bob, unless you guys have more evidence than what I've seen, you don't have a case here," he told Monahan. "Why are we going into a 32? We ought to at least be able to work this out at an NJP (nonjudicial punishment, such as an admiral's mast)."

"No way," said Monahan. "We're going to hammer those guys. They're all guilty. We're going to nail them."

"I don't see the evidence," said Rae. "I really don't. I don't think you should put these guys through it."

The argument fell on deaf ears. Monahan was adamant. Tritt was going to court.[51]

Following Tritt's pretrial hearing, investigating officer Cmdr. Larry McCullough filed the required report with Reason on July 12. McCullough recommended dropping the assault charges as well as the government's charge that Tritt had organized a mini-gantlet of his fliers to grope women coming out of the VAQ-129 suite.

But although admitting the evidence was flimsy—"There is no direct evidence that the accused committed this offense," McCullough wrote—he ruled that there was enough evidence to provide reasonable grounds to believe that Tritt had seen women get pinched and grabbed.

McCullough also said the government should charge Tritt with failing to stop misconduct by subordinates and making a false official statement to investigators.[52]

Now it was Capt. Jeffry Williams's turn. As Reason's top lawyer, it was his job to analyze the findings of McCullough and Seaton; then, to advise Reason on whether to go to court-martial, and on which charges.

Given the government's aggressive prosecution to date, a trial seemed a foregone conclusion.

On Tuesday, August 10, 1993, in a crisp, matter-of-fact court-martial hearing that lasted barely twenty minutes, Miller stood before Capt. William T. Vest, a military judge, and pleaded not guilty on all counts.

When Tritt's court-martial was convened August 12, the original eight charges had been reduced to five. But despite McCullough's recommendations, Tritt was still being charged with two counts of assault—one on Ponikowski, the other on "females, whose names are unknown"—along with one count of conduct unbecoming an officer for touching those unknown females, one count of failing to stop subordinates from doing so, and one count of making a false official statement.

Tritt withheld his plea pending the court's ruling on several defense motions.

The following day, papers were served on Lt. Cole Cowden. Despite a prosecutor on his case being fired for telling superiors the case lacked merit, despite the pretrial recommendation that all charges be dropped, and despite a letter written to Adm. Frank B. Kelso by the flier's congressman, Rep. Malcolm Wallop, R-Wyo., who called the continued prosecution of Cowden "outrageous," Cowden, thirty-two, was going to trial.

8

Counterattack

As far as the defense attorneys for Miller, Tritt, and Cowden were concerned, the remarkable aspect of their impending trials was the decision in each case to prosecute despite strong pretrial recommendations to the contrary.

It was Capt. Jeffry Williams who had recommended pressing the cases. But it was Vice Adm. J. Paul Reason, the lawyers knew, who made the final decision to do so.

The big question, lawyers asked themselves, was, why? What was Reason thinking? These cases had obvious flaws. Was Williams that influential? Robert Rae, representing leg-shaver Rolando Diaz as well as Tritt, suspected something else: that Reason was being pressured from above to produce some convictions to assuage Congress and the public.

Rae decided to go after Reason.

The influence, Rae would argue, had been spawned by powerful sources. Members of Congress were angry. Certain high-level defense officials and members of Reason's own chain of command felt a similar outrage. The need for a change in attitude towards the opposite sex had been expressed in Navy-wide messages condemning sexual harassment. A July 1992 "ALNAV" message quoted acting Navy Secretary Dan Howard telling senior Pentagon officials that "the attitudes that led to" Tailhook "have absolutely no place" in the Navy. "I'm directing immediately that we take certain steps to drive them out," Howard said. The messages, Rae said, made it impossible for the Navy to conduct an unbiased internal probe.

Reason, Rae concluded, had to be feeling the pressure.

The day prior to Diaz's first pretrial hearing, Rae told a reporter that he was about to ask the Navy to remove Reason as head of the investigation. Reason couldn't possibly be impartial, Rae argued, because he had had ongoing conversations about Tailhook with senior Navy and Pentagon officials, including a daily chat with Adm. Frank B. Kelso, chief of naval operations.

"I've never seen such high command interest in a case," said Rae. "These things have been preordained and are politically destined. They need some convictions, and they don't care who it is. They're going to get them."

In particular, Rae questioned the dismissal of Lt. D.J. Hansen from the Cowden case after Hansen advised against a court-martial, and the convening of courts-martial against Tritt and Miller in the face of indecisive testimony from largely drunk witnesses.

"They forgot that you need evidence to prosecute," Rae said. "You have to have some ID, some victim, some reason to convict someone at a court-martial."

Undue command influence is a two-way street. Rae knew he couldn't prove that Reason was on the receiving end unless he could also prove who'd been leaning on him.[1]

On August 3, one of his clients took the counterattack's first shot. Diaz fired a broadside heard all the way to Washington, D.C.

While the courtroom filled up for the Diaz hearing, Alba Bragoli, a Norfolk-based freelance courtroom artist who often sketched courtroom scenes for local newspapers and TV stations, was looking over Diaz's charge sheet. The sheet included the charge of "wrongfully shaving the pubic area of two unidentified females."

She turned and remarked to a reporter, "How do you *rightfully* shave the pubic area of females?"

After a pause, Bragoli cracked, "with a safety razor."[2]

During the hearing, Diaz freely admitted shaving women's legs. But he denied ever being told by Cmdr. Christopher Remshak, the officer in charge of the VAQ-129 suite, that he was not to shave legs above the mid-thigh.

As his hearing drew to a close, the investigating officer, Cmdr. Steven Seaton, asked Diaz if he wanted to make a statement. Standing beside Rae, Diaz, reading from prepared remarks, spoke clearly and without hesitation.

"I am being charged for behavior that was encouraged and fostered by my seniors," he said. "What I did was viewed by the highest-ranking officer in the United States Navy."[3]

During Tailhook and through the present, the top officer in the U.S. Navy was Frank B. Kelso. He'd told agents he hadn't seen a thing.

This was history. A Navy lieutenant was accusing the top officer in his chain of command, an officer seven pay grades his senior, of lying.

The ramifications of the accusation were huge. Kelso, as acting Navy secretary, had directed to Reason and Krulak the case files of 140 officers suspected of sexual misconduct at Tailhook '91, ordering them to both investigate and see that justice was done.

But if Kelso was guilty of any of the offenses any of the 140 were suspected of committing—even if it amounted to no more than knowledge of misconduct and tacit approval of same—he would have no moral or legal grounds for having ordered the investigation, since he would have a personal interest in the outcome.

In the event of such a finding, the judge would have no choice but to throw out the entire investigation.[4]

In addition to the statement's far-reaching implications, it made for sensational courtroom theater.

"If the Department of Defense Inspector General cared about the truth, my charge sheet would have read as follows: 'Lieutenant Diaz is charged with conduct unbecoming an officer because we failed to find anyone who assaulted Paula Coughlin,' Diaz said."[5]

Although the charge against Diaz may ultimately have been grounded in political correctness, it was also true that Coughlin's alleged assailant had still not been formally accused. Another week would pass before the Marines would announce a pretrial hearing for Capt. Gregory J. Bonam, the F/A-18 pilot who Coughlin had picked out of a lineup at Camp Lejeune, N.C., as her assailant.

"There was no conduct unbecoming on my part," Diaz continued. "The conduct unbecoming occurred when the senior leadership present at Tailhook averted attention from themselves and onto their subordinates."

Diaz then implicated Kelso and kept going, his voice full of anger.

"While I cannot condone the actions of a few officers who may have been involved in non-consensual acts, I cannot stand by and be falsely accused of disobeying an order I never received. I understand that Commander Remshak had to protect his career. But he is mistaken when he states he gave me a direct order not to shave above mid-thigh.

"I fully cooperated with investigators from the start of the inquisition," Diaz said. "I never lied or omitted facts about my behavior. I shaved many women's legs at Tailhook. Several were naval officers, and one was Lieutenant Paula Coughlin. None of the women complained."[6]

This angered Diaz far more than feeling as though he was one of the scapegoats for a failure to find Coughlin's assailant. Here he was, about to be court-martialed for shaving women's legs at Tailhook '91, and she, he claimed, had twice been one of his customers, once while she was in uniform. A poster on the wall behind his leg-shaving booth had allegedly been signed, "You made me see God. The Paulster."[7]

Diaz couldn't understand why officers who shaved legs at Tailhook were being punished, but officers who had had their legs shaved were not. He also felt there was evidence that Coughlin had committed adultery that weekend; She later admitted that Lt. Scott Wilson, aide to Rear Adm. Don W. Baird and a married man, had spent a night in her suite at the Paddle Wheel Hotel during the Tailhook weekend. She said he had slept on the couch.[8]

"Lieutenant Coughlin lied to the investigators and even though the DOD-IG had evidence, they covered it up," Diaz said, referring to the Pentagon investigation. "She has not faced the scrutiny for her actions that I have. Like Lieutenant Warnick, Lieutenant Coughlin lied but is protected by the authorities."

Warnick was the officer who claimed she had been raped by Cowden.

"This is selective prosecution, encouraged by the DOD-IG and railroaded through by the special interest groups in Congress at the cost of naval readiness and morale," Diaz continued. "The DOD-IG has falsified statements by omission of facts, buried evidence, and protected female officers because it was politically correct.

"The Navy's solution to Tailhook '91 is a disgrace," Diaz said. "While I would expect this to be possible in Castro's Cuba, I would have never believed the country I swore to defend 16 years ago would turn on me just to appease Congress."

He ended with a flourish. "There is no backbone in the Navy's present leadership," he said. "The warriors are dead; the politicians have taken over."[9]

The statement was aimed directly at the Tailhook attendees that

Barbara Pope had said were ignored during the Navy's own investigations: senior officers. But Diaz didn't mean suite commanders. He meant the admirals.

That afternoon, the Office of the Chief of Naval Information, or CHINFO, wasted no time firing off a return salvo to what it termed Diaz's "unsworn statement."

Kelso, according to a CHINFO statement, "did not visit any of the squadron suites, nor did he see or hear of any misconduct or inappropriate behavior. Admiral Kelso has testified *under oath* that the only time he spent on the third floor of the Las Vegas Hilton was in the pool/patio area on Friday evening, when he spent about forty minutes visiting with naval aviators."[10]

A week after Diaz stood up, Miller's civilian attorney Don Marcari told reporters he also planned to move for dismissal on grounds that Reason had been unduly influenced. He also planned to move that excessive pretrial publicity made finding an impartial panel of peers impossible.[11]

At a separate hearing the same day, Rae moved for dismissal on grounds that the Navy had engaged in selective prosecution by targeting Tritt and none of the more senior Navy officers who'd attended the convention.

During that hearing, Capt. William T. Vest, the military judge, told the court he had been troubled by the wording on one of the charges against Tritt. It stated that Tritt "unlawfully touched females, whose names are unknown . . . "

"Not knowing names, in my opinion, is a serious deficiency in pleadings," said Vest. In addition, Vest wanted to ensure that the pleadings were "sufficient." If Tritt were found not guilty on a vaguely worded charge, it could leave him open to additional charges for the same offenses if, for instance, the names of victims became known. "I want to protect him against double jeopardy," Vest said.[12]

Vest, a short, wavy-haired, soft-spoken Virginia native, would be at the center of the Navy's Tailhook hearings. A twenty-nine-year Navy veteran, he had begun his career as a reservist in Vietnam, a fast-boat skipper who intercepted enemy supply trawlers and fired on shore-based enemy positions during riverine operations in 1967–68.

In 1972, he received his law degree from the University of Louisville, and began his career as a Navy lawyer. The master of laws degree followed, awarded in 1978 by George Washington University.

Working his way up the Navy ladder, Vest in August 1989 became chief trial judge of the Navy's Norfolk-based Tidewater Judicial Circuit, its largest and busiest.

SurfLant fell into his district. So, accordingly, would all of the Tailhook cases sent to trial.

Vest was regarded as the best judge in the Navy. He had a reputation as a straight arrow, a man of unquestioned integrity who was intensely loyal to the Navy and the nation.[13]

Vest admired detail and thoroughness, and it showed in court. He expected attorneys to do their homework before standing up to argue a case. More than a few young Navy attorneys had left his courtroom with their tails between their legs, his soft Southern twang ringing in their ears.[14]

The day after Rae made his motions, Marcari filed documents with Vest that made essentially the same arguments on nearly every count against Miller. The "observed officers" he had allegedly gathered on the Hilton's pool patio, and the "females whose names are unknown" who had been accosted—who were they? Without names, Marcari argued in his brief, how could Miller properly prepare for trial, evaluate exculpatory evidence, present a defense, and be protected from improperly investigated allegations?

The defensive counterattack was in full swing. On August 12, during Tritt's arraignment, Rae had asked Vest to dismiss all charges because undue influence had been exerted on Reason, and on the grounds that the Navy was selectively prosecuting Tritt and ignoring more senior officers who'd attended the convention.

Rae wanted to question Reason. But he needed more evidence to put him on the spot.

Theoretically, the defense at any trial has the right to review the same evidence held by the prosecution in order to prepare a proper defense. The process is known as "discovery." The right to such discovery is magnified when that evidence is exculpatory—that is, when the evidence might exonerate the defendant. In civilian courts, the requirement for compliance with defense requests for discovery varies by state. In the military, compliance is an absolute requirement.

Rae had fired off three straight requests for discovery, felt the government was dragging its heels on compliance, and said so to Vest. Lt. Cmdr. Mike Ritter, the assistant prosecutor on the Tritt case, rose to tell Vest the most recent request had come in just the previous night, and Reason hadn't had a chance to respond. Vest said he would defer ruling until Reason could do that.

Rae was asking for a lot. He wanted every piece of information with a bearing on Tritt's case. That included the DOD-IG's entire Tailhook database—the "ZY index"—along with every photo in DOD-IG's possession, printouts of electronic mail, and transcripts or notes from conversations between Reason and his staff and senior naval and Pentagon officials in Washington.

Vest wanted to know why Rae was demanding so much material. Rae replied that he needed the information to prop up his motions to dismiss charges for undue command influence and selective prosecution. He said he had learned that Reason had been communicating frequently with Kelso and Dalton about Tailhook, and felt his sources were solid. But he knew his claims were baseless unless he could get ahold of the actual phone records, the kind routinely kept by aides of calls made by senior leaders.

In addition, said Rae, the motions were all intertwined to some extent. Navy training on sexual harassment in the wake of Tailhook, he argued, amounted to a form of undue command influence that made it impossible to find an impartial jury of peers to sit in judgment of Tritt.

Vest said he would issue a ruling on the 18th as to whether Reason had exercised his "independent discretion" in bringing Tritt's case to trial. He wanted briefs two days prior. That, said Rae, was too much of a pinch.

"On the 18th, you want witnesses and everything?" he asked Vest. "I mean, we can't possibly have the witnesses that we're going to need for that kind of a session at this point in time. We just can't do it."

Vest disagreed, and told prosecutors he wanted a determination on whether Reason would be available to come and testify on the 18th on the motion.

"Then," said Vest, "the burden is going to be on you, Mr. Rae, to show me that there's been any influence counter to the exercise of that independent discretion, if that is the case," Vest said.

If, Rae asked Vest, Reason's testimony leads you to believe there hasn't been any exercise of undue command influence, but later discovery indicates otherwise . . .

"Then you can reopen it," said Vest. But if that happened, he said,

Reason could not be recalled to testify.

Not fair, said Rae: he couldn't adequately question Reason without the discovery evidence.

"Well, again, Mr. Rae, you're asking the government to provide you with thousands of documents," said Vest.

"Yes, sir," said Rae. But Rae wasn't backing down. "There's a decision-making process there that has been influenced by the highest levels," he argued. "The records are going to show it, or they're not." The defense had previously refused to provide the ZY index. "That would expedite the trial if we had that," Rae said.

Vest tried to close the door. "I am not going to allow the defense to seek the discovery of thousands and thousands of documents that have absolutely no bearing on the issue," he said.

"Your honor, you don't know they have no bearing on the issue," argued Rae. "You don't know that. They're just giving us what the DOD-IG has given them and said is relevant to our case. We need a chance to be able to go in there and do that."

"Very well," said Vest. He said he'd rule on the motion on the 18th, and adjourned the court. That afternoon, Reason informed Vest he'd be available on the 18th to testify.[15]

The day before Reason took the stand, the first legal hearing in Paula Coughlin's eighteen-month quest for justice began 165 miles to the north: Col. Steven S. Mitchell, a Marine Corps Reserve judge, rapped his gavel on the bench in a courtroom at Marine Corps Combat Development Command headquarters in Quantico, Va. Capt. Gregory Bonam's Article 32 hearing was under way.

Until now, the Marine Corps' Tailhook proceedings had sailed along fairly quietly behind the closed Quantico doors of Lt. Gen. Charles C. Krulak, Reason's Marine counterpart. That had been the plan. As detailed in a leaked Marine Corps legal memo concerning its Tailhook hearings, the Marine plan was to "handle matters like the Navy. That is, to keep the media out of it and to keep the accused at NJP (nonjudicial punishment)."[16]

If that was the Navy's plan, it failed. But as much as the Navy had been blasted for the way it had handled Tailhook to date, the Marines stood to take a much bigger hit if they mishandled this highest-profile case.

Coughlin's story of her assault had remained consistent from the outset. But attempts to identify her primary attacker had brought mixed results. Her recollection of the attacker's shirt had ranged from orange to a floral Hawaiian pattern. The attacker himself had gone from a deeply tanned white to a light-skinned black. During an early photo lineup, she had pointed out a man who hadn't even attended the 1991 convention.

The Navy felt it knew the identity of Coughlin's attacker, but didn't have absolute proof, according to that same Marine Corps memo. Despite the lack of proof, the memo implied, the government felt it had no choice but to take the case to trial, even though it was already apparent that Bonam would be found innocent.

"The government acknowledges a weak case, but has bowed to the politically correct feminists and will put Coughlin on the stand to be cut up by the defense," the memo stated.[17]

Coughlin was the first witness. In explicit detail—and with little variation from previous testimony—she described her ordeal at the 1991 Tailhook convention. Coughlin had identified her attacker as a man with coffee-colored skin, pale eyes, and very short hair—a description, it was worth noting, that wasn't far removed from Navy Lt. David Samples' appearance, although Samples was more her height than Bonam's.

In court, Coughlin reaffirmed the identification she had made at the 1992 lineup. "I recognized Captain Bonam as the individual," she said.

But under cross-examination by Bonam's attorney, Patrick J. MacKrell, she recounted her hesitation about pointing at Bonam when, following the lineup, she had told Lt. Cmdr. Hank Sonday and NIS agent Beth Iorio, "What is bothering me is I'm afraid I have this minor shadow of doubt. . . . I remember him being larger. He weighed more."

She also acknowledged having picked a man who hadn't even attended the convention out of a photo lineup in November 1991.

Coughlin had testified that her attacker was wearing a burnt orange T-shirt, and, possibly, short pants. Other witnesses recalled Bonam on Saturday night wearing a shirt with a green-and-black, zig-zag design on it and "Bonner," Bonam's call sign, over the left breast pocket.

MacKrell showed Coughlin a snapshot of three Marines posing together at Tailhook on Saturday night. In the picture, Bonam is wearing shorts and the green-and-black shirt. Standing next to him is Lt. Timothy Durst, wearing an orange shirt, and Capt. Scott Harrison. Durst and Harrison are Caucasians.

Coughlin said she had told DOD-IG agent Matthew Walinski that she didn't think the light-skinned black man on the right wearing the green-and-black shirt was the man who assaulted her. Although she now knew it to be Bonam, she said, "I'm still not convinced. Even looking at him in the courtroom and looking at the photograph, I'm not convinced that is Captain Bonam."[18]

Bonam had returned to full duty following what apparently was successful surgery in the spring of 1992 on his cancerous back. When he took the stand, he pointed himself out in the photo, noting that he was wearing the same watch in the photo that he now had on. He also identified his clothing.

Bonam remembered Coughlin from flight school; both had attended in 1986, but they had never been introduced. That said, he flatly denied assaulting Coughlin.

"I did not see Lieutenant Coughlin on the evening of September 7th," he said. "I did not touch her. I did not touch any female that night."

If he had seen her being assaulted, Bonam said, he would have brought it to a halt.

"If I saw a woman begin assaulted, my response would be to help her," Bonam said. "If I would have seen Coughlin assaulted, I would have assisted her whether that involved having to physically intervene or not. I would have done something to keep the attack from continuing."[19]

Other witnesses backed him up. "I have seen him break up fights between people he didn't even know," said Matthew Long, a former Marine officer. "I saw him stop traffic to help an ambulance get through. He's not the type of person that would go out of his way to hurt someone."

Bonam's commander agreed. "His reputation as to thoughtfulness and peacefulness is very well known, and exceptional," said Cmdr. Stewart Ashton of Training Squadron 7, out of Meridian, Miss. "He is an active member of his church, and demonstrates the conviction of his faith in his everyday life."

His relations with women, both said, were equally even-keeled.

"I never saw any aggressive nature toward women," Long said. "He helps women out when he can. For example, I was dating this girl, and he would protect her from other people who would try and hit on her. I also had a girlfriend that he didn't particularly like, but he never said an unkind word to her."

"As far as the practice of equality," Ashton said, "I found that Bonam in particular was one who supported it when it was sometimes difficult for me to get up and make statements to the effect that people had to live with this. But I found him one of the few to be quite supportive from Day One on this issue."

Bonam testified that nearly all of his time Saturday night was spent in the Rhino suite. He admitted going into the third-floor hallway about three times, but only briefly. On one of those trips, he accompanied Capt. Ray Allen, the officer who'd said he had seen Navy Secretary Lawrence Garrett in the Rhino suite, down to the VMFA-121 suite.[20]

The Rhino suite was close to the tail end of the gantlet. The VMFA-121 suite was across from the VAQ-129 suite—right where the gantlet began.

Bonam wasn't asked what time he was in that end of the hall. But he denied seeing "any gauntlet-type activities" while he was at the convention.

"I believe they occurred," he said, "but I did not witness any of them because I generally stayed out on the patio and out of the hall."

Bonam was dismissed. After closing arguments, Mitchell announced that if the defense had further evidence to be considered and his report hadn't been completed, he had reopen the investigation.[21] All Coughlin could do now was wait.

Wednesday, August 18, was a busy day at the Norfolk Naval Legal Service Office. The Navy announced that Diaz would be court-martialed. In a separate pretrial hearing, two lieutenants testified against suspected gantlet participant Lt. David Samples.

But the main event would be held that afternoon down the third-floor hallway in the Powers courtroom, the largest in the NLSO. Vice Adm. J. Paul Reason, the Navy's consolidated disposition authority for Tailhook, was coming over from SurfLant to testify at his own inquiry.

The room was packed full of reporters, Navy lawyers and, right in their midst, Miller, Cowden, and Diaz. At the defense table, Tritt sat alongside Rae. As at all the Tailhook courts-martial hearings, Vest presided.

Vest, noting that Reason wouldn't arrive for another half-hour, said he would rule on the matter of the questionnaire.

At an earlier hearing, Rae had tried to introduce a lengthy, in-depth questionnaire to be filled out by members of the panels, as military juries are called. He felt the initial questionnaire wasn't sufficiently detailed enough to weed out prejudiced officers. Non-aviators, he felt, might be biased; females might carry a grudge into the courtroom. The longer questionnaire would take about an hour to complete, he told Vest, but the alternative was a longer grilling in court.

The matter seemed trivial, but it was of great concern to Rae. Although the burden of proof during a trial would be on the prosecution, the success of any defense would depend wholly on how the members of the panels perceived the evidence. And Rae was worried about the makeup of the panels; he felt sure that Jeffry Williams and Capt. Lorry Hardt, the SurfLant Inspector General, were hand-picking them.[22]

Prosecutor Lt. Cmdr. Carole Gaasch argued that Rae's questionnaire was an attempt by the defense to "indoctrinate the members into their theory of the case." Vest didn't disagree, but said he felt many of the questions on the questionnaire were so subjective that they needed to be asked in the courtroom, under oath, where he could judge the responses. Vest denied the motion, telling Rae he had given it "careful consideration.

"Commander Rae, I can assure you and Commander Tritt that no member will be seated to hear this case unless I am convinced that member is qualified in all respects as an impartial trier of fact."

Rae had served twenty years as a Navy lawyer; Vest addressed him by his former military rank on several occassions during the hearings. It was impossible to determine whether he was being playful, or was speaking out of habit. Rae didn't appear amused, but later said he didn't mind.

Rae then began his argument that Reason, who'd convened the Tailhook investigation on Adm. Frank B. Kelso's orders, was being unduly influenced to refer officers to trial.

"Superior commanders and staff officers, as well as military and civilian legal officers, must never directly or indirectly interfere with the convening authority's exercise of its lawful duty," Rae argued. "It is not only unprofessional, but a fraud on this system, for a superior to send the word down to a convening authority and ask for a desired result in a criminal case which will please the leadership of our own forces.

"And if ever there's been an environment conducive to this kind of action, the Tailhook investigation is, and that's the foundation to which we rest our motion," Rae said.

Vest thanked Rae. Then he laid down the law for Reason's cross-examination. Questions would be limited strictly to whether Reason "exercised his sole discretion" when referring Tritt's case to court-martial. He said he had no evidence that Reason "had been deprived of his independent decision-making ability," and for the purposes of this motion, put the burden of proof on the defense.

Reason was called in, sworn in, and sat on Vest's right. Large, tall, and broad-shouldered, Reason carried himself proudly, almost regally. It was a big moment. One senior Navy legal officer said he had rarely seen an admiral testify in any venue, and never a vice admiral.

"Admiral, in the course of your duties . . . have you had occasion to speak with the secretary of the Navy?" Rae began.

"In conjunction with my duties as CDA?" Reason asked. "No, not really."

Reason said he had spoken to the secretary "maybe three times, never in private, really, attendant to his swearing-in and assumption of duties." He was referring to John Dalton, he said.

Rae asked if Reason had spoken to previous Navy secretaries or acting secretaries about Tailhook. "To the best of my knowledge, I never did," Reason responded.[23]

This was all a bit of hair-splitting. Dalton and Reason had spoken while the latter was in charge of the Tailhook investigation, and had done so while Reason was conducting Tailhook business. But Dalton wasn't yet officially the Navy secretary. And, a Dalton spokesman later said, they didn't talk about Tailhook.

The two men were good friends. Dalton had graduated from the Naval Academy in 1964, Reason the following year. It was said that Reason, a nuclear propulsion expert, helped Dalton get through the Navy's nuclear power plant school back when both were on active duty. They remained friends while working as officials in the Carter administration.

In April, the White House announced its intention to nominate Dalton to the top Navy post. Dalton then began effectively serving in the position as a "contractor." Dalton wasn't officially nominated until July 1, and was confirmed as Navy secretary on the 21st.

When the CDA team was holding briefings for Reason at Little Creek May 10-11, Navy attorneys recalled that he was interrupted several times over the two-day period to take calls from Dalton. A petty officer would enter the room to bring Reason messages. Reason would stand, announce that he'd gotten a call from "Secretary Dalton," and walk out.

In response to a June 1996 query, a Dalton spokesman confirmed that according to phone records, Dalton phoned Reason on May 11, and that Reason called Dalton on the 12th. Dalton, the spokesman said the two men recalled, was seeking advice on an officer he was considering for a slot within the secretariat. The person in question was, like Reason, a surface warfare officer.

Reason didn't provide such detail at the hearing. And it's hard to believe that if the two men had talked, Dalton didn't at least ask Reason how his investigation was going. But if he and Dalton had indeed not spoken about Tailhook, Reason had told Rae the truth.[24]

Reason was animated during his forty-five minutes on the stand, often smiling and arching an eyebrow at Rae's questions. But he spoke in a calm and self-assured manner, and his answers were short and to the point. "There has been no effort to influence me in any direction," the articulate Reason told Vest in his deep, resonant, slightly monotone voice. "I have had no direction from any higher authority."

He told Rae he hadn't read the Tailhook report so he could remain unbiased. He also admitted he hadn't read "every page" of Cmdr. Larry McCullough's pretrial hearing report on Tritt, but had reviewed the report with Capt. Williams, his top lawyer.

Reason told Rae that before the hearing, he had read over the questions Vest had ordered Rae to submit, but that "some were not, you know, understandable."

"Just like the charges," Rae shot back.

Reason said he had spoken a half-dozen times with Kelso during the past year, and Tailhook had come up only once. That was the call in which Kelso gave him his marching orders to run the investigation, he said.

He had also spoken several times with Adm. Stanley R. Arthur, who'd succeeded Jerome Johnson as Kelso's vice chief of staff; once with Derek Vander Schaaf, the acting inspector general, about a request for a grant of immunity for an accused flier; and with Don Mancuso, who had headed up the DOD-IG investigation, about acquiring the actual Tailhook files. He hadn't spoken with Defense Secretary Les Aspin since 1988.

He said he had "never had the pleasure of meeting" Rep. Pat Schroeder, D-Colo., and hadn't spoken with former assistant Navy Secretary Barbara Pope since the previous summer. He also said Tailhook had come up briefly during a party conversation with Rep. Bobby Scott, D-Va., a few days prior to the hearing.

"He had seen my name mentioned in the newspaper," said Reason, "thanks to you, probably."

"You're welcome," said Rae, smiling.

Though he hadn't read the DOD-IG report, Reason said he had read several of the case files, including Tritt's. Rae asked, "If you were to find out these reports of interview were incorrect, misleading, or distorted, would you desire to have this court send these charges back to you for review?"

Ritter objected. Vest interceded. He decided not to allow the question. "Hypothetical," Reason chimed in.

Vest was keeping a tight lid on things. He shot down questions on how Reason determined what constituted conduct unbecoming an officer and whether Jeffry Williams had advised him about potential problems in the area of command influence.

Rae tried a different tack. He asked Reason about the admiral's mast he had held for Capt. Kenneth "Kilo" Parks, the highest-ranking flier Reason had reprimanded administratively. Just prior to charging Parks, Rae claimed Reason had told the captain: "We never could, but even now, we can't do it even more, because of all the heightened attention we've all received. Maybe that's after the horse is out of the barn. I do hope that you will find a way to recognize, at least, the position I'm in. This is conduct unbecoming an officer in the United States Navy." Had he?

Reason couldn't recall. After a few more questions, Vest thanked him, and he was dismissed. Vest wasted no time denying the motion.

Rae, who appeared unfazed, repeated his request for more discovery material, including the DOD-IG's computerized ZY index that contained the statements of the more than 2,900 people interviewed about Tailhook.

"The government has used these to their advantage," Rae told Vest. "Commander Tritt is the one on trial." Rae asked for all statements collected from patio area victims. Vest ordered prosecutors to produce them, but limited discovery to victims from Saturday, September 7, 1991—the same day Tritt was alleged to have committed his misdeeds.[25]

Earlier in the day, the Navy announced that Diaz would be court-martialed on one charge: conduct unbecoming an officer, for "wrongfully and dishonorably" giving two women "bikini cuts" at his leg-shaving booth. The charge of willfully disobeying Cmdr. Remshak's alleged order had been dropped.

And at Junior Samples' pretrial hearing, also held earlier, two officers who'd partied hard during Tailhook told the story of lifting drunk teenager Julie Rodgers into the air and carrying her down the third-floor hallway on the convention's final night. Lt. Greg "Goose" Geiss said it was "like passing her down, like at a football game."[26]

But their stories differed in one major respect. Lt. Frank Truong said Samples helped carry the young woman. Geiss didn't remember seeing Samples take part.[27]

Geiss and Truong both admitted drinking heavily that night. Both were also immune from prosecution on anything they said.

Mike Kmetz, Samples' attorney, decided to question Truong's integrity in an effort to give pause to investigating officer Seaton concerning Truong's testimony.

"During the first three interviews, according to your testimony here today, you lied," he said.

"Yes, sir," replied Truong.

"On the fourth interview, you told the truth."

"Yes, sir."

"Other than your good word, lieutenant, how do we know that?"

"I wanted to close that chapter and get on with my life," replied Truong.[28]

So did Greg Tritt. But the mild-mannered flier was beginning to boil over. Janssen's testimony, Reason's testimony, the overall weakness of the government's case against him and the sense of betrayal by the system he felt he had honorably served for nearly twenty years had taken Tritt and his wife Rosa to the breaking point. The day after Reason had taken the stand, Tritt, a naval officer in the midst of being court-martialed, stepped away from the Navy's public affairs umbrella and took the highly unusual step of holding a press conference.

At a long rectangular table in a back room at Rae's Virginia Beach office, Tritt and Rosa let it all spill out for more than an hour in front of broadcast and newspaper reporters. They portrayed themselves as a conservative, middle-class couple, high school sweethearts who had spent twenty-five years together as a Navy family but who now unexpectedly found themselves in the middle of the sordid Tailhook affair.

"It makes me feel a little bit bitter," said Tritt, wearing an ever-calm demeanor. "Up to now, I've always let the system work. I've always trusted and had faith in the system."

Although he had been to four Tailhooks, Tritt said he wasn't tuned in to the convention's bawdy side. "I didn't go there thinking activity like that would go on," he said. "I didn't see the leg shaving, the Rhino suite, the molesting of women.

"I've discovered that I'm a little bit naive," Tritt said.

What Tritt lacked in fire was more than made up for by his wife. Rosa Tritt was especially riled at Reason, who had admitted on the witness stand the previous day that he didn't read "every page" of the investigating officer's report on Tritt, but was "familiar" with it.

"My husband spent 20 years in the Navy, and he can't read the report?" she asked angrily, her eyes flashing. "If it was at all fair, he would have accepted the I.O.'s report."

Rosa Tritt was also incensed about the testimony of Janssen and LoGuidice. It's "pretty bogus and incredulous," she said, that two young men the family had tried to look after had testified against her husband.

"The IG put words in their mouths," she said. When Janssen gave his testimony at Tritt's first pretrial hearing, she said, "He wouldn't look me in the eye."

Tritt denied seeing or taking part in any unwanted touching of females. If he had seen something like that, he said, he would have tried to stop it. Of Kim Ponikowski, the woman who saw "an old bald guy" at the doorway to the pool patio try to grab her on the rear end, Tritt said in a flat, unemotional voice, "I've never seen that woman in my life."

Like other officers being investigated, Tritt said that DOD-IG agents tried to browbeat him into admitting his involvement in sexual hijinks. "I didn't appreciate it, because the investigators who did the thing were unprofessional, getting as low and debasing as they could in their techniques."

And Tritt expressed unhappiness at the quality of the witnesses against him. "We know for a fact that people have changed their statements under oath at Article 32 hearings," he said. "What's happening to those people?"

Asked what he thought his chances were, Tritt said, "I think they're great. I'm confident that the truth is going to win. Am I being naive again?"

Although Tritt may indeed have been innocent—and he certainly didn't seem nearly outgoing or forward enough to be grabbing women's rear ends at a party—it didn't deter him from using a few techniques of his own to counter the aggressive investigators.

At survival, evasion, escape and rescue, or SEER, school, Tritt had learned, as all military fliers do, to insulate himself from pressure. "I wasn't going to start agreeing with the things they were suggesting," he said. "From the beginning, their efforts were very, very antagonistic.

"Part of your training is training to resist," explained Tritt. "It's for your own protection that we're trained that way. You don't tell untruths, but you keep your answers as short and sweet as possible."

It was a technique DOD-IG agents suspected many fliers of using, and Tritt said he was aware of that suspicion. "There's probably an unconscious desire to protect your fellow officers," said Tritt. "But it's in our inherent nature to be ethical people." The main thing they had been taught at SEER school, he said, was "don't lie. Because eventually it'll catch up with you."[29]

Despite Vest's ruling that Reason had exercised his "sole discretion" in the Tritt case, Cole Cowden's attorney decided to question just how objective he had been. On August 20, Lt. Cmdr. Jeffrey Good told Vest during an arraignment hearing that he would make a similar motion to dismiss charges, claiming that Reason had expressed an opinion about Cowden's guilt prior to being briefed on the case. He also planned to move that Cowden was the victim of selective prosecution, and that Jeffry Williams, Reason's top legal advisor, had exhibited personal bias against Cowden during the pretrial process.

In addition, argued Good, Reason was too close to the prosecution. And Cowden "had no way of knowing that the government was going to claim that his conduct was criminal." Finally, he argued, Lisa Mattiello, the woman DOD-IG insisted on calling a victim, wasn't bringing any charges against Cowden.

"She didn't make an accusation," Good said later. "There is no victim. I was surprised that they would take an act that had no victim and bring it to general court-martial."

Vest, concerned about pretrial publicity from the frequent news reports about Cowden's case, also placed a gag order on the officers who'd been notified they might serve on the military jury that would hear it.

Afterward, Cowden seemed agitated and more hyper than usual. Perhaps Good's litany of motions had exacerbated Cowden's anger at being prosecuted.

"My amazement grows every day," he said in his rapid-fire style. Asked if he thought he would get a fair hearing, he replied, "It's not like I have a lot of choice now." Still have faith in the system? "I'd like to have my faith improved," he said.[30]

9

Chasing a Blue Angel

Rough-around-the-edges Tailhook defendant Tom Miller was regarded by his fliers as a solid commander, one they were proud to serve with. But he'd be the first to admit he was no poster boy for naval aviation.

He'd leave that role to fliers like Bob Stumpf.

1991's Persian Gulf War had given the Navy its first modern-day heroes since Vietnam. And they didn't come any greater than Stumpf. Air power—mostly Air Force power, actually—had played a huge role in the Allied operation that drove Iraq out of Kuwait after invading its tiny neighbor the previous summer. But Navy fliers produced some showcase performances of their own. More than a few were turned in by one of Navy aviation's brightest lights: Cmdr. Robert E. Stumpf.

An F/A-18 Hornet pilot, Stumpf had flown twenty-two strike missions from the decks of the USS *Saratoga* during the course of that war. His efforts earned him six Air Medals, three Navy Commendation Medals for combat achievement and the Distinguished Flying Cross, one of the nation's highest awards for combat heroism.

The DFC was awarded for planning and leading a twenty-four-plane attack on a Scud missile storage site in Central Iraq. Despite heavy cloud cover and intense anti-aircraft fire, Stumpf located the target and delivered four 2,000–pound bombs with pinpoint accuracy, according to the citation.[1]

Tall, blond, and athletic, Stumpf looked the part, as well. But he was more than just a courageous fighter pilot. The father of three daughters, friends called him a devoted family man. His fellow officers hailed him with accolades like, "the best commander I've ever served with," "a truly remarkable officer," "an outstanding individual."[2]

In 1992, he had been selected over dozens of other cream-of-the-crop officers to command the Blue Angels, the Navy's precision flight demonstration team.

"Commander Stumpf was head and shoulders above all the applicants," said retired Rear Adm. William R. McGowen, then the chief of Naval Air Training, or CNATRA. "And all the other applicants were superstars."[3]

But by the summer of 1993, it began to look like Stumpf's brilliant career was about to be swallowed up by the Tailhook quagmire—along with the careers of four other senior officers: Capt. Frederic G. Ludwig, Jr., Capt. Richard F. Braden, Cmdr. Gregory E. Peairs, and Cmdr. Robert C. Yakeley.

Ludwig had been the 1991 president of the Tailhook Association; he was felt by some to be accountable for the whole mess. Braden was in line to command the Pacific Fleet's Airborne Early Warning Wing. He had been in charge of inspecting and assessing suite damage at Tailhook, and was suspected of being in the third-floor hallway while an assault was taking place.

Peairs was in line to become executive officer of the aircraft carrier USS *Carl Vinson*. And Yakeley was a staff officer at the Naval Air Systems Command in Washington. Investigators thought both had streaked on the convention's final night.

Stumpf's case was the most tantalizing of them all. Investigators said he had watched a stripper perform oral sex on one of his fliers while attending a Saturday night party in an upstairs Hilton suite at Tailhook.[4]

Reason, however, didn't have much to go on. None of the five had a case file strong enough to support a court-martial—or even an admiral's mast, for Stumpf, Ludwig, and Braden.

Mast was offered to Peairs and Yakeley, both Rae clients. Reason adviser Jeffry Williams told the pair that a nonjudicial hearing wouldn't hurt their chances for promotion.

To a point, that was true. If charges at mast are dismissed, or a nonpunitive letter is issued, nothing is added to a service member's personnel file indicating that what amounts to a counseling session has taken place. As far as official records are concerned, it was as if the mast never happened.

But Rae didn't trust Williams, and felt that if Peairs and Yakeley agreed to go to mast, Reason, given his aggressive pursuit of the five officers, would hammer his clients with punitive letters of admonition or reprimand. Such letters would be entered into their service records, end any chance of future promotion and effectively end their careers. He advised them to decline.[5]

Reason, in turn, had denied their subsequent requests for courts-martial, which they made knowing that a pretrial investigating officer would recommend dropping the weak cases. Reason, frustrated, then asked his friend and Navy Secretary John Dalton to hand down letters of censure to all five. These powerful letters would bring their careers to a dead halt.

But Reason was rebuffed. Adm. Stanley Arthur, Kelso's deputy and a highly decorated Navy flier, intercepted the requests before they reached Dalton's desk and ordered that the cases be handled in a more conventional manner.[6]

Undaunted, Reason, in late August, ordered five new investigations.

The Navy calls them formal fact-finding boards, convened to investigate "all facts and circumstances" in a particular case. Witnesses testify under oath before a panel of senior officers—these would employ a two-star admiral and two captains—but the boards are nonadversarial. Although the officers being investigated are allowed legal representation, the Navy attorney advising the board on legal matters is supposed to steer clear of a prosecutorial role.

When news of new investigations was leaked, the Navy was still hard in the grip of a long, hot summer of criticism over its handling of Tailhook. Critics said Tailhook was a failure of leadership. But only one officer above the rank of commander had been investigated, and his case was disposed of at an admiral's mast.

Now, nearly two years after the convention, barely thirty-five officers had been fined or given punitive letters—mostly for indecent exposure, not failure to lead or sexual assault, the hot-button issues—with nonpunitive letters going to another ten. Out of thousands who had attended the Tailhook convention in 1991, only four were being court-martialed. And their cases were being dragged out interminably as defense attorneys deluged the court with motions.

In the midst of this slow road to justice lay five high-profile, high-ranking targets whose punishment would make clear to Congress and the American public that the Navy was serious about policing itself in matters of sexual misconduct.

None were higher-profile than Stumpf. The Blue Angels commander was clearly the biggest sacrificial lamb of the bunch.

"I can't wait to take your client to trial," Jeffry Williams told Stumpf's Washington, D.C.-based attorney, Charles W. Gittins, in late May 1993. Reason was convinced that Stumpf had witnessed the sex act. Even if he hadn't, Reason believed Stumpf knew what was about to happen and had tacitly condoned it by saying nothing and leaving the room.[7]

In September 1991, Stumpf was still commanding Strike Fighter Squadron 83, the unit he had led during the Persian Gulf War. After the war, VFA-83 had been named the Navy's top F/A-18 unit of the year, and Stumpf went to Tailhook to pick up the Estocin Award on behalf of his unit.

Stumpf planned to fly to Las Vegas on Friday, September 6, aboard a Navy C-9 passenger jet with the rest of his unit, and had official orders in hand to make the trip. But the plane had developed problems, and its arrival at Cecil Field was delayed. Stumpf and the others also learned that the late C-9 wouldn't return as scheduled on Sunday, but a day later.

Stumpf had to be back on Monday to begin a predeployment training exercise. So he decided to go via F/A-18, a trip that he could authorize for two days of cross-country flight training. Stumpf and Lt. Langhorne Sias, another unit pilot, took off from Cecil Field, Florida, landed at George Air Force Base, Nevada, and rented a car for the 150–mile trip to Las Vegas.

Nellis Air Force Base had been declared off limits for tactical aircraft during Tailhook.[8]

Meanwhile, on the delayed C-9 flight to Vegas, Lts. Scott Bubeck and Victor Weber decided they would use their hotel room to throw a party in honor of their recent promotions.

Bubeck had more than the promotion to celebrate; he had had a pretty good year. The popular flier had joined VFA-83 earlier in the year, smack in the middle of the Persian Gulf War. A green-as-grass ensign straight out of the flight training cycle, he had made his first out-of-school catapult shot off the *Saratoga* in an armed-for-bear F/A-18 bound for a six-hour bombing run over Iraq. Bubeck had never flown with so much ordnance, never undertaken an aerial refueling, never flown more than two hours at a clip.

The most junior pilot in the squadron, he was the first to get an air medal for Gulf War combat. He received it aboard ship during a visit by Chief of Naval Operations Adm. Frank B. Kelso.[9]

Military promotion parties are sometimes called as "wetting downs," after the postpromotion ceremony tradition of dousing the new rank and its wearer with some sort of liquid, usually alcoholic. Such rites of passage are practiced with varying degrees of intensity throughout the U.S. military. Prior to the mid-1980s, new Army NCOs in combat units often received a "blood promotion" in which their new rank, normally pinned and fastened to the uniform's collar, was instead mashed through the shirt into the promotee's chest. The practice continues among certain submariners, Navy SEALs, and Marine and Army airborne and special operations units.

Officers typically give money instead of blood. New promotees, regardless of rank, typically donate a month's increase in pay to fuel the promotion party.[10]

At the Hilton, Stumpf shared a room with Sias and Lt. Stephen Frick. Two other VFA-83 lieutenants, Michael Sadler and Carl Trahan, also roomed together.[11]

When Bubeck and Weber checked into their Hilton suite, they found some pamphlets on an end table touting local attractions. One advertised exotic dancers who delivered their wares on site. Seemed like a good idea. After comparing a few ads and calling around for the best price, they made their choice for Saturday night, hoping they had chosen a "class act."[12]

It was around noon Saturday when Lt. Christopher "Gator" Gates woke up over at his hotel. After freshening up, he ambled over to the Hilton and "milled about smartly," poking his head into the flag panel seminar. He wasn't yet a member of VFA-83, but he had orders to report September 24. Gates planned to spend his evening making friends with his future cohorts.

That evening, he attended the Secretary of the Navy awards banquet, although he arrived late. At the banquet, Stumpf accepted the Estocin Award. Afterwards, Gates ran into Carl Trahan, who invited him to attend the party upstairs. Gates figured it was a "pat on the back" party for the unit's winning the Estocin.[13]

Participants were in general agreement about what happened from this point on. But as with other Tailhook testimony, the times and events were fuzzy. Many had been drinking and partying all day long Saturday; hard to remember clearly what happened last night the next day, much less two years later.

By about 10 p.m., Bubeck and Weber, not feeling much pain at this point, left the third floor to go start the party. They called and placed their order for the exotic dancers. Weber ordered more beer from the hotel; a keg was delivered, tapped, and placed by the door. Chairs lined the wall. The bed was folded back onto the wall.

Guests filtered in. One was Stumpf, who brought the squadron's new trophy upstairs and set it on a table. Some of the crowd was older. Weber thought they looked like senior officers, although he didn't recognize any of them. "There were heavies in the room early on," he later testified. "Above my rank, anyway."

All told, about thirty people filled the suite at the party's height.

At what most figured to be around midnight, two hours after the order had been placed, two dancers showed up. One was tall, thin, and black; the other was shorter, overweight, and white. Bubeck said he and Weber haggled over finances with the women, who wanted an up-front tip. Weber didn't remember that.

Gates had met Stumpf the night before, and recognized him at the party; at the time, Stumpf wore a mustache. But Gates said that when the dancers arrived, Stumpf left. During testimony, Bubeck and Weber recalled him being there earlier, but couldn't say for sure whether he had been there when the dancers were in the room. Trahan didn't remember Stumpf being there at all. Nor did Sias. Nor did Lt. Cmdr. Eli Hertz, a former member of the squadron and supposedly the government's key witness. Frick didn't attend the party. Only Michael Sadler and Lt. Henry Gibson, a Cecil Field pilot with a different squadron, remembered Stumpf being in the room when the strippers were present.

The story of those who couldn't place Stumpf at the party went like this. After the payment was settled, the black woman, wearing a tank top, began dancing and stumbling around the room, "looking a little high," recalled one observer. The white woman also began working the room. They were performing "lap dances," up-close-and-personal shows for individuals in an effort to elicit more tips. Most observers remember some or all of the dancers' clothes eventually coming off.

The black woman, not a striking woman and less than appreciated by the group, left first. Weber had felt sorry for her, and followed her out, "partly for her safety." When she got on the elevator and left, Weber returned to the room.

When he came back inside, he passed Bubeck, who had posted himself near the door to keep unwanted partiers out. Straight ahead, he saw someone sitting in the middle of the room's left side, seated on a barstool facing away from Bubeck and the door.

Gates was surrounded by other fliers. Several fliers were chanting his call sign: "Ga-tor! Ga-tor! Ga-tor! Ga-tor!"

Gates didn't recall being surrounded by people. He just remembered the white dancer beginning to fondle him. Bubeck said Gates was on the receiving end of a lap dance, and the white woman "rubbing up against him." Bubeck then saw her kneel down between Gates's legs.

She slipped a condom on Gates. Then she looked up and said to Gates, "This isn't going to happen in the middle of everyone."

"That's why we went in the bathroom to finish the job," Gates testified.

No one could remember why Gates had been singled out; he said the sex had "just happened." The government was trying to make the case that the oral sex was some sort of command-sanctioned initiation.

When they came out, only a few people were left. The white woman drifted out of the room.

"She just kind of left," said Gates. "I went back down to the patio area, and that was the end of the evening."

"A sexual act was performed on you without your permission," Stumpf attorney Gittins remarked while questioning Gates during the hearings. "Are you a victim in the Tailhook report?"

"No," Gates said. "I don't feel like a victim."[14]

Sias testified that Stumpf was due to fly the F/A-18 back to Florida the next morning, and was meticulous about getting the proper amount of crew rest before flights. Frick, who said he hadn't partied, testified that Stumpf returned to their room sometime after 9:30 p.m. and went to sleep. That would have given Stumpf enough time to leave the awards banquet, take the trophy upstairs, hang around for a few minutes, and leave.[15]

The recollections of Gates and the others didn't give prosecutors much to chase Stumpf with. Gibson's story did.

Gibson, a 1984 Naval Academy graduate, attended Tailhook in 1988,

1989 and 1991, the latter as a member of VFA-106 out of Cecil Field. He had flown to Las Vegas with the fliers from VFA-83.

At about 11 p.m., Gibson and another officer drifted upstairs to the impromptu party "because the third-floor patio had gotten quiet." He'd had eight to ten beers and a few margaritas by that point, and he was pretty drunk.

Gibson remembered a bunch of out-of-uniform officers milling around the suite. He didn't recall seeing the Estocin trophy. He may made a few trips downstairs and back, but he wasn't sure. Sometime during that next hour, he said, the strippers showed up.

Gibson was standing near the door. Stumpf, he said, was seated to his left. One of the dancers—Gibson didn't remember which one—approached Stumpf and tried to solicit a tip. Stumpf wanted no part of it. "I remember him making a gesture for her to go away," Gibson said.

Later, he saw Gates seated in the center of the room, surrounded by ten to fifteen people, the white stripper performing oral sex on him. Gibson didn't remember Stumpf being in the room at that time. Gibson left before the stripper had finished her work.[16]

Sadler agreed that Stumpf had been in the room when the strippers were present. He had also seen Stumpf wave off the stripper when she approached him. Stumpf, he said, then turned and left.[17]

The board members surely saw a pattern. Everyone who served with Stumpf or recognized him, except for Sadler, said he wasn't there during the striptease. Gibson, who said he was, had only met him once. And Gibson, like Janssen, LoGuidice, and dozens of other witnesses, had gotten drunk that night. Nonetheless, the evidence against Stumpf was weak.

If anyone out of that group seemed culpable, Gates certainly did. Gates testified that he had first come to Norfolk on May 28 after being told by his commander that he would be facing admiral's mast for conduct unbecoming an officer. He met with Jeffry Williams, who told him what his options would be. Gates asked about a court-martial. Instead, said Gates, "He was pushing mast."

After conferring with his attorney, Gates went back to Williams and refused mast. Williams hedged a bit, then replied that he was looking for more statements. Williams knew he didn't have enough to court-martial Gates.

"This is what we're after," he finally told Gates. "We really don't want you. We want Commander Stumpf."

"I kind of let out a sigh of relief," Gates recalled. He asked Williams, "What's in it for me?"

"We can give you immunity," replied Williams. The only stipulation was, of course, that Gates agree to another interview with DOD-IG.

He hadn't mentioned the oral sex in his first interview.

Gates conferred with his attorney, Lt. Cmdr. William G. Sweeney. "Can they do this to me?" he asked. "To be honest," Sweeney replied, "I don't know anything." Sweeney's advice: "Take the immunity and run."

Gates, now known as "Pearly," was given testimonial immunity for all Tailhook-related matters, and transactional, or total, immunity for the Saturday night party.

He then told Williams the same story he repeated in court.

"What was Williams's reaction?" asked Gittins.

"None, sir."

"Think he was disappointed in you?

"I assume he was," said Gates. He then gave a second interview to DOD-IG, and repeated the same story with his attorney present. He hadn't seen Stumpf during the sex act.

"You can't be prosecuted for anything else arising from this incident?" asked Gittins. "Is that true?"

"I hope it's true, sir," Gates replied.[18]

DOD-IG had taken it easy on Gates, which was unusual, given the war stories making the rounds. A lot of heat was being applied to the fliers of VFA-83.

At the first of Gibson's three interviews with DOD-IG agents, in September 1992, agents began questioning Gibson even though his military attorney hadn't yet arrived.

At first, he said, "They were trying to put words in my mouth." When Lt. Andrew Williams showed up, Gibson said, the tone "went from a very intimidating nature, very leading, to very conciliatory, very professional." He didn't sign a statement as asked.

In January 1993, Gibson again met with agents without an attorney present. He wasn't read his rights. They asked if he had any other information to provide. When he said no, Gibson said the screaming began. Accusations flew.

At one point, one of the agents waved a red envelope with "Not Cleared" printed on it, angrily telling Gibson he was on the "not cleared list." He was told to wait out in the hall.

There, he overheard them accusing another officer, a friend of his, of having sex with a woman there. Gibson got angry. "That guy's not even married!" he blurted out.

One of the agents burst back through the door and got in Gibson's face. "What you said in there wasn't relevant!" he screamed. "This isn't over for you! You're a disgrace!"

On Friday, May 28, 1993, Gibson was summoned to Norfolk and given three days to decide whether to accept mast on the charge of conduct unbecoming an officer. Andrew Williams, his attorney, had been on vacation in California and couldn't make it to Norfolk until Tuesday afternoon.

Gibson drove up to Maryland over the weekend to see his brother-in-law, a patent attorney; he accompanied Gibson on the four-hour drive back to Norfolk.

Since Monday was Memorial Day, the calendar bought them an extra day. They spent most of Tuesday at Gibson's temporary quarters at Little Creek Naval Amphibious Base, considering options. Late in the afternoon, Williams arrived. He told Gibson he could only stay until the next afternoon because of a previously scheduled trial commitment back in California.

A quick call was placed to the SurfLant headquarters to request a meeting with Capt. Jeffry Williams.

The request was denied. The two men were told to come to Williams's office at 11:30 Wednesday morning. Once there, they were subsequently told to wait until 1:30.

By mid-afternoon, Gibson's brother-in-law had to leave to attend to business back in Maryland. At 5, his military attorney could wait no longer, and left for the airport.

At 5:01, Gibson was called into Jeffry Williams's office. Present were two DOD-IG agents.

"We discussed my potential knowledge of activities in an upper-level suite," Gibson testified. "I excused myself, went across the street to a pay phone, called my brother-in-law, and asked him to call and talk with Williams. We also talked about refusing mast."

Williams held firm. Gibson was alone, and he felt trapped. On Thursday night, he decided to accept mast, which was administered in Norfolk in June. Afterward, he was given the standard offer of immunity, an order to testify, and a third interview with DOD-IG.

At the Stumpf hearing, attorney Gittins asked Gibson: Did he believe it was a coincidence that Williams found time to see him one minute after his attorney had left?

"In my mind, I was convinced it was not a coincidence," Gibson replied.

Later, Gibson was asked to compare what he saw at the VFA-83 party with what he had seen at Navy officers clubs; Gibson had been stationed at Oceana Naval Air Station, once famous for its erotic dancers, in 1988–89.

"Considerably less provocative," Gibson said.[19]

Scott Bubeck had refused to answer the first round of questions from DOD-IG, when agents had interviewed fliers aboard the USS *Saratoga* in October 1992. He hadn't been read his rights, and, he said, "I didn't feel like talking with them about something that didn't have anything to do with the assaults and things I'd heard of."

In June 1993, Bubeck agreed to talk with DOD-IG investigators in Jacksonville, Fla., but not without presence of Mike Powell, his civilian lawyer. The Tailhook team's Cmdr. Don Risher handed Bubeck an order signed by Reason giving the flier testimonial immunity and ordering him to testify, told Bubeck he didn't need to have Powell present, and sent him in to meet with the agents.

Bubeck was concerned about a possible attempt to intimidate him, and wanted Powell in the room. He refused to talk to the agents, who sent him back over to talk with Risher. Risher told Bubeck that since he was immune, the only way he could get into trouble was by refusing to cooperate or lying.

Risher, Bubeck said, seemed to be intimating that Bubeck was missing the boat. "He knew my case had been placed in a no-action file," said Bubeck. "He was concerned that I was creating 'unnecessary problems' for myself by insisting on counsel being present."

That may have been Bubeck's perception, Risher later said. "But with the grant of immunity, he wasn't going to be prosecuted, so there wasn't any 5th Amendment right to be concerned about," Risher said. He told Bubeck that he didn't have the right to have counsel present. If he wanted to talk to counsel, that could be arranged.

Jeffry Williams wasn't too pleased about Bubeck's refusal to testify. Within the week, Bubeck was issued orders to report to Norfolk for questioning. When Bubeck arrived in Norfolk, it got a little wild. Agent Matthew Walinski was so pumped up during questioning that his hands and chest were vibrating. "This is our interview," he yelled at Bubeck when the flier objected to the line of questioning. "You will not ask questions!"[20]

Walinski and agent Tom Bonnar also tried baiting Bubeck—but with Powell's presence, at the insistence of Williams and Monahan, to their credit. During a calmer moment, Bubeck was told that his version of the party "did not fit the fact pattern for common sense."

"Were the agents trying to get you to agree with their version of events?" Gittins asked Bubeck at a hearing.

"Absolutely," Bubeck replied.

"Did you feel threatened at that interview?" asked Gittins.

"Yes, I did," said Bubeck.

Had he? Had agents really browbeaten all of the fliers, or were the fliers now simply spouting the party line?

On the witness stand, Bubeck seemed credible. He admitted he had had a great time at Tailhook. "For three days straight, I partied my ass off," he testified. But when he was interviewed, he said, "It was very clear to me what the DOD investigators wanted me to say. I've told the absolute truth here. I'm angry about what's happening here."

It wasn't just the investigation, Bubeck said, but the public's perception of it. "It's almost to the point where I feel our Navy's shooting itself in the foot," he said. "Fifteen years down the road, we're going to look back and see that we made decisions for political expediency. That has hurt us, and hurt our combat capabilities."[21]

When Victor Weber was interviewed on June 3, 1993, in his commander's office at Cecil Field, Florida, he asked DOD-IG agents Mike Parker and Jack Kennedy if he could tape his own interview so he could be sure he wasn't misquoted. He was told it wasn't DOD-IG policy.

During the interview, the agents became angry when Weber told them he'd been going to see nude dancers with fellow officers for years.

Looking down on the table, Weber noticed a grant of immunity with his name on it, though he hadn't been told he had be receiving one.

"What does that mean?" he asked.

"I fucking ask you the questions, or I'm gonna have those wings!" Parker screamed. "You're the worst liar I've ever seen! You're a disgrace to the Navy." The tirade continued, Weber said, for five to ten minutes.

At a subsequent interview in Norfolk, Weber asked Cmdr. Robert Monahan, Williams's top assistant, if he was being accused of wrong-doing. If so, Weber wanted to be read his rights. DOD-IG Special Agent Thomas Bonnar, also present, agreed that would be appropriate.

Bonnar remarked, "Chris Gates says you escorted the white woman out of the room." Later, Weber said, "I found out he didn't do that." [22]

The DOD-IG's badgering tactics and mind games concerned leaders like Cmdr. George E. Mayer, who served as Stumpf's executive officer during Tailhook and followed him as VFA-83 commander. During the agency's visit to the squadron in June 1993—more than a month after the Tailhook team met with Reason at Little Creek to decide what to do to whom, and a month after Stumpf had been pulled off the Blue Angels pending completion of the investigation—agents had interviewed nine of Mayer's officers. All were granted testimonial immunity. Five had not attended the 1991 Tailhook convention.

"I was very concerned about the safety of the squadron," Mayer testified. He convened a "human factors board" at which several of the officers were interviewed, "just to make sure they're focused on the job at hand." Mayer also lodged a complaint with the Office of the Chief of Naval Personnel. [23]

Human factors—a euphemism for safety—were an especially big concern for the Blue Angels. Team members take part in harrowing, close-quarters aerial routines that require exceptional skill and precision, so much so that members never fly in any other formation slot but the one to which they are assigned that particular season. No one else had been freshly trained to take Stumpf's place in the Number One jet.

"We had to cancel two weekends of shows," testified retired Rear Adm. William R. McGowen, who, as the chief of naval air training, used to oversee the Blue Angels. [24]

At that point, two of Stumpf's officers had already appeared before Reason. They were told by Jeffry Williams, Mayer said, that "mast would not affect their careers; they would still be screened for command, and that they should accept mast because it would show that the Navy legal system was fair." Neither was disciplined. [25]

Testimony in the Stumpf hearings, held in early September 1993, lasted five days. Throughout the investigation, the stoic, chiseled expression of Rear Adm. Archie Clemins, seated at the panel's center, rarely changed.

But as the parade of witnesses alternately singing Stumpf's praises or saying he did no wrong at Tailhook wore on, Clemins looked increasingly like he was losing patience with the proceedings, which also had been moved three times in one week. On the final day, Clemins's joke about the living room-sized courtroom where they had been situated for the final day of testimony seemed like an unintended metaphor for the government's fading case against Stumpf.

"It's always nice to deal with the Navy legal system," he deadpanned. "We started in the big courtroom, we moved to a smaller courtroom, and today we're in this courtroom. If we continue Monday, we'll be over in the head."[26]

In addition to questions about Stumpf's activities, panel members repeatedly asked about VFA-83's JOPA, or Junior Officers Protective Association. DOD-IG agents suspected it and other JOPAs like it had been formed after Tailhook by officers who closed ranks and made sure their stories dovetailed. But every officer questioned said the JOPA was no more than a harmless clique for younger fliers in the rank of lieutenant and below to air mutual concerns. Said Weber, "I can't remember the last time there was a JOPA meeting in the squadron."[27]

The panel was also curious about the propriety of Stumpf flying an F/A-18 Hornet cross-country to Nevada instead of taking a government C-9 flight. McGowen told the panel it was wholly justified. Such cross-country flights have real training value, he insisted, and unit commanders are responsible for ensuring such training periodically takes place.[28]

Questioned about Stumpf's views on alcohol consumption, Weber said the squadron had a conservative alcohol abuse policy that, while unwritten, was strongly reinforced. "We were constantly reminded, by comparison with other squadrons I'd rather not name, as to what was an unacceptable type of behavior."[29]

"One drink affects your health," Hertz told Clemins. "And Tailhook '91 affected all of the Navy."[30]

During McGowen's testimony, panel counsel Cmdr. James E. McPherson pressed him about the improper activities that investigators said took place at his own CNATRA suite at Tailhook.

McPherson said that on one occasion, a hired stripper was allowed to perform to two songs "behind closed doors" at the suite. McGowen replied that the money had been raised to pay her, the stripper had arrived, and that the decision allowing her to go ahead and perform briefly was the right one.

"I thought that was very properly handled," said McGowen, adding that he took no action against any of the participants.[31]

That was the sort of casual attitude that, critics maintained, indicated the presence of a cultural mindset—the kind that led directly to instances of sexual harassment and assault. Such critics had to look no further than the comments of Eli Hertz, who said the VFA-83 party hadn't been remarkable.

"I didn't think I'd witnessed anything unusual that hadn't happened at previous Tailhooks," he said of the public oral sex administered to Gates. "It was just another sort of Tailhook happening."[32]

To counter the picture of Stumpf's presence at the risqué party, Gittins called a parade of impressive character witnesses on the flier's behalf. In addition to McGowen, they included Vice Adm. Robert Kihune, chief of naval air and training, and Capt. Joseph Mobley, a Vietnam veteran who spent five years in a Hanoi prison camp and knew Stumpf from when both served aboard the *Saratoga* during the war with Iraq.

These and other witnesses all gave resounding appraisals of Stumpf's character: "He leads by example," "Outstanding military bearing," "Didn't tolerate misconduct among officers."

Said Mobley: "I believe in his integrity, his leadership skills, and his morality."

"With all due respect," said Sias, "I ask that you right the wrong that has been done so far, acquit him, and put him back in the Number One jet of the Blue Angels." [33]

As far as Stumpf's fliers were concerned, his case, despite the appearance of impropriety, seemed to perfectly illustrate the degree to which the government's desire to lay the blame at someone's—anyone's—feet had overwhelmed what seemed to be a lack of the concrete evidence necessary to convincingly do so in a just manner.

"This looks a lot like a vendetta," said Lt. Cmdr. Dave Stewart, the Blue Angels's executive assistant, during testimony. "It makes the probe look more like a witchhunt than ever. If there's evidence against Commander Stumpf, present it. But there is no evidence, and three fruitless probes seem to point that out.

"Two years after the fact, Tailhook still haunts the Navy," said Stewart, "and in particular, naval aviation."[34]

Said McGowen, "I think the best thing to do is dismiss all the actions against Commander Stumpf and all the others, get back to work, and quit wasting the tax dollars."[35]

Stumpf was never called to testify. During a July 1996 interview, he flatly denied being in the room when the sex act between Gates and the stripper took place.[36]

In October, the panel cleared Stumpf. But Reason was still convinced of the flier's guilt. He forwarded the investigation transcript to Arthur—along with a request that Stumpf be relieved of command.[37]

Reason's frustration was felt even more powerfully by the DOD-IG, which, for all its work, had spent the summer of 1993 getting pounded in court and in the press.

DOD-IG agent Peter Black had testified so frequently at Tailhook hearings that he had become synonymous with the investigation—for better or for worse. By now, it was obvious that Black was frustrated and angry about the continual pounding his investigation had received in court and in the press. He was sure there were hundreds of naval officers who had taken part in sexual misconduct. Collusion, he felt, was the reason they were getting away with it.

During the fact-finding hearings for Capt. Richard F. Braden and Cmdrs. Robert C. Yakeley and Gregory E. Peairs, Black gave voice to those frustrations.

At Braden's Sept. 7 hearing, Black was asked if the investigation had been focused on assaults or on general misconduct. Assaults, Black replied. Unprompted, he added, "In preparing cases for criminal assaults, our feeling was that there was a whole generation of Navy and Marine Corps officers who don't understand the word, 'integrity.'

"As a former Army officer, I was concerned there were people who stood by and did nothing," Black said.

Black, who always seemed tightly wound upon first taking the stand, growing increasingly exasperated as time wore on, angrily painted a third-floor hallway picture of "200–300 naval aviators, pounding walls, grabbing women, their breasts and buttocks, and in some instances, knocking them down.

"I think what we're trying to do here is rewrite history," Black said. "Beyond the 200 who did it, 500 watched it, and 2,000 knew it was going on. Naval aviators, in order to prove their manhood, had to take part in this.

"They didn't go there for the seminars," said Black. "They went there to get drunk."

The Braden panel was headed by Rear Adm. Byron Tobin, the commander of Norfolk Naval Base. Tobin, low-key yet affable, was also an aviator, and he calmly took exception to Black's statements in a later exchange.

"You've made some rather sweeping statements about naval aviators," Tobin said, a slightly wry tone to his voice. "Is that how you feel about all of them?"

"No, sir." But he went on to tell Tobin that he found that the simple process of asking questions of fliers to be enormously frustrating. "It would sometimes take an hour-and-a-half to get an answer to a simple question. . . . I would say that we found very deliberate attempts to obstruct our investigation." Officers, he said, "consistently changed their stories."

Black said he had concluded that for naval officers, lying was institutionalized. When agents asked fliers who had graduated from the Naval Academy about that, Black said they would reply, "That's part of our honor code." He had no notes to back that up, he said.

Tobin responded in measured tones. "I understand your concern pursuant to the investigation," he said. "But I question how you can condemn such a large group of people. . . . " With that, Black stepped down.[38]

10

Technicalities

Despite the extra workload, the four fact-finding boards didn't prolong the Navy's Tailhook cases against Gregory Tritt, Thomas Miller, David Samples, Cole Cowden, and Rolando Diaz. That was being accomplished by a succession of aggressive motions introduced by the defense teams that were forcing the government to spend more time justifying the charges the Navy had brought than proving the defendants' guilt.

In late August 1993, that doggedness began to pay dividends for the defense.

On August 25, military judge Capt. William T. Vest dismissed one of the two assault charges against Tritt, concurring with a motion by Tritt attorney Robert Rae that the charge of touching females "whose names are unknown" was too vague to fairly prosecute.

Without a named victim, Vest told the court, Tritt would "be unable to conduct a pretrial interview of any alleged victim and will be deprived of any right of direct confrontation at trial"—critical, Vest said, for a defendant to properly prepare his defense. Vest also ruled that if Tritt was cleared on the charge as worded, he wouldn't have double-jeopardy protection from future prosecution by a named victim who might come forward in the case.[1]

Tritt still faced charges of lying under oath, two counts of conduct unbecoming an officer, and the charge that he assaulted Ensign Kim Ponikowski, the gantlet victim who couldn't pick him out of a lineup.

That charge seemed likely to stay, given a named victim and current political sensitivities. Dismissal would provide even more fuel for the Navy's ongoing public relations bonfire. Dismissal would also mean that of the thousands of fliers who had attended Tailhook '91, two black men, Samples and Marine Bonam, could end up being the only officers court-martialed for assault out of the predominantly white male fraternity that is Navy and Marine Corps aviation.

Vest, however, now turned to a Rae motion to dismiss one of the conduct unbecoming charges—worded nearly identically to the charge just dropped for vagueness. The legal argument that ensued addressed the greater question of whether there was a different standard for conduct unbecoming an officer at the 1991 Tailhook convention. Was it less than that expected anywhere else, at any other time?

The answer had already been determined on a lesser scale, in dozens of instances, by Vice Adm. J. Paul Reason during admiral's mast hearings in his Atlantic Fleet Surface Force office. Now, for the first time at the Tailhook hearings, the question would be openly debated.

Vest told attorneys that while lack of consent by the "victim" is an essential consideration of assault, it is not necessarily so when considering the charge of conduct unbecoming an officer; it is possible to have engaged in unbecoming conduct without knowing a victim's name, he said.

"The question for the trier of fact in the ultimate sense is whether or not the conduct, under the circumstances, somehow dishonored the status of that person as an officer and a gentleman," Vest said.

That's exactly the tack Lt. Cmdr. Mike Ritter took in arguing for the prosecution. It didn't matter that Tritt grabbed women without their consent, he argued. The government's theory "is that whether or not they consented, the conduct falls below the standard that's required of an officer in the United States Navy."

Ritter also argued that Tritt, because of his grade and position, essentially should have known better. What might might have been disgraceful conduct for a commander at Tailhook might not have been for an ensign; the latter would presumably lack the seasoning assumed to be possessed by the former.

Rae stood to argue that the charge against Tritt should be voided for vagueness because, contingencies aside, it was still essentially the same charge as the assault charge Vest had just dismissed. It "subjects the government to the same types of proof," he said. Rae also argued that such vagueness would make it impossible for Tritt to mount a defense.

After follow-on arguments, the courtroom fell silent as Vest looked down, pored over the documents on his desk, and considered the arguments for several minutes.

Finally, he denied the motion.

"I find that neither . . . the consent of or the identity of any individual allegedly touched by Commander Tritt is necessarily essential to the government's case," he said. The charge made it clear what Tritt must defend against, Vest added, and protected him against double jeopardy.[2]

Two days after the Tritt hearing, on August 27, Coast Guard Lt. Cmdr. Jeffrey Good introduced his multiple motions to dismiss charges against Cowden, the officer who had been photographed licking Lisa Mattiello's chest. Good charged that Reason had prematurely expressed a belief in Cowden's guilt, that Cowden was the victim of selective prosecution, and that Cowden couldn't have known in 1991 that licking a woman's chest at a Tailhook party would later be construed as criminal conduct.

But more than anything else, Good wanted to prove that Jeffry Williams, Reason's top legal adviser, had exhibited personal bias against Cowden during the pretrial process.

Eleven members of Cowden's Norfolk-based unit sat together on the right side of the courtroom; they had come to provide moral support. Vest presided.

Good called Lt. Ronald Hocevar, the military attorney assisting Rae on the Diaz case, to the stand. Hocevar had been Cowden's first attorney, but had passed the case off to Good to prevent a possible conflict of interest.

Two days later after doing so, Hocevar said, he and Diaz were sitting with Cowden and Good in a conference room at SurfLant, waiting to speak with Reason after Cowden and Diaz had told Williams they were refusing mast. Williams, said Hocevar, came in and told the two officers that Reason was "surprised" at their decisions.

Reason, however, had said nothing of the sort.

Vest interrupted. "Are you certain that Captain Williams said it was the admiral who was surprised?" he asked.

"Yes sir, I am," Hocevar replied.

The prosecutor, Lt. Cmdr. Christopher Morin, declined to cross-examine Hocevar. Cowden then testified, corroborating Hocevar's story.

Morin called Williams to the stand.

Williams affirmed that as force judge advocate for Reason, he had reviewed the DOD-IG files, had made recommendations to the Little Creek Tailhook team as to which cases should go to mast, and had ultimately approved the mast packages, including Cowden's.

Williams said the reason Cowden and Good had to wait for six-and-a-half hours to meet with Williams the day that Cowden refused mast was because so many cases were being handled at the same time. It was crazy, he said, and fairly hectic.

"We had to make a choice as to who to consider first," he said, saying that some officers had flown in from other parts of the country, and he wanted to give them a chance to meet with counsel before making a choice. In addition, he said, "a senior officer was coming that afternoon, and I wanted to meet with him." Reason also had to leave twice that day on other business, he said, but Williams finally got in to tell the admiral that two officers had refused mast.

"Did Admiral Reason seem surprised?" asked Morin.

"No. I did," Williams replied. "I'm not sure I mentioned Cowden by name. I did refer to the photograph that did exist in his case file."

Asked for Reason's reaction, Williams replied that he'd had none. Reason then asked, "Do you think I should see them?"

"No sir. I'll see them," Williams recalled saying. Asked what he had said to Cowden and Diaz, he replied, "I don't remember what I did say."

Good stood up to cross-examine Williams. "How are you?" he asked.

Stone-faced, Williams didn't reply.

Good asked him to repeat what he had said to Cowden and Diaz on May 27.

"I believe what I said to you was, 'I think the admiral was surprised that your client refused mast,' because as I recounted to you, 'There's a photograph of your client licking a woman's breast,'" Williams said.

Williams said that Reason may have heard some discussion of Cowden's case during the May briefings. Good asked if Reason had been briefed on Cowden's case before the flier was summoned to Williams's office.

"Yes, sir," replied Williams. "He was part of the deliberation process."

"Was the admiral part of the screening process?" asked Good.

"You bet," said Williams. "It was his discretion that was being exercised."

Why, Good wanted to know, had Williams said the admiral was surprised, and not himself?

"I wanted these individuals to know that their time had not been wasted," said Williams.

"Were you upset when they refused?"

"Surprised. Let's go with surprised," said Williams. "I could not believe that when faced with that photograph, he refused mast."

Vest interrupted. "When was the decision made to refer Lieutenant Cowden's case to court-martial?"

Williams couldn't pin it down. Vest wanted more clarification. "You said Lieutenant Cowden is here today because he refused mast."

Said Williams, "If you're asking me if we were predisposed to bring this case to court-martial, the answer is no."

"As a matter of routine," asked Vest, "does Admiral Reason decide how to dispose of a case prior to an Article 15?" Article 15 is the section of the Uniform Code of Military Justice that governs nonjudicial punishment like admiral's masts.

"In four or five instances, yes," said Williams. Vest asked who made the decision to refer Cowden's case to an Article 32 hearing, the normal preface to a court-martial. Admiral Reason, Williams replied.[3]

The hearing took place over the course of two days. After the first day's testimony, Good wasn't optimistic. "Actually, it's one of my weaker motions," he said. He was more interested in the government taking a longer look at Lt.j.g. Elizabeth Warnick, the officer who had changed her story so frequently during interviews by government agents.

"Why isn't she being charged?" Good asked. "She admitted under oath making false official statements, and false swearing. And there's very good evidence she perjured herself at the 32."

It was a good question. But behind the scenes, there was a feeling that prosecuting the seemingly fragile Warnick would be more trouble than it was worth. There was a sense among the trial counsel that she viewed herself as another Paula Coughlin, and that her case ought to be attracting as much attention. If they failed to gain a conviction, prosecutors could end up making her out to be even more of a victim than she was trying to be. Basiscally, it was a case everyone just wanted to be done with.

Good was also concerned that Reason literally wasn't seeing the whole picture. The photograph of Cowden and Mattiello shown to

Reason, Good said, had been greatly enlarged and then cropped tightly to cut out Mattiello's hand on the back of Cowden's neck.[4]

During the Cowden hearing, a Navy judge still on active duty sat in the front row, passing advice to Good on small notepad sheets. Morin objected to the "gentleman in the front row assisting the defense," but Cmdr. Alan Bergstrom was on "terminal" leave en route to a September 1 retirement. Legally, he had been cleared after beginning that leave on August 8 to act as a consultant to Cowden—and to Tritt, Miller, Diaz, Yakeley, and Peairs.

When the Norfolk NLSO first learned in early March that it would be handling the Tailhook courts-martial, Bergstrom was Vest's deputy circuit court judge. Since the NLSO was expecting as many as 25 courts-martial, Vest decided to split up the caseload: Bergstrom would hear the cases of O-4s, or lieutenant commanders, and below, and Vest would take commanders and on up.

Vest also wanted to eliminate any possibility of prejudicing the cases. He told Bergstrom, as well as Larry McCullough and Steven Seaton, the two judges who would conduct Article 32 pretrial hearings, not to read anything about Tailhook and to excuse themselves if conversations turned in that direction.

But it became rapidly apparent that the caseload would be far less than expected. Bergstrom, a twenty-year veteran, had already planned to retire later in the year. By May, he had decided to go work with Rae, who had retired from the Navy the year before. Bergstrom and Rae were old friends; they were two years apart at the Naval Academy.

Although he kept working at the NLSO, Bergstrom said his move didn't give Tritt an unfair advantage.

"I was disqualified from anything to do with the cases," Bergstrom said. "I knew I was going to Bob's. I told them not to tell me anything." Bergstrom said he also avoided reading about the Tailhook cases.

What Bergstrom did bring to the defense was the experience he had gained in the area of Navy-Marine Corps procedural guidelines. Bergstrom had spent the previous three years helping to rewrite those guidelines, and there wasn't a procedural question he didn't know—a big advantage in the area of motions and objections. Bergstrom also reinforced the defense conviction that Jeffry Williams "was screwing things up" for the Navy.[5]

On September 10, Vest essentially confirmed that assessment during a subsequent hearing for Cowden. "This court finds that by his words and actions, Captain Williams exceeded the permissible bounds of his official role as a legal adviser, and therefore he must be disqualified from acting as the staff judge advocate in this case," Vest said.

Vest asked Reason to appoint a "neutral and detached" staff judge advocate to again review McCullough's Article 32 investigation, and to then prepare new advice for Reason.[6]

On September 20, Cmdr. Thomas R. Taylor published his review of Cowden's case. His decision: dismiss all charges. Reason accepted his recommendation.[7]

Cowden was a free man. Good, reached for comment, could hardly contain himself.

"I'm real pleased, obviously," said Good, just a year out of law school at the University of Hawaii. "I obviously would have preferred that it didn't get this far. But at least he's spared from going to a court-martial."

Cowden, having a beer with squadron buddies at the naval base's Breezy Point Officers Club that afternoon, wasn't as happy as expected. "It's kind of a relief, but it really hasn't sunk in," he said. "It's bittersweet. It should never have happened in the first place."

The first order of business for Cowden was to accept his long-delayed promotion to lieutenant commander. The next was to begin flying again, even though he had now been saddled with the call sign "Rocky" after the 1960s cartoon character. He had gained the new name thanks to news articles that included Monahan's August reference to Cowden as "that little squirrel."

"Hopefully, that, too, shall pass," said Cowden.[8]

Lost in the Tritt-Cowden shuffle was a change in the Samples case. On September 2, a new charge sheet was released minus the allegation that the flier had made a false official statement.

Investigating Officer Cmdr. Steven Seaton noted in his ruling that Samples hadn't confessed to taking part in the assault on Julia Rodgers in his post-mast statements. But, he wrote, "a statement that is merely incomplete, even intentionally incomplete, does not support a criminal charge."

At the same time, Seaton said he would press forward on the indecent assault charge.[9]

In Quantico, Lt. Gen. Charles C. Krulak had disposed of most of the nonjudicial Tailhook business facing the Marines—although the

Coughlin case still cast a long shadow across his desk. But on September 10, Lt. Tony Eaton was back in Quantico. Eaton, the flier accused of lying on the floor in a party suite under a naked stripper, had asked for another personal interview with Krulak.

Eaton's case was still in limbo. Charged with conduct unbecoming an officer, he had never signed the paperwork refusing nonjudicial punishment, and hadn't been referred to court-martial.

The mood was tense; Krulak wanted to find Eaton guilty, and honed in on a photograph, published in the DOD-IG report, of a stripper dancing over a man on the floor. At the same time, he tried to put Eaton at ease. "If I find you guilty and give you a nonpunitive letter of caution," he told the flier, "nothing will appear in your records."

Eaton and Mike Powell, his attorney, knew that in a previous hearing for Maj. Phil Gabriel, Krulak hadn't paused between his pronouncement of verdict and sentence to give Gabriel a final chance to refuse nonjudicial punishment and go to trial. Still, they were prepared for a quick exit: If Krulak suddenly announced a verdict, Powell planned to loudly interrupt, tell Krulak, "That was what you did to the major," and walk out.

Krulak questioned Eaton for roughly forty-five minutes. At one point, he asked, "How can you say you weren't part of the act?"

Replied Eaton, "I wasn't part of the act because I never took my clothes off."

When Krulak was finished, everyone left the room except the general and Col. Dave Hague, his personal lawyer. Five minutes later, Eaton and Powell were summoned and stood before Krulak's desk a full minute while Krulak deliberated.

Finally, he looked up. "I find that the offenses are not warranted by the evidence, so I'm awarding no punishment," he said. Krulak paused. "But I'm giving you a letter of caution."

Despite his acquittal, Eaton's promotion to captain was held up. In November 1994, he was finally promoted. Eaton left the Marines in September 1995.[10]

Ten days after Eaton's meeting with Krulak, Gabriel, the Marine upon whom Krulak levied punishment June 18 without pausing, filed an appeal of his June 18 office hours hearing on those very grounds. Krulak granted the appeal, wiping Gabriel's record clean.[11]

On September 24, Diaz dropped from the Tailhook scene when he decided to accept admiral's mast—the same sort of hearing he had rejected back in May. Taylor, the same officer who had recommended dropping all charges against Cowden, had performed a similar court-ordered review of Diaz's case after Rae had alleged bias on Williams's part.

Taylor, however, had recommended a court-martial for Diaz. The trial was scheduled to begin October 18.

Diaz had changed his mind a couple of weeks before the announcement, Rae said. Reason had granted his client a private audience at which Diaz was allowed to tell his side of the story. "Diaz left that meeting very, very impressed with the admiral, and we get through sources that the admiral was very impressed with Diaz," Rae said.

A few days later, Reason, suitably impressed, handed Diaz a punitive letter and a $1,000 fine, and the flier was on his way back to his job at Naval Station Roosevelt Roads, Puerto Rico.[12]

To date, the strategy to dismiss charges by nailing Reason for being unduly influenced by superiors had failed. But the effort had refocused the defensive counterattack on the officer who attorneys regarded as their clients' real nemesis. Jeffry Williams still had much to answer for, and further embarrassments awaited.

On September 30, Tritt received another boost. McCullough, in a review ordered by Vest, recommended tossing out the charge of conduct unbecoming an officer that alleged Tritt had failed to stop others from taking part in the Saturday night "mini-gantlet" on the pool patio.

"The sharp contrast between the testimony of the government and defense witnesses is remarkable," McCullough wrote. "A question that cannot be ignored is whether Lieutenants LoGuidice and Janssen gradually formed a basic impression or concept of the events of 7 September as it became clear the behavior of themselves and others would almost certainly be focused on by the investigation into Tailhook 1991. From this basic mental construct they may have embroidered a picture of the evening's events."

McCullough said there was "probable cause" to believe that some sort of groping offense was committed. But, he said, "the evidence presented by the government establishes only that and little, if any, more.

"The government's case against Commander Tritt is not persuasive and is far from compelling," McCullough wrote. "I recommend, therefore, that the specification not be referred to trial by court-martial."

It was a small victory. Tritt still faced a charge of making a false statement to DOD-IG agents, as well as the remaining assault charge.

That same day, Jeffry Williams testified before Vest on a Rae motion requesting an entirely new investigative report on Tritt. Rae argued that Williams hadn't remained impartial while advising Reason on Tritt's case, and had done so in an incomplete and misleading fashion.

Throughout the testimony, Rae and Williams kept up a running verbal sparring match, Williams practically snarling his answers, Rae pressing for more. More than just a day in court, it was an inevitable clash of egos between two of the Tailhook investigation's biggest players.

"You get guys like Jeff Williams and Bob Rae in the same room, you're bound to get broken dishes," D.J. Hansen later remarked. Hansen also felt that the antagonism that developed between the SurfLant lawyers and defense attorneys such as Rae and Good was largely responsible for the continued drive to press the cases despite their weak underpinnings.

"It became a face-saving thing," Hansen said.

It also sometimes became comical. During Williams's testimony on the 30th, Rae was asking about a pre-hearing "closed-door" conversation Williams had conducted with former prosecutor Hank Sonday. Rae established that prosecutor Ritter had briefed Sonday about the line of questioning he could expect this day, and thought that Williams and Sonday had talked about that very same thing; Williams said it had been an innocuous conversation about Sonday's work at the U.S. Attorney's office in Norfolk.

"I think we could leave it at that, but you did determine that it was necessary to close the door and have a closed-door session when you discussed it with him," Rae said.

"No, not at all," Williams replied.

"Who closed the door, sir," Rae asked.

"He walked in through a closed door."

"He walked in through a closed door?"

"I was, in fact, I was napping in the room, you know, when he arrived," Williams said.

"He didn't walk through a closed door, right?" Rae asked.

"Right, that's right," Williams said.

"Now, and the door was closed behind him?"

"The door closes behind him, if that's what you mean. Yes, the door was closed," Williams said.

"Well, the door doesn't close by itself, sir?" Rae asked.

"Some does," Williams said.

"Somebody closed the door?"

"No, I think it does," Williams said. "It has one of these, you know, automated critters on it."[13]

On October 1, DOD-IG acting chief Derek Vander Schaaf issued a statement of his own, but one that he would just as soon not have been forced to make. Back in May, a group of DOD-IG auditors, partying at an Alexandria, Virginia bar, decided to have a little Tailhook-style fun with a Marine colonel. Groping him as he walked past the bar, the civilians shouted "Let's play Tailhook," and joked about forming a "gantlet." Vander Schaaf issued a public apology, and said disciplinary action was being considered against thirteen of the forty-four employees who had been at the bar.

Of the thirteen, five were men, eight were women.[14]

From the day he was sworn in, Navy Secretary John Dalton knew he would soon be forced to deal with a most unpleasant piece of unfinished business: the files the DOD-IG had compiled on the 35 flag officers who had attended the 1991 Tailhook convention.

After being sworn in July 21, the Office of the Secretary of Defense transferred the files no one wanted to Dalton, who began poring over them. Dalton also conducted personal interviews with about half of the officers.

On the afternoon of Friday, October 1, Dalton completed his review. As the day wound down, he sent Defense Secretary Les Aspin a memo containing his decisions: reprimand thirty-two of the thirty-five flag officers, and fire Kelso.

Since the service chiefs are presidentially appointed, firing Kelso would require a nod from President Clinton. But Clinton, not on the best of terms with the military following his initiatives to allow gays to serve in the military and to give women a combat role, apparently wanted no part of that. White House spokeswoman Dee Dee Myers was quoted by *The Washington Post* as saying the decision "was up to Secretary Aspin."

It was an awkward moment for the administration. Clinton and Dalton were close friends. Aspin held Kelso in high regard. And Kelso had tendered his resignation once before, in 1992, in the wake of the

Tailhook-related resignation of Navy Secretary H. Lawrence Garrett. But he had been turned down by then-Defense Secretary Dick Cheney.

Aspin, architect of the massive post-Cold War reduction in U.S. armed forces, wasn't universally admired by the troops either; if he advised Clinton to fire Kelso, his stock would plunge even further.

Aspin spent the weekend agonizing over Dalton's request. On Sunday, he met with Kelso for an hour, and also spent an hour at the White House discussing the matter with Clinton.

On Monday, Aspin rejected Dalton's recommendation. While generally praising Dalton's report for its fairness, Aspin said the time had passed to fire Kelso just because he was "captain of the ship" at the time of Tailhook. And, he noted, "an evaluation of his record under the criteria you have offered does not suggest to me that he should be asked to retire." Aspin also asked for a clarification of the criteria used to recommend discipline for the other thirty-two admirals.[15]

On October 15, Dalton decided to give Kelso a letter of caution instead of a pink slip.

"It is clear to me that there was a failure of appropriate leadership at Tailhook '91," he wrote in a revised statement. "I strongly believe in the principle of accountability and responsibility."

At the top of the list, Dalton said, was Vice Adm. Richard Dunleavy. "More than any other individual, Admiral Dunleavy was responsible for the failures at Tailhook," Dalton wrote. He also fired darts at Dunleavy's deputies, Rear Adms. Riley Mixson and Wilson Flagg.

"There were ample signals that trouble could arise—precedents of unacceptable conduct at prior Tailhook conventions, visible use of alcohol to excess, resistance and hostility toward women entering what many aviators considered to be a male-only professional domain, and widespread attendance at the event for the sole purpose of having a good time," Dalton wrote. "That potential was heightened by an atmosphere in which rank and the rules of propriety and deference toward rank were set aside for the purposes of Tailhook."

Dalton handed down secretarial letters of censure—the same kind of letters Reason wanted Dalton to give the five officers who had been reinvestigated—to Dunleavy, Mixson, and Flagg. He also took a star from the now-retired vice admiral, knocking Dunleavy down to rear admiral and making a substantial dent in his retirement pay and pride in the process.

Thirty of the remaining thirty-two flag officers—including Adm.

Frank B. Kelso, his own service chief—were given nonpunitive letters of caution. Dalton spared two flag officers who came to Las Vegas and left after one afternoon symposium.

The group of thirty included some of the naval service's top officers, including Adm. Robert J. Kelly, commander-in-chief of the Pacific Fleet; Vice Adm. William C. Bowes, commander of Naval Air Systems Command; Vice Adm. Anthony A. Less, commander of the Atlantic Fleet Naval Air Force; Vice Adm. Jerry L. Unruh, commander of the Pacific Fleet's 3rd Fleet; and Marine Lt. Gen. Duane A. Wills, deputy chief of staff for Marine Aviation.

The group of thirty flag officers hadn't personally engaged in any wrongdoing, he wrote. "However, with regard to Tailhook, their performance was not all that could have been."

Most took their medicine and kept quiet. Dunleavy was the only flag officer who stood up—albeit belatedly—and acknowledged his role, a move that only boosted his stock with Navy fliers. Mixson, in a statement released along with Dalton's, said he was being held accountable because of his position.[16]

In a preretirement interview conducted the following spring by the independent Norfolk weekly newspaper *Soundings*, Less, while acknowledging that Tailhook was a "major problem," seemed intent on diluting the issue. "The crime was such that the Las Vegas police wouldn't even touch it," he told the paper. And he refused to characterize Tailhook as a failure of leadership. Not so much that, he said, "as maybe an oversight."[17]

In the midst of the Dalton-Aspin standoff, Stumpf appeared to finally escape the Tailhook quagmire during an October 7 meeting with Adm. Stanley R. Arthur, the vice chief of naval operations.

Arthur had been designated to hear appeals of nonjudicial Tailhook rulings. Stumpf had been cleared by his fact-finding board, but Reason had sent the findings to Arthur along with a request to relieve Stumpf of his command.

The word on the street was that Arthur was looking favorably upon the cases of Gulf War veterans; he had commanded naval fliers during the brief conflict. Arthur gave Stumpf a nonpunitive letter of caution—his advice on how Stumpf could have better handled the Tailhook incident—and cleared him of any wrongdoing, giving Stumpf immediate clearance to rejoin the Blue Angels in the team's Number One jet.

"I'm elated," said Stumpf, reached at his Pensacola home that night.

"I don't think it's sunk in yet. Like I told my wife when I got off the plane today, this was as good as coming back from an eight-month cruise."

Stumpf's future looked bright. He could now resume his command. In 1994, he would be selected for promotion to the rank of captain, with orders to become the deputy commander of a carrier air wing. Stumpf looked for all the world like he was back on track to become the admiral everyone thought he eventually would be.

Reason, undeterred, asked that the Naval Bureau of Personnel attach the investigation results to Stumpf's personnel file as a "matter of interest." That, too, was rejected.[18]

The same day Arthur cleared Stumpf, Vest ordered a new review of Tritt's original Article 32 pretrial hearing, ruling that, as in Cowden's case, Williams had once again stepped over the line.

Williams, said Vest, had acted as "the investigator, the prosecutor, and the . . . reviewing officer" in recommending to Reason that Tritt be court-martialed. He asked Reason to appoint a new judge advocate to review the results of the original Article 32 hearing. He also delicately urged Reason to review the Samples and Miller cases "to determine if it would best serve the convening authority and the accused" to order similar new reviews.

Samples and his attorney Mike Kmetz had a similar motion pending before Vest to dismiss the flier's assault charge because of bias on Williams's part.

In his decision on Tritt's case, Vest said that Navy lawyers acting as Tailhook prosecutors were "personally directed" by Williams. While not impermissible, Vest said, it demonstrated the degree of control Williams wanted to exercise.

"The perception of 'fair play' must be carefully guarded and maintained," Vest wrote. "This perception was distorted," Vest said, by Williams's "total domination of the prosecution, and his actions indicating an inflexible bent as to the accused's guilt" prior to Tritt's pretrial investigation.[19]

Strike two for Williams.

Despite the prosecution's setbacks, the long process was beginning to takes its toll on Miller. One day, after another in what seemed like an endless series of motion hearings, he turned resignedly to his attorneys Don Marcari and Lt. Cmdr. William C. Little. "I wish I could say I was lying, so I could end this," he said.[20]

As it pressed forward with Miller's motion-riddled case, the Navy was trying desperately to come up with something that would indicate Miller was a less-than-truthful individual. In an apparent effort to find a smudge on Miller's character, prosecutors coerced an officer at Miller's old Whidbey Island unit who had helped investigate the 1992 EA-6B crash involving Miller into telling them some of what he had learned.[21]

Information gathered for mishap investigations is considered sacrosanct. The military feels that finding out exactly why an accident occurred is more important than indicting a possibly negligent participant. By telling interviewees up front that it will not prosecute for human error, the military dulls any temptation the guilty may have to lie to protect themselves. The investigation results are of such a privileged nature that unauthorized release is a criminal offense.[22]

In early August, Lt. Cmdr. David Green, the executive officer of VAQ-139, had been summoned to Norfolk to be interviewed by the Navy attorneys prosecuting Miller. Green, prosecutors learned, had taken the original statement from Lt. James P. Hogan, the ill-fated Prowler's pilot in 1992. During questioning, Lt. Cmdr. Mike Ritter brought up the crash and asked for details.

Green told Ritter, "I can't tell you. It's privileged." Ritter replied, "Well, I can get an order from a three-star to release it."

After lunch, Ritter produced a letter signed by Cmdr. Robert Monahan that identified him as "the Assistant Staff Judge Advocate for Commander, Naval Surface Force, U.S. Atlantic Fleet." In the military, invoking the commander's title implies that the letter writer bears the authority of the commander.

Reason or Tailhook were never mentioned in the letter. Instead it stated that Ritter "is a trial counsel in the cases of CDR Thomas R. Miller, USN, and CDR Gregory E. Tritt, USN, and as such, is authorized to inquire into information he deems relevant to those individuals and their respective cases."

It went on to say that Ritter, "as an officer of the Department of Defense with a need to know," was authorized to obtain the mishap report involving Miller, "within the provisions of the Privacy Act." Monahan concluded by advising Green "to cooperate fully with LCDR Ritter and reveal such information to him, regardless of any designation of such information as 'privileged.'"

Green bought off on it, and answered Ritter's questions.[23]

On October 5, Green, who had become concerned that he had done something improper, decided to call Lt. Dawn Jordan, the top lawyer at the Navy Safety Center in Norfolk, and tell her about the SurfLant probe. The center is where all the service's accident records are collected, analyzed and maintained. Jordan told her boss, Rear Adm. Andrew A. Granuzzo.

Granuzzo was livid. He ordered Jordan to retrieve Ritter's notes.

As she was in the process of reacquiring the notes, Monahan, in Williams's presence, asked her not to tell the Miller defense team what had taken place.

Jordan relayed that to Granuzzo, who decided that in the name of fairness, Miller should be told what had transpired by the Tailhook staff. Jordan's October 7 memo to Williams documenting Granuzzo's decision carried a reminder that since the contents of the report were privileged, "the contents cannot be revealed." She also noted that since Miller's court-martial was scheduled to start the following week, Miller should be informed by the following day: Friday, October 8.

Five days passed. On Wednesday, October 13, Jordan told the Miller defense team what had happened. On the 14th, the prosecution followed suit.

Reason learned what his Tailhook prosecutors had done the following day, during his second appearance in Vest's court to defend charges that he had exerted unlawful command influence on the investigation.

"Have you since August of 1993 been informed of the status of Commander Miller's case?" asked Lt. Cmdr. William C. Little, Jr., Miller's military attorney.

"To some extent, yes," Reason replied in his calm, deep voice. "It was usually coupled in the same breath with Commander Tritt's case, you know, and just where they are in the process."

The wiry, studious-looking Little asked Reason if he knew that results of a privileged accident mishap report had been obtained by one of his prosecutors "for Commander, Naval Surface Force, U.S. Atlantic Fleet."

Reason's eyebrows shot up. "Was that done in my name?"

"Unfortunately, that is correct, sir," Little replied.

Vest ordered Little's editorial comment struck from the record. But he ended up drawing the same conclusion.[24]

It was strike three for Williams. Vest kicked him off Miller's case, and wasted no time ordering a new review of the original pretrial findings by a "neutral and detached" staff judge advocate. The review was assigned to Cmdr. Joseph P. Callahan.

The prosecution's misstep had gone largely unnoticed by the public. Much bigger waves were being generated northward in Quantico, site of the Marine Tailhook investigation.

Nearly two months had gone by since Capt. Gregory Bonam's testimony had closed out his day in court on charges he had assaulted Paula Coughlin. But Col. Steven Mitchell had yet to produce his recommendations for Lt. Gen. Charles C. Krulak, who as head of the Marines' Tailhook investigation would ultimately decide whether Bonam should be court-martialed.

In August, Mitchell had promised Bonam attorney Patrick MacKrell he could reopen the investigation if he had new evidence.[25] MacKrell had an eyewitness: fly-on-the-wall James T. Kelly, the Navy civilian who had stood in the third-floor hallway on Tailhook '91's final night and watched as Coughlin was sexually assaulted by a group of men down near the elevator area.

Kelly had first testified about Coughlin's assault during a September 23 hearing in Norfolk for Tailhook president Capt. Frederic Ludwig. He had talked about the assault, but it hadn't been the focus; the Navy fact-finding board wanted an overview of the Saturday night third-floor scene, which Kelly provided. Now, the Coughlin assault could be explored in greater detail.

Kelly's version of the assault differed slightly from Coughlin's account. Some of the differences would prove significant.

On October 14, Mitchell reopened the Bonam hearing. MacKrell had requested that Coughlin be present, but the prosecutor announced that she was sick in quarters, "as verified by a flight surgeon," and excused from attending. Kelly, a civil servant with the aircraft division of the Naval Air Warfare Division and a P-3 Orion tactical coordinator with the Naval Reserve, was the first witness.

Kelly had gone to Tailhook for the briefings—"the finest naval aviation professional seminars that I had ever attended," he called them—as well as the nighttime parties. On Saturday night, he tried to see it all. He wound his way across the patio, through the various suites, and ducked into the third-floor hallway about six times, he recalled. He didn't drink much—two or three beers all night, he said.

On two of the six visits to the hallway, Kelly said, he watched the gantlet in action.

The first time, he parked himself up against the wall between the VAQ-129 and VAW-110 suites, not far from the main elevators. Here, he had a bird's-eye view of an officer he called the "master of ceremonies" who was standing about twenty feet up the hall, between the VS-41 and HS-1 suites. This "MC" was encouraging women to enter.

The MC was 5'7" to 5'9", about 160 pounds, and white. It was a perfect description of Lt. Greg "Goose" Geiss. Kelly also remembered a black male standing next to the HS-1 suite door. The military-looking man was about 5'8", 165–170 pounds, and very stocky. At one point, he said, the man grabbed a woman's rear end as she passed by.[26] The description and timing meshed with testimony placing Lt. David Samples near Geiss, but Kelly didn't identify him further.[27]

"A number" of women were doing so willingly, Kelly said. He remembered a group of four college-age women entering the gantlet, giggling and pushing one another through.

Some weren't giggling. On one occasion, Kelly said the MC lifted a woman up and placed her at the mouth of the gantlet; on another, he lifted a woman up onto his shoulders and carried her in. Two Hilton Hotel security guards were standing nearby, Kelly said, but took no action. He also saw two women fight back; one with an open-handed slap, another with a punch. Both continued on through the gantlet.

Kelly then saw the assault on Julia Rodgers, the teenager who had had one too many in the HS-1 suite. According to Kelly, she hadn't been carried out but had staggered out on her own. She turned left—at the exact point where the gantlet began. She was immediately descended upon, Kelly said. He moved to the center of the hallway to get a better look.

Within moments, Kelly recalled, a pair of underpants flew into the air. Almost immediately, the crowd began to disperse; Kelly had to get out of the way to keep from being run over. He looked back. Rodgers was sitting half-naked on the floor, slumped over, her hair covering her face. She looked very drunk, Kelly said. After the hallway cleared out, he said, the security guards went to Rodgers and, grabbing her by the arms, picked her up and helped her down the hall.

Kelly went back out onto the patio to get another beer. He returned to the hallway, but the gantlet wasn't happening. He drifted off to another suite.

A bit later, he returned to the hallway. He had been up in the chief of naval aviation training or CNATRA suite, which was on the opposite end of the hall from the main elevators, on the other side of the fire exit from the Rhino suite, owned by the Marines of the deactivated VMFP-3.

As he worked his way through the crowded, noisy hall and came alongside the Rhino suite, he heard someone shout, "Clear deck!" meaning to make a path through the hallway. Kelly backed against the wall closest to the Rhinos. CNATRA was to his right, the elevators far down to his left.

As he backed up, he saw what looked to be a civilian male with long hair to his right, groping a woman being handled by men standing behind her. Kelly couldn't believe it. He looked to his left and saw Coughlin, about twenty to forty feet away.

"Her right biceps [sic] was in the grasp of the left hand of the master of ceremonies, and they were having a conversation of sorts," Kelly testified. "I could lip-read the word "lieutenant" that she spoke to this guy that had her by the arm, and he was speaking to someone to his right." It appeared to be, he said, a confrontation.[28]

In his statement to DOD-IG, Geiss couldn't say whether he—or Samples—had been in the hallway at this time. He also didn't recall hearing any chants of "admiral's aide."[29]

Neither did Kelly.

Kelly looked back at the woman being assaulted in front of him. She was falling into the opposite wall, her angry eyes riveted on the man's face. The long-haired man was still groping her. Kelly turned back to his left to look in Coughlin's direction.

"Very abruptly, someone came up behind her, and I observed arms being thrown around her shoulders/sternum area and being grasped in the front," Kelly said. "I could see the bare arms and hands of the individual . . . I did not observe any arms down her blouse. The hands were clasped, hand-to-wrist . . . . I did not see the individual's face. The arms were of lighter skin color; white, oriental, Hispanic, I don't know, but they were not dark-complected."[30]

Coughlin hadn't testified about a conversation with the master of ceremonies, and had said someone had forced their hands inside her blouse and grabbed her breasts. She had also said that when she turned, her assailant looked to be more than six feet tall. Bonam was 6'1".[31]

Kelly contradicted that. "Paula Coughlin's body blocked the assailant's body from my view," he said. "The individual's relative height was slightly taller than Lieutenant Coughlin. I would say it's fair to say she is five-four; she's about that tall. The individual with his arms around her was five-six to five-seven, perhaps. Her head completely blocked this individual's head, except for just the top of it."

As they struggled, Kelly said, her assailant moved against the wall, still holding onto Coughlin, his chest to her back. Struggling, they began to descend, sliding down the wall.

Kelly decided things were getting just a little too hairy. And he didn't want Coughlin, whom he knew from Patuxent River, to see him. He didn't like her, hadn't gone to her aid, and didn't want to be accused of taking part in the gantlet. He turned to the right and walked through the fire exit onto the patio.

All of about a minute had passed from the time he had seen Coughlin get grabbed.

About ten minutes later, Kelly recalled, he was out on the patio in front of suite 357, on the opposite side of the elevator entrance, when he heard several crashing noises. It was the sound of glass shattering on the patio. Someone had pushed out an 8th-floor window by pressing their bare buttocks against it, sending the pane five floors down to the patio.

Strangely, Kelly invited himself to sit at breakfast with Coughlin and her boss, Rear Adm. Jack Snyder. Not a word was spoken about the previous night, he said.

MacKrell fixed the times of events Kelly said he had seen. The Las Vegas Hilton security blotter contained an entry for Saturday, September 7, at 11:15 p.m., that referred to guards picking up Rodgers.[32] The broken glass was noted in an entry dated September 8, at 12:29 a.m.[33]

MacKrell then produced two additional witnesses. Both provided alibis for Bonam's activities on Saturday night.

Marine Capt. Barry Kragel, a friend of Bonam's since 1985, said he had spent most of Saturday night out on the patio with Bonam. Kragel arrived on the patio around 10:30–11:00 p.m.; a half-hour later, he ran into Bonam. They spent the better part of the next two hours together, Kragel said. Bonam wasn't out of his sight more than five or 10 minutes. They were both on the patio when the window broke, he said.

Kragel hadn't seen any scars or bruises on Bonam, he said. Coughlin said she had bitten her attacker hard on the left forearm and right hand.[34]

MacKrell then called ex-Marine Matthew Long back to the stand. He had spent much of the evening in Bonam's company, he said, up through when the window broke; Long recalled seeing Bonam on the pool patio most of the night, although Bonam had testified he had spent the bulk of his time in the Rhino suite.

"At the time it broke, I was in Greg's company; he was standing to my left side," said Long. "Immediately prior to that, he had been in my company for a period of time. I'd say at least 10 minutes before that."

Bonam "was acting himself" that night, Long said. "We were just having normal conversations, joking around with people, like normal." He hadn't seen any marks on Bonam, he said.[35]

The following day, Mitchell recommended dropping the charges. Krulak's top legal adviser concurred. The advice forced Krulak to make a decision with explosive implications.[36]

Coughlin was the focus of the entire Tailhook scandal. The entire nation knew her name. If any case demanded that justice be done, it was Coughlin's. Even if Bonam appeared innocent, it would be tough not to send him to court-martial. That, in fact, would be the easy way out for Krulak: to let a military judge decide if Bonam was guilty.

That next day in Norfolk, Reason cleared Capt. Richard Braden, who had been in charge of inspecting and assessing suite damage at Tailhook, and was also suspected of having seen an assault in the gantlet.

The subdued Braden, reached at his home in San Diego, said he was glad it was over.

"But it's cost me my career," he said, noting that the long legal process had forced the Navy to give the command he had been slotted for to someone else. "It's great to be a person of mistaken identity, but I sort of feel the way Captain Bonam must have felt in Quantico yesterday. The damage has been done."

Braden's attorney also had mixed feelings. "I'm actually ecstatic for him and his family that it's finally over," said Lt. Jeff Horwitz. "But I'm disappointed that it took this long to clear him. It was evident from Day One that this was the result that should have occurred. Anyone who just took time to look at the case would have come to the same conclusion."[37]

On October 21, Krulak, after a 100–hour review of the Bonam case, announced his decision: Case dismissed. Bonam was a free man.

"It's the right decision for the right reasons," MacKrell told reporters. "It would just be incredible to believe that Greg had anything to do with this. I'm glad the general had the courage to do the right thing."

In a statement, a Marine spokesman made it clear that Krulak sympathized with Coughlin, whose chances for satisfaction from the military in the matter had just evaporated.

"The decision to dismiss the charges against Bonam reflects the facts of this particular case," said Chief Warrant Officer Robert Jenks, a spokesman. "While the identity of her assailant may remain undetermined, this in no way diminishes the seriousness of the incident nor the moral courage of Coughlin in reporting the incident and insisting that it be fully investigated. Her indignation at what took place at Tailhook 1991 is shared by the Marine Corps."[38]

Anne Merritt, at least, was able to face her attacker. She did so, however, out of court—at her insistence.

Merritt, who had been manhandled during Tailhook on the pool patio at the Las Vegas Hilton by a drunk Marine captain, never turned in her assailant. Her reticence stemmed from two sources: She had been raised in the military, the daughter of an Army sergeant major and an Air Force civilian, and had always been treated well by military men. In addition, her father, Donald Merritt, warned his daughter that "things could happen" if she reported the assault; he told her he didn't want anything to happen to his little girl.

Merritt decided she just wanted an apology, and a promise that he would never do it again.

The incident had shattered Merritt, who never expected to get assaulted by someone she knew. Four months after Tailhook, she was assaulted by another drunken officer after giving him a ride home. This assault she reported; the man received nonjudicial punishment. Merritt began going to psychological counseling.

Meanwhile, Merritt was on the lookout for someone in the Marine community who would tell her assailant of her desire for an apology. In the summer of 1992, she corralled a Marine colonel at at the Officers Club at Mather Air Force Base, told him what had happened at Tailhook, and who had done it. The colonel agreed to forward the request—but not without first "hitting on her."

Months later, she called the colonel and asked why she hadn't heard anything. The colonel apologized on behalf of the captain. That wasn't good enough for Merritt, who said she would turn in the captain if the apology wasn't made. Several other senior Marines also became aware of Merritt's complaint.

Late that summer, Merritt received a phone call from her assailant. His voice cracking, he explained he had been drunk and had no memory of the assault, and shouldn't be hurt for it. Merritt poured out her feelings, and the captain apologized. She told him if he ever assaulted another woman and she heard about it, she would report the Tailhook assault.

For Merritt, the call was cathartic. For the first time since Tailhook, she stopped crying about her assault.

Merritt's name was subsequently passed to DOD-IG agents by a different colonel. She refused to reveal her assailant's name, but agreed to review a photographic lineup of six officers. None, she said, were her assailant.

DOD-IG agents persisted, and tracked down one of the colonels she had spoken with about the incident by obtaining her phone records and figuring out who she had called.

It was a false trail. The captain was never identified, and never brought to Quantico.[39]

The day after Bonam was cleared, Callahan handed Reason the new Article 34 advice Vest had ordered in Miller's case.

Callahan's recommendation: Skip the court-martial.

Callahan more or less agreed with Cmdr. Steven Seaton's original report to Reason: dump the indecent exposure charge and move forward on all the others. That would leave one count of dereliction of duty, four counts of conduct unbecoming an officer, and one count of impeding an investigation pending against Miller.

But, Callahan advised, press the charges at an admiral's mast.

"The allegations here reflect extremely poorly on Commander Miller's judgment and deportment in command," Callahan wrote. "Even so, I believe that initial attempts to redress personal leadership shortcomings should not take place at a felony-level trial."

Like Seaton, Callahan recommended dropping the unbecoming conduct charge that addressed Miller's alleged instances of indecent exposure, calling it "fatally speculative." He said the Honolulu incident, where Miller had allegedly walked on an outdoor penthouse roof, was more than 100–150 yards from the ground or the nearest hotel. Someone who chanced to look in Miller's direction is "unlikely to have been able to distinguish anatomical details with the unaided eye." The evidence, he said, was "far short of reasonable proof" that Miller intentionally exposed himself to the general public.[40]

Attorneys for Tritt and Miller had the government reeling, and Mike Kmetz was now hot on the trail. With Samples' court-martial set to begin October 27, Kmetz, his attorney, was peppering Vest with motions to dismiss charges on by-now familiar grounds: that undue command influence had persuaded Reason to refer Samples to court-martial, and that Samples was a victim of both selective and vindictive prosecution. But Kmetz thought his best chance for dismissal lay with conflicting government statements about what type of immunity the Navy been granted to Samples.

The Navy insisted—and documents verified—that after Samples had gone to mast before Reason, and been given a subsequent order to testify, he had also been given testimonial immunity. That meant that when he took part in the standard post-mast interview with DOD-IG, he could "come clean." Even if he revealed a heretofore unknown fact that implicated him in a crime, he couldn't be prosecuted for it. Someone else would have to do that.

Kmetz argued that Cmdr. Robert Monahan, Jeffry Williams's right-hand man, had implied to Samples that the flier had in fact received *transactional*, or total, immunity.

The grant of immunity had stated that Samples was granted immunity from the use of his testimony, and could only be prosecuted for perjury, giving a false statement, or failure to comply with an order to testify.

The order to testify had read in part, " . . . no testimony or other information given by Lieutenant David Samples or *any information directly or indirectly derived from such testimony or other information can be used against him in any criminal case*" (italics added).[41]

All of that seemed clear enough. But, Kmetz said, Monahan had told Samples after the flier had gone before Reason that, in essence, "If you're honest, if you're truthful, you have nothing to worry about"— implying that Samples was now completely immune.[42]

On the witness stand October 19, Monahan denied that allegation, but flip-flopped on the details of his discussion with Samples throughout his more than three hours in the witness stand. He admitted using the term "transactional" as a "jumping-off point" in order to explain that type of immunity to Samples as a preface to describing what was meant by testimonial immunity.

Later, he amended that comment, saying, "I don't remember having used the term "transactional." He said he didn't tell Samples he would be free from being further prosecuted. But Monahan repeatedly told Kmetz and Vest that he couldn't remember the specific words he had used, instead saying he could only remember what he had generally said to all the officers he had briefed after admiral's mast.

Monahan spent much of his day in court verbally sparring with Kmetz and avoiding direct answers, to the point of forcing Vest to warn Kmetz to stop arguing with Monahan, and to admonish Monahan for not being responsive. One exchange went like this:

"Commander, did you read the statement of Lieutenant Samples after he was given the grant of immunity?" Kmetz asked.

"I don't recall having done so, in fact, I believe I did not," said Monahan.

"Did you read the statement of Lieutenant Frank Truong after he was given immunity?" Kmetz continued.

"My answer would be the same," said Monahan. "I . . . I don't recall and I believe I did not."

"Well, you know, that's sort of an ambivalent statement, Commander," said Kmetz. "I mean, it's either yes or no . . . "

Lieutenant Cmdr. Chris Morin, the prosecutor, cut in. "Excuse me sir," he said to Vest. "Again, we would object and ask that counsel not argue with the witness."

"Well . . . ," Vest began.

"I'm not arguing," Kmetz interrupted. "It's an ambivalent answer."

"I . . . I am . . . I am not ambivalent," said Monahan. "I do not recall. I believe I did not . . . "

"Excuse me," said Vest. "Commander Monahan, you're not listening again. If you would just listen, and if you'd please, sit up."

Later, when Vest began questioning Monahan, the lawyer was able to specifically recount the manner in which he had described the immunity grant to Samples: that it was "a protection against the event, the incident itself."

Lt. Cmdr. Mike Ritter then testified that he had questioned Samples the day after his mast hearing, but primarily to get information on Miller and Tritt, the top two officers in Samples's squadron during Tailhook '91.

Before they began, Ritter told Samples it was OK to come clean. "You've got immunity and at this point, you can tell us anything that happened. And as long as you're honest, there's no problem. The only problem you can get into is if you make false statements."

"So you told him that you don't have to worry about prosecution or disciplinary action as long as you're telling the truth?" asked Kmetz.

"That's right," said Ritter.

During closing arguments on the motions on October 20, Kmetz said that Samples had been identified as being near the assault as early as January 1993 by Geiss, making him a suspect in the government's eyes. But the government had then deliberately deluded Samples about being given total immunity, he argued, in order to obtain an incriminating statement—that he had seen the tail end of the undressing of Julia Rodgers.

Morin explained that the government had not scheduled Truong two days after Samples in an attempt to nail Samples on a lie, knowing that Truong might implicate Samples in the assault.

"It wasn't a setup," said Morin. "The government had no inkling that Lieutenant Truong knew of the Julia Rodgers assault." He did note that Truong had previously lied several times to investigators about the assault.

"This is a case where the . . . key piece of evidence fell out of the blue in an immunized debrief," Morin said.

Kmetz also attacked Monahan's veracity. When the Navy lawyer was on the stand the day before, Kmetz said, "We dodged, we ducked, and then finally at the very end of his testimony he, in answer to the military judge's questioning, all of a sudden, he miraculously comes up with these exact words. Well, quite frankly, your honor, I don't believe Commander Monahan. I don't believe him. I believe he was untruthful on that stand. I don't believe a word of his testimony other than, "I don't recall . . . "[43]

On Monday, October 25, Vest denied three of Kmetz's lesser motions for dismissal. On Tuesday, the same day Cmdrs. Robert Yakeley and Gregory Peairs were cleared of any wrongdoing by their fact-finding board, Vest rejected Kmetz's ace in the hole. Samples, said Vest, must have known he had been given testimonial immunity.[44]

Vest's 2 p.m. rejection meant Samples' court-martial would begin as scheduled the next day. Kmetz called co-counsel Lt. Timothy Keck to see if the Navy lawyer knew anyone up in appellate defense at the United States Court of Military Appeals in Washington. Keck did, but that attorney was working another case.

Without an insider to help smooth things, Kmetz called appellate defense at around 4 p.m. to ask if they would consider accepting an appeal of Vest's ruling, and by the way, would they request a stay of Samples' court-martial?

Appellate defense accepted the case. Kmetz spent the evening in his Norfolk office, talking with Lt. David P. Sheldon and faxing him documents relating to Sample's case.

At 8 a.m. Wednesday, Sheldon entered the Washington court to file a request to stay Samples' court-martial. At the same time, Kmetz, Keck, and the Navy prosecutors were in Vest's office in pretrial session.

Kmetz told Vest that a petition for extraordinary writ was being filed as they spoke, but Vest didn't seem too concerned. "Well, that's your right," he said, in his soft drawl.

At 9 a.m., Vest brought the court to order and announced that Kmetz had asked for an extraordinary writ from the U.S. Court of Military Appeals to abate the Samples court-martial while they ruled on his appeal of the immunity issue.

Kmetz was confident the petition was going to be accepted quickly, but he needed to buy some time. So he asked Vest to reconsider his denial of the immunity motion, saying the testimony of Monahan, Ritter, and Walinski proved Samples had been given *de facto* transactional immunity.

"In what respect?" asked Vest.

"Judge, I don't want to . . . I don't want to argue with you, judge, but . . . "

"Well, you're going to have to," said Vest.

" . . . we disagree with your findings," said Kmetz. The testimony of Monahan, Ritter and Walinski, he said, made it clear that Samples had been given "a grant of *de facto* immunity."

Vest countered that he had cited case law to back up his findings. As he reiterated those findings, a Navy legalman entered the court and leaned over the bar to whisper something to Keck. Out of the corner of his eye, Kmetz got a thumbs-up and a smile from Keck.

Vest concluded, adding that he wouldn't alter his findings.

"Yeah, I understand, judge," Kmetz said.

"Do you have any further specific aspects that you would like me to address?" asked Vest.

"Judge, it's my understanding that the Court of Military Appeals has stayed the proceedings as we speak, and that you'll be receiving a phone call momentarily," said Kmetz.

Vest was visibly irritated, but remained composed. "Very well. And who did you receive that information from?"

"I believe it was from the Appellate Defense up at NAMARA," Kmetz replied.

Keck jumped in. "Commander Cave just called a few moments ago, your Honor."

"Say again?" said Vest.

"Commander Cave, judge," said Kmetz. "I guess he's the assistant department head for Appellate Defense."

Vest nearly cut him off. "Well, the motion to reconsider is denied," he said, loudly. "The court will stand in recess."

That's the way it stood. Little more than an hour later, Vest announced that the high court had indeed accepted the case. Samples' court-martial had screeched to a halt barely ten minutes after it had begun.

The appeals court's acceptance of the case wasn't a judgment of the motion's merit, Kmetz said. They recognized there was a problem, and they wanted to review it.

Asked afterwards how he felt about possibly being cleared on a technicality, Samples said he wouldn't characterize the appeal that way. "I'm aware of when I think my rights were violated," he said. "I wouldn't want my case dismissed for something I didn't understand. In that case, I'd want my name cleared."[45]

Yakeley, cleared the day before, went back to Naval Air Systems Command in Washington, D.C., to continued working in the F/A-18 program branch. Peairs lost the job as the USS *Carl Vinson*'s executive officer due to the long delay in settling his case, but landed the same position aboard the carrier USS *Abraham Lincoln*. His long-delayed promotion to captain, he figured, couldn't be far behind.[46]

On October 30, the remaining assault charge on Tritt was dropped. Cmdr. Mark S. Utecht, who had been appointed by Reason after Vest had kicked Williams off the case, said Lts. Janssen and LoGuidice had failed to place Tritt at the spot Kim Ponikowski had said she was assaulted.

"Most compelling, however," Utecht wrote, "is the inability of Ensign Ponikowski to identify the accused as her assailant." Reason accepted his recommendation to drop the charge.

Utecht also recommended dropping a charge of conduct unbecoming an officer, and to handle the remaining charges of failing to stop subordinates from groping females and making a false official statement at an admiral's mast.[47]

Dropping the assault charge against Tritt left just one officer out of the original 140 Navy and Marine Corps suspects from Tailhook '91 who faced an assault charge: Samples.

The same day, Capt. Frederic Ludwig was cleared. Reached afterward, he took a positive tack. "I still love the Navy, and I love naval aviation," he said. "And I've learned that the Navy's justice system works if given the chance. I feel like I was treated fairly."[48]

All five of the officers who had been reinvestigated in Norfolk were now off the books. The remaining Marine cases at Quantico would end up being handled administratively. That left Samples, Miller, and Tritt on the Tailhook court-martial docket.

It was small consolation to Miller. He'd had it. He had been off the USS *Independence* since May, and had been stuck in his room at Little Creek since June. His career was dead-ending fast, and the legal bills were piling up. Plus, the Navy was refusing to reimburse him for temporary living expenses, saying he was in a disciplinary status.

On the morning of Friday the 29th, he told Don Marcari, his civilian attorney, that he would accept admiral's mast instead of proceeding with his trial. Then, he said, he would turn in his retirement papers.

Friday afternoon, he had a change of heart.

"We're going to court," said Marcari. "Maybe he got a little discouraged, but he got to thinking about it, and he's back on track."[49]

The following week, on November 4, Jeffry Williams and Robert Monahan, the number one and two lawyers for Tailhook convening authority Reason, were dismissed by Vest from any involvement with the Tailhook cases for their role in trying to cover up the attempt to obtain the privileged information on the 1992 crash of Miller's EA-6B.

That same day, Vest ordered the government to produce the written statement of the Prowler pilot taken by Lt. Cmdr. David Green—the same statement Ritter and Monahan had made a back-alley attempt to obtain.

Vest wanted to "protect" the information by ensuring that it was shared by defense attorneys. That knowledge would eliminate any temptation by the prosecution to use the information gained from the statement in court. Even though Ritter's notes of his discussion with

Green had been destroyed, Vest ordered that Miller attorney Lt. Cmdr. William Little be allowed to review the statement. He also ordered the government to produce Green so Little could conduct an interview.

There was only one person who could legally approve Little's review of the statement: Navy Secretary Dalton, who had to decide whether to invoke "executive privilege." If he invoked it, the information would remain protected, and Ritter would join Williams and Monahan on the sidelines. If he didn't, Little could read the report, and Dalton would in essence validate what Ritter and Monahan had done.

"The government can't do it," said Little. "It would set a dangerous precedent if it was released. If it's opened up in this case, the government would have to release it in other cases." The results of safety investigations, he said, "can't even be used in criminal investigations."[50]

On November 5, Little filed a motion to dismiss Miller's case for prosecutorial misconduct. Williams, Monahan and Ritter, Little wrote, violated military law "and the ethical responsibilities of an attorney." Invoking Reason's name to get the information, he wrote to Vest, "is more reprehensible."[51]

11

Where's Kelso?

For months, Robert Rae and the other defense attorneys had tire-
lessly banged the same old drum: We cannot properly defend our
clients without getting the discovery evidence, and we're not getting it
quickly enough.

The attorneys were especially anxious to get their hands on the
DOD-IG's Tailhook database. This "ZY index" contained nearly the
entire Department of Defense Inspector General investigation. With
roughly 3,000 statements on its disks, it was invaluable. Computer
searches for data would speed the discovery process immeasurably.
But until attorneys could actually get their hands on it, the statements
it contained weren't of much use.

When the database was finally produced in mid-October per the
order of military judge Capt. William T. Vest, the defense teams went
to work. For weeks, attorneys burned the midnight oil. In addition to
poring over statements, they quickly learned how to reset the database
to more easily cross-reference names and places.[1]

The results began paying off with the onset of Cmdr. Thomas Miller's
court-martial November 8. After unsuccessfully moving that Miller's
Article 32 pretrial investigation be re-opened, co-counsel Lt. Cmdr.
William C. Little asked Vest to dismiss charges because unlawful
command influence had been exercised in the case.

And on what grounds? asked Vest.

"Admiral Kelso was in the area of the pool patio on the evening of
Sept. 7, 1991," Little replied.

Prosecutor Lt. Cmdr. Carole Gaasch popped out of her chair. According to Kelso's statement, she said, he was not on the patio on Saturday
night; he had spent forty minutes there the night before.

Little countered that he had witnesses who said otherwise. One, Cmdr. Richard L. Martin, had seen Kelso, Navy air warfare chief Vice Adm. Richard M. Dunleavy, and Secretary of the Navy H. Lawrence Garrett III on the pool patio on Saturday night.

Gaasch questioned the relevancy of their presence to Miller's case. Little replied that Kelso was not only guilty of unlawful command influence, he also was an "accuser."

The basis of Little's motion, really two motions in one, was simple: Kelso, as acting Navy secretary, had illegally referred the charges for investigation since he himself was in the vicinity of and had seen the sexual hijinks and assaults the prosecution contended that Miller had seen but failed to stop. He was what was known legally as an "accuser."

And Kelso, Little noted, had already been disciplined by current Navy Secretary John Dalton for Tailhook. By not forwarding to Reason the investigation files of the admirals who had attended, including his own file, Kelso had exercised unlawful command influence on the proceedings.

Vest pulled out Kelso's interrogatory, or sworn written statement. Kelso went to dinner Friday night, it read, and afterward, took the elevator to the third floor and walked out onto the patio at about 10 p.m. He spent thirty to forty minutes there, speaking with Dunleavy, Vice Adm. John Fetterman and several junior officers.

"I see no reference to attendance on the pool patio on the 7th of September," Vest told Little.

Replied Little, "There are other statements."

Vest questioned the relevance. Little was ready.

"It goes to the ability of a subordinate to review this case or any case," he said, referring to Reason, the consolidated disposition authority or CDA, and his subordinate status to Kelso.

"Admiral Kelso may be a witness to this," Little argued. "He has an interest, and that interest would flow to anyone below him in the position of reviewing that case. Admiral Kelso, by appointing Vice Admiral Reason as CDA, has appointed a subordinate to call for a general court-martial in a case in which he has an interest."

Miller, the government claimed, had failed to stop subordinates from sexually harassing women on the patio. "If Admiral Kelso was on the patio at the same time, would he not have a similar duty?" Little asked.

"The patio is a huge area," said Gaasch. "These events happened in a small area."

Vest interrupted. Referring to Saturday night, he said, "The government's position is that Kelso was not on the patio. The defense position is that he was. I've got to resolve it. I think the defense has made a valid point. I've got to know the facts."

In his statements to DOD-IG, Kelso hadn't said that he *wasn't* on the patio on Saturday. He had only said that he *was* there on Friday.

Former Assistant Navy Secretary Barbara Pope had wanted senior commanders punished for allowing Tailhook to happen. Now, if the defense could produce the witnesses, the most senior officer present at Tailhook could go down in flames. And if Kelso went down, the government realized, so could the entire Tailhook investigation.

Little and Don Marcari, Miller's co-counsel, wanted to call fifty-three witnesses. Vest wasn't going to allow every one of them, but said he wanted to hear from the eleven the defense said could place Kelso on the patio on Saturday night.

Every statement had been hidden inside the long-withheld DOD-IG reports tucked away in the ZY index.

Vest asked the government to further explore the wording in Kelso's DOD-IG statement. "It's important for two reasons," said Vest. "I need to determine that to rule on the motion, and I need to know whether Admiral Kelso was there to rule on the case's merits."[2]

That afternoon, Navy damage control shifted into high gear. Kelso, spokesman Steve Pietropaoli said, left a Saturday night banquet for Secretary Garrett "around 9:30 or so. He then went to the casino, left, and went back to the hotel to get his stuff to check out, then left for Nellis (Air Force Base). So from 9:30 to about 11 p.m., he was in the casino."[3]

With Kelso back in the news, more than a few witnesses began to get sweaty palms about the statements they had first provided to investigators. The first witness to hedge did so that same evening. Rear Adm. James H. Finney had originally told investigators that he had seen Kelso on Saturday night. Reached at his Colorado Springs home outside Cheyenne Mountain, Colorado, where he now headed up North American Air Defense Combat Operations, he now said he'd been steered to that conclusion—and was having second thoughts.

"I can't tell for sure whether I saw him Saturday night or not," he said. "Obviously, I swear to my statement, and I took an oath to that effect. But during the testimony, I was led to believe then that I was incorrect."[4]

The taped interview went like this:

Question: "Did you see anybody you knew out on the deck that you recall seeing?"

Finney: "Oh, yes."

Question: "A lot of people?"

Finney: "A lot of people. And you asked me before, did I see the CNO Friday night. I saw him Saturday night out there."

Question: "About what time?"

Finney: "I'd say around 11:00, but that's, you know, plus or minus a few."

Question: "You sure?"

Finney said he was.

Question: "You sure that's not Friday night?"

Finney: "Yeah."

Question: "We think he left before Saturday night."

Finney: "You do?"

Question: "Yeah."

Finney: "OK. Well, maybe it was Friday night. I don't . . . "

Question: "I'm not trying to get you to change your mind. I'm just trying to get a sense for how firm your recollection is at this point."[5]

Another admiral, Vice Adm. William C. Bowes, had also placed Kelso on the patio on the convention's final night. Investigators here also appeared to attempt to steer the Sept. 8, 1992 interview. It was conducted by DOD-IG agent Mike Suessmann.

"Did you see the secretary on Saturday night?" Suessmann asked. Yes, Bowes responded. "Out on the deck?" Yes, again.

"Who was with him?" asked Suessmann. Bowes replied, "I think Dick Dunleavy and the CNO. I know there was a group there, and I don't think I even chatted with them. I stood nearby, but I don't think I . . . "

Suessmann interrupted. "Are you sure of the CNO? I don't think he was there then."

"Well, OK," said Bowes.

"Think about that," said Suessmann.

"OK. Maybe I'm . . . maybe it was the night before . . . "[6]

DOD-IG investigators had come under repeated criticism during the earlier hearings for leading witnesses with questions and inaccurately portraying their interviewees' answers in the reports of interview. Now, it looked as though they may have been doing so during some taped interviews, as well.

If the agents weren't steering, interviewees were doing some serious postinterview waffling. During the next several weeks, nearly every officer or official personally or professionally close to Kelso ended up either making changes to their original statements or claiming they had been misunderstood.

The next day, November 9, Vest told counsel for both sides to submit written questions to send out to Cmdr. Richard L. Martin, who was cruising through the Pacific Ocean aboard the aircraft carrier USS *Abraham Lincoln*.

Prosecutor Lt. Cmdr. Mike Ritter then called his first witness on the Kelso "accuser" motion. It was Maj. Michael T. Edwards, Kelso's Marine aide at the time of Tailhook, who was now assigned locally to Norfolk's Marine Security Force Battalion.

Edwards looked picture-perfect, his hair cut high and tight, his brown dress uniform crisp and impeccable. It was Oliver North at his 1987 Senate-hearing best.

Marines pride themselves on their integrity, on telling it like it is. Edwards was the perfect opening card to play.

"Admiral Kelso never went to the third floor on Saturday night," Edwards said firmly.

"Are you sure?" asked Ritter.

"I'm positive," replied Edwards, impassive, statuelike.

Edwards, as Kelso's traveling aide, testified that he, Kelso, Kelso's executive assistant Capt. Phil Howard and the rest of the entourage arrived at Las Vegas on Friday, September 6, at 5 p.m. After Kelso attended a banquet in his honor, Edwards accompanied admirals Kelso, Dunleavy, and Fetterman to the third floor patio for forty minutes.

On Saturday evening, Edwards said he lost sight of Kelso only while the admiral was attending a banquet honoring Garrett. Edwards had escorted Kelso to the banquet at 6:30 p.m., and then went back to Kelso's room to pack his belongings. He checked Kelso out of the hotel and returned to the banquet hall.

At 9:30, Kelso emerged and he, Adm. Robert J. "Rocky" Spane and Spane's son, a lieutenant junior grade, went to the adjacent casino to play craps "for an hour or so." Edwards said that he and Kelso then played slots for a while. At 11 p.m., Edwards said he and Kelso walked the "20 or 30 yards" from the casino to the main entrance. They were driven to Nellis, boarded the admiral's assigned Navy airplane and flew back to Washington.

Little asked Edwards if he had ever discussed Tailhook with Kelso. Edwards replied that while home in Mississippi on leave, Kelso had called him "about the time that Secretary Dalton was recommending Admiral Kelso's relief."

Kelso told him that reporters were asking to talk to Edwards about Kelso's actions at Tailhook, and, said Edwards, Kelso wanted to know if he could release his name to them. Edwards said he agreed.

Kelso, said Edwards, then asked: "And you can confirm that I was not on the third floor on Saturday night?"

"Absolutely," Edwards replied.[7]

A week later, the defense team for Cmdr. Gregory Tritt asked to join the Miller motion to dismiss all charges because Kelso's attendance at Tailhook gave him a personal interest in the Tailhook investigation. A similar motion was already pending in the Tritt case. But the Tritt motion, argued attorney Robert Rae, asked whether Kelso was on the pool patio on Friday night, as well. If he had been and it could be proven he had seen or been in a position to see misconduct, it could also be argued that Kelso had "failed to take appropriate action"—just as Tritt and Miller had been charged.

Vest joined the cases together. Rae then called his first witness against Kelso. It was the man who had directed the DOD-IG investigation.

No penetrating questions here. Rae simply asked Donald Mancuso about his April 15, 1993, interview with Kelso.

To put the interview in perspective, Mancuso said that he and agent Mike Suessmann had interviewed Kelso in July 1992, just after the agency's investigation had begun. Kelso recounted his basic story: He spent about forty-five minutes on the pool patio on Friday night. On Saturday, he left the Secretary of the Navy banquet, entered the casino to gamble for a bit, and then left for Washington without going back upstairs.

During the succeeding year, said Mancuso, the agency found that "there were a number of witnesses where when we reviewed their statements, particularly an aide that he had, Captain Howard . . . who appeared to indicate that Admiral Kelso may have been at some time on the pool patio area on Saturday evening."

At the outset of the 1993 meeting, Mancuso read Kelso his rights, advising him he was suspected of false swearing and giving a false statement. Kelso, however, said he had no recollection of being on the pool patio.

Mancuso told Kelso's attorney, Capt. Donald Guter, that the DOD-IG had no further need to speak with Kelso.

The agency did follow up, but hardly in the tough investigative manner taxpayers might have hoped for. Capt. Phil Howard, Kelso's executive assistant, had originally told agents that he and Kelso had gone up on the patio after the banquet.

He was given an opportunity to provide a revised statement. Howard then told agents that while he had been on the pool patio on Saturday night, he was unaware of Kelso's presence. And a second interview with Spane, Kelso's gambling partner and long-time friend, also corroborated Kelso's story. But although they had spent ninety minutes gambling together Saturday night, Spane hadn't mentioned Kelso at all in his first statement.

Rae said the defense had stipulations of expected testimony from nine witnesses who said they had seen Kelso on the patio that night. He asked Mancuso why these witnesses weren't also reinterviewed. The agency, Mancuso said, saw no reason that Kelso, Spane, Edwards, and Howard—the second time, anyway—"would have intentionally given erroneous information."

But Kelso, said Mancuso, appeared to undergo considerable anguish while being questioned the second time. "I recall him, you know, shaking his head, thinking and trying to say, 'How could I have been? Maybe I went to change my clothes. Could I have possibly found my way to the third floor and crossed the patio?" Mancuso said. And Kelso never stated with absolute certainty that he hadn't been on the patio on Saturday night. Kelso had said he didn't visit the patio "to the best of my recollection."

After a recess, Vest began hearing opening arguments on the motion that would make or break the government's case. Was Adm. Frank B. Kelso an accuser? Was his personal interest in the case such that he had no right to have, in essence, ordered the investigation? Lt. Cmdr. Christopher Morin, the government prosecutor, argued otherwise. "There's no evidence before the court that that's the case here," Morin said.

To counter Morin, Rae stood and read the text of a charge still facing both Tritt and Miller, changing the name, rank and title of the accused in the process.

"In that Admiral Frank B. Kelso, U.S. Navy, chief of naval operations, while assigned as chief of naval operations, in attending the 1991 Tailhook Annual Symposium at the Hilton Hotel, Las Vegas, Nevada, did, on or about 7 September 1991 and 6 September 1991, wrongfully and dishonorably fail to take appropriate action to stop a group of officers of the United States Navy, including subordinates assigned to his command, who were gathered together on the pool patio area outside suite 302, Hilton Hotel, and were engaged in touching females whose names are unknown on the buttocks with their hands."

Kelso hadn't been so charged. Rae's point was that the government could easily substitute Kelso for Tritt or Miller on the charge sheet, even if he had only been on the patio on Friday night, as he had claimed.

"He's in the same boat Friday night," argued Rae. "He's just as exposed as Commander Tritt and Commander Miller.[8]

On November 19, Vest ordered Kelso, Garrett, Howard, Spane, Dunleavy, and Fetterman to testify in Norfolk. He also ordered that the "flag files," the investigative files on all thirty-five admirals and generals who had attended Tailhook, now back in the DOD-IG's possession following Dalton's rulings, be turned over to counsel for both sides.

All of a sudden, Gregory Tritt, Thomas Miller, and David Samples had faded almost completely into the background. It was Frank B. Kelso who was on trial.

On Monday the 29th, the Powers courtroom at the Norfolk Naval Legal Service Office was filled with Navy lawyers and Kelso's entourage. Local reporters were joined by out-of-towners who made the trip down from Washington. In front of the rail, the tables were crowded. To the left of the onlookers sat the prosecutors: Lt. Cmdrs. Morin, Ritter, and Gaasch. On the right, several tables were pushed together to accommodate the defense teams: Little, Marcari, and defendant Miller, sitting alongside Rae, fellow attorneys Alan Bergstrom and Lt. Cmdr. Diane Karr, and Tritt, the co-defendant.

Vest opened the session at 9:44. Prior to Kelso's arrival, Little rose to tell Vest that the defense still had not received some of the discovery evidence Vest had approved for transfer. Little asked for a court order releasing "all documents maintained by the DOD-IG, the Navy inspector general, and the Naval Criminal Investigative Service."

Vest agreed. "It is being observed by the court that government counsel have been slow in producing—or receiving information from various sources," Vest said in his soft Virginia drawl. "I feel it's time that all information held by the government be released to the defense."

After telling defense attorneys that he wouldn't allow argumentative questioning of Kelso, he told the bailiff to bring him in.

Kelso, although not a tall man, looked impressive in his full dress blue uniform, his eyes wide open and intense, his trademark bushy gray eyebrows partially obscured by gold metal frame glasses. Ritter swore him in and, for the record, asked him to tell the court his position with the Navy.

"I am the chief of naval operations," he said in a soft, calm voice.

Kelso was aggressive on the stand, often not waiting for the questions to be finished before beginning his answer. Ritter asked what room he stayed in at Tailhook. Kelso replied, "Can I make a statement?" Vest said he could.

"I was in Rhode Island a week ago, and I don't remember what room number or floor I was on, either," said Kelso. He also later told prosecutor Ritter, "That hotel is so large, I wouldn't have known how to get to the area they call the pool patio without some help." The comments, defense attorneys later remarked, seemed aimed at casting Kelso, a brilliant man, as a slightly preoccupied and befuddled character—a sort of nutty professor.

Kelso then reiterated his itinerary, identical to the official Navy version. When Ritter asked Kelso how sure he was that he hadn't gone up to the third floor patio on Saturday night, Kelso cut him off.

"I'm positive I was not," he said.

"Sir, a number of people say that they saw you on the pool deck on Saturday night. What do you say to that?"

"I say they're mistaken," said Kelso, firmly.

"Do you have any personal interest, that is, anything other than official interest . . . "

"I have no personal interest in the case," Kelso said. "I have an official interest."

Miller attorney Little rose to ask Kelso to define what constituted personal interest. Kelso said that would be "if I had some desire as to what the outcome must be. I have no desire. I want the outcome to be fair under the Uniform Code of Military Justice."

Kelso had already testified he had been on the pool patio on Friday night. Garrett had told investigators he was there on Saturday. Little asked how much Kelso socialized with Garrett. Kelso said they spoke at the Saturday night banquet but emphasized, "I was not . . . on the pool patio with Mr. Garrett at any time," said Kelso. And, he added, "I was not in any suites at Tailhook."

"Do you recall when Secretary Garrett denied being in the admin suites on the third floor on Saturday evening?" Little asked.

Unbelievably, Kelso said no, but he remembered when a witness's statement was deleted from a Naval Investigative Service report because agent Beth Iorio thought it wasn't relevant.

"I talked to Mr. Garrett about that," said Kelso. "He was surprised. He did not know this information existed."

"Do you know why Mr. Garrett may have resigned as secretary of the Navy?"

"Objection again as to relevance," prosecutor Chris Morin chimed in.

"Overruled," said Vest.

Kelso said he told Garrett, "Sir, I think this is a relevant part of this investigation, it needs to be included as part of that investigation. We need to make sure it is."

It was about at that same time, in June 1992, that Kelso became aware that anyone, including himself, could be investigated, he said.

Rae rose to question Kelso. Who prepared the itinerary of his Tailhook activities? Kelso told Rae it had been prepared on June 9, 1992, by his public affairs spokeswoman, Cmdr. Debra Burnette, and his aide Howard, in response to a query from *New York Times* reporter Eric Schmitt. Other reporters, including the *Chicago Tribune*'s David Evans, had also requested the information.

Kelso also acknowledged that although Vice Adm. Reason had the authority to investigate flag officers subordinate to Kelso, the flag files had been withheld. Who specifically possessed the files wasn't explored. Kelso said the decision to hold them back came from the Department of Defense, but he couldn't say which office had done so.

Kelso then once again reviewed his Saturday night activities. His account was consistent with what he had previously stated.

He told Rae he couldn't accurately recount where different parts of the hotel were, saying, "the hotel is so big . . . I'm not familiar with the hotel."

He also said that although he had been standing on the patio twenty-to-thirty feet away from the party suites at one point on Friday night, he didn't see the fifteen feet by one foot sign over the sliding glass doors of one suite that read, "FREE LEG SHAVES!" Nor did he see any of the ten assaults investigators said took place on the patio that night—although at this point, anything the investigators had said on the subject of assualts was open to question.

He didn't hear a window break. He didn't know what was going on in the "Rhino" suite. And he hadn't known anyone had been assaulted at Tailhook until after he returned to Washington and finally heard that Lt. Paula Coughlin had been victimized on Saturday night.

Kelso was a career submarine officer. The 1991 convention was only his second Tailhook; he had also attended in 1986. But, he said, "I didn't realize or have any idea that there'd be the kind of problem we had in this Tailhook Symposium."

Rae wanted to verify Edwards's statement that he never lost sight of Kelso, especially on Saturday night. "So, is it possible, sir, that there was a period of time that Major Edwards was not with you that evening?"

"I suppose it was possible, but I doubt it," replied Kelso.

Rae asked Kelso whether he had received counseling from Dalton following the secretary's October reprimand of 33 admirals and generals. Said Kelso, "I was *provided* a letter of caution."

He showed Kelso Tritt's charge sheet, telling Kelso that Tritt had been charged with failing to stop subordinate officers who were accosting women on the pool patio.

"Now admiral, isn't it true that on the 6th of September, you were in the area outside of Suite 302 as well, in the—in other words, pool patio area?" said Rae.

Kelso didn't recall the date, then said he had been out there on Friday night for 30–40 minutes.

"Yes sir," said Rae. And if he had seen inappropriate conduct while out there, Rae wondered, "wouldn't it be fair to say that . . . you too could be subject to criminal prosecution?"

"Objection," said Morin. "He's asking for a legal conclusion."

"Sustained," said Vest.

Rae turned to the Mancuso's DOD-IG interviews. "Mr. Mancuso

testified last week that you could not state with absolute certainty that
you had not gone to the pool patio area," said Rae. "So, would he be
inaccurate in that regard?"

"I don't know what Mr. Mancuso said," said Kelso. "All I can tell
you is what I . . . what I remember I did."

"In fact," said Rae, "Mr. Mancuso stated that you agonized over
thinking about where you may have gone."

"I agonized, counselor, only in the sense that this was a very big
hotel," replied Kelso. "And to traverse it . . . the aide is normally set up
to move me from one area to the other." He said he didn't remember
specifics, but that "if I'd been on the third deck or the pool patio area as
I was on Friday night, I would have recognized it. And I wasn't there."

He also said he didn't think he had been with Spane the whole time
he was in the casino Saturday night, that he might have been out of his
sight for fifteen to thirty minutes.

Rae noted that in the initial DOD-IG interview of Howard, conducted by Special Agent Jack Kennedy, Howard had stated that he
"went to the third deck" with Kelso Saturday night after the banquet.

"That's a false statement as far as I remember," said Kelso.

"Were you aware of the DOD-IG policy not to investigate or prosecute adultery cases in the Tailhook investigation?" asked Rae. No,
said Kelso.

"Were you aware of Admiral Reason's policy of not prosecuting
women in any of these cases?" asked Rae. After an objection was
overruled, Kelso first replied that he "never talked to Admiral Reason
from the time he started until today about any cases . . . that he's had
to deal with." Then, he added, "There was no discrimination between
men and women as far as how he would deal with the cases."

"Admiral, do you know Admiral Paul Parcells?" Yes, said Kelso.
"Are you aware of his statement that he said he was in your company,
as well as the SecNav's company, on the third-floor patio area on that
Saturday night?" asked Rae.

He had heard that, said Kelso. And he knew of no reason for Parcells
to lie. But, said Kelso, "He's mistaken in this case."

Another admiral had also seen Kelso that night. Rae said that Vice
Adm. William Bowes had seen Kelso with Secretary Garrett in the
suites on Saturday night.

Replied Kelso, "I have no reason to believe he would not be truthful. But he was mistaken also."

What about Rear Adm. James Finney, asked Rae. He also claimed to have seen Kelso on the third-floor patio on Saturday night.

"I don't know what he said," said Kelso, "but if he said I was up there on Saturday night, he was mistaken."

Vest adjourned the hearing at 11 a.m. All told, Kelso had spent two hours on the stand.[9]

Outside, Kelso's entourage plowed through the swarm of reporters standing near the curb to a waiting car. He paused long enough for two questions. His brief replies: "I consider this a fair process," and, "I was not on the (third) floor on Saturday night. Thank you."[10]

That afternoon, former Navy Secretary H. Lawrence Garrett III took the stand. He told the court that after the Saturday night banquet, he had asked Kelso if he was "going down to the third deck to mingle with the troops." Kelso told him, he said, that he wasn't going to do that.

Later that night, Garrett told the court that "I'm absolutely positive I didn't see him." But when asked later by Rae if Garrett could have missed spotting Kelso in the midst of the pool patio throng, Garrett responded, "Yes, it's possible."[11]

Kelso's inner circle continued to file into Vest's courtroom over the next few days. The day after Kelso and Garrett testified, Capt. Philip G. Howard, then Kelso's top aide and principle adviser and now commander of Carrier Air Wing 17, took the stand.

Howard's story dovetailed almost perfectly with the Kelso-Edwards version. Kelso stayed on the patio Friday night, and didn't visit any suites. Kelso didn't visit the patio at all on Saturday, he testified.

Howard was simply reiterating the substance of his second interview with DOD-IG, conducted the day after Kelso was interviewed a second time.[12]

Howard's first statement, taken December 8, 1992, was not tape-recorded. As with nearly every other Tailhook interview, the interviewing agent took notes and later produced a report of interview.

After Howard's interview, special agent Jack Kennedy had written: "Saturday morning, CAPT Howard accompanied the CNO on a classified mission in another part of the state. They returned in the afternoon. . . . During the evening, he attended the banquet, made a short visit to the Las Vegas Hilton casino and went to the third floor, all with the CNO. Again, he estimated their entire time on the third floor did not exceed 45 minutes." At 11:30 p.m., wrote Kennedy, Kelso and Howard left the Hilton to fly home.[13]

In court, Howard explained how the second interview had come about. On April 14, 1993, Air Force Maj. Gen. John P. Jumper, then the top military aide to Defense Secretary Dick Cheney, had told Howard that "some people" had placed Kelso on the patio on Saturday evening.

The next morning, Kelso was reinterviewed by Pentagon agents who informed him that he was suspected of false swearing and making a false official statement.

Afterward, Kelso's top lawyer, Capt. Don Guter, told Howard that he was one of those people. "There's a disconnect there," he told Howard. "They think you escorted him up on the third floor on Saturday night."

Howard said he then called the DOD-IG's office on Army-Navy Drive in Arlington, just a stone's throw from the Pentagon, and asked to see the report of his interview and to talk to Kennedy.

An error had been made, he said. "Not once did I say that Admiral Kelso was on the third floor on Saturday night," he said, telling the court, "I wanted to go on the record with an accurate statement."

On Saturday night, he and Maj. Edwards had escorted Kelso from the banquet to the casino area, he said. "At some point," Kelso saw longtime friend Rocky Spane, and they started playing craps.

"I went up to the third floor," Howard said, spending about a half-hour out on the patio. He then went to the VX-4 suite, where he spent another thirty to forty minutes. He didn't see Kelso, he said. When he returned to the casino at roughly 11:30 p.m., he didn't see Kelso, either. Edwards, he said, told him, "He's playing slots."

Vest asked, "You were not aware of the CNO's whereabouts for a considerable amount of time while you were on the patio. Is that correct?"

"That is correct," replied Howard. He added that upon his return to the casino, he asked Edwards, "Have you been with Admiral Kelso the entire time?" Replied Edwards, "He has not left my sight."

At the defense table, eyebrows shot up. Why, on the night of September 7, 1991, would Howard have expressed concern about whether Edwards knew of Kelso's every move? Didn't he trust Edwards to do his job properly? Why would he bother to ask the question?

Howard was also questioned about his role in recreating post-Tailhook itineraries for Kelso. One had been written in response to the *Times* and *Tribune* queries. But another was created as sort of a crib sheet for Kelso's first interview with DOD-IG, in July 1992.

When that itinerary was given to Kelso for his review, Howard testified, Kelso remarked, "There's no way I could have gone on the third floor on Saturday night, right?"

"Now, why . . . why would he say that?" Vest asked.

"Because he depended on us to, in fact, account for his whereabouts and make sure he was at the right place at the right time," Howard replied.

"Well," said Vest, "why was that an issue?"

"You want an honest answer?" said Howard. "The man is so honest that he wouldn't want to give a wrong . . ."

Vest cut him off. "I'm not questioning his honesty, Captain. I'm questioning why this was an issue at the time."

"I don't think it was an issue, sir,"

"Well, why was the question asked if it was not an issue?"

Howard couldn't say. He recalled that Kelso had also remarked at the time, "Major Edwards is the key to my whereabouts."[14]

Afterward, Miller was steaming. "How come out of 3,000 people, he's the only one allowed to review his notes and change his story?" he blurted out in a hallway outside the courtroom.[15]

Actually, that wasn't true. Every admiral and senior official had been allowed to review the results of their interviews, whether recorded or in a written report of interview.

At the tail end of Howard's testimony on November 30, a non-Kelso issue briefly surfaced. Dalton had been advised by the new Navy Judge Advocate General, Rear Adm. Rick Grant, to delay a response to Vest's order for a decision on whether or not Dalton would allow the onetime use of the report on the March 1992 mishap that had involved Miller. Grant reportedly advised Dalton that "the time wasn't yet ripe."

Up until now, Vest had been cutting Dalton some slack on the issue. After all, Rick Grant was Vest's boss. But the wording of the reply didn't go down well with Vest.

"Apparently, the secretary feels the time is not ripe for a decision," Vest told prosecutors in a scolding tone of voice. "The time *is* ripe. I *expect* a decision."[16]

When Howard completed his testimony, he was followed to the stand by the naval officer who Navy Secretary John Dalton had said "was responsible for the failures at Tailhook."

Tall, confident, and now retired *Rear* Adm. Richard M. Dunleavy strode into the courtroom, nodded at Vest, and immediately seated himself in the witness stand before Morin could swear him in.

"This is a hell of a club," he said, looking around with a sort of deadpan incredulity.

Dunleavy affirmed that he was the senior naval aviator present at Tailhook. He had visited the third floor patio twice on Friday night, spending only one-and-a-half hours there before calling it a night. "I'm getting old," he cracked. "I couldn't do it like I used to."

For all the criticism one could level at Dunleavy for having condoned Tailhook's wild party atmosphere, he was, of all the Tailhook figures, the one senior officer who remained highly admired by the aviation community. That was because when he learned that the DOD-IG was interested in his story, Dunleavy had voluntarily gone straight to Army-Navy Drive to acknowledge his presence and leadership position at Tailhook. To aviators, Dunleavy didn't try to weasel his way out of the Tailhook mess. He was, as they termed it, "a stand-up guy."

"I was the senior naval aviator present, and the way I interpret it was I had to assume responsibility for my brothers, my shipmates," he told the court. "It's like the captain of a ship: You run it aground, you've got to take the hit. I was the responsible guy, and I've said that a thousand times."

That brutal honesty, plus Dunleavy's spirited personality, combined to create a memorable appearance in court.

Dunleavy described how he generally made his way around the third floor at Tailhook. In addition to walking about the patio, Dunleavy, often accompanied by his "partner," Vice Adm. John H. Fetterman, also made a point to visit his favorite suites: Attack Squadron 128, Strike Fighter Squadron 125, the "Top Gun" suite, and then back down the third-floor hallway.

"It looked like a Mardi Gras," said Dunleavy.

Dunleavy acknowledged that women and combat aviation had been an issue at Tailhook '91, particularly at the Saturday afternoon flag panel. He said he had heard booing and hissing at the mention of women flying combat jets, and had felt compelled to speak up.

"Hey, guys, this is a democratic society," he said he told the fliers.

Dunleavy spent a lot of time on the third-floor patio at Tailhook, he said, because he felt like it "was my duty to be there." He said he roamed the patio—"I'm a moving target"—in order to talk to as many different JOs, or junior officers, as possible.

"I almost make a ritual of staying away from the senior officers," he said. "I see them all the time. I always considered ourselves guests of the JOs."

Dunleavy said that after the Secretary of the Navy banquet, he had asked Kelso if he wanted "to make one more swing on the third deck to see the JOs." Kelso, he said, replied, "No. I'm tired. I've been at it all day. I have an early flight. I'm out of here."

Vest told Dunleavy that a number of witnesses had placed Kelso on the patio on Saturday night.

"To the best of my recollection, I do not remember seeing Admiral Kelso there," he said. Asked if he could have missed seeing him, Dunleavy replied, "Oh, sure."

But on Friday night, said Dunleavy, he had accompanied Kelso during his visit to the third floor.

"Yes, in fact, I escorted him, and we walked around," Dunleavy said. "From the patio, finally made a swing through the suites down the passageway, up to another suite and back out on the patio."

That directly contradicted Kelso's assertion that he didn't visit any of the suites at Tailhook.

Dunleavy tossed off a few more good lines. Asked by prosecutor Chris Morin if he felt like he'd been under suspicion of wrongdoing when first interviewed by DOD-IG, he replied, "That office suspected everybody in uniform. If you were west of the Mississippi and you were at Tailhook, you were guilty."

He also acknowledged that while he had never seen the actual leg-shaving, he remembered telling leg-shaver Rolando Diaz in 1990, "You did such a good job that we'll have to get you a bigger place next year."

When he was excused, he stood up and shook hands with Vest, and waved goodbye to Tritt and Miller, seated at the defense table. Even Vest was smiling at the irrepressible flier.[17]

By placing Kelso somewhere where he said he hadn't been, Dunleavy was the exception among the senior officers. And if others had previously implicated Kelso in statements, they, like Howard, were soon changing their tune. Others made finer, but significant, adjustments that brought their statements into lock-step with Kelso's itinerary.

On December 1, Vice Adm. Robert J. Spane took the stand. He had worked for Kelso when Kelso had been commander-in-chief of Atlantic Fleet; they were old friends.

Spane, a native of Ely, Nevada, enjoyed gambling. After the banquet, he testified, he went straight to the first craps table and played for an hour and a half. Kelso and Spane's son joined him "shortly" after he had begun to play. Kelso had testified that after he finished gambling, he left the hotel.

During cross-examination, Miller attorney Little noted that during his first statement for DOD-IG investigators, Spane hadn't said a word about being with Kelso on Saturday night.

"I wasn't asked," he replied. "That interview was about my actions at Tailhook, and I did not think it was appropriate to use Admiral Kelso to establish my whereabouts on Saturday night."[18]

At the next interview, held on April 17, 1993, a week before the second part of the DOD-IG's Tailhook report was released, Spane told the same story he now was recounting in court. His recollection of elapsed time was vague. He had told agents Kelso departed "right around midnight . . . it wasn't two in the morning and it wasn't eleven."

He had also said that Kelso arrived "certainly within 30 minutes" after he had begun gambling. "I mean, it wasn't an hour later, and it wasn't five minutes later. Something like that."[19]

Tritt attorney Robert Rae tried to pin him down on the time. "So it wasn't more than 30 minutes?" he asked.

Spane seemed much more certain. "No," he replied.

"No possibility?"

"No."

"Could it be 30 minutes plus or minus five minutes?" asked Rae.

"No, it couldn't," said Spane.

"Could you say how long you've been on the witness stand?" asked Rae.

"No, I couldn't," said Spane, smiling. It had been about fifty minutes.[20]

A curious trend was developing. Spane never mentioned Kelso before, but then could recall a specific amount of time spent with him in the casino. Kelso, wracked with uncertainty at his second DOD-IG interview, was suddenly absolutely positive about his whereabouts at the 1991 convention. Investigators were steering interviews. Initial statements were getting changed.

On the surface of it, the latter development wasn't surprising. In the early Tailhook hearings, the defense had pointed out repeated discrepancies between what DOD-IG agents had written in their reports of interview and what those same witnesses said they had said when seated in the witness stand.

These were different. Spane and Howard had been tape-recorded. There was no question about what had been said the first time. And while the prosecution would also call a number of witnesses who hadn't been taped and who said their statements didn't reflect the truth as they now recalled it, none blamed sloppy or erroneous note-keeping by DOD-IG agents. That had been the basis for most of the complaints in the early Tailhook cases.

Now, most simply said they must have been mistaken.

Despite the flip-flops, prosecutors hoped those who changed their statements would come across strongly enough to help convince Vest of the truth of Kelso's claim that he hadn't seen or committed any acts or wrongdoing at Tailhook.

Defense attorneys hoped that under cross-examination, changes made by those same witnesses would help make a clearer case that undue command influence had caused them to change their minds—and had been exercised throughout the investigation.

This portion of the case was the prosecution's strongest. Most of its witnesses were high-ranking and high-powered. Nearly all had good reason to be near Kelso at the convention. Their words carried a lot of weight.

But with full-time access to the ZY index, the defense now had its hands on several dozen statements that placed Kelso exactly where he said he hadn't been: on the third floor on Saturday night. Here the prosecution could only hope to cast doubt on the veracity or character of the witnesses.

The defense team's biggest task was to come up with witnesses who would back up their original statements—and would agree to appear in court. Like any judge, Vest would place more credence on in-court testimony than on sworn statements.

For those witnesses still in the Navy, it was asking a lot. Testifying against Kelso while still in uniform would take a lot of guts.

For retired Capt. Daniel P. Whalen, testifying on Kelso's behalf was a gut-wrenching experience. It was almost painful to watch.

Whalen, somewhat of a look-alike to famed actor Jimmy Stewart, had told DOD-IG agent Jack Kennedy during a December 9, 1992, interview that he had seen Kelso on the patio on Saturday night. The time Whalen said he had seen Kelso agreed with the roughly half-hour gap that Spane had testified existed between the time he had last seen Kelso at the banquet and the time he saw Kelso in the casino.[21]

Now, following Spane onto the witness stand in Norfolk, he was changing his story.

"Are you as positive now as you were prior to coming here that you had seen Admiral Kelso on the 7th?" asked Little.

"Am I as positive?" said Whalen. "No, I'm not."

When Little asked him why, Whalen replied that he now knew there was sworn testimony from Kelso and Howard stating otherwise.

Little showed him the report of his DOD-IG interview. "And in that interview, do you recall telling the agent that you saw Admiral Kelso on the pool patio on Saturday evening?"

"Yes," Whalen replied.

During cross-examination by prosecutor Ritter, Whalen was asked to explain his lack of certainty about seeing Kelso that night.

"Because I'm absolutely trustful about Frank Kelso," Whalen said. "If he says, 'I wasn't there on Saturday night,' then Dan Whalen's got a problem." Kelso, he said, "has a damn good memory." And, he said, there weren't "two more honest people" than Kelso and Howard.

"We appreciate your opinion," Vest said softly, "but this court wants to hear what you saw that night while you were on the third deck. It's either, you either did see him, or you did not." What's it going to be?

"If it's going to be that black-and-white," said Whalen, "then I'm going to have to say I didn't see him on Saturday night."

"Are you being honest?"

"Yes, sir, because I don't believe . . . I believe if Kelso says he wasn't there . . . "

Vest interrupted. "Have you discussed your testimony with anyone else, except counsel?"

"No, sir," Whalen said.

As Whalen waffled, Vest repeatedly reminded him that he was under oath and was expected to tell the truth. Whalen denied that he had discussed his original story with anyone other than prosecutor Ritter.

Vest asked if Whalen remembered standing at the convention with former Pentagon co-worker Margaret Handy, a secretary. He said yes. "Are you aware that she's made a statement?" asked Vest. Whalen said no.

"Would it surprise you if she related that she saw Admiral Kelso on the third deck on Saturday night?" asked Vest. Whalen, appearing distraught, looked down and shook his head, replying, "No . . . no."

After a couple of questions by Tritt attorney Rae, Vest cut in once again, asking Whalen if he was having a difficult time testifying. Whalen said he wasn't.

But Whalen, who once worked for Kelso on a Pentagon-based leadership improvement team, admitted, "I'm strongly influenced by him." He repeated his conviction about Kelso's honesty, saying that if Kelso had been on the patio on Saturday night, "He'd sit right here in this chair . . . and tell you he was out there."

Vest cocked his head. "If Captain Whalen is under oath, sitting in that chair, will Captain Whalen be as honest as Admiral Kelso?" he asked.

"Yes, sir," Whalen replied. "I'm being as honest as Admiral Kelso."

The grilling continued for an hour. Whalen admitted that if he hadn't learned of Kelso's testimony, he'd still be standing by his original statement.[22]

Nearly as torn up was Lt. Ellen E. Moore, who told investigators on September 15, 1992, that she had seen Kelso on the pool deck area early Saturday evening.[23]

On the witness stand, her voice shaking badly, Moore tried to recant her story. "Currently, I do not have a specific recollection of seeing Admiral Kelso on the pool patio that Saturday," she said.

"Do you recall telling the IG that you saw Admirals Kelso and Dunleavy at the pool area on Saturday evening?" Little asked.

"I don't recall specifically addressing that with investigators," she said.

Asked to stand next to a map of the patio and circle the general area where she had hung out, she marked the same general area where other witnesses had said they had seen Kelso on Saturday night. She did remember seeing a group of people "around a senior officer, an elderly gentleman," but said she didn't recognize the man. She added that she wouldn't recognize Dunleavy or Kelso.

Vest read the pertinent part of her original statement out loud. "I believe it could be inaccurate," Moore said.

Vest leaned over the right side of the bench toward Moore, peering down over the top of his brown bifocals. "Have you talked with anyone about your testimony?" he asked.

"With my boss at work, Commander Don Morehead," she said.

"Why?" asked Vest.

"I have an ambiguous recollection," she said. "I would feel more comfortable if I had clearer recollections."

"Were you aware during that conversation that Admiral Kelso's location was an issue in this trial?" asked Vest.

"Yes," said Moore. She had heard through the media.

"You understand that as a witness, you're sworn to tell the truth," said Vest.

"I have a problem with my potentially getting caught up in misrepresenting my ambiguity," said Moore, creating one of history's all-time ambiguous answers. She told Little she was concerned that she would be the only witness who could place Kelso on the patio on Saturday.

Later, she told Rae, "I have no reason to disbelieve the agents. But I have no current recollection of making the statement."[24]

Far more composed was Margaret C. Handy. A tall, soft-spoken civilian Navy secretary, she had worked for Dunleavy for two years, and been flown to Tailhook at taxpayer expense. She had told DOD-IG investigators she had seen Garrett with Dunleavy and Kelso on the poolside patio on Saturday night "after the dinner."

In court, that changed. "I remember Admirals Dunleavy, Fetterman, and Kelso walking through the patio one evening," she said. "I don't recall which evening."

Before and after Handy's testimony, Vest said he was becoming concerned about "the institutional pressures that I think have been demonstrated at least several times in this court."[25]

At this point, nearly every witness produced by the prosecution had been either a senior officer close to Kelso, a trusted aide, or a long-time Pentagon employee. Only Moore was an outsider, and her weak performance on the stand lacked credibility.

The defense had received an unexpected bonus from Dunleavy. Now, its parade was about to begin in earnest, boosted by a string of favorable interview reports culled from the ZY database.

Cmdr. Kathleen Ramsey, a military judge in the Bremerton, Wash., district, told agents she saw Kelso, Garrett, and Dunleavy on the patio at around 10 p.m. Saturday.

Cmdr. Richard Martin, an air operations officer with Carrier Group 3, believed he remembered seeing Kelso and Dunleavy on Saturday, and thought the third person with the two officers was Garrett.

Robert Nordgren, a retired captain, pilot, and a former vice president of the Tailhook Association, saw Garrett on the patio deck in the vicinity of the VAW-129 suite on Saturday night. Garrett, he said, was with Kelso and Dunleavy. The group went into suites in the vicinity of the VS-41 suite, third from the main elevators, and VAW-110, home of the free leg shaves, to get beer, he said. Kelso left around 10:45 p.m., with Garrett fifteen minutes behind. Nordgren hadn't been drinking.

Cmdr. David Cronk said he returned to the patio on Saturday at 9 p.m. and noticed Garrett, Dunleavy and Kelso talking just outside the VX-5 suite, on the opposite side of the elevators, closer to the swimming pool. He saw Cmdr. Kenneth "Kilo" Parks, the only senior officer eventually called before Tailhook convening authority Vice Adm. J. Paul Reason for admiral's mast, go up and chat with the three men.

Lt. Brian Lawler said he was speaking with Fetterman at about 11 p.m. Saturday night when the admiral introduced him to Dunleavy and Kelso.

Lt. John Wood said he saw Garrett, Dunleavy and Kelso chatting together near the pool on Saturday night.

Lt. Jack Moriarty saw Garrett and Kelso out on the patio sometime after 9:30 p.m. Saturday.

Lt. James Quinn got out of an elevator at the third floor after the Saturday night banquet and followed Garrett, Kelso and Dunleavy, who'd gone up before him, out onto the patio. Dunleavy introduced him to Garrett, with whom he briefly chatted.

Cmdr. John Hoefel saw Garrett on the patio after the banquet, talking with Kelso and Dunleavy. They were only there a few minutes, he said, before walking toward the elevators.

Marine 1st Lt. Adam Tharp was introduced to Kelso and Fetterman on the patio sometime after 7 p.m. Saturday.

Lieutenant Junior Grade Mike King saw Kelso and Dunleavy on the patio on Saturday night for a short time.

Jill Cooke, a Navy civilian budget analyst, saw Kelso, Dunleavy and others on the patio in the early evening Saturday.

Lt. Cmdr. Larry Rice saw Garrett and Kelso at around 8 p.m. Saturday, hobnobbing with people in the patio area.

Cmdr. Michael Sturm saw Dunleavy and Kelso in the Naval Strike Warfare Center suite Saturday night after the banquet.

Cmdr. Charles Nesby saw Garrett and Kelso on Saturday night while cruising around the patio.

Retired Marine Col. Ray Powell said he had been chatting with Garrett for about twenty minutes in clear view of the leg shaving suite. Also standing with them was Kelso who, he said, walked in front of the window to the suite.

Ex-Marine Capt. Ronald Rives said he recognized three admirals who were on the patio on Saturday: Kelso, Dunleavy, and Fetterman.

Lt. Joe Fordham saw Kelso on the patio on Saturday night.

Lt. Cmdr. Richard Scudder saw Garrett, Dunleavy and Kelso outside suite 305, two doors away from the leg-shaving suite, on Saturday night after the banquet.

One witness, retired Marine Capt. Eugene "Mule" Holmberg, had told investigators he had seen both Garrett and Kelso in the "Rhino" suite early Friday evening. He had obviously mixed up his nights, since Garrett didn't arrive at Tailhook until Saturday afternoon. He also thought he had seen them in the suite on Saturday, but told agents he couldn't swear to it.

Holmberg also told an investigator that he had read a newspaper article quoting Garrett as saying he had only stuck his arm into the Rhino suite to get a beer. Holmberg later said this was "bullshit."

Holmberg's Tailhook roommate was retired Navy Senior Chief Petty Officer Robert Lawson. Lawson said he and Holmberg briefly visited the Rhino suite on Saturday along with Lawson's mother, Mrs. Sally Day, an eighty-year-old with fifteen Tailhooks under her belt. He said he never saw Garrett or Kelso in the Rhino suite, but thought he saw Kelso walking onto the patio from the doors leading from the central elevator.

The times witnesses said they had seen Kelso on the patio didn't all agree with his early evening schedule. Kelso had unquestionably attended the banquet, and was not on the patio from 7 p.m. to around 9:30 p.m. But most placed him on the patio following the banquet. And, just as significantly, in most of the same places.[26]

The defense certainly had the numbers. But what mattered most to Vest was how those witnesses would testify in court. While the original statements of Howard, Whalen, Handy, Moore, and Finney changed on the witness stand during the next couple of weeks, the contrary witnesses remained remarkably consistent with what they had told investigators.

"I saw Vice Admiral Dunleavy and Admiral Kelso and a civilian officer, Secretary of the Navy Garrett," Scudder testified. "I distinctly remember seeing those people when I emerged from the elevators after the banquet."

"I remember someone saying, 'Hey, there's the CNO,'" said Cronk. "I looked over and I distinctly remember seeing Admiral Kelso."

Said Nordgren, "I firmly believe that's the individual I saw departing the area on Saturday night."

"It was just a remarkable event," said Capt. Thomas J. Terrill. "At one point, just after a conversation ended, I looked up, and at one arm's length to my left was Admiral Kelso; at one arm's length to my right was Mr. Garrett."

Retired Marine Capt. Ronald Rives also saw Kelso on the patio after the flag banquet. "I was walking right toward him," he said.

"Does it surprise you that Admiral Dunleavy has said he didn't see Admiral Kelso on Saturday night?" asked prosecutor Lt. Cmdr. Carole Gaasch.

"It doesn't surprise me," replied Rives.

Vest cut in. "Why is that?"

"Because of the politics involved, sir," said Rives.

Asked if he knew Fetterman hadn't seen Kelso that night, Rives said that didn't surprise him, either.

"Do you believe Admirals Fetterman and Dunleavy are lying?" asked Gaasch.

"Well, somebody is," said Rives

"Is that a yes or a no?" she asked.

"That's a yes," said Rives.

Gaasch played her only trump card. "Captain, isn't it true that you were involuntarily separated from the Marine Corps?" A cheap shot, to be sure, but one that intimated that Rives could be holding a grudge against the Navy's top leader because he had been overseeing the congressionally mandated reduction in Navy personnel, part of the ongoing defense drawdown.

"Yes," he replied.[27]

By the second week in December, everyone's patience was wearing a bit thin. Someone dubbed it, "The hearing that wouldn't die." But the near-daily grind continued.

One story was particularly damning to the Kelso cause. Navy Reserve Capt. Robert L. Beck didn't see Kelso on Saturday, but had been chatting with him on the patio on Friday night when a group of nearby Navy fliers gathered around a couple of women and began chanting to get them to remove their bikini tops.

"Tits! Tits! Tits!" the men chanted. A crowd quickly grew.

"It was obvious the men were trying to get the young women to show their breasts," said Beck. The admiral said, 'Am I hearing what I think I'm hearing?'"

"If you think you heard the word, 'tits,' you're absolutely right," Beck replied.

Beck, a commercial airline pilot, 1966 graduate of the Naval Academy, and member of the same midshipman company there as Navy Secretary John Dalton, said he and Kelso couldn't see exactly what was going on in the center of the group. Suddenly, Beck said he and Kelso saw the top of a girl's bathing suit being held up triumphantly.

"I guess that's the end of that," Beck recalled Kelso saying. Beck replied, "Well, maybe, maybe not, admiral."

At this point, a new chant began. "Bush! Bush! Bush!" The fliers now wanted the bottoms removed. At this point, said Beck, the admiral began walking away to the left, hotel security arrived, and the crowd dispersed.

Beck told Rae that he had become aware of Kelso's denials the weekend before he testified. He had come to Norfolk with his reserve unit for a drill weekend, and had read a copy of *Soundings*, a local independent weekly newspaper aimed at Navy readers. The lead story, he said, was about the testimony of Kelso and Dunleavy, "specifically about Admiral Kelso and what he saw or didn't see that night."

"Are you up for admiral?" asked Rae.

"Eventually, yes," replied Beck.

"Does your testimony today alarm you in regards to that?"

"Yes," said Beck.[28]

Two admirals hedged a bit, but didn't completely refute their statements to investigators that they had seen Kelso on Saturday night. Said Rear Adm. Paul W. Parcells, "I still feel that I saw him there. But my degree of confidence in those feelings is very, very low."

"Sir, at the time you made the statement, did you believe it to be true?" asked Rae.

"Yes," Parcells replied.

And Vice Adm. William C. Bowes agreed that he had sworn to investigators that he had seen Kelso, Garrett and Dunleavy on the patio on Saturday night following the banquet. In court, he said, "I can't remember precisely seeing him there. I thought I had seen him."[29]

Marine aide Edwards was called back to testify. Edwards seemed as firm and assured as before. Friday night, Kelso, Fetterman and Dunleavy had gone up to the third floor for forty minutes.

No suites. "No. Absolutely not," Edwards said. No "tits, tits, tits" chants. "No sir. It didn't happen. There's no doubt in my mind."

On Saturday, he said he stayed "on the periphery" as Kelso and Spane gambled. Master Chief Roger Wise, Kelso's "flag writer," was getting the luggage at the front door area, about 100 feet away from the casino. Edwards said he went over to check with Wise, and did so two or three times while the pair gambled. It was very crowded, Edwards said.

He said that Kelso "was not as enthusiastic" as Dunleavy about visiting with naval aviators. "If Admiral Dunleavy had not been as enthusiastic as he was, we wouldn't have stayed a second night," said Edwards.

He also admitted he saw the "Free Leg Shaves" sign on Friday night. "It's fairly hard to miss, sir," he told Vest. "It's a fairly large sign." Like Howard, he said he never mentioned the sign to Kelso.

Late that Saturday night, Edwards said he knew it was time to go when a Tailhook representative came up and told him the van was ready to take the Kelso party to Nellis Air Force Base.

"How did that Tailhook representative know to find you in the casino?" asked Vest. Edwards didn't seem to understand.

"What time did the car arrive?" asked Vest.

"Sir, I don't know," said Edwards.

"Who was the driver?"

"I don't know."

"Did you tell them where you were going to be located?" asked Vest.

"I don't recall the details of that," said Edwards.

"That's a big hotel," said Vest, pressing. "How did they know where you'd be?"

"During the process of getting the luggage and checking out, we told a Tailhook representative," said Edwards.

Vest wasn't satisfied. "You seem to have a good recollection of other details, but you don't remember this. . . . You can remember

Wise asking you about Admiral Kelso's whereabouts. That's a very specific detail. And you can't remember who your driver was?"

"I don't remember everything crystal clear," said Edwards.

The Marine also reiterated that while at home in Mississippi on leave, Kelso had called, and that he had returned the call. Kelso had told him that Dalton, the new Navy secretary, had recommended that Kelso resign. "Look, I'd like to give him your name and number so he can call you," Edwards quoted Kelso as saying.

"He never once called me about his activities at Tailhook," said Edwards.

In a closing statement, Edwards said he had "the deepest admiration and respect for Admiral Kelso, but even more so for the naval service. I would never compromise my integrity for the service."[30]

Some particularly damning statements had been collected by the DOD-IG from a married couple. Lt. Cmdr. Paul Larocque said he had seen Garrett, Dunleavy, Kelso and Fetterman at the patio on both Friday and Saturday night. But his wife Karye provided an even more intriguing statement. She had seen Garrett and Kelso on the third floor sometime between 8 p.m. and 10 p.m., and thought it might have been in the VX-4 suite, up past the Rhino suite near the chief of naval air training party.

After she finished her DOD-IG interview, she had walked back into the room to speak again with agent Wayne Cooper. She said she had seen Paula Coughlin, dressed in a short leather mini-skirt, drinking in the third floor hallway with an unknown man. She was, said Larocque, "chugging" a bottle of champagne and rubbing her breasts up against several different men.[31]

In court on December 9, her husband's testimony corroborated his original statement. Then Karye Larocque took the stand.

After being sworn in, she told Miller attorney Little that she had not only seen Kelso and Garrett on the third floor on Saturday, but that she had seen them in the Rhino suite, where they watched two women drink liquor from a dispenser that ran through the large dildo attached to the rhinoceros mural. That corroborated Eugene Holmberg's recollection of their whereabouts, although Holmberg had possibly mixed up his nights.

It was sensational testimony. But when Rae rose to ask questions, problems began.

"Mrs. Larocque, would it be more appropriate for me to call you Dr. Larocque?"

"Whatever," she replied.

"Isn't it true that you're a surgeon?"

"Yes."[32]

Rae was asking in order to establish her attention to detail. The move backfired.

Two days later, with the help of a few phone calls by DOD-IG agent Peter Black, who was still in Norfolk assisting the Tailhook team, government prosecutors made a discovery: Larocque wasn't a doc.

No mention could be found of her at two of the three universities she had cited as attending. She had said she graduated from medical school in 1978, which would have made her twenty-two at the time, far too young to have earned such a degree. She said she had received an undergraduate degree from the University of Arizona, but the school's records showed her being dropped from the rolls there in 1978 for cutting classes.

"A fraud has been perpetrated on this court," prosecutor Lt. Cmdr. Carole Gaasch told Vest on December 14. "We move that her testimony be stricken." Vest gave the defense two days to counter.

Larocque had taken the defense by surprise. Alan Bergstrom, co-counsel for Tritt, tried this tack: "Mrs. Larocque testified as a person. She was not testifying as an expert witness."[33]

Reached by the Associated Press at her Florida home, she denied lying about her credentials. "Government attorneys are trying to use scare tactics," she said. "I made it clear in court that I was no longer a practicing physician, and haven't practiced since the late '80s. I made it clear that I was testifying as a Navy wife. I came forward because I felt very strongly that the truth was being masked.

"This whole thing is pretty ridiculous," she said, which was the perfect comment.[34]

The promised proof never materialized; Vest struck her testimony. Morin had fun with this one the next morning, greeting defense attorneys outside the courtroom with, "Hey, did you guys hear the good news? She really IS a surgeon. A tree surgeon!"

Rae was undaunted. "Even discounting Larocque's testimony, you have very, very credible witnesses placing him there on Saturday night. We've got enough to prosecute him for perjury right now," Rae told a reporter. "I think he's lied under oath."[35]

The hearing that wouldn't die heard its final testimony on Dec. 17, when former Assistant Secretary of the Navy for Manpower and Reserve Affairs Barbara S. Pope took the stand,

Pope had been called to testify by Vest to illuminate the atmosphere at the highest levels of the Navy during the Navy's Tailhook investigations. Pope hadn't attended Tailhook '91, although she had been invited by Richard Dunleavy.

Pope smiled widely as she was seated, projecting an aura of self-assurance. When Vest asked if he should address her as Madam Secretary, she said "Ms. Pope" or "Barbara" would do just fine.

Pope basically reiterated what she had told DOD-IG agents during a long, taped interview: When the Naval Investigative Service and Naval Inspector General reports were to be issued in April 1992, she had become concerned "that there was a broader issue, an issue of leadership and accountability that wasn't addressed, that was falling through the cracks between the NIS and the IG's investigation."

Pope said that in the spring of 1992, she was concerned "that not a single naval aviation flag, an aviator, had stepped forward and said, you know, 'I accept responsibility,' that said we've known this has been going on." She especially had wanted such an officer to speak to the aviation community at large, reasoning that coming from one of their own, such a statement might induce junior officers to be more forthright with investigators.

She expressed that concern to Kelso, she said.

His response, she said, "was that undue command influence was a concern."

Pope said she had known Kelso was going to attend Tailhook. Vest asked about a line from her taped DOD-IG statement in which she had said that in a post-Tailhook conversation with then-Navy Secretary Garrett, "We talked about he and the CNO going up, you know, after the banquet and having a drink on the patio."

She told Vest she had assumed that when Garrett had used the term "we," he meant that he had gone up to the patio with Kelso.

"I didn't realize he wasn't there on Saturday night," she said.

"Is that realization coming about because of his testimony or because of your lack of memory about this statement?" Vest asked.

"No, it was his . . . his testimony," Pope said. Later, she said she considered Kelso "a honorable man of integrity," and that she didn't believe he would lie.

Little asked Pope if it was true that she had been angry that senior officers weren't held accountable for what happened at Tailhook.

It was. "I didn't believe that nobody saw anything," she said. "I found it hard to believe."

"Now, were you so incensed that you had, in fact, threatened to resign your position?" asked Little.

Pope said that after being briefed on the reports, she went straight to then-Navy Secretary Garrett after he returned from the two-week trip to Australia. "I told him that if we didn't . . . do another report and look at what we needed to do about accountability and responsibility and the larger issues at hand, I would resign."

Little asked if then-Defense Secretary Dick Cheney had been aware of her demand. Pope said no.

"Were you aware of a threat to fire Secretary Garrett and Admiral Kelso if you did resign?" Little asked.

"I'm not aware of that," she said.

Little asked Pope to revisit the high-level concern over undue command influence. She had been told, she said, that it meant that if any of the charges went to trial, "they would be thrown out of court."[36]

Pope was excused, and final arguments began. Lt. Cmdr. Chris Morin began by arguing that the testimony of admirals Edwards, Fetterman, Dunleavy, and Spane "gives the best available snapshot" of Kelso's doings at Tailhook.

"The defense is relying on memories that are two or more years old," he said, although, it hardly needed to be argued, the memories of prosecution witnesses weren't any fresher.

Vest asked if Morin thought the defense witnesses had been untruthful.

"The government believes that every witness has been truthful to the best of his or her own recollection," he said.

Morin then ran down the list of defense witnesses, taking shots as he went. To attack the most credible witnesses, Morin noted that there had been discrepancies in minor details, such as how Kelso had been dressed after the Saturday banquet. Kelso had said he was in a coat and tie at dinner and didn't change; but some remembered him on the patio in a polo shirt.

Morin also took note of the amount of liquor some defense witnesses had consumed. Cmdr. David Cronk had admitted being drunk on Thursday, about half of a beer on Friday, and to drinking steadily on Saturday to the point where he "wouldn't have passed a breathalyzer test."

The strongest witnesses of the group—Cmdr. Kathleen Ramsey, the military judge; Navy Reserve Capt. Robert L. Beck, who had been standing with Kelso during the chanting that urged a woman to remove her top; and retired Marine Col. Ray Powell, said Morin, "were refuted by the testimony" of Kelso and others.

Although the subject was never broached in court, Ramsey, married to a Navy flier, had a reputation as a mighty wild Tailhook partier during her days as a young Navy lawyer. But one fellow lawyer said she was "far more circumspect in 1991 than in the old days." More importantly, no one questioned her truthfulness.

Of his own witnesses, Morin said that Lt. Ellen Moore was "anguished," and was suffering a "genuine conflict of interest," whatever that meant. Dan Whalen, asked three times in court if he had seen Kelso on Saturday night, had each time denied it.

And Kelso, said Morin, "is in the best position to know what his whereabouts were that evening." Kelso, he said, saw nothing untoward and didn't take part in any misconduct or inappropriate behavior.

As far as Saturday night's activities were concerned, Kelso couldn't be an "accuser," that is, essentially accusing Tritt and Miller of something he himself was guilty of, because "he wasn't there." Nor was Kelso's patio appearance on Friday night indictable, said Morin.

Citing case law, he told Vest the test of bringing such a charge was dependent on Kelso's being "so closely connected to the offense that a reasonable person would conclude that he had a personal interest in the matter." Kelso didn't do anything wrong, said Morin, so he didn't have such an interest.

And although Kelso had been read his rights prior to an April 1993 interview with DOD-IG agents, that didn't make him an accuser, either, Morin argued.

Vest seemed unswayed by Morin's course of reasoning.

"The government's position is that the evidence demonstrates conclusively that Admiral Kelso was not on the third deck on Saturday?" asked Vest.

"Absolutely, yes sir," Morin said.

"The evidence shows conclusively that Admiral Kelso was never in a position to see any inappropriate conduct?" Vest asked.

"Yes sir," said Morin. "There's no evidence he participated in any criminal misconduct, there's no evidence he observed any criminal behavior."

How could Morin say there was no evidence? Vest asked. Morin reluctantly admitted Beck's testimony qualified as such.

"We're using a reasonable man test here, aren't we?" said Vest. He made Morin reread the case law that he had just quoted, stating that the test for an "accuser" motion should hinge on whether a reasonable person, based on the evidence, would conclude that Kelso had a personal interest in the matter.

"The issue is whether or not he was ever in a position to observe what may be deemed to be inappropriate conduct and whether or not, if that occurred, he failed to take action to stop it," said Vest. "And then that would be conduct similar to, if not the same, as misconduct charged against the accuseds."

Morin said Beck was the only witness who saw misconduct on the third-floor patio.

"How do you explain Captain Beck's testimony?" Vest asked.

"The government simply believes he was mistaken," said Morin.

"Is he a liar?" asked Vest. "What's the government's position?"

"The government hesitates to call him a liar," Morin said. "The government thinks he was mistaken, just as these other witnesses are mistaken."

"Why was he mistaken?" asked Vest.

Ultimately, Morin admitted, he had no explanation "other than the passage of time, the nights being blurred."

After a recess, it was the defense's turn.

"The government hangs its hat totally on one issue," Little said. "Was Admiral Kelso present on the pool patio on Saturday, and . . . did he witness any misconduct? The defense position is that the issue of command influence goes much further than what the government projects to the court.

"Our position is that if you could be a witness, if you could be an accused, a victim or have some other personal responsibility or interest in the case, you are disqualified because it is a personal interest.

"Why . . . was Admiral Kelso interviewed?" Little asked, rhetorically. "He was interviewed because he would have knowledge or could have some knowledge of what was occurring there."

Kelso, Little said, "could be an accused. He was read his rights. He has a personal interest."

It was also a matter of personal involvement, Little argued. The defense was initially led to believe that the case files came directly from DOD-IG to the Tailhook team. But the DOD-IG, he said, first sent them to the secretary of the Navy. Kelso, he said, was acting secretary of the Navy.[37]

"There's a filter there," Little argued. "There were no referrals of admiral files here. No one senior to a captain was ever referred for any disciplinary action, even though we would ask the court to assume that there were people, admirals junior to Admiral Reason, that could have been referred. The appearance of impropriety, the appearance of . . . partiality. The appearance that when the public looks at all of the facts and circumstances, it would conclude that there is unfairness in the prosecution."

The government was arguing, said Little, that there wasn't enough evidence to put Kelso on the patio. The same evidence, he said, was being used against Miller and Tritt.

Then Rae rose to address Vest. What it all came down to, he said, was how much stock Vest wanted to put in the testimony of Kelso's inner circle.

"Here we have a question of, does their gold outweigh our numbers?" Rae asked. The prosecution's entire argument, he said, was based on the premise that "since Admiral Kelso said he didn't do it, he didn't do it." And, Rae argued, the court already had enough evidence for a pretrial investigating officer to recommend court-martial for Kelso on charges of making a false official statement.

Captain Beck, said Rae, is irrefutable. Lt. Cmdr. Richard Scudder, he said, was "virtually unrefuted."

"Whether one believes that Admiral Kelso is a perjurer is actually irrelevant," said Rae. "In appearances, he is nothing but a witness—a witness who has provided information that is very, very incredible when it's weighed against the other facts of this case.

"You've had the opportunity to see how unshakable many of the defense witnesses were," Rae said. The defense witnesses still in the Navy, he said, "have come here at much personal expense and very, very real exposure."

He turned back to Kelso's veracity. "Can we say that Admiral Kelso is wrong or mistaken? I don't care what we say, whether it's mistaken, lying, wrong. He is absolutely in a position that is untenable.

"We have the CNO, who was acting as the secretary of the Navy at that the time that the consolidated disposition authority was appointed," said Rae. "His testimony was that everyone below Admiral Reason was to be handled by Admiral Reason. This court knows that Admiral Reason did not receive everyone's files below that. Who took them? Where did they go? Back to the CNO, back to the SecNav."[38]

But trying to determine who had influenced whom was a nearly impossible task for the defense, Rae argued. "Acts of omission are very, very difficult for us to ferret out in this process." Even in the ZY index that was finally produced by the government, he said, "pieces of information that are critical to the defense are left out.

"So, where does this whole investigation go, and what do these last four weeks mean?" Rae asked. "It means that the entire system is on trial here. It means that these two individuals are not receiving—or cannot receive a fair trial here in this type of a situation because of Admiral Kelso's involvement.

"We have to assume that people are going to act honorably," he told Vest. "When there are appearances that show that people do not act honorably, then the court must step in.

"The government's burden is clear in this case," Rae said. "And it's by a very high standard, a preponderance of the evidence standard. They have not done that."

Kelso had been the focus of the recent hearings. But Rae wanted to make sure it was clear before the court what he felt the ultimate outcome should be if Vest ruled for the defense.

"The government has . . . conceded the fact that if Admiral Kelso is disqualified, that Admiral Reason is disqualified as well," said Rae. If Reason was disqualified, his entire investigation would go with him, and Tritt and Miller would be cleared.

"Well, there's no question about that," Vest said. But he added, "I do want to make it clear . . . there's no evidence before the court that Admiral Reason has in any way acted as an accuser in his own right." Rae agreed.

In conclusion, Rae pointed out, it was ultimately irrelevant whether Kelso's Saturday night activities as alleged by the defense had ever occurred. Kelso, by his own admission, had visited the patio on Friday night. He had an interest in the cases.

"The atmosphere of this trial should be free from the influence of any superior officer," Rae said, "and that's very, very key to the prosecution of these two officers. The Code demands that. I don't believe the government has met its burden of proof in this case. We would argue . . . that their arguments sometimes fall on the somewhat absurd premise that all of our witnesses are lying and all of their witnesses are telling the truth, We would ask that you weigh the credibility of each."

The soft-spoken Chris Morin stood up to rebut. "There has to be more than an appearance of evil in the air," he said. "There has to be some articulable, tangible proof. It's the government's position that there simply is no such proof in this case."

Morin argued that Kelso, Garrett, Spane, Dunleavy, Fetterman, Edwards and Howard "would have had to have engaged in the grossest conspiracy to come up with their (the defense's) version of events. It's fantastic to believe that happened."[39]

Finally, it was over. Only a ruling remained. Vest excused Tritt and Miller for the holidays.

On December 21, Dalton finally decided that the time was ripe for his decision on the release of a portion of the safety investigation on the 1992 EA-6B crash involving Miller. As expected by the defense, Dalton directed the trial counsel to assert "executive privilege" on his behalf to prevent further disclosure of James Hogan's witness statement—unless the government chose to allow Vest to view the information *in camera*, or in private, and then to share the information with the defense to ensure parity in the trial. Vest would decide that one after Christmas.[40]

For the time being, he had more important things on his mind. William T. Vest was facing the biggest decision of his judicial career. He loved the Navy. He was intensely patriotic. A decision for the defense would hit hard at all he held dear.

Moreover, Vest, unknown to most, had great respect for Kelso, an officer he deeply admired. Being placed in the position of having to judge Kelso's integrity was the most difficult call he had ever faced.[41]

For the next six weeks, Vest essentially sequestered himself, poring over the hearing transcripts, trying to exercise what Edmund Burke had termed, "the cold neutrality of an impartial judge."

12

Crash Landing

Was Frank Kelso lying? Was he guilty of a poor memory? Or could he really have gone to Tailhook and not seen what so many witnesses near him had seen?

Here was another possibility: submarine officer Frank B. Kelso both saw and heard at least some of what he was suspected of seeing and hearing, but simply didn't believe it was happening.

To an outsider, that was hard to swallow. Did Kelso, the chief of naval operations, really have absolutely no idea what took place at the annual convention of his aviation branch, even though he had attended one other Tailhook?

In Kelso's defense, his reputation for honesty preceded him. And despite his lofty position, Kelso was notoriously naive about shenanigans such as Tailhook featured; asked once how he could have missed the leg shave sign above a window on the third-floor pool patio, he replied, "Why would men want to get their legs shaved?"[1]

Researcher Pat Gormley may have been right when he called Kelso "a good guy with his head in the sand."

Kelso also had two physical shortcomings that could have had a significant effect on his ability to perceive what was happening at Tailhook.

Kelso was hard of hearing; late in his tenure as CNO, he began wearing a hearing aid. Kelso also wore glasses. When he was in large crowds and socializing, he tended when speaking with someone to take off his glasses and lean forward, focusing his attention and trying to hear.[2]

Without glasses, "Free Leg Shaves" might have been a blur. So much of what was being said could have been so much white noise.

There's no record of whether he followed his custom at Taihook '91. And even if he did, that didn't explain his reaction to the loud chant Beck said they heard together, or Powell's recollection of Kelso walking right past the window of the leg-shaving suite, or the trip to the Rhino suite Holmberg said Kelso made.

It was up to Capt. William T. Vest to sort it all out, and he had a literal file cabinet of information to sift through before he could rule on the motions. The pressure was enormous. Whatever he decided, he knew, would set off waves of protest.

Vest had demonstrated on the first day of Lt. David Samples' November court-martial hearing that, like any judge, he most definitely did not care to have his decisions appealed. That meant that the forthcoming decision would be a carefully written, appeal-proof ruling that wouldn't be too quick in coming.

The post-Christmas news lull out of Norfolk came to a temporary end on January 11, when the all-civilian U.S. Court of Military Appeals announced that it had denied Samples' motion to dismiss his case because he believed he had been issued what amounted to complete immunity from prosecution before facing an administrative hearing the previous June.[3] Mike Kmetz couldn't believe it.

"It sort of came as a shock, actually," Samples' attorney said. "I thought the facts were in our favor, and so was the law." He called the court's decision "intellectually dishonest."[4]

Samples' previous testimony, said Judge Robert E. Wiss, made it clear the flier had understood that his immunity was partial, despite Vest's ruling that (a) Cmdr. Robert Monahan, in briefing Samples on his immunity, had made a "partial misstatement of the law"; (b) prosecutor Lt. Cmdr. Mike Ritter's statement to Samples that "you don't have anything to worry about prosecution . . . as long as you're telling the truth"; and (c) DOD-IG agent Matthew Walinski's statement that if Samples told the truth his case would become a "washout."

Although the court denied the motion, the decision wasn't rendered without some embarrassingly harsh words for the Tailhook prosecutors—words that served as an indictment, at least in these cases, of the government's blinders-on approach to the judicial process.

"The assembly-line technique in this case that merged and blurred investigative and justice procedures is troublesome," Wiss wrote. "At best, it reflects a most curiously careless and amateurish approach to a very high-profile case by experienced military lawyers and investigators. At worst, it raises the possibility of a shadiness in respecting the rights of military members caught up in a criminal investigation that cannot be condoned.

"Where were the defense lawyers during all of this?," Wiss continued. "Why would seasoned military lawyers like Captain (Jeffry) Williams and Commander Monahan not ensure that petitioner's lawyers were at hand just to make sure that, as a practical matter, no problems ensued?" And, he argued, "why would a seasoned lawyer like Commander Monahan take it upon himself to 'explain' the grant of immunity in the first place? After all, it was clear and unambiguous; and any 'explanation' of it to the grantee should come from his own lawyer, rather than from a lawyer at the center of the investigative/prosecutorial effort."[5]

The Navy's shabby prosecution stood in stark contrast to the Marine effort at Quantico. Despite the idiosyncracies of Gen. Charles C. Krulak and one case in which a defense attorney had been verbally bullied, the Marine investigation was for the most part handled in a far less combative and over-reaching manner. The Navy, obviously, had a far larger caseload, but the pressure to finish it off quickly seemed largely self-induced.

As with the Navy, there were undoubtedly Marine fliers who had gone unpunished or gotten off more lightly than they should have. Krulak had to deal with the same lack of evidence that faced Reason. But instead of trying to reinvent the wheel, Krulak played the cards he was dealt, and avoided the reinvestigation debacle in which the Navy became mired. Even the highly sensitive and controversial decision to exonerate Capt. Gregory Bonam was seemingly handled properly. And when Krulak realized he had mishandled a hearing, as in Gabriel's case, he wasn't afraid to correct the mistake.[6]

For Navy prosecutors and the DOD-IG, the Court of Military Appeals ruling was an embarrassment, but a victory all the same. Samples was going to be court-martialed, pending the outcome of the Kelso motion.

The next two weeks brought no further news as Vest continued deliberating. Defense attorneys remained cautiously optimistic, but really didn't seem to know which way Vest would go.

On Friday, January 28, Samples and Kmetz asked to join the Miller-Tritt motion dismissing all charges.

Vest opened the session by noting that the appeals court had sustained his original ruling—flashing a quick victory smile at Kmetz in the process—and had returned the case to Vest for further action.

Vest then noted that at the end of the last session, the government was still short of fully complying with his previous order to produce all of the remaining files in the DOD-IG and Navy Inspector General offices. Some of the delay in reaching a decision on the Kelso motion, he said, was "due to the government delay in delivering additional evidence to the defense."

Vest was reluctant to let Samples join at this late date, but allowed Kmetz to argue his case. Kmetz briefly reiterated the accuser and unlawful command influence arguments already made by the Thomas Miller-Gregory Tritt team.

"I have several concerns about your request to join in the motion," said Vest, leaning forward and peering over the bridge of his brown-frame bifocals, as he tended to do when about to take some one to task. "There is a voluminous amount of evidence before this court—a record of trial approximately 1,500 pages in length, and thousands of pages of documents. Have you had a chance to review this?"

"We're in the process of doing that," said Kmetz. "We can file an affidavit that we have reviewed documents."

In a bit of a surprise, Tritt co-counsel Alan Bergstrom objected to the Samples motion, briefly displacing the notion that the defendants were "all in this together." But Bergstrom said nothing about the merits of Samples' case; he said he was concerned about the "speedy disposition" of the case against Tritt. Miller and his co-counsel Don Marcari, however, offered to let Samples in.

Vest then reviewed the Miller-Tritt motions for the court, ruling on each. First, he let stand the motion for appropriate relief claiming Kelso was an "accuser" and had exerted unlawful command influence on the investigation. He had denied the motion claiming selective prosecution—"there's no evidence of that before this court." Also denied was the motion based on vindictive prosecution—"it is without merit and is denied." And the motion claiming unconstitutional denial of due process, said Vest, "somewhat merges" the first two motions he was allowing. He took it under advisement, along with a motion protesting lack of a speedy trial. A motion for unconstitutional detailing of court-martial members, or military jurors, was "not ripe for consideration at this time."

With that, Vest ruled in favor of Samples. The last three Navy officers now accused of Tailhook misconduct were all in it together. In addition, Vest promised to expedite matters. "The military judge will not delay a decision any longer than necessary," he said. Kelso's version of the Tailhook story would stand or fall on February 8.

Vest then turned to the illegally obtained information contained in the report of the 1992 air crash involving Miller that Navy Secretary John Dalton had decided in late December to protect by authorizing prosecutors to assert "executive privilege."

According to Vest, a complex legal argument boiled down to this: the prosecution has to share the information it illicitly gained with the defense; if it doesn't, the defense can exercise the privilege and exclude it from use in the trial.

"My interpretation is that the government has invoked executive privilege," said Vest.

Morin moved for reconsideration. Vest promptly denied it.

"If the government wants to preserve the integrity of the investigative process, I can appreciate that," said Vest. "The court has a great understanding of the critical nature of the aircraft mishap investigative process and the confidentiality that attaches. A breach of the confidence attached to that investigative process is inexplicable.

"I have a duty to preserve the integrity of that process, but I also have an equal duty to protect the rights of the accuseds," Vest said. "The motion to reconsider is denied and the remainder of my ruling becomes effective immediately."

Morin asked if Vest was willing to consider an additional legal analysis.

"I'm not," said Vest. "Commander Morin, I'm not going to play games. You have invoked executive privilege."

Morin protested. He, personally, hadn't invoked the privilege.

"Are you going to make the information available?" asked Vest. "I'll reconsider."

Morin said the prosecution would not turn over the notes. Vest granted the defense motion to protect the information. It was the end of the line for Ritter, the prosecutor who had actually interviewed the source of the information.

"Commander Ritter is disqualified from any further involvement in this case," Vest said.

"This case," said Morin, "specifically, the case of United States versus Miller and Tritt . . . "

"And Tritt," said Vest.

Rae stood to twist the dagger. "Your Honor, I guess we, at this time, move to disqualify Lieutenant Commander Ritter and have him depart the proceedings."

Ritter rose to leave the courtroom. A deeply religious man, he was shattered. But Vest, not wanting to embarrass him any further, said Ritter could remain for the remainder of the hearing.

Rae asked Vest to issue an order preventing Ritter from passing on his case notes. Morin argued that Ritter should be free to do so. Vest disagreed, saying Ritter was bound by the rules protecting such information.

"Whatever information is held by Commander Ritter at this time is within the purview of the regulation," Vest said. Passing his notes to the prosecution, said Vest, would be a violation of that regulation.

"I do not sit in judgment of Commander Ritter," said Vest. "That's not my job. I get no pleasure, counsel, in having to take such action. I gave the government every opportunity to provide me with an acceptable alternative. The issue went all the way to the secretary of the Navy."[7]

The judging would be left to others. With the firing of Ritter, a total of three Navy lawyers had now been left in Tailhook's dust. The vindictive Williams, who had tried and failed to dominate the prosecution; the underling Monahan, who had displayed so little conviction on the witness stand that Vest himself actually had to remind the man in court to sit up straight and stop dodging the questions; and Ritter, who, apparently through inexperience or naiveté, had no idea such mishap reports were privileged information—at least, until he had been ordered by Monahan to get the information.

"We won a small victory today," said Miller attorney Don Marcari afterward. "He's probably the best prosecutor they have. He plays well in front of a judge."

Marcari, like Rae and Kmetz a former Navy lawyer, might have felt a little bit of empathy for the embattled Ritter. "You hate to see that happen," he said, diplomatically. "But it's clear that you can't use that information. It says so right on the front cover sheet."[8]

February 8 was overcast, cold, and a bit blustery. In the parking lot of the Norfolk Naval Base pass office, a small one-story building across Hampton Boulevard from Gate 5, the usual group of local print and broadcast reporters was swelled with out-of-towners. After the media passes were distributed, SurfLant spokesman Archie Galloway led a caravan of cars out of the lot to the right and down Hampton Boulevard to Gate 2. Once through, it was another four blocks to the Norfolk Naval Legal Service Office.

Inside, the Powers courtroom was packed. In front of the railing, on the spectators' left, Gaasch and Morin took their customary seats at the prosecution table; Ritter was conspicuously absent. On the right side, three tables had been pushed together to contain Miller, Tritt, Samples and their eight civilian and military attorneys. At 9 a.m. sharp, Vest brought the court to order.

"This has been a very difficult motion for this court," Vest opened, "and I appreciate both counsel's efforts. I have spent thousands of hours reviewing a 15–hundred-page record of trial, and hundreds of documents. I took nothing lightly. The findings are not designed for oral presentation."

The courtroom audience was rapt, on the edge of their seats. Vest's words crackled through the dead silence.

"It is hereby ordered, based upon the findings of this court, that Admiral Kelso is an 'accuser' within the meaning of Article 1 (9), UCMJ, with regard to each accused and (2) that there has been both actual and apparent unlawful command influence in each case. The charges against Commander Thomas R. Miller, U.S. Navy, Commander Gregory E. Tritt, U.S. Navy, and Lieutenant David Samples, U.S. Navy, are hereby dismissed without prejudice to the government's right to reinstate court-martial proceedings against the accused for the same offenses at a later date."

As nearly everyone's mouth hung open, Vest went on to disqualify Reason as convening authority, although he found his conduct "above reproach." He left Reason with three options: take no further action; take administrative or nonjudicial action, or forward the charges to "an authority senior in rank and command to Admiral Kelso" for disposition and possible reinstatement of charges.

It was Tuesday morning; Vest said Reason had until Friday morning to make a decision.

And that was it. "This hearing is adjourned," said Vest.

At the joyous defense table, there were handshakes and hugs all around. Greg Tritt leaned over the rail to hug and kiss his wife Rosa. Even Gaasch was smiling as she hurriedly left the courtroom, wearing the look of a person very relieved and anxious to get back to her family in San Diego.

This was historic, incomprehensible, momentarily numbing. A sitting military judge had ruled against the highest officer in his chain of command, dumping a multimillion dollar investigation in the process.

Afterwards, Tritt, standing on the lawn in front of the NLSO with his wife, Miller, Samples, and their attorneys, all in the midst of a throng of reporters and cameramen, said he wasn't yet ready to celebrate. "I'll be more thrilled Friday," he said. But his wide grin said otherwise.

Rosa Tritt was ecstatic. "I just want to thank God, my family and our lawyers for serving us," she said.

Samples seemed somewhat relieved, but wondered how to put his life back on track. "People don't realize how much this has affected my career," he said.

The resolute Miller wasn't yet ready to celebrate. "Absolutely not," he said, saying he still feared administrative action by Reason.

"It's been part of our life for the past year," Miller said. "A lot of people want to say things but have chosen not to. Admiral Dunleavy was the only one who came in and stood up early on. And Admiral Kelso . . . boy, would we like to talk to him."

Said Tritt, "I would like an invite to the Pentagon, and have the secretary of the Navy . . . apologize for this situation." And, he added, "those people who were given immunity should be brought back."

Rae said he couldn't imagine Reason prolonging Tailhook any further. "I think it's all over," he said. "I don't see the military wanting to jump back into the tar pit."

Rae said he couldn't see the government filing an appeal of Vest's decision. "That 111–page finding was written with appeal in mind," he said, which was true. In his analysis, Vest had leaned heavily on legal interpretations issued by both the U.S. and Navy-Marine Corps Courts of Military Appeal to support his findings.

New mast proceedings were not an option. A two-year statute of limitations exists on the imposition of nonjudicial punishment for a given incident.

"We could waive that," said the smiling Rae, "but we're never going to do that."

But, like Miller and Tritt, Rae was feeling a bit vindictive. "Secretary Dalton tried to fire Kelso before," he said. "He was overruled. But now he's got enough to court-martial Kelso, or bring him up on charges, or fire him. Here and now, I call for his resignation."

Rae added that the defense was considering filing civil suits against selected members of the prosecution "on a contingency basis."

One word kept cropping up in post-hearing comments about Vest's decision: "Gutty." Said Rae, "He has probably saved the military justice system in the Navy and all the services from appearing to be a pawn of those in power."[9]

It was certainly unprecedented. Apparently, "their gold," as Rae had termed it, had not outweighed the long and substantially credible line of defense witnesses.

Vest didn't exactly call Kelso a liar, although that was the essence of his far more diplomatic and legally correct finding. "Based on the convincing nature of the testimonial evidence and the many corroborating facts and circumstances surrounding such evidence, this court finds Adm. Kelso is in error in his assertion that he did not visit the patio on Saturday evening," Vest wrote.

Vest castigated Kelso for failing to forward to Reason the files on the admirals who had attended Tailhook, including his own, until ordered by the court, apparently basing this finding on the testimony of DOD-IG agent Don Mancuso. Kelso "attempted to shield his personal involvement at Tailhook '91 by denying he ever observed any inappropriate behavior on the part of junior aviators during his visit to Tailhook '91," Vest wrote. Withholding the files, he said, amounted to an effort to influence the investigation.[10]

Vest also ruled that the investigation by the DOD-IG was seriously flawed by inaccuracies in its reports—compiled, generally, from handwritten notes after talking with witnesses. "This novice approach to criminal investigation," he wrote, "resulted in the wholesale repudiation of the reports by many of the witnesses."[11]

By 12 noon EST, the story was all over the country. In Washington, officials seemed too stunned to react. Navy spokesman Steve Pietropaoli said that Dalton and Kelso were "reviewing" Vest's decision, and that "the first reactions should come from Admiral Reason."[12]

But in the national press, the battle lines were quickly drawn.

Editorialists wasted no time slamming Kelso and the Navy. John Hall of Media General News Service said if upheld, Vest's ruling would add up to "a massive cover-up and a deliberate manipulation of the Navy system of justice to shield the top brass," with Kelso at the top of the ladder. The Navy had bungled the investigation into the 1989 gun turret explosion aboard the USS *Iowa*; now they were at it again. Here was a prime example, said Hall, of the Navy's inability to competently handle internal investigations.[13]

On the opposite side, former Navy Secretary Sean O'Keefe fired a broadside at Vest via an Associated Press piece written by Suzanne Schafer. In her story, O'Keefe complained that it was his idea to appoint Reason, and said that Kelso shouldn't be punished for putting O'Keefe's plan into action.[14] But O'Keefe's argument was specious. Kelso was secretary of the Navy when the investigation was ordered; it was Kelso's investigation.

Other news stories quoted sources who questioned Vest's judgment, or were effusive in their praise for Kelso, widely and rightly recognized as having become a strong advocate of a more active role for women in the Navy. Other editorialists took a protective tack along the lines of, "The Frank Kelso I know would never lie."

One wondered if any of the critics had bothered to read the ruling— or knew of the high regard Vest had held for Kelso. Certainly, none of the quoted Kelso supporters, other than Barbara Pope during her own testimony, had ever attended a Tailhook hearing.

In his findings, Vest wove a meticulous reconstruction of Kelso's activities at Tailhook, giving the greatest weight to in-court testimony and drawing from some unlikely sources.

Much stock was placed in the testimony of Vice Adm. Richard Dunleavy, who said that he had escorted Kelso through the suites on Friday night. Dunleavy had testified that "we swing out through the patio and then up, usually 128, because for me it is the walkway in there, and then back out again."

Dunleavy meant that the group had entered suite 307, that of Fighter Squadron 128, from the patio through its sliding glass doors. They could then enter the third floor hallway and visit other suites and come back out the way they had come in. The "Rhino" suite was adjacent to 307.

Vest said that Kelso aide Edwards corroborated that to an extent, testifying that on Friday night, the Kelso party had entered the patio "from the doorway near room 308, the Rhino suite." Since Kelso had testified that they had first entered the patio from the central bank of elevators, they must have left the patio at some point to have reentered it as Edwards had testified.

Vest also found that Kelso witnessed leg-shaving activities. He based this mostly on the sworn statement of Marine Col. Raymond Powell, who said while on the patio from 10 to 11 p.m. on Saturday night that he had spent twenty minutes talking with Navy Secretary Garrett and a group of admirals that included Kelso.

They were standing "approximately 20 feet from the leg-shaving suite" . . . and "women were lined up waiting to get into the suite," said Powell. Powell added that someone in the group said that "the girls must like having their legs shaved." And Kelso, he said, walked in front of the window.

Kelso testified that he had told DOD-IG agents, "I didn't see any" leg shaving.

And Vest gave weight to what he termed Beck's "undisputed" testimony that he and Kelso had witnessed the "Tits! Tits! Tits!" incident on Friday night. The incident itself, wrote Vest, was corroborated by an October 27, 1992, statement given to the DOD-IG by Lt. Joseph Fordham.

In all, Vest found that thirty-four attendees had mentioned seeing Kelso on the patio on Friday or Saturday evening; almost all had placed him in the same general area and at nearly the same time; and a number of them placed Kelso on the patio with Garrett, who was only there on Saturday evening.

Of the thirty-four, Vest recapped the recollections of nineteen. Six—Thomas Terrill, Richard Scudder, John Hoefel, David Cronk, Robert Nordgren, and Ronald Rives, testified in court that they had seen him on Saturday night; one, Navy judge Kathleen Ramsey, confirmed her sighting in a written stipulation of expected testimony; the statements of five were confirmed either by the witnesses or by checking agents' notes. Four testified they could no longer clearly remember details, but confirmed the accuracy of their original statements. Three saw Kelso, but were unsure of the night.

Vest said that finding Kelso "in error" was supported by the "highly contradictory, and often implausible, nature of the testimony presented by the government."

When asked in court if he was on the patio Saturday evening, Kelso had replied, "I am positive I was not." But Vest found that "the degree of certainty expressed by Adm. Kelso . . . was much more definite than it was during his sworn statement to Mr. Suessmann, DCIS, on 15 April 1993, some nine months earlier." Kelso had told Suessmann he *could* have gone back to his room after the banquet, and that he didn't visit the third floor "to the best of my recollection."

According to Howard's testimony, Kelso had said to him during the reconstruction of his itinerary, "There's no way I could have gone on the third floor on Saturday night, right?"

Vest noted that Vice Adm. Robert Spane, who vouched so convincingly in court for having taught Kelso how to gamble that Saturday night, had never mentioned Kelso's presence during his October 14, 1992, DOD-IG interview. Spane later said he had not considered it appropriate to use Kelso to establish his own presence that night. He hadn't been so shy, noted Vest, about using others to do the same thing. He had also been told prior to his second DOD-IG interview, Vest said, that the agents were trying to establish Kelso's movements and whereabouts.

Vest took note of Kelso's September 1993 call to Edwards to ask if the major could confirm his movements on Saturday night. And Edwards had testified that he had been contacted by Capt. Donald Guter, Kelso's personal lawyer, to tell Edwards that his name had been mentioned during the second Kelso interview.

Vest also found contradictions between the cocksure Edwards and Master Chief Roger Wise, Kelso's flag writer. Edwards had said he had gone to Wise's room during the Saturday night banquet to check on luggage; Wise said the bags had already been collected. He also denied he had ever been asked by Edwards to move the flight home to an earlier time, as Edwards had testified.

And Howard had testified that when he returned to the casino area Saturday night from the third floor, he had found Edwards in the lobby, not the casino. When he asked about Kelso's whereabouts, Edwards had said he was playing craps. "He's about finished, and he's asked me if the plane was ready to return to Washington," Howard quoted Edwards as saying. Kelso, said Howard, showed up about ten minutes later.

The stories of Howard, Edwards, Kelso, and Spane intersected nicely. Too nicely, thought Vest,[15] who came very close to charging Edwards with perjury.[16] "This court also finds," wrote Vest, "unlike typical witness evidence concerning events several years past, Capt. Howard's in-court testimony is *noticeably aligned* with that of Adm. Kelso and Maj. Edwards regarding their activities immediately after the banquet." He also found that Howard's in-court testimony is "conspicuously different" from his first statement to DOD-IG.

In his original statement, the agent who had interviewed Howard the first time, Jack Kennedy, had written that Howard had said: "During the evening I attended the banquet, made a short visit to the Las Vegas Hilton casino, and went to the third floor, all with the CNO."

In his April 15, 1993 statement, Howard said that everything in the first statement was correct except for the phrase, "all with the CNO." And Kennedy later said he had made an error when typing up his original notes two weeks after the first interview. He had misread the symbol "w/" to mean "witness," as in, "witness to third floor," not "*with* someone to third floor." Nor had he mentioned Kelso in that area of his notes. He testified that he hadn't made such a transcription error in 19 years as an investigator.

His boss, Don Mancuso, testified that "w/" is routinely used to mean "with"—much as the rest of the English-speaking world uses it.

Finally, Vest noted a conversation related by Barbara Pope to DOD-IG agents on June 30, 1992, in which she had had a conversation about Tailhook with Navy Secretary Garrett and apparently spoken with him about activities of his that she had previously learned of in other briefings. "That was the first discussion we had," she told the agents, "I mean, right when all that came public about Paula Coughlin having been assaulted and her letter. We talked about his being there. We talked about he and the CNO going up, you know, after the banquet and having a drink on the patio."

Kelso's post-Tailhook knowledge had begun with weekly briefings on the Navy NIS and IG investigations. When receiving a final briefing from then-NIS chief Rear Adm. Mac Williams, Kelso had asked point-blank: "Is there anything in your investigation that's going to place the Secretary on the third floor at Tailhook?" Williams apparently lied and denied it, but the question itself, said Vest, "signaled Adm. Kelso's personal concern for any information that might link him to such conduct" and "discloses an early appreciation for the potential embarrassment."

To back up Kelso's version of events, his staff had produced an itinerary for consideration by the court. The original had been prepared in response to a media request for a "minute-by-minute, detailed account" of his time at Tailhook '91. Ultimately, wrote Vest, it lacked credibility because (a) it was prepared so long after the actual events; (b) it was "prepared at a time when official concern and press interest had been raised"; and (c) that "the rationale for its creation as an assist during the DCIS interview is obviously incorrect and misleading." Kelso's initial interview didn't take place until two months later.

Vest also found that although Kelso controlled the DOD-IG flag files, which were sealed for delivery to the next Navy secretary, he didn't give them to Reason to consider along with the other 18 Navy cases. They were only passed down to Norfolk, noted Vest, after a court order was issued near the end of 1993, well after John Dalton had assumed the top spot.

In his legal analysis, Vest wrote that according to military law, an accuser is someone with "an interest other than an official interest in the prosecution of the accused." That was more narrowly defined in a 1952 ruling by the U.S. Court of Military Appeals that "the test should be whether the appointed authority was so closely connected to the offense that *a reasonable person* would conclude that he has a personal interest in the matter." The interpretation was reiterated in 1981 and 1992 rulings by that same court.

In determining whether Kelso had observed sexual misconduct at Tailhook, Vest ruled that the admiral's interest was more than official. "Based on the totality of evidence presented and this court's related findings of fact, the answer can only be yes," Vest wrote.

He also ruled that since Kelso had been read his rights on one occasion, and that since "numerous, credible witnesses" had placed him on the third floor on Saturday evening, "a reasonable person would be forced to conclude that Adm. Kelso had a personal interest in this litigation."

In summary, wrote Vest, the "protective spirit" of the Uniform Code of Military Justice, Article 1 (9) "dictates that any military commander convening a court-martial calling a subordinate to account for an act of misconduct in violation of the UCMJ, *must be free from any suspicion of involvement*, directly or indirectly, in the same or any related act of misconduct.

"This is a matter of fundamental fairness," Vest wrote.

Vest ruled that Kelso, by withholding the flag files, "manipulated the initial investigation process and the subsequent CDA [consolidated disposition authority] process in a manner designed to shield his personal involvement in Tailhook 91." This, said Vest, amounted to unlawful command influence.

If it could have been determined that Kelso hadn't done so, said Vest, he still exerted *apparent* unlawful command influence. He quoted a 1983 U.S. Court of Military Appeals ruling: "Nothing erodes public confidence in the military justice system as quickly as the perception that the outcome of a trial, be it findings or sentence, is preordained by the improper exercise of command position."

When doubt exists about whether such influence has been wielded, Vest quoted the high court as saying, "the doubt must be resolved in favor of the accused."[17]

On the Friday following Vest's ruling, Navy Secretary Dalton released a statement praising Reason and calling Tailhook "a painful lesson for us. It is time to move on." He then added, "Before making a decision as to how to proceed with respect to Admiral Kelso, I want to carefully review the facts." It sounded as though Dalton, rebuffed the previous September when he had tried to fire Kelso, was now about to finish the job.

That same day, the Navy announced that Paula Coughlin had submitted a letter announcing her intention to resign her commission. The Navy provided no other details,[18] but NBC News obtained a copy of the letter and quoted Coughlin as saying the Tailhook assault "and the covert attacks on me that have followed have stripped me of my ability to serve."

It was also very nearly the end of the line for the Marines' Tailhook investigation at Quantico. On February 10, the Marines dismissed all charges against Lt. Col. Cass D. Howell.

Then a professor of military science at UCLA, Howell had been charged with sexual harassment, conduct unbecoming an officer, false swearing, and obstruction of justice. After DOD-IG agents discovered that the married Howell had spent Tailhook '91 with his girlfriend, they added an adultery charge. Howell had admitted she spent the night, but denied they had sex; the charge was later dropped.

Howell, a former Rhino, hadn't taken too well to being targeted, and was literally up in agents' faces during questioning. An internal Marine Corps memo characterizing its cases described Howell as "extremely disliked by all involved."

"The government plans to hammer him above all others," the memo read. "He will be the exhibit to show everyone the DON (Department of the Navy) is serious." Other than a long wait to be cleared, the hammer never fell.

Behind the scenes, the Marines were still trying to identify the captain who had assaulted Anne Merritt by tracking down some of the senior officers she had confided in concerning the assault.

Nothing ever officially came of the effort. But sources said that as of the spring of 1996, the captain's scheduled promotion to major had been held up by the Marines.[19]

On Friday morning, February 11, 1993, Tailhook officially crash-landed. In a press conference at SurfLant headquarters, the imposing Reason, resplendent in his dress blues, strode purposefully to the podium to deliver his decision on Vest's ruling in his deep-voiced, deliberate style.

"I have determined not to seek an appeal from his ruling," Reason told the gathering of reporters and camera operators. "I will take no further judicial action.

"The officers involved have been informed of this decision, and each has been directed to return to his normal duty assignment," Reason said. "As the convening authority for these courts-martial, it is properly my role to respect the ruling of the court and the judicial process."

Reason, acknowledging that he had been disqualified as the convening authority, emphasized that the disqualification was based solely on a technicality.

"At no time, and in no way was any attempt made, direct or indirect, real or implied, to influence my deliberations in Tailhook matters," he said.

This, he said, was it.[20] Only three cases were sent to court-martial. More than forty officers had stood before Reason during administrative "admiral's mast" hearings. Of these, twenty-eight received nonjudicial punishment. Miller, Tritt and Samples would all get "a letter," he said without elaboration; spokesman John Tull later said the letters would be nonpunitive and impermanent.[21]

Reason told reporters that he was happy with the work of his legal staff. Capt. Jeffry Williams, sitting in the rear of the room, said nothing.

Finally, asked if he thought there were fliers who had gone unpunished for their activities at Tailhook, Reason, choosing his words with his usual meticulous care, replied, "Yes. I'm almost certain of it." He paused, then continued.

"What would you have me do about that?" he said, sardonically. "Evidence is a requirement."[22]

Reason couldn't possibly have meant what he had said about the work of Jeffry Williams—unless he was loyal to his subordinate to a fault. His own decision-making aside, it was, in tandem with the Pentagon investigation, the work of his legal staff that had heaped so much criticism upon the investigation—and Reason in particular. Reason, a busy commander, had delegated the legal work and trusted his staff to handle it properly and expeditiously. As he had testified back in October, "They don't give me the details. I'm waiting for the results."[23]

Said a senior Navy official familiar with the case, "Vice Admiral Reason was a good man who received and acted on extremely bad legal advice."[24]

13

Repercussions

In Washington, the same day that Reason held his press conference, the embattled Kelso finally spoke out on Vest's ruling, and it wasn't pretty. "I said from the beginning I didn't see anything untoward at Tailhook and I stick by that," he angrily told ABC News. "I did nothing to influence the process. I'm going to continue to serve in my job."

By Tuesday, Kelso changed his tune, and announced that he would step down as the Navy's chief and retire two months early. The change of heart was the result of a high-level deal in which Kelso, in making his announcement, would at the same time receive ringing public endorsements from Dalton and new Defense Secretary William Perry.[1]

Perry also apparently agreed to take a shot at Vest.

The issue is the independence of the judiciary, a basic tenet of fair and open government. When high-ranking public officials blast judicial decisions, the charge of inappropriately wielding influence is difficult to duck. When President Clinton in March 1996 criticized U.S. District Court Judge Harold Baer, Jr., his own appointee, for tossing out a drug dealing case after ruling that police had no business stopping the car of the alleged dealer, he in turn was accused of applying untoward political pressure—especially when Baer later reversed his decision and admitted the evidence. Despite the criticism, Clinton maintained that "it is proper for the president to personally say if he disagrees with a judge's opinion."[2]

Perry, in openly criticizing one of the Navy's top jurists, apparently felt likewise. At Kelso's press conference, he quoted Pentagon Deputy Inspector General Derek J. Vander Schaaf as saying there was "no credible evidence that Admiral Kelso had specific knowledge of the misconduct, and no evidence that Admiral Kelso sought to thwart the Navy's internal investigation."

At this point, of course, Vander Schaaf and his agency didn't have a lot of credibility left. Perry's statement ignored the fact that the investigation had been sloppily conducted to begin with—one could hardly expect Vander Schaaf to admit that his own investigation had been botched—and that investigators had on many occasions put words in witnesses' mouths. It also grossly oversimplified Vest's ruling on the issue of Kelso's manipulation of the investigation.

But Perry's endorsement apparently was good enough for Kelso, who turned aside suggestions for a board of inquiry to clear his name.

"I clearly have become the lightning rod for Tailhook and I think it's in the best interest of the Navy if I proceed on and retire and we can get on with this business," he said. "I greatly regret that I did not have the foresight to be able to see that Tailhook could occur."[3]

Representative Patricia Schroeder, D-Colo., was equally regretful, but not out of sympathy for Kelso. The investigation, she said, was "mishandled from its tawdry beginning to today's embarrassing finale, with Defense Secretary William Perry defending the chief of naval operations, Frank Kelso. The Tailhook scandal should have been investigated by an outside, non-naval authority," she said. "What we now know, sadly, is that the Navy is incapable of investigating itself."[4]

Senator John Warner, a former Navy secretary, took a more diplomatic tack. The Virginia Republican said that Kelso "has wisely stepped up to one of the oldest traditions of the sea: As captain, he accepts full responsibility for all actions on his watch."[5]

That evening, on the Public Broadcasting System program, "The MacNeil/Lehrer Newshour," Jim Lehrer focused on Kelso and Tailhook. His guests were a retired vice admiral, a female Navy flier, and two powerful guests guaranteed to set off sparks: Schroeder, and former Assistant Secretary of the Navy Barbara Pope.

Schroeder opened by characterizing Vest's decision as "very clear." A few minutes later, Pope fired back. "I think the kinds of decisions the judge made were without a lot of validation," she said. The battle was joined.

"Is there anywhere else in society," said Schroeder, "where someone could be so damned by a decision—and this was a very damning decision about Admiral Kelso's role in this and the role in the cover-up—can you think of anyplace else where you could just say, 'Well, we don't go along with that decision, that decision wasn't right? Of course, we're not going to appeal it and prove we were right because, you see, it would just take more time and money. Everything is fine. I'll just retire a couple of months early. Have a nice day.'"

Later, Schroeder noted that even the independent newspaper *Navy Times* had called for Kelso's resignation. "Look at all the things that didn't work," she said. "The Navy Criminal Investigation Service had to be removed. That didn't work. The Navy investigators had to be removed. We had trouble with the inspector general in the Defense Department. And now we have this courageous captain down there who tries this case and says, 'Look, this was all about throwing over some younger officers to preserve some admiral's tail.'

"Now, I think that judge was right. And I think we ought to be talking about him. He really is saying, this is a government of laws and not of admirals, and he should be the hero here. And yet, I hear everybody trashing him and saying, 'Well, no, no . . . but no one wants to test his decision in a court of law outside the military system."

Pope disagreed, attacking Vest's ruling. "I think the judge has made two very serious errors in his decision," she said. Pope said that O'Keefe had put Kelso in an untenable position by leaving him the responsibility of referring the charges. She also slammed Vest because "he chose to believe the aviators who testified at the hearing above Frank Kelso . . . 1,500 of them who'd been interviewed by the Department of the Navy, more than that by the Department of Defense—they lied!"

Replied Schroeder, "Well, if they're so confident, why don't they appeal this decision?" She later noted that Pope had changed her own testimony. "You said you assumed he was out on the patio. Why would you say that in sworn testimony if you didn't think he was out there?"

Pope didn't answer, letting Lehrer change the subject.[6]

Some of the thirty-four reports of interview originally cited by the defense to support the Kelso motions included the very fliers Pope was talking about. Their reports of interview included statements that, like Kelso, they'd been read their rights because the DOD-IG suspected them of making a false statement or of criminal involvement.

Vest, however, placed the greatest weight on the testimony of

Dunleavy, Ray Powell, Beck, Terrill, Scudder, Hoefel, Cronk, Nordgren, Rives, and Ramsey.[7]

None were read their rights. None were given immunity to testify. None went to mast. While Pope had once said she had known Dunleavy to lie on aviation issues, the others were strong witnesses without apparent axes to grind. And Ramsey was a sitting military judge. If Barbara Pope couldn't believe her, who in the Navy could she believe?

After a week of editorials and speeches in Congress, the Tailhook headlines temporarily faded. But the scandal continued to surface as an major issue during congressional testimony and during Senate consideration of promotions and retirements.

And although an unfair association for the entire sea service, Tailhook and the Navy had now become so synonymous that the scandal earned a mention in any story having to do with women and every story concerning the social consequences of life in the Navy.

For instance, the previous year's decision to allow women to sail aboard combat ships produced a spate of stories in late spring, when the first sixty female crew members of the Norfolk-based aircraft carrier USS *Dwight D. Eisenhower* reported for duty March 7, and in the fall when, on October 20, the carrier's full complement of 415 women set sail for the Mediterranean, part of a crew of more than 5,000 men. Nearly every woman and a good number of the men on board were questioned before, during, and after about what it was like to sail aboard a combatant with a gender-integrated crew.

By all accounts the cruise was a success.[8] Much to the Navy's chagrin, nearly every story included a Tailhook reference.

All four military services were sullied on March 9, when four female service members testified before the then-House Armed Services Committee about being victimized for reporting sexual harassment—retaliation that took place in the supposedly more-enlightened climate that followed Tailhook. Military spokesmen pointed out that the cases were all a year old at the time, but all the services had been stressing equal opportunity a lot longer than that.

The women were a former Army private who left the service after superiors ignored her charges of harassment; an Air Force sergeant who received poor performance ratings after refusing to have sex with a superior; and a Marine Corps staff sergeant who, in the course of seeking justice against a fellow noncommissioned officer she accused of sexual harassment, was harassed by defense attorneys who questioned her sexual history.

The worst case, however, involved a Navy Reserve attorney. Lt. Darlene Simmons had accused her commander of harassment on two separate occasions, in 1991 and 1992. For her trouble, she was forced to undergo three days of psychiatric tests.

"Commanders in the field still may not say, loudly enough or often enough, that sexual harassment will not be tolerated," said Edwin Dorn, the assistant secretary of defense for personnel and readiness, testifying at the hearing.[9]

The subsequent nominations of two four-star admirals—one to retire with all of his stars intact, one to a prestigious command— were directly affected by the Simmons case.

Admiral Henry H. Mauz, Jr., like any three-or-four-star officer, had to gain Senate approval to retire at his final active-duty rank—otherwise, he'd receive a two-star pension. Simmons had accused the outgoing commander of Atlantic Fleet of failing to properly handle her sexual harassment case, and of suppressing the findings of his own command inquiry into the case.[10]

Vice Chief of Naval Operations Adm. Stanley R. Arthur, nominated to take the top spot in Pacific Command, stood accused of refusing to accept a formal complaint from Simmons alleging Mauz had been derelict in this duty.[11] Arthur was also taking flak for his ruling that a female officer, Lt. Rebecca Hansen, didn't make the cut in flight school not for her complaint of sexual harassment but for her failure to meet training requirements.

Independent inquiries by the Navy and the DOD-IG came to the same conclusion as did Arthur. But on June 24, the Navy bowed to Hansen's GOP Minnesota Sen. Dave Durenberger and withdrew Arthur's name.

The following Tuesday, Sen. Daniel K. Inouye, D-Hawaii, took exception to the nomination's demise on the Senate floor.

"Have we come to this—where the facts no longer matter, where appearances and imagery rule, where symbolism and symbolic value drive out realism and truth? Mr. President, we all decry sexual harassment. We were all appalled by the Navy's Tailhook scandal. But we have to stop this cycle of character assassination by insinuation. Enough is enough."

Mauz survived his September retirement hearing on a 92–6 vote, but only after four female senators withdrew their objections in return for closer scrutiny of military nominees. Said Sen. Patty Murray, D-Wash., "I remain deeply troubled by the difficulty I experienced when trying to get straight information and straight facts from the Navy" about the Mauz case.[13]

In mid-April, Perry and Joint Chiefs of Staff Chairman Gen. John Shalikashvili asked the Senate to allow Kelso to retire with four stars. "Shali," at least, admitted his endorsement was "likely to fuel charges that we in the services are operating an old boy network."

The issue, as framed in a *New York Times* editorial, wasn't the illustrious quality of Kelso's career, particularly his progressive attitude toward women's role in the Navy. It was, the *Times* argued, "his captaincy of the ship—what happened on his watch—and the signal his performance sends to the Navy and to the world."

That signal, said the *Times*, was this: that "the American military's old-boy network is, despite the general's disclaimer, operating at full tilt."[14]

Kelso, like Mauz, got his four stars. He left the Navy April 30.

In early May, William T. Vest announced that he would retire. A Navy statement said the retirement wasn't related to his handling of the Tailhook hearings. Vest, the Navy said, had applied months before to become a U.S. administrative law judge with the Social Security Administration's Office of Hearings and Appeals in Nashville, Tennessee. Vest praised "the integrity of the military judicial process, as well as the complete and total independence of the military's trial judges in fulfilling their judicial responsibility."[15]

Another thread that ran through the year's Tailhook news was the continuing saga of Paula Coughlin. On May 31, her resignation took effect. On September 8, she settled a lawsuit against the Tailhook Association—still alive and kicking, amazingly—out of court. The award was $400,000.

The following week, Coughlin took the Las Vegas Hilton and Hilton Hotels to court, claiming the resort failed to provide adequate security during the convention. Early on, Coughlin's defense was dealt a blow when U.S. District Court Judge Philip Pro ruled that the DOD-IG report, in which she was the only victim named, was replete with hearsay, not subject to cross-examination, and too unreliable to be admitted as evidence at her trial.

Ultimately, it didn't hurt. Nor did defense claims, voiced by attorney Eugene Wait, that Coughlin had been drinking with male fliers since 1984 and should have had the foresight to avoid the gantlet. "Miss Coughlin knew more about drinking aviators than the Hilton" did, Wait said at one point. Nor did the claim raised during videotaped testimony by Lt. Rolando Diaz that he shaved her legs while in her Navy uniform, and that Coughlin was drunk and "partying as hard as everyone else."

On October 28, the four-man, four-woman jury, after two days of deliberations, awarded Coughlin $1.7 million in compensatory damages for emotional distress. But the panel also ruled that the hotel and corporation had acted with malice, thus deciding to award punitive damages as well. Three days later, they handed Coughlin an additional $5 million in punitive damages, bringing the total award to $6.7 million.

"I think justice was served," Coughlin told reporters afterward. "This sends a message that you can't tolerate abusing women, even for making money."

Coughlin, now unemployed, said she didn't know what was next. "I'm hoping to slip into obscurity," she said. "I want to paint my house. I just want to go home."[16]

The following March, Pro, on appeal, decided to subtract the $400,000 Coughlin had received from the Tailhook Association from the compensatory damages awarded in the Hilton lawsuit; in addition, Nevada law limits punitive damages to three times the compensatory award. As a result, the total award was reduced to $5.2 million.

Eight other women filed suits against either the Hilton, the Tailhook Association, or both, among them Anne Merritt and Kim Ponikowski. Their settlements were not made public, but were said to be "significantly less" than Coughlin's.[17]

Still, Tailhook wouldn't die. Over the next two years, two ongoing story lines would dominate Tailhook's aftermath. One was an uncanny string of sexual harassment and assault cases that would continually pinch the sea service, despite its best official efforts to the contrary, right where it hurt.

The other was what amounted to the U.S. Senate Armed Services Committee's closed-door prosecution of the Tailhook cases.

The SASC is simultaneously the military's best friend and worst enemy. It is where money is appropriated for budget items ranging from funding for pay raises to favored weapons systems. It is also the final approving authority on all field-grade officer promotions—

and rightfully so, given the U.S. Constitution's insistence that the nation's military be subordinate to civilian leadership. Congress has the power to raise and support armed forces; and the president is the nation's commander in chief.

The Senate had paid an increasing amount of attention to upper-level Navy and Marine officer promotions since 1987, when a couple of rubber-stamped retirements and promotions backfired. Subsequently, the secretary of defense was required to notify the Senate Armed Services Committee, which handled military retirements and promotions, when general officer nominees or retirees had committed a crime. The intent was simple notification, not a report. But it escalated to the point where simply being charged with misconduct was enough to get the letter attached to one's file.

Greater and greater amounts of information were being required when, in 1992, the Navy's first Tailhook report was released. The Senate Armed Services Committee began requiring that the Navy Department tell the SASC whether nominees had been implicated in the Tailhook scandal. Gradually, the committee began requiring the complete investigation on each tainted nominee.

The SASC received its first notification about the Tailhook involvement of nominees in a letter attached to each promotion packet in which an assistant secretary of defense was required to state whether a nominee had or had not been "identified as potentially implicated in the Tailhook incident or in any cover-up," and so on.

By the DOD-IG's determination, there were 140 fliers implicated in Tailhook misconduct. Their names were maintained on special Marine and Navy rosters; Naval Bureau of Personnel staffers took to calling theirs the "wrong place, wrong time" list. When one of these officers was selected and approved for promotion, their promotion packet was flagged with a letter—and contained a synopsis of the results of the DOD-IG investigation into their case.[18]

Inclusion on these Tailhook Certification Lists meant that the screening of nominees' service records by Senate staffers would include an examination of the information DOD-IG had gathered on their Tailhook activities, even if they had been cleared or never charged with Tailhook misconduct.

Robert E. Stumpf had been cleared. It didn't matter.

While back in the seat of the Blue Angels' Number One jet during the 1994 season, Stumpf in March was nominated for promotion to captain. His nomination quickly sailed through the SASC, and he was confirmed by the full Senate on May 24.

In June, someone in the Navy realized the service had neglected to tell the SASC about Stumpf and Tailhook—although, given the level of interest in the scandal and the number of headlines Stumpf's case had generated less than a year before, it was difficult to believe that the flier's name didn't ring a bell with any of the committee's twenty-two members.[19]

The Navy informed the SASC.[20] Senators Sam Nunn and Strom Thurmond, then the respective chairman and ranking minority member of the committee, wrote Dalton and asked that Stumpf's appointment be delayed until the Navy forwarded "a complete report on this matter." The report, the senators told Dalton, was to contain all relevant information about Stumpf in both the Navy and DOD-IG reports, "a complete description of the conduct, review, and disposition of the allegations," an "analysis of CDR Stumpf's degree of cooperation with each investigation," everything that was considered by his promotion board, and "a step-by-step explanation for the failure of the Navy" to tell the Pentagon and the SASC why none of the above had been made available.[21]

The Navy was greatly upset by this renewed interest in Stumpf's case. But the SASC's power makes it difficult to complain about the handling of an officer's promotion when a service secretary such as Dalton has to turn around and ask the committee for billions in, say, new ship construction. Dalton tread carefully.

Nearly two months later, Dalton replied by letter that there was "no intent to avoid disclosure" about Stumpf's Tailhook involvement, and that he was apologetic for "this administrative error." At the same time, Dalton said, he wholeheartedly supported Stumpf's selection for promotion to captain. Dalton wrote that he had conducted an "exhaustive review," and was "convinced that CDR Stumpf did not engage in misconduct while attending Tailhook '91." The letter was accompanied by responses to specific questions raised by Nunn and Thurmond.[22]

The year turned and the committee, now headed by Thurmond following the Republican landslide in the 1994 elections, still wasn't satisfied with the level of response. The Navy, the committee felt, hadn't provided "all relevant information" about Stumpf contained in the investigations.[23]

Senior Pentagon officials refuted that accusation, saying the Navy wasted no time sending over the entire investigative report on Stumpf.

"That's bullshit," said one. "It's been over there since Day One," said the other.[24]

Whatever the answer, the committee remained displeased. Said one source close to the SASC, making an oblique reference to a hit movie about Navy fliers, "this guy is the Jesus Christ of 'Top Gun-dom.'" Out of all the suspects' files that had Tailhook letters attached, the source said, the only one missing the letter "just happens to be this guy's. We wonder just how much of a coincidence that is."

Another concern, the source said, was the lack of a sworn denial from Stumpf. "Did he ever say this stuff under oath?" the source asked. He hadn't; Stumpf never testified during his board of inquiry.[25]

The Stumpf review was centered in the SASC's Personnel Subcommittee, chaired by Sen. Daniel Coats, R-Ind. When promotions were being considered by the full committee, members would naturally defer to the subcommittee chairman's judgment, making Coats's opinion critical.

Coats was angry about the conduct reported at Tailhook, and wanted more information. He told Charlie Abell, the SASC's majority staff chief and chief of Coats's professional staff, to get it.[26]

Abell, a retired Army officer, asked the Navy for more information in two key areas: Stumpf's F/A-18 flight to Tailhook '91, and whether he was present during the convention in a Las Vegas Hilton hotel room when a junior officer received oral sex. While the issue seemed to have been beaten to death two years before in Norfolk, the committee apparently still didn't have a copy of the 1993 Navy board of inquiry into Stumpf's case.

Abell had some help in focusing his questions. They had originally been posed, noted the Navy chief of legislative affairs, Rear Adm. Robert J. Natter, in a March 29, 1995, letter accompanying the Navy's replies, at a meeting attended by Abell, Personnel minority staff chief P.T. Henry, and Vice Adm. Frank "Skip" Bowman, Navy personnel chief.

The source of the questions? Wrote Natter, "I forward responses to the two issues raised by recent anonymous telephone calls to your staff."[27]

One senior Navy official eyed such language with suspicion. Anonymous calls, he said, are a tool that staffers can use to raise favored issues. It's a game, he said: one calls another "anonymously," and the recipient can claim to have actually received an anonymous call.[28]

Although the information on Stumpf was trickling in, there was an additional obstacle to expeditious consideration of Stumpf's case. As the year advanced, debate intensified on the fiscal year 1996 defense authorization bill, taking up an increasing percentage of the committee's time. In the grand scheme of things, defense spending is a far higher priority than officer promotions.

While stymied on his promotion, Stumpf was still on an upwardly mobile career track. In the spring, he became deputy commander of Carrier Air Wing 3—a captain's slot.[29]

On April 4, 1995, the Navy, according to the committee, finally forwarded everything the committee wanted on Stumpf's case.[30] By late June, the full SASC still hadn't reviewed the documents, and wanted the Navy to delay promoting Stumpf until the review was complete. Since the Senate had already approved the promotion, the SASC could only ask.

The Navy, of course, bowed before the powerful committee. "They told us not to promote him," said Capt. Bill Harlow, Dalton's spokesman.[31] On June 28, three days before the promotion was to take effect, Stumpf received a letter to that effect from Bowman, who explained that promotions can be delayed "when there are questions about the professional qualifications of officers."

That scotched the job at CVW-3. But the Navy gave Stumpf a similar assignment, as deputy commander at Carrier Air Wing 17, also at Oceana Naval Air Station.

Stumpf's attorney expressed outrage not only at the Senate committee, but at the Navy for not standing up for the officer who many regarded as its top flier.

"I think it's unconscionable that the Navy is holding this up," said Charles Gittins. "The Senate already confirmed him. By the Constitution, they're done. The Constitution says, 'advice and consent.' Once they've done that, they're out of the picture."[32]

Stumpf wasn't the only officer in limbo.

The Navy confirmed in late August that the scheduled promotions of seven other officers—several of whom, like Stumpf, were cleared or never charged—were similarly being put on hold at the request of the SASC.[33]

On August 30, Dalton asked the SASC to promote the seven, saying he had reviewed their cases and that each had his "personal support." They were Cmdr. Christopher Remshak, who'd been in charge of the leg-shaving suite at Tailhook; Cmdrs. Thomas F. Nagelin, Jr. and Thomas G. Sobieck; and Lts. Michael S. Cushanick, Bryan J. Lower, Robert W. Ernst, and Mike Bryan.

Ernst, a helicopter pilot, told agents during questioning that he may have served alcohol to underage partiers while tending bar in the Tailhook party suite of HS-1, the suite out of which Julia Rodgers was carried into the hallway on the convention's final night. He was never formally charged, and was never brought to Norfolk to meet with Vice Adm. J. Paul Reason. His name had also been deleted from the Navy's promotion list at the Senate's request.

"Why is his name not on the list?" asked an incredulous Mike Powell, Ernst's attorney. "It shows me that something's wrong here. If they would do such sloppy work of pulling someone's name off the list who wasn't punished, that says, why did you have the CDA thing in the first place?

"When does it ever end?" Powell asked.[34]

Navy Lt. Mike Bryan was in the same boat as Ernst. Bryan, an A-6 Intruder pilot, told agents he had spent a few minutes in the third-floor hallway at Tailhook, at the entrance of what later became the gantlet, before walking out onto the patio. After two hours of highly antagonistic questioning, Bryan gave the agents a sworn statement that he hadn't seen any sexual misconduct. He was assured he was free and clear—agents even called his commander on the spot to tell him so.

Bryan was never charged, and didn't hear anything more about Tailhook until a month after the day he learned, in October 1994, that he had been selected for promotion to lieutenant commander. In November, assigned to the USS *Independence* and ashore in Japan, he got a call from Washington. His name hadn't been submitted to the Senate.

His name was finally submitted in May 1995. But two months later, no action had been taken, and Bryan, now training to fly the F/A-18 at Cecil Field, Florida, went to Washington to visit members of Congress, including Sen. John McCain, R-Ariz., to see what was up. Nothing changed.[35]

Dalton hadn't become a blind advocate for his fliers. In the wake of the Stumpf debacle, Dalton was also pulling those he felt undeserving off the promotion list.

California-based flier Lt. Cmdr. Jack Marshall was one of the latter. Marshall seemed at first glance an easy choice. He received a letter of admonition at his 1993 admiral's mast hearing in Norfolk for his day-glo dance with a stripper. He was subsequently forced to appear before a "show cause board," a panel of three captains, one of them a female. The board found no misconduct, and Marshall retained his commission.

Although the letter of admonition remained in his permanent personnel file, Marshall was in March 1995 selected for promotion to commander. On May 1, he received a letter from the chief of naval personnel stating that, because of the punitive letter's presence in his file, the Navy secretary would have to decide whether to recommend Marshall to the Senate for promotion.

Marshall, through attorney Alan Bergstrom, filed a petition in May 1995 with the all-civilian Board for Correction of Naval Records asking that all references to the nonjudicial punishment be removed from Marshall's file.

In July 1995, the B.C. & R. board decided on a 2 to 1 vote that Marshall was not guilty of conduct unbecoming an officer because he was never placed on notice that a dance with a stripper at a private party constituted same. The board ordered Marshall's record purged of the damning letter.

That sparked a long-distance, summer-long confrontation between Marshall and the assistant Navy secretary for manpower and reserve affairs, Bernard D. Rostker, that resulted in another B.C. & R review by a brand-new panel. In September, that panel also recommended clearing Marshall's record.

In October, Dalton wrote the SASC and recommended Marshall for promotion.

On December 7, Rostker ruled that Vice Adm. J. Paul Reason, who had originally heard Marshall's case in Norfolk, was "in a better position" to evaluate whether misconduct occurred. And as a lieutenant commander, Marshall, Rostker said, "should have known better." Rostker overturned the B.C. & R. decision.

Bergstrom was steamed. "We have a board of officers saying that Reason was wrong," he said. "We have a selection board saying he was wrong. And two B.C. & R. panels saying Marshall wasn't guilty."[36]

The Marines were also reviewing officers' files at the SASC's behest. One officer, a Marine who was questioned but never charged during the 1993 hearings at Quantico, was selected for major in 1995.

But his name was pulled off the promotion list before it was ever forwarded to the Senate.

Marine Capt. Jerry "Popeye" Doyle, an F/A-18 weapons officer with eleven years, two commands and an outstanding service record under his belt, figured the move was Tailhook-related, but he waited to learn exactly what "adverse material" the Corps had used to arrive at its decision.

A month later, the adverse material was in his hands. It was a copy of the old report of interview completed by the DOD-IG.

Doyle, a forward air controller with an infantry outfit during the Persian Gulf War, had partied in the Rhino suite, had admitted to drinking heavily at Tailhook. But he said he hadn't touched or groped anyone, and felt strongly that those who took part in the gantlet should have been severely punished: "Oh God, yes," he insisted.

"My response was that it was sort of double jeopardy," Doyle said of the withdrawn nomination. "General Krulak had seen everything they now presented to me, and he didn't take any administrative or criminal action. And now, suddenly, somebody other than the general officer appointed by the commandant was looking at the same material, saying I was not worthy of promotion."

Despite the promotion snafu, despite the investigative inaccuracies, despite being told by Marine lawyers during the infamous 1992 briefing at El Toro that he couldn't protect himself legally, Doyle, amazingly, said he wasn't bitter. "It would take more than one incident to make me bitter toward the Marine Corps," Doyle said, saying he had gotten the support of many senior Marines while trying to get reconsidered.

"Annoyed," Doyle finally termed his state of mind. "I'm not happy about it at all. I think it's wrong."[37]

The Marines pulled two others off promotion lists in the fall. One, Maj. Phil Gabriel, was found guilty at a June 1993 office hours hearing in Quantico, but Lt. Gen. Charles C. Krulak granted his appeal six months later, clearing his record. The other, Lt. Col. Daniel Driscoll, was found guilty of withholding information from government agents about the party suite he had supervised, but Krulak gave him no punishment, keeping his record clean, and later specifically recommended him for promotion.

In March 1996, both received letters from the Marines saying their promotions were being held up.[38]

None of the fliers so rebuffed had greater cause for complaint than Cmdr. Gregory E. Peairs. He had been waiting to sew on captain's stripes since 1992.

The approved promotion was put on hold pending the outcome of the Tailhook investigation. In 1993, Peairs was cleared by a Navy board of inquiry similar to Stumpf's. The female whose rear end he was accused of biting had admitted, in writing, that she in fact had bitten Peairs, not the other way around.

Two years later, he was still waiting for his promotion when, on June 15, 1995, he received a letter from Dalton saying his name had been deleted from the promotion list. In the interim, he had served a normal tour of duty as the executive officer of the aircraft carrier USS *Abraham Lincoln*—a job reserved for Navy captains.[39]

Another flier Dalton didn't boost seemed to have perhaps the strongest argument possible that he was innocent as charged. The DOD-IG said Lt. John M. Cooney had lied when he had denied seeing the gantlet form at Tailhook '91 on Saturday night. The charge was based on the statement of another lieutenant who said Cooney looked on that night as drunk fliers formed the gantlet.

Cooney, however, wasn't in Las Vegas on Saturday night. He was in San Diego. He had flown back on Saturday afternoon, and had receipts and witnesses to prove it.

On Thursday, September 5, Cooney and two buddies flew from San Diego to Las Vegas and Tailhook in a rented Cessna 172. They spent a day and two nights at the convention, taking in a Las Vegas revue after partying on Friday night.

The next morning, they returned to the airport, gassed up, and returned to California, arriving that afternoon.

That's the story he gave DOD-IG agents on two separate occasions. At the conclusion of the second interview, he was told he was "not going to have any problems." But on the Tailhook Referral Questionnaire agents completed for each of the original suspects whose files were forwarded to the Navy and Marines, agent Stephen Bankhead accused Cooney of making a false statement, saying Cooney "denied witnessing or having any knowledge concerning assaults" at Tailhook, yet "was reportedly present in the hallway during the gauntlet and did observe assaults."

Reason apparently didn't think much of Cooney's case because the flier was never charged nor brought to Norfolk for questioning. But two years later, Cooney learned in a June 1995 letter from the Naval Bureau of Personnel that because of his "involvement in Tailhook," his request to be transferred from the Naval Reserve to the regular Navy had been delayed until his case could be approved by the Senate."[40]

No one will ever know if Cooney witnessed misconduct on Friday night, and the witness, like many questioned long after the fact, was simply confused. But there is no proof Cooney did so, or had lied about same. Still, even with an alibi and witnesses, he was flagged down by his own service based on what amounted to innuendo.

On October 25, the SASC met in closed session to consider Stumpf's promotion, among others. The F/A-18 flight to Las Vegas by Stumpf and another flier was a concern. But Coats and the subcommittee members were much more concerned about Stumpf's presence in the Tailhook suite where the strippers performed. To Coats, this was immoral behavior, not be be condoned from any officer.

Stumpf's flight to Tailhook had been found during his 1993 hearing in Norfolk to be a standard cross-country military flight with legitimate training purposes, and one that, according to Navy instructions, Stumpf, a squadron commander, could authorize. The Navy, however, had neglected to include a copy of that instruction in the five-inch-thick folder of Stumpf documents that was being circulated.

The committee was also made aware of a statement by the Atlantic Fleet Naval Air Force released one month before Tailhook '91 that prohibited the use of tactical aircraft for travel to Tailhook, and the use of Nellis Air Force Base, near Las Vegas, for Tailhook travel, "unless operational/tactical commitments dictate otherwise."

Stumpf had orders to fly to Tailhook, and the Navy passenger jet he was to take had broken down. He was also required to be back at Cecil Field, Florida, on Monday, to take part in a predeployment training exercise. He and his wingman landed at George Air Force Base, not Nellis, and rented a car to get to Las Vegas.

But without the missing Navy instruction, members of the SASC questioned the legitimacy of the flight and Stumpf's authority to order it. During an executive session, closed to the press and public, the impression was additionally and mistakenly conveyed that Stumpf's flight had violated someone's direct orders.

That, plus Stumpf's presence in the room, painted the picture of an officer with fatally flawed judgment who did not deserve to be promoted.

There didn't seem to be much doubt about which way the committee would lean.[41]

In a letter produced out of that session, Dalton was advised that if the SASC knew what it now knew about Stumpf's activities at Tailhook '91, it would not have recommended that the Senate confirm his nomination. He was also advised that since the Senate had already confirmed Stumpf, "the decision to promote him rests solely with the Executive Branch."

Dalton received a letter stating same on November 13.[42] The group of seven fliers he had recommended for promotion were brushed off. Three days before Christmas, Dalton removed Stumpf's name from the promotion list, telling the committee in a memo that he did so "in light of my duty to maintain the integrity of the promotion process."[43]

Stumpf couldn't believe it. "I am completely chagrined that four years after the Tailhook convention it is still taking down good men who had no part of any of the misconduct involved," he said.[44]

Stumpf's attorney took a harder tack. "What is extremely sad is that the secretary of the Navy, and the secretary of defense, do not have the moral courage to do what they know is right," Charles Gittins said. "That is the essence of poor, weak, pathetic leadership. It is a message they are sending to the entire Navy."[45]

Critics felt the SASC was beating a dead horse to fulfill a political agenda. And many questioned whether information gathered from an investigation deemed by a federal judge as "replete with hearsay" was justifiable grounds upon which to deny advancements. Those associated with assaultive or sexually harassing behavior, or lying, clearly did not deserve promotion. Similar punishment for party antics seemed repressive. One officer, referring to the woman who in October 1991 accused Supreme Court nominee Clarence Thomas of sexual harassment on national TV, called it "applying post-Anita Hill standards to the 30-year history of Tailhook and, really, to the entire history of maritime tradition."

Denial of the promotion forced the Navy to pull Stumpf out of his deputy command slot at CVW-17, and the officer many in the Navy considered one of its rising stars instead began pushing paper. Stumpf became a special projects officer at Oceana's Atlantic Fleet Fighter Wing, re-writing the training syllabus for the T-34 trainer airplane. The last time he had flown an F/A-18 was in August.[46]

Dalton's handling of the Stumpf case wasn't winning him any points in the naval aviation community. On January 25, during a visit to the Jacksonville area, Dalton made a stop at Cecil Field, Florida, Stumpf's old stomping grounds.

Dalton was brought to "Ace's Place," an old auditorium at Cecil Field, to address base personnel with the sort of typical quick state-of-the Navy speech such visits demand—"It's people like you that make this the finest naval service in the history of this country"—with a question period to follow.

A group of fliers had gathered in the back, and several were egging on Lt. Mike Bryan to ask Dalton what was happening with his stymied promotion. Instead, Cmdr. Mark Fox, the commander of VFA-81, rose to ask Dalton to explain the Bob Stumpf situation.

Dalton explained that promotions were "a three-step process," and that Stumpf hadn't made it through the third step, the Senate. The fliers knew that wasn't technically true, since the Senate had confirmed Stumpf. Then Dalton said, "The message that should be taken from this incident involving Commander Stumpf is, if you find yourself in a position of having to explain yourself, don't do it. In the case of Stumpf, he found himself in that position."

The room got real quiet—"like a silent groan," Bryan recalled. For a lot of the Cecil Field fliers, Dalton had lost all credibility.[47]

So had the SASC, in the minds of many. Stumpf had been cleared by the Navy. On what was it basing its decision?

The incomplete record the committee had based its October decision upon notwithstanding, there were other documents that had never been made public that could be negatively influencing the committee.

By now, the committee certainly had a copy of Stumpf's DOD-IG file, as it did on every Navy and Marine Corps nominee. This information, discredited by two courts, hadn't been made fully public. One revelation focused on by the committee was a statement that one of the strippers in the upstairs suite had at one point been rubbing a piece of ice on her genitals as she danced, and that Stumpf had been in the room at the same time.

The committee also had the results of the 1993 board of inquiry, hearings which, thanks to Stumpf's Blue Angels connection, had been widely reported.

Another possible influence on the committee were the endorsements added to the 1993 board of inquiry's findings by each level of the chain of command as they were forwarded up through the Navy

Department. The first such endorsement on Stumpf's results, like those of the other four officers who faced such boards in Norfolk, would have been J. Paul Reason's—an endorsement prepared for him by Capt. Jeffry Williams. In Stumpf's case, especially, it was unquestionably negative.

Critics charged that the committee's claim of "new information" in the case was a smokescreen, raising questions of the fairness of the process. If there wasn't anything new, if the promotions were being quashed out of a sense that the conduct of individual officers, whether they had assaulted women or not, whether they were cleared or not, was simply too questionable to approve a promotion, that was the SASC's prerogative, critics said. But at least, they argued, come out and say it.

By now, the committee realized it had opened a huge can of worms. The SASC was getting scorched in the press by editorials and news articles alike. The retired community was bombarding the committee with calls and letters protesting its handling of the Stumpf case.

Key players such as Nunn were now well aware that Stumpf's F/A-18 flight was legitimate. But the "new information" that arose out of a renewed inquiry in February was a real concern. And the same media blitz that raised questions about the validity of the questions the committee was asking had helped create a bunker mentality among its members. [48]

During an amazing committee hearing held March 12, 1996, Sam Nunn lashed out.

He aimed his remarks at critics of the promotion process for officers tainted by Tailhook, and again declared that new information in Stumpf's case had caused the committee to deny his promotion. But, he revealed, the Navy had asked the committee not to release it.

The hearing, held to review the Navy's 1997 budget request, was being held in the accustomed spot, an ornate but cramped meeting room in the Russell Senate Office Building.

The Navy Department's top leadership was on hand: Dalton, Adm. Jeremy M. "Mike" Boorda, who succeeded Kelso as Navy chief, and Krulak, making his first appearance before the Senate as the Marine Corps commandant. In his opening statement, Dalton acknowledged that the Navy was still having problems adjusting to the increasingly visible role of women. "The Navy Department is making significant strides in that regard," Dalton said. "Obviously, cultural change presents a challenge. I'm confident we'll meet that challenge . . . ."

For two hours, committee members fired questions about spending levels and budget priorities at the trio. Finally, Sen. John McCain, R-Ariz., a Stumpf backer, entered the room for the first time. When recognized, he asked Dalton and Boorda if they'd seen the editorial in that morning's *Wall Street Journal*—an editorial that revealed that the committee's rejection of Stumpf was based on new information an inside source said it possessed, but which lambasted both the Senate and the Navy for holding up Stumpf's promotion. McCain also wanted to know where the two stood on the case.

Only Boorda had read the editorial. Both said they believed Stumpf should have been promoted.

Boorda said he had just finished reexamining the entire Stumpf case. "We in the Navy made a lot of mistakes [in Tailhook] and it tainted us," he said. "But those actions have been completed, and like it or not, it is time to move on from Tailhook."

Boorda also said a service member's entire record should be taken into account for promotion consideration. "We need to look at more than just a few minutes of a person's career," Boorda said.

After a few more questions, McCain turned toward Nunn—the most senior member at the hearing since both chairman Thurmond and Sen. John Warner, R-Va., had left—and said, simply, "Senator Nunn?"

The sense was that McCain was throwing the meeting over to Nunn in order to adjourn. Nunn, however, went off like a fuse had been lit under him.

"What I deeply resent is the pounding this committee has taken on procedure," Nunn said. "This is not one that slipped by the committee in the night."

Nunn said he was frustrated that the committee is being "beat over the head" as if "you've got some kind of McCarthy trial going on."[49]

That was an ironic statement, because that was sure how it looked, given that Nunn had earlier made a cryptic reference to information the committee had but was not releasing publicly because the Navy had asked that it be kept confidential.

Stumpf said he was sure there wasn't anything new. "That's smoke," said Stumpf, reached later at his Virginia Beach home. "I think that's a red herring. It's just a way of not dealing with the issue. There's nothing in the past that causes me concern." He said a professional lobbyist he and Gittins had hired to work the SASC had reviewed the records and reported that "there's nothing else in there."[50]

At the hearing, Nunn, continuing his cryptic ways, said the information was being withheld to protect an individual, but it wasn't clear whether he was referring to Stumpf. He also said that "if it all becomes public, it will be a different perspective," once again unclear. Finally, he added, "The more you try to protect an individual in this town, the more excoriated you are for not putting the full record out there."

Nunn asked Dalton and Boorda if they would object to "putting the entire record out there." Dalton said no. Said Boorda, "We have to do what is right," later adding, "for us, there is nothing in that case to be proud of.

"We need to learn the lessons of Tailhook, and all of us need to get the individual pieces behind us," Boorda said.

Nunn took the Navy to task for its handling of the scandal, stating that Navy investigators had proven themselves "incapable" of handling the investigation. The Navy then went to the other extreme, Nunn said, rushing to judgment on Tailhook attendees without providing due process.

Nunn also suggested that admirals and "top gun" fighter pilots who were at the convention got preferential treatment from the Navy.

"If this had been just enlisted people," he said, "I'm afraid I'd have to come to the conclusion that heads would have been rolling all over the place."

As an example of the committee's fairness, Nunn said the SASC had already confirmed fifteen officers who were the subject of administrative action stemming from Tailhook—although he didn't say if they'd been cleared. Another nine were rejected for promotion, Nunn said.

That night, the committee went into closed session to consider the Stumpf case.[51] If all went well, Stumpf said, he'd not only make captain; the committee would decide once and for all to stop asking the Navy and Marines to tag the files of officers who had gone to Tailhook '91.

During his two-year quest to climb the ladder, Stumpf had been treated like an interdepartmental ping-pong ball. Still, he expressed equal concern about the effect the process was having on down the line.

"I don't think that until recently, they've understood the impact it's had on the fleet," Stumpf said. "The young mid-grade guys look at that and say, 'Is this the treatment I can look forward to as a senior officer?'"[52]

Stumpf's future in the Navy became clearer the next day. In a terse statement signed by Thurmond and placed into the Congressional Record late the following night, the committee essentially killed the promotion. The statement alluded to the information on Stumpf that Nunn had mentioned, but said that Boorda "has testified that he believes such confidentiality should be maintained" (a strange contention, in that both Boorda and Dalton had told Nunn they had no objection to putting the whole record out in public). The committee's 1995 recommendation to cancel the promotion was made "on information that was made available by the Navy."[53]

As far as Gittins was concerned, that information consisted of the board of inquiry transcript, the endorsements, and the DOD-IG report—the latter a questionable set of documents, which had been widely discredited.[54]

The statement also noted that Dalton had pulled Stumpf's name from consideration, and that the SASC had been advised by the Navy General Counsel that Dalton's action was final and irreversible.

The Navy was welcome to try again and resubmit Stumpf's name, the statement said.[55]

Nunn, it was clear, hadn't lost any of the outrage he had expressed as far back as 1992, when he told the committee he then chaired, "This kind of behavior is not tolerable now, nor would it have been tolerable 50 years ago, nor would it be tolerable under any circumstance."[56] Other Democrats, including the SASC's Sen. James Exon, D-Neb., and Robert C. Byrd, D-W.Va., also seemed convinced that Stumpf did not deserve the promotion.

But sources said Nunn, who had been behind legislation in the fall of 1995 to get the SASC out of the business of approving three- and four-star retirements, didn't have it in for Stumpf. Rather, he was simply acquiescing to the desires of Coats and Byrd.[57]

There were many other possibilities. Besides the Democrats, they included one or more Republican members of the committee, now in the majority and in a stronger position to express moral outrage over Tailhook; senior active-duty officers who saw an opportunity to administer a backhanded payback to officers they felt should have been found guilty; and committee staffers with individual agendas.

Reason certainly seemed a strong senior officer possibility, given his original zeal for prosecuting Stumpf. But one high-ranking Pentagon official in a position to know said he felt sure it wasn't Reason, now at the Pentagon as the deputy chief of naval operations for plans, policy and operations, or his lawyer, Capt. Jeffry Williams.

"They harbor some real grudges against Stumpf," the official said. "They don't think he should have gotten a lawyer. I think it was an emotional reaction." But while Reason had once lobbied Dalton intensely to censure Stumpf, the official said, "I just don't think Paul would be up on the net playing again."[58]

But there were quite a few officials and interested observers who felt strongly that one or more SASC staffers was raising havoc behind the scenes.

The Navy's Harlow, while choosing his words cautiously, said, "Frequently, in any organization, people start wearing their bosses' stars. Whether that's the case here, I don't know. Sometimes, there's so much stuff the Senate has to consider that staffers take on increased authority."[59]

That theory became increasingly plausible on March 27th, when Rowan Scarborough of the *Washington Times* reported that the Navy had given the SASC a previously undisclosed document concerning Stumpf—the nonpunitve letter of instruction that Arthur had handed to Stumpf following the 1993 meeting at which Arthur had cleared the flier.

The Arthur letter, released by the Navy on February 6, was the admiral's personal advice to Stumpf on how he could have better handled himself at the 1991 convention. This was, unquestionably, the "new information" alluded to by Nunn—and very likely was the piece of paper he was waving around during the budget hearing.

It was also privileged information. According to the *Times*, the information was obtained at the request of Abell—according to another letter signed by Natter. But by Navy regulation, nonpunitive letters are private matters between the giver and receiver, and are not supposed to be placed in the receiver's personnel file.

The committee felt otherwise. "It's entirely appropriate," spokeswoman Chris Cimko said of the committee's review.[60]

Only two copies of the letter had existed: Arthur's, and Stumpf's.

According to Arthur, there were only two ways the letter could have been discovered: either he had left it behind in the vice chief's legal file—"really shabby work on my part" if that was the case, he said—or a copy had been made.

"How that got transmitted to a staffer on the Hill is a great concern,"

Arthur said. "And how that came to be asked for by name is too, and the fact that the Navy didn't come to me and ask permission.[61]

On the Pentagon's E Ring, it was common knowledge in 1993 that Arthur had given Stumpf the letter. The scuttlebutt was that someone in the Pentagon who knew of the letter had it in for Stumpf, and passed the letter to the SASC.

But several, including Stumpf, Gittins, a Pentagon official close to the investigation and other insiders also pointed fingers at SASC minority staff director Arnold Punaro.

"There is a problem with the staff over on the Hill, and it's primarily Arnold Punaro," said the Pentagon official of Punaro, also Sam Nunn's staff director. "I don't think the members are totally aware of what games are being played behind the doors."

Punaro, a Marine Reserve brigadier general, had maintained for reasons unknown an adversarial relationship with the Navy that dated back to the John Lehman years. Sources also said he blamed the Navy for the Marines' Tailhook troubles, and was the person who tried to keep Nunn wound up on the issue.

Punaro was also powerful—influential to the point that when people wanted something from the committee, they lined up in front of his office, not former majority staff director Richard Reynard's. It was said that Punaro ensured that Marine nominees with Tailhook connections found a smoother path to promotion than their naval brethren.

Gittins said that during the fight for Stumpf's promotion, the professional lobbyist they had hired was told by Punaro that it didn't matter if Bob's name came up again because "he's not getting promoted." "The allegations," Punaro later said, "are all untrue."[62]

Stumpf, a twenty-two-year veteran, had held out to the bitter end, confident the system would correct itself. Thurmond's letter was the last straw. On Friday, March 16, Stumpf and Gittins filed suit in Federal District Court in Alexandria, Virginia, calling for a judicial review of Dalton's decision to acquiesce to the Senate and overturn Stumpf's promotion.

"It's unfortunate we had to litigate," Gittins said. "We tried to work the political process as diligently as we possibly could. The bottom line is, when push came to shove, character didn't matter to the Senate Armed Services Committee."

Dalton had sixty days to respond. A federal judge would then decide whether Dalton violated federal statutes and/or Navy instructions that govern procedures for delaying an officer's promotion, and for removal of an officer from a promotion list.[63]

On the evening of the 19th, Nunn and Coats took the committee's case to the Senate floor along with Exon and Byrd, all lashing out against critics and news media coverage, singling out the *Washington Times*. The *Times* had run a December 19 editorial by Gittins in which he said the committee's rejection of Stumpf was based on "rumor and innuendo and anonymous phone calls."

Nunn rejected that notion, saying, "The committee's recommendation was based on the records of the fact-finding board."[64]

By the time the *Times* story appeared, the story had taken two more turns. First, a Navy selection board freshly recommended Stumpf for promotion to captain.[65]

And on March 22, Stumpf had made good on his claim that his past caused him no concern. In a letter to the SASC, he authorized the committee to release all documents related to his case. "I have nothing to hide from the Committee or the public," Stumpf wrote. In turn, Strom Thurmond wrote John Dalton to say the SASC "has no objection" to the Navy's release of the Stumpf documents, to include the findings of the board of inquiry, the endorsements by the chain of command, and "the final disposition of the matter" by the Navy.[66]

On April 19, U.S. District Judge Albert Bryan granted a government motion and dismissed Stumpf's case outright.[67]

A subsequent Navy promotion board recommended that Stumpf be promoted to captain. In May, Dalton ordered the Navy's assistant general counsel to take a "fresh look" at Stumpf's case. Stumpf and Gittins stomped out of their mid-June meeting with Joseph G. Lynch, complaining that it had become "prosecutorial."

"It was clearly an effort to find some reason not to promote" Stumpf, Gittins said.

On July 12, 1996, one of the most contentious promotion fights in naval history came to an end; Stumpf gave up the ghost and announced his retirement. "It's been a tough three years," he said. "We're all kind of worn out."[68]

Stumpf had remained hopeful throughout his ordeal, but began to see that the writing was on the wall. In addition to his Senate difficulties, the shocking May 16, 1996, suicide of Boorda, one of his strongest backers, was a real blow. "That's the end of my support on the uniformed side," Stumpf thought.

He was also stunned when, after the current commander of the Blue Angels bowed out in late May 1996, citing "personal training difficulties," Stumpf wasn't recalled to temporarily take his place. "That was a pretty significant sign," Stumpf said.

Asked what he would tell SASC members if he were to be granted an audience, Stumpf said, "I would ask them, 'What is it in my record that you have a problem with?'"

If the SASC had a problem with the letter of caution Stumpf was given by Stan Arthur—the "new information" that wasn't part of Stumpf's official records—the committee didn't even blink at a similar letter given Vice Adm. Jay L. Johnson when it recommended him to succeed Boorda. Johnson, one of the thirty-five flag officers who attended Tailhook '91, was one of the thirty given a letter of caution by Dalton for "a failure of appropriate leadership." Johnson was confirmed by the full Senate July 31, 1996; he received his fourth star in the process.

On allowing the strip act to take place, Stumpf said, "The rules at that time didn't even cover that sort of thing. This sort of activity happened at officers clubs throughout the Navy. As far as I know, all of the services had tolerated this kind of activity routinely, and it didn't even occur to me that there was anything untoward or could be a problem."

Stumpf said he saw no connection between allowing the strip act to take place and the sexual misconduct at Tailhook. "Absolutely not," he said. "It had nothing to do with any kind of sexual harassment."[69]

The outcomes for many in Tailhook's diverse cast of characters were predictably varied and, in some instances, unbelievably ironic. As of May 1996:

Gregory E. Tritt had a bad run of luck following the Tailhook hearings. He retired from the Navy on July 31, 1994. The following winter, on February 25, 1995, he and son Jeremy, who was driving, were returning from a skiing trip to Mount Baker in northern Washington. They struck an oncoming car. Tritt, who was asleep at the time, suffered serious injuries, breaking his back, hip, pelvis, and foot. That December, his wife Rosa, while driving Tritt up to the mountains, was struck by an oncoming car, and she suffered whiplash, and shoulder and chest injuries.

Tritt, for the most part recovered from his injuries, began working as a flight instructor for Loral Aerospace Corporation at the EA-6B flight simulator at Whidbey Island, Washington. He lives with Rosa and Jeremy in nearby Oak Harbor.

Cmdr. Thomas R. Miller remained in the Navy, and was teaching command and control warfare at the Armed Forces Staff College in Norfolk, Virginia.

John LoGuidice left the Navy to work as a dispatcher for an airline in Chicago.

Lt. Dan Janssen planned to leave the Navy in May 1996, destination unknown.

Paula Coughlin now lives the civilian life, address unknown.

Capt. Gregory Bonam was flying F/A-18s for VMFA-323 out of El Toro Marine Corps Air Station in California. Despite being cleared in court, sources doubt that he'll make major.

Greg "Goose" Geiss faced a post-Tailhook "show cause" board at Pensacola (Florida) Naval Air Station in August 1994 at which three Navy captains found that he committed misconduct—the charges were indecent assault, conduct unbecoming an officer, and substandard performance—"but in their view the circumstances did not warrant separation." Geiss left the Navy in September 1995.

Lt. David Samples expected to be augmented from his status as a naval reservist—that is, made an active-duty naval aviator—but the approved move was reversed. He was flying EA-6Bs for VAQ-135 out of Whidbey Island.

Rolando Diaz left the Navy in October 1995.

Cole V. Cowden was promoted to lieutenant commander almost immediately after Vice Adm. J. Paul Reason accepted fresh legal advice and threw out his case. He was flying E-2C Hawkeyes for a Norfolk unit.

Elizabeth J. Warnick, the ensign and self-described "player" at Tailhooks '90 and '91, was promoted to lieutenant in June 1994. She completed flight school and, as of April 1996, was flying helicopters for a San Diego-based squadron.

Lt. John M. Cooney's file was purged in April of its "Tailhook tag," clearing him for possible augmentation as an active-duty naval aviator.

Frederic G. Ludwig, Jr., retired from the Navy in May 1995.

Navy Reserve Capt. Robert L. Beck, who testified against Kelso, was, as he feared would happen, passed over for promotion to admiral. His current whereabouts are unknown.

Michael S. "Wizard" Fagan was promoted to colonel.

Hank Sonday was practicing law in Kansas City, Mo.

William T. Vest remains an administrative law judge for the Social Security Administration, but transferred to Norfolk, Virginia.

Robert Rae, Mike Kmetz, and Don Marcari continue to practice law in Virginia Beach and Norfolk, as do Mike Powell and Charles Gittins in the Washington, D.C. area; Jeffrey Good and William C. Little still practice law for the Coast Guard and Navy respectively; Alan Bergstrom became an administrative law judge for Social Security in Pittsburgh, Pennsylvaniia.

Frank B. Kelso retired and was promptly struck down by a rare viral disorder that for a time confined him to a wheelchair. After intensive treatment at the Mayo Clinic, he is back on his feet and is, friends say, recovering nicely.

Gen. Charles C. Krulak was the commandant of the Marine Corps.

Adm. Joseph Paul Reason was nominate in May 1996 for his fourth star and command of the Atlantic Fleet. He was scheduled to assume that command in December 1996.

Jeffry Williams, who was awarded the Legion of Merit for his tour of duty at SurfLant, rejoined Reason at the Pentagon as his staff judge advocate. In 1996, he transferred from the Navy to the civil service where, as a GS-15, he was teaching criminal procedure and rules of evidence at the FBI Academy.

Robert Monahan became a litigator for the Central Intelligence Agency.

Mike Ritter, who nearly resigned his commission after being kicked off the Tailhook cases by Vest, was promoted to commander and was working in Washington, D.C.

Robert E. Stumpf retired from the Navy in October 1996.

Lt. Scott Bubeck, the VFA-83 pilot who helped organize the up-stairs party at the Las Vegas Hilton that caused so much trouble for Stumpf, died less than three months after William T. Vest brought the Tailhook hearings to an end. On April 28, 1994, while *Saratoga* was sailing in the Adriatic Sea, Bubeck's F/A-18C was launched skyward. As the Hornet cleared the edge of the deck, it made an uncommanded roll to the right—a flight control malfunction. The Hornet crashed into the sea, and Bubeck was killed. The Navy said the cause of his death was an "unsuccessful ejection."[70]

14

A Hard Lesson to Learn

A failure of leadership, deceptiveness, institutional entrenchment, loyalty over truth, abuse of power, outright incompetence: These and other reasons explain why Tailhook took place, and why its ugly aftermath continues, five years later, to have a powerfully detrimental effect on the Navy and Marine Corps.

Tailhook the event was a military culture gone out of control, a culture of self-aggrandizement and alcohol abuse and lack of respect for anyone outside of it and any woman trying to get into it.

Tailhook the aftermath resulted from a failure by the Navy's macho culture to stand up and accept responsibility for its actions when the first stories of sexual assault at the conventions surfaced—to admit the times had changed and that, despite the lip service being paid to "zero tolerance," it hadn't changed with them.

Tailhook was dozens of naval officers who considered themselves part of that macho culture, but didn't stand up for the females being groped at its conventions.

Tailhook was the hundreds of naval officers who lied to investigators out of anger, out of a sense of loyalty to fellow fliers, but also out of the sense that, guilty or not, they were targets of a politically driven witchhunt.

Tailhook was a gross failure of leadership.

Tailhook was an abuse of taxpayer dollars and the public trust.

Tailhook was investigative abuse driven, in part, by all of those factors.

Tailhook was and is a U.S. Senate that softened its certification requirement in September 1996 but continues to flog the Navy Department over Tailhook, long after past the time the whole matter should have been dropped—gropers and liars notwithstanding.

Tailhook was and continues to be an overreaction by the nation's civilian leadership that has forced social changes down the military's throat—some good, some detrimental. It is a climate of political correctness that has in some cases lowered training standards, sometimes endangering others and dulling morale.

It all could have been handled so much differently.

Kelso and Garrett took the Tailhook scandal's biggest dives. They deserved to, but their performances could have been far more graceful. The investigation would have undoubtedly played out in a radically different fashion if the two leaders had taken a more proactive stance after first hearing of Paula Coughlin's assault. Both had been at Tailhook, true. But was the only alternative to risking a charge of undue command influence sitting back and hoping fliers would cooperate—fliers who are taught, at least at the Naval Academy, that loyalty comes first?

Kelso had a particularly rich opportunity to challenge the aviators's status quo. On the afternoon of September 7, 1991, Frank Kelso was at the Tailhook flag panel. He had to have heard the catcalls and hissing when the women in combat issue was raised.

There's no record of the chief of naval operations standing up to challenge those fliers. But Kelso had to have realized then, if he hadn't before, how deeply the problem ran in his Navy.

Garrett, Kelso, and Dunleavy in particular, could have stepped up following Paula Coughlin's letter to Navy officials and admitted to the nation that Tailhook had been a long-standing, accepted tradition and that the Navy had a long-standing problem. Then, of course, they would have had to disassociate themselves from any subsequent investigation.

That sort of forthrightness, together with some good-of-the-Navy-style prodding and promises that only those officers who'd actually assaulted women or lied would be hammered, might have actually produced some cooperation from the officers who had attended the convention.

Instead, the Navy tried to hide its dirty little secret, and lay the blame at the feet of its junior officers. The resulting avalanche of political and media criticism, and the roughshod tactics employed by DOD-IG investigators, created a sense on the part of fliers that suddenly, all were suspect.

Fliers, most of them in no mood to cooperate with an investigation into women being groped, received precisely that message. The sense that a witchhunt was taking place fomented widespread resistance. Many officers—though certainly not all, as Barbara Pope intimated—lied or obfuscated details of their involvement. This group included the secretary of the Navy and the chief of naval operations, neither of whom set much of an example to follow.

One of the gantlet's major players said the resistance could have been greatly softened. "I would have set out some kind of format," said Lt. Greg "Goose" Geiss. "'Hey, if you were one of the grab-assers, and you did this and that, come tell us. The Navy can learn some good lessons from it. You're going to be punished, but we're not going to ruin your life, because we realize you're not some hardened criminal.'

"Hey, we got out of hand, but set up a format to allow us to fairly come forward and talk about it," said Geiss. "Don't set up a guillotine and say, 'Your head is chopped off.'"[1]

The Navy, through the statements of Dan Howard and many others, set up the guillotine; it probably had no other choice, given congressional and public pressure. But its narrow-scope investigation couldn't crack the code, especially given the lack of cooperation. Only three fliers were accused of misconduct; at least two of them were eventually exonerated.

Enter the Department of Defense Inspector General. Imbued with a sense that it had a congressional mandate to deliver senior officers at all costs and anxious to prove it could produce a valid report in the face of the widespread stonewalling—and a far better one than the Navy managed, it hoped—the agency frequently exhibited all the professionalism and class of a rabid wild boar, abusing witnesses' rights during hotbox sessions in aircraft carrier ready rooms and off-base hotel suites.

In their defense, the Navy's fumbling and the subsequent lies made the job inordinately difficult. But the agency produced a report that was rife with errors. The only punishments were handed down by Reason and Krulak, behind closed doors. The court cases disintegrated. As Reason himself noted, evidence is a requirement.

Investigators accumulated tons of evidence. But much of it was wasted when the worst offenders—like Geiss—were given immunity in exchange for their testimony against senior officers. The Navy and the DOD-IG deserve heavy criticism for having agreed so readily to this trade-off.

Instead, the Navy ended the careers of several dozen officers who had "ballwalked"—one-time offenses for which the punishment hardly seemed to fit the crime—while handing out nonpunitive letters of caution to the admirals who had condoned and ignored the behavior.

It was the gropers who deserved to get booted out of the service. Sexual misconduct, an intermittent problem at past Tailhooks, exploded in the hot Las Vegas night, fueled in 1991 by a macho, post-Gulf War euphoria being cooled for some because they hated the idea of female fliers trying to earn seats in combat jets. Such attitudes produced the ridiculous Tailhook T-shirts like "Women are property," and "He-man Women Haters Club."[2]

Thanks to the grants of immunity and the cover-ups, most of the gropers didn't get punished.

Judging from most reports, much of the sexuality reported at the 1991 Tailhook convention was consensual or at least not regarded as offensive. But while the DOD-IG overstated the number of assault victims it purported to discover, there were undoubtedly other victims who never reported their assaults.

No matter what the numbers, it is absolutely unbelievable that adult males—military officers—escorted women into situations like the Rhino suite or the gantlet, knowing how the women would be treated; even more so, that they would knowingly assault female naval officers.

It is equally unbelievable that males in the vicinity of assaults didn't step in to stop others from humiliating or abusing people. Macho, at least in the civilized world, used to mean standing up for women, not knocking them down. Officers and gentlemen? In many instances, what was practiced at Tailhook was more like the manners one associates with Attila's Huns than with latter-day American warriors. Attendees who took part in assaulting women or who saw assaults and did nothing showed a total lack of guts, of character, of respect for the opposite sex.

Our nation's military needs people who have the self-assurance and drive to handle the pressure that comes with life on the edge—in training and in war. But just as bravery doesn't equate with foolhardiness, a high degree of self-confidence doesn't grant one a license to sexual assault. The world is full of men and women with powerful sex drives who restrain themselves from touching members of the opposite sex on a whim in hopes of gaining a cheap thrill or coercing some quick satisfaction.

There's nothing wrong with consenting adults doing adult things. Consent and setting are the obvious keys.

In the end, while none of the accused officers was convicted at court-martial, many paid a price for their Tailhook activities. Forty Navy officers received nonjudicial punishment; of these, twenty-seven paid fines ranging from $500–2,000, and twenty-four received punitive letters of reprimand, which were placed into their permanent files and darkened their Navy futures.[3]

Eight Marine officers went to nonjudicial hearings; the Marines refused to release their punishments or redacted transcripts of their administrative hearings, citing privacy concerns. One officer resigned after receiving what was likely a punitive letter; nine others were counseled; four cases were dismissed.

Given Tailhook's scope, it all seemed to come up a little short. That perception led to what amounted to an inquisition by the Senate Armed Services Committee.

Unquestionably, certain officers connected with Tailhook did not deserve to remain in the service, much less by advanced, and it is the Senate's just place to make such decisions. But the Senate needed and still needs to draw the line between serious crimes, such as assaultive behavior and lying, and retroactive, politically correct application of current social standards to the 1991 Navy. More importantly, the Senate should not judge officers solely on the basis of the flawed DOD-IG investigation—unless the information was derived from taped and transcribed interviews, from reports backed up by sworn testimony—or, subsequently, from verbal admissions during administrative hearings. And in the name of fairness, the Senate should allow the affected officers to stand before it and answer their critics. The Senate continued to refuse to allow this, although the committee decided in late September 1996 to allow promotees to submit material on their own behalf.

That same month, the SASC belatedly promoted sixteen officers who'd been held up, bringing the Tailhook Certification List total to thirty-one promoted, eight rejected.[4]

Naval aviation wasn't the service's only branch bruised by Tailhook. Thanks to the efforts of a chosen few, the Navy legal and investigative branches, their recent history not exactly sterling, ended up being sullied once again.

In 1987, the combined efforts of the Marine Corps and Navy investigators and prosecutors, for instance, helped bring about the dismissal of all charges against two of the three Marines charged with espionage at the U.S. Embassy in Moscow, and of related charges against a fourth Marine. The case against one guard collapsed when prosecutors waited too long to file charges in a military court; another guard's case was dropped after being mishandled by Navy investigators; yet another's, for fraternization, was also dropped. Only Sgt. Clayton J. Lonetree was found guilty of espionage. He received twenty-five years, a total later reduced to fifteen.[5]

In 1989, a gun turret on the battleship USS *Iowa* exploded during test firing, killing forty-seven crew members. The combined $4 million efforts of an informal board of inquiry and the Naval Investigative Service determined that a suicidal gunner's mate, Clayton Hartwig, had sabotaged the gun. NBC News subsequently broadcast leaked allegations of Hartwig's homosexual link to a sailor he had named as beneficiary in a life insurance policy.

But subsequent tests by the Energy Department showed the explosion may have been the result of over-ramming the powder bags in the gun. In response to howls of protest from members of Congress, the news media, and family members, the investigation was reopened. In October 1991, the Navy concluded, after spending another $25 million, that the exact cause of the blast couldn't be determined, and Kelso formally apologized to Hartwig's family.[6]

Tailhook appears to be just another point along the same line of incompetence, poor focus, and rushing to judgment.

Tailhook's prosecutorial abuses were shameful. Williams and Monahan, in particular, stepped far over the line and abused their power.

"Williams became so personally involved in the investigation of the cases that he lost all objectivity and abandoned his role as staff judge advocate," said a senior Navy legal official. "Any conflict with the way he wanted things to go was a challenge to his masculinity. When he was removed as the SJA by the military judge, he gave the entire JAG Corps a black eye."[7]

Monahan's subordinate Mike Ritter, some would say, belonged in the same category. But he, along with many of the other relatively young Navy lawyers working for Williams and Monahan, suffered in part because of the bunker mentality established at Little Creek.

"If Mike Ritter had been able to talk with anyone other than Monahan about the safety report," the legal official said, "he would have been told to leave it alone. He was a very inexperienced trial counsel who needed to be able to bounce problems off more experienced JAGs."[8]

Prosecutors and defense attorneys alike are expected to exercise good ethical judgment. The law demands it, and their clients—their fellow service members—deserve it.

Ultimately, Vest helped atone for those shortcomings by ruling against the abuses and influence peddling. So did Lt. D.J. Hansen, who had the guts to tell a superior that Lt. Cole Cowden's case wasn't worth prosecuting. So did the Navy attorneys who worked, in many cases alongside civilian counterparts, to defend their clients.

But although Vest's verdict prevented a miscarriage of justice, justice didn't carry the day. Miller, Tritt, and Samples were spared a court-martial, but their names were cleared on technicalities, which was no vindication. Judging from the numbers reported in the third-floor hall-way, most of the officers who took part in the gantlet escaped punish-ment—especially the culpable who were given immunity. The women who lied or took part in misconduct weren't punished at all, weren't even charged. And Paula Coughlin, Anne Merritt, Kim Ponikowski, Julia Rodgers, and the other women whose assaults were corroborated never had the satisfaction of seeing an assailant brought to justice.

"The sad thing is, all the women's groups are no better served by this than our clients were," said Don Marcari, Miller's co-counsel. "I still think the Navy has a great system, and if they'd let it function like it was supposed to, it would have worked."[9]

It didn't, and given the Navy justice system's record, it is highly questionable whether it can when a high-profile case presents itself.

It is ironic that one of Frank Kelso's last official acts was to sign off on a new sixty-four-page handbook on how to recognize, prevent, and deal with sexual harassment. One measure of how seriously the Navy was taking the problem: the handbook's recommended "last resort" for frustrated victims is to write to Congress.

This is a significant departure from the norm. In most military circles, going outside the normal chain of command to contact a mem-ber of Congress invites instant contempt and ostracism.

But if the Navy really is serious about changing its behavior, about repairing its tattered social image, it needs to get equally serious about changing the way it investigates itself. If the Navy—if the Defense

Department—can't be trusted to competently scrutinize themselves, why even have a Naval or Defense Criminal Investigative Service? Why not, at the first sign that an internal criminal investigation will be required, simply call the FBI, to ensure that a completely independent investigation will be conducted? Why not try all courts-martial in civilian federal court? At the very least, military trial and defense counsel should work for separate commanders who answer not to their base or ship commander, but directly to a civilian authority in the Department of Defense—a military justice command under the Joint Chiefs of Staff, perhaps.

Something needs to change. The former crew of the USS *Iowa*, the Marine guards at the Moscow embassy, and the victims and accused of Tailhook demand it.

The Navy could also start realizing that no one expects it to be perfect. Military public affairs officers are taught to deal with ugly incidents or accidents with the following dictum: maximum disclosure, minimum delay. But they can only tell the public what their commanders allow them to say. The Navy, like all branches of the military, owes honesty and forthrightness to the taxpayers who fund it.

The next time a ship runs aground, a bunch of midshipmen cheat on an engineering exam—or even in the unlikely event that a group of female aviators once again gets sexually assaulted by their male peers at a drunken convention—why couldn't the service involved step back, take a deep breath, and decide on a measured response? Can't it get the story out quickly and proactively, tell the truth, mete out the appropriate level of justice without regard to the political winds, and get on with the business at hand?

This is a tall order for the military, where information is strictly compartmentalized on a "need-to-know" basis. But one of Tailhook's most powerful lessons should be that tragic or scandalous episodes are rarely matters of national security. You build trust by admitting your mistakes.

Despite pronounced efforts to change attitudes, sexual harassment is still a significant problem for the military. In a survey of 90,000 service members released by the Pentagon in July 1996, 53 percent of Navy women said they'd been sexually harassed at least once in the previous year. For all the services, the figure was 55 percent. Those numbers had dropped thirteen and nine percent, respectively, from a 1988 survey of all services. An improvement, to be sure, but one that also magnifies how far the services have to go to make life tolerable for most of their women.

The military isn't the only segment of society facing this problem. Sexual harassment in the military might be more pronounced than it is in society at large, but the military is hardly alone in treating women as sex objects. Tailhook-style conventions aren't limited to the Navy, or the military.

In May 1995, for instance, following a national vigil for slain officers, groups of New York City police officers staying at the Hyatt Regency and other Washington, D.C., hotels reportedly went on a drunken rampage. At the Hyatt in particular, witnesses said police, some of them in their uniforms, groped women coming out of elevators, slid naked down beer-soaked escalator handrails, tried to force their way into the rooms of attractive women, and sprayed fire extinguishers on upstairs walls. About $30,000 worth of damage was reported at the Hyatt Regency alone.[10]

But even if everyone is doing it—and if they are, most aren't making a big enough mess to make the news—it still doesn't excuse what happened at Tailhook.

And with Tailhook five years gone, questions remain about whether the scandal's lessons will ever completely sink in. Given the gush of adverse incidents that marred 1995, one might have thought Tailhook had never even given the Navy anything to think about. A married admiral based in Portugal, Rear Adm. Ralph Tindal, was censured, demoted, and forced to retire early following an admiral's mast ruling that he had sexually harassed a subordinate with whom he'd had a year-long affair. A captain who used to head the Navy's equal opportunity office, Everett Greene, lost his promotion to admiral for an "unduly familiar" relationship with a subordinate that reportedly included giving her his used gym shorts as a gift.[11]

Even sadder was the October 27, 1995, commercial airline flight upon which witnesses said a male petty officer who was drunk repeatedly groped a female sailor sitting next to him. Reportedly, none of the twenty or so sailors and officers seated nearby did anything to stop him.[12]

But these incidents were overwhelmed by the midsummer 1995 rape and murder of a woman in Virginia committed (they were convicted) by two Virginia Beach-based SEAL trainees,[13] and the rape by a sailor and two Marines of a twelve-year-old girl on Okinawa.[14]

A comment on that rape lost Adm. Richard Macke his position atop Pacific Command in November. Macke, in response to reporters' questions, said, "I think it was absolutely stupid."

Then he added, "I've said several times, for the price they paid to rent the car, they could have had a girl."

Within hours, Macke was forced into early retirement for his remarks. Although critics in and out of the military were quick to point out that what Macke had said was basically true, the remarks of this four-star admiral trivialized the twelve-year-old's rape; other critics viewed them as extremely insensitive and disrespectful.[15]

Still, what amounted to the firing of Macke raised hackles within the service. "We should never tolerate needless misconduct, because we are better than society as a whole," said Rear Adm. David R. Morris, outgoing deputy commander in chief of U.S. Naval Forces Europe, speaking at his February 28, 1996, retirement ceremony in Norfolk aboard the carrier USS *John C. Stennis*. "Yet we need to stand up to the window of capricious unfairness and push back the pendulum back to the middle, where an individual can say it like it is and be different without fear of career incrimination, or getting sacked."[16]

But it was the rejection of Stumpf that really had the aviation community up in arms. One of the Navy's top fliers spoke for many at his March 15, 1996, retirement ceremony when he acknowledged Tailhook's devastating effect—and, in effect, asked the Senate to look at his community in a different light.

"We are not bad people!" said a forceful Vice Adm. Richard C. Allen, the outgoing Atlantic Fleet Naval Air Force commander, speaking to a huge crowd seated in the hangar bay of the Norfolk-based USS *America*. "We are proud citizens of this great nation, and we are grateful to have the opportunity to serve."

The crowd included three people who'd been deeply touched by Tailhook: Vice Adm. J. Paul Reason, who would soon be tapped to return to Norfolk as commander of Atlantic Fleet; retired Rear Adm. Richard Dunleavy; and Chief of Naval Operations Adm. Jeremy M. Boorda, who Allen, in an obvious reference to the Stumpf case, turned to thank "for the tough stand you are taking on Tailhook problems, which have emasculated naval aviation since '91."

Afterward, speaking to reporters, Allen replied to a question by asking, "How long do we have to put up with this? We've suffered, we've learned, we've taken our moral issues to our heart, we have changed. We need to be allowed to get on with our future, and quit worrying about Tailhook."[17]

Tailhook apparently was only one of the many darts being thrown in the spring of 1996 at the personable Boorda, who had been criticized for what some termed politically correct leadership—the withdrawal of Stan Arthur's nomination to lead Pacific Command, for instance. Boorda was about to be questioned about improperly wearing two combat decorations from his days in Vietnam when he shot himself to death at his Washington Navy Yard home on May 16.

One of his harshest critics was former Navy Secretary James Webb. During an April 25 speech at the Naval Academy, Webb, without mentioning Boorda by name, blasted the Navy's senior leadership for what he said was its failure to stand up for the officers still being scrutinized by the Senate for their attendance at Tailhook '91. His remarks were said to have badly stung Boorda.

During another speech at Annapolis less than four weeks after Boorda's death, Webb, an academy graduate, again called upon military leaders to stop leaning with the political winds.

"The number one problem for the Navy to fix right now is the strength of the leadership at the top and its obligation to defend the military culture," Webb said. He mentioned Boorda by name only once, saying, "One thing I hope will come out of Admiral Boorda's tragedy is the ability for everyone to sit down and look hard at where things are and to agree to move forward toward solving a lot of the problems that were surrounding the Navy at that time and are still here now."

Webb also criticized the Senate's continued sharp focus on officers who attended the 1991 Tailhook convention, Stumpf's case in particular.

"It is not acceptable, and indeed it is harmful, when the political process decides to use the military as a controlled laboratory for social experimentation, when it intrudes into command prerogatives, and when it decides, as was done recently after the Tailhook debacle, that it has either the authority or the expertise to take apart the results of lower-level promotion boards and voice political judgment in otherwise political matters," Webb said.[18]

Webb's position is right on point—with an exception. If standards are not softened, women deserve the same military opportunities as men, except in a direct hand-to-hand combat role. The physical demands of infantry duty would preclude an overwhelming majority of women. And it doesn't take a genius to figure out that forty-member platoons with only one or two women present would be extraordinarily problematic.

When standards are softened, as was apparently the case in a high-profile 1994 crash, the results can be tragic.

It took a 1993 decision by the late former Defense Secretary Les Aspin—made at about the same time that Tailhook prosecutors were deciding which fliers to court-martial—to give women the opportunity to fly combat jets.

Women were immediately allowed to apply for the essential schools. The first graduates have spent the past four years joining squadrons that were home to some of those same hooting, hissing junior officers who so vehemently opposed their presence during the Tailhook '91's flag panel and gantlet. One of the first was a woman who was assaulted at Tailhook: Lt. Kara Hultgreen, a former A-6 bomber pilot who had cross-trained over to the F-14 Tomcat.

On October 25, 1994, Hultgreen crashed on approach to the USS *Abraham Lincoln*, an incident that Navy spin doctors were quick to blame on engine problems; although her landing grades placed her slightly below average for the air wing, she was fully qualified in the F-14, they said. But a leaked Navy Safety Center report found fault with Hultgreen's performance, saying she had failed to line up directly on the carrier's center line and waited too long to correct the error, "contributing to left engine stall."

Hultgreen had accumulated 1,242 flight hours but only 218 in the F-14; there also were whispers that she had been helped through flight school. Even if that were true, Hultgreen could hardly have been the only flier, male or female, ever given a break in the midst of that expensive training. But the Navy was again heavily criticized for appearing to spin the story instead of telling the whole story.[19]

Despite such incidents, the Navy is making every appearance of trying to strike a healthy balance between mission accomplishment and the reality that boys and girls will be boys and girls. With the aircraft carrier *Dwight D. Eisenhower* leading the way, women were by mid-1996 sailing aboard more than forty combat ships.

Some women seem to have fit in, and managed the delicate dance of being themselves while being one of the guys. Others have found the going a bit rude. A male sailor on the *Eisenhower* told a new female crew member, "This is a man's world."

She chewed him out, backing him down.[20]

The Navy says the transition will be smooth, that the groundwork has been laid by more than twenty years of women sailing on noncombat Navy ships. And in the fleet, the macho attitude appears to be slowly softening, especially in the enlisted community. The shock therapy provided by Tailhook was the catalyst, but an apparently more genuine command commitment to equal opportunity is carrying it through. Most importantly, ship commanders seem openly committed to making their mixed-gender combat ships a success.

At this point, of course, they really have no choice. Congress has spoken.

The reality, however, is that the Navy is still a man's world. The ranks are still laced with senior officers and sailors who, for all the lip service being paid, still want no part of women in the military, but who are quick to bow to political pressure.

If the Navy is going to stand up for itself before the nation's civilian leadership, it needs to do so while making an honest account of itself and its needs.

And while it weaves women more densely into its organizational fabric, it needs to enforce honest standards. In this way, the Navy—the entire military—can produce the best possible soldiers, sailors, airmen, and Marines, and at the same time strengthen morale and mutual respect among service members.

The Navy's efforts at mending its ways seem admirable. Stretched to the limit with fewer ships, fewer sailors and operational requirements nearly identical to those maintained during the Cold War, it continues to perform exceptionally well. It has in many instances shown that it has the ability to change with the times. Still, the problematic five years that have followed Tailhook '91 have shown that the jury is still out. Weeding out the dinosaurs, it appears, will take quite a few more years.

Interviews

Much of this book could not have been written without the help of many people who agreed at one time or another to share their experiences and/or opinions regarding the Navy Department's Tailhook scandal. Some were interviewed at length; others for but a few minutes. Some were at Tailhook '91 or involved in its aftermath; others were not, but were nonetheless affected.

Not all are mentioned in the text. All contributed to its making.

Special thanks are also due several active and retired Navy and Marine Corps officers who spoke with me at length, but felt their careers or positions would be imperiled if their names were published. I have honored their requests.

Don Abenheim
Lt. Gene Ager
Vice Adm. Richard C. Allen (retired)
Adm. Stanley R. Arthur (retired)
Alan Bergstrom
Peter T. Black, DOD-IG
Maj. Paula Bogdewic, USMC
Adm. Jeremy M. Boorda
Capt. Richard F. Braden
Lt. Mike A. Bryan
Lt. Carl Chebi
Airman Malissia Chester
Chris Cimko
Lt. Ed Cook
Paula A. Coughlin
Lt. Cmdr. Cole V. Cowden
Lt. Rolando A. Diaz
Cmdr. Ryland Dodge

Capt. Jerry "Popeye" Doyle, USMC
Rear Adm. Richard Dunleavy (retired)
Rear Adm. Marsha Evans
Al Fancher
Mike Fasanaro
Walt Felton
Rear Adm. James H. Finney
Maitland Freed
Archie Galloway
Lt. Joe Gelardi
Charles W. Gittins
Lt. Cmdr. Jeffrey Good
Lt. Cmdr. Susan Haeg
Lt. Susan Harvey
Lt. James P. Hogan
Lt. Jeff Horwitz
Cmdr. Lin Hutton
Chief Petty Officer Chris Jackson
Lt. Dawn Jordan
Michael Kmetz
Lt. Cmdr. William C. Little
Capt. Frederic G. Ludwig Jr.
 (retired)
Don Marcari
Lt. Cmdr. Janet Marnane
Lt. Cmdr. Charles "Chip" Meade
Cmdr. Thomas R. Miller
Lt.j.g. Jerry Morick
Charles C. Moskos
Lt. Pete Nette
Lt. Jim O'Brien
Lt. Kathy Owens
Rear Adm. Kendall Pease
Petty Officer 2nd Class Suzan Peterson
Lt. Vicki Peterson
Cmdr. Steve Pietropaoli
Barbara S. Pope
Mike Powell
Robert Rae

Don Risher
Jeffrey P. Ruch
Lt. David Samples
David Segal
Hank Sonday
Cmdr. Robert E. Stumpf
Lt. Lisa Tarner
Cmdr. Gregory E. Tritt (retired)
Rosa Tritt
Cmdr. John Tull
Cmdr. Kevin Wensing
Lt.j.g. Bill White
Capt. William T. Vest (retired)

Notes

The material for *The Mother of All Hooks* was gathered over a three-year period, both while covering the continuing Tailhook story for my newspaper, the *Daily Press*, and during many weeknights and weekends while working out of my home. The story is drawn from my coverage of the Navy's Tailhook hearings in Norfolk, which lasted nearly nine months, interviews with many dozens of participants and interested parties, and thousands of pages of documents obtained both by private means and through the federal Freedom of Information Act.

In a perfect world, every source used to develop this story would be identified in the notes. Covering the military and political arenas and getting to the heart of the story, however, doesn't always allow for full disclosure. Several key sources used here are still on active duty or working closely with highly placed protagonists. If their names were revealed, they would pay dearly for their honesty and candor.

The material they supplied, however, has been invaluable; they have both helped confirm the observations of named sources concerning events in Norfolk, Quantico, at the Pentagon and on Capitol Hill and, in some few instances, been the sole source of information. The inclusion of their material was necessary, I felt, to more fully paint the Tailhook picture. I can only assure the reader that each source is of impeccable character, and that I have full faith in their veracity.

The notation, "various other sources," is a catch-all that denotes a consensus of opinion on particular facts or events that the author has developed over time by drawing on a wide range of people and/or documents. It is sometimes used to back up other sources—especially information garnered from the notoriously problematic Reports of Interview written by Department of Defense Inspector General agents—but rarely to stand on its own.

Through it all, the goal has been to produce a book that is as close to the truth as an outsider can get, one that not only tells a story but helps enrich the ongoing debate over Tailhook's legacy.

Chapter 1

1. Court proceedings detailed in this chapter are drawn largely from author's notes taken at the Article 32 hearing for Cmdr. Gregory E. Tritt at the Naval Legal Service Offce, Norfolk Naval Base, Norfolk, Va., July 7, 1993.
2. Charge sheet signed out by Atlantic Fleet Surface Force assistant force judge advocate against Cmdr. Gregory E. Tritt dated June 14, 1993.
3. Tailhook Referral Coversheet on Lt. John LoGuidice, February 1, 1993, Department of Defense Inspector General (DOD-IG).
4. Tritt Article 32 hearing.
5. Department of Defense, Office of the Inspector General report on Tailhook 91, Part 1, September 1992, 2.
6. Consensus of dozens of Tailhook attendees and testimony of sexual assault victims.
7. Ibid.
8. Transcript of taped testimony of Peter T. Black, DOD-IG, at Fact-Finding Board for Capt. Richard F. Braden, September 7, 1993, 34.
9. Transcript of taped testimony of Black at Fact-Finding Board for Cmdrs. Gregory E. Peairs and Cmdr. Robert C. Yakeley, September 13, 1993, 37.
10. Gathered from statements of members of Congress and senior Navy officials, 1992–93.
11. Transcript of taped interview with Lt. John J. LoGuidice by DOD-IG, March 10, 1993.
12. Report of Naval Investigative Service on Tailhook, April 30, 1992.
13. DOD-IG report, Tailhook 91—Part 2, February 1993.
14. Ibid.; numerous other sources.
15. Transcript of taped testimony of Vice Adm. J. Paul Reason at Article 39(a) session in general court-martial of Cmdr. Gregory E. Tritt, August 18, 1993.
16. Leaked, unofficial memo of summation of conversations between Lt. Col. Geoffrey Lyon and Maj. Phil Seymour indicates only nineteen of the twenty-two Marine Corps cases were being pursued by the U.S. Marine Consolidated Disposition Authority, 1993.
17. Variety of sources including transcripts of taped Article 15 hearings for twenty-three officers conducted by Vice Adm. J. Paul Reason, May 20–June 4, 1993.
18. Interview with Robert Rae, attorney, March 22, 1996.
19. Tritt charge sheet.
20. Based on interviews with variety of people who know or who have worked with Tritt. "Old bald guy" reference from transcript of taped testimony of Lt. Daniel F. Janssen at Tritt Article 32 hearing, July 7, 1993.
21. LoGuidice interview with DOD-IG, March 10, 1993.
22. Transcript of taped testimony of Black at Article 32 hearing for Cmdr. Thomas R. Miller, June 14, 1993.
23. Ibid.
24. Transcripts of taped testimony of Black at Fact-Finding Boards for Braden, Peairs, and Yakeley.
25. Transcript of taped testimony of Black at Fact-Finding Board for Braden, 50.

26. DOD-IG report, Tailhook 91—Part 2, and photographs within.
27. Ibid.
28. LoGuidice interview with DOD-IG.
29. Report of interview with Janssen by DOD-IG, January 20, 1993.
30. Report of interview with Janssen, February 16, 1993.
31. Transcript of taped interview with Janssen by DOD-IG, February 16, 1993.
32. LoGuidice at Miller Article 32, June 14, 1993, 104; at Tritt Article 32, September 17, 1993, 233.
33. LoGuidice at Miller Article 32, 103–4; transcript of taped testimony of Lt. Mark C. Nye at Article 32 hearing for Tritt, September 16, 1993; interview with Lt. James P. Hogan, April 6, 1996; numerous other sources.
34. Ibid.
35. Janssen interview.
36. Interview with Cmdr. Thomas R. Miller, February 2, 1994; interview with Tritt, March 28, 1996.
37. LoGuidice at Tritt Article 32, September 17, 1993, 250.
38. Ibid.
39. Interview with Rae, June 8, 1993.

Chapter 2

1. Letter from Capt. Frederic G. Ludwig, Jr., Tailhook Association president, to aviation squadron commanders, October 11, 1991.
2. Transcript of taped statement by then-Vice Adm. Richard M. Dunleavy to DOD-IG, July 28, 1992.
3. Department of Defense, Office of the Inspector General (DOD-IG) report on Tailhook 91, part 1, September 1992, 2–3.
4. Ibid.; Report of Interview with retired Senior Chief Robert LeRay Lawson by DOD-IG, August 20, 1992.
5. Transcripts of taped interview with Lt. Gregory J. Geiss by DOD-IG, January 25, 1993, 37, and January 26, 1993, 167.
6. Naval Inspector General Report of Investigation: Department of the Navy/Tailhook Association Relationship, April 29, 1992, 6.
7. DOD-IG report, part 1, 2–3.
8. Review of Naval Record of Lt. Cmdr. John W. Marshall, Board for Correction of Naval Records, September 28, 1995, 4–5 (cites unnamed retired vice admiral interviewed by DOD-IG).
9. Lawson interview report. Lehman essentially confirmed his conduct during at least one previous Tailhook convention while being questioned during the broadcast of ABC-TV's "This Week with David Brinkley" on May 26, 1996. Lehman told reporter Sam Donaldson that he thought the incident where he was lying on his back under a woman, as described in Gregory Vistica's 1995 book *Fall From Glory*, "was 1981" but then turned his reply to the topic of "gutter reporting." Pressed as to whether he was denying the incident, Lehman replied, "I am flattered by the attention, Sam, fifteen years after, and at the risk of hurting my reputation in some quarters, I have to say that the description is far more lurid than the fact." When reporter Cokie Roberts asked Lehman whether or not it was important that a Navy secretary was lying on the floor under a nude woman with members of his command watching, Lehman said, " . . . I think that what happened 15 years ago at a convention is certainly a matter of passing interest."

Lawson said he thought the Lehman incident occurred "during the same year that naval aviators were again authorized to wear brown shoes," which was 1986.

10. Various sources and reports.
11. Ibid.
12. Geiss, January 26, 193, 159–160.
13. Ibid., 164; corroborated by transcript of taped interview with Lt. John J. LoGuidice by DOD-IG, March 9, 1993, 66–68.
14. Various sources and reports.
15. Inspector General Report, 2,4.
16. Tailhook Association report on the 1991 Symposium, November 30, 1992.
17. Interview with Cmdr. Thomas R. Miller, February 2, 1994.
18. Ibid.
19. Inspector General Report, 1.
20. Geiss, January 25, 193, 15–16; various sources.
21. Ibid.
22. DOD-IG report, part 2, V-8 (photo and text).
23. Photograph in DOD-IG report, part 2, X-4 (figure 16); Naval Inspector General Report: Personal Conduct Surrounding Tailhook '91 Symposium, 2, 5.
24. Ibid.
25. James P. Stevenson, *The Pentagon Paradox: The Development of the F-18 Hornet*, Naval Institute Press, 1993, 206–304; Michael R. Gordon and Gen. Bernard E. Trainor, *The General's War: The Inside Story of the Conflict in the Gulf*, Little, Brown and Company, 1995, 96–98, 312–20.
26. Naval IG Report: Personal Conduct, 4; numerous other sources.
27. Transcript of taped interview with Assistant Navy Secretary Barbara S. Pope by DOD-IG, June 30, 1992, 4–7.
28. Various sources; author's observations during visit to the Philippines, 1992.
29. Ibid.
30. Various news articles by Dave Schad, *Pacific Stars and Stripes*, 1992.

Chapter 3

The Tailhook convention activities and general demeanor of Lt. Gregory J. Geiss are drawn in large part from the nearly 300–page transcript of taped interviews with Geiss conducted by agents of the Department of Defense Inspector General, January 25–26, 1993.

1. Geiss, January 26, 1993, 132; Kerry DeRochi, "Flier's deal to tell about Tailhook irks lawyers," *The Virginian-Pilot*, October 3, 1993.
2. Geiss, 142.
3. Ibid., 161–62.
4. Geiss, January 25, 1993, 2–3.
5. Ibid., 6.
6. Ibid., 4–5.
7. Ibid., 5.
8. Ibid., 6.
9. Ibid., 24.
10. Ibid., 7–8, 11–15.
11. Ibid., 20.
12. Ibid., 26–27.
13. Ibid., 29–31.

14. Ibid., 34.
15. Ibid., 35, 39.
16. Author's notes of testimony of Rear Adm. Richard M. Dunleavy (retired) during hearings to determine if Adm. Frank B. Kelso II was an "accuser," November 30, 1993.
17. Geiss, January 25, 1993, 63.
18. Author's notes of Dunleavy; Geiss, 58–60.
19. Geiss, 41–42.
20. Ibid., 62–64, 73; Transcript of taped interview with Lt. Mike A. Bryan by Department of Defense, Office of the Inspector General (DOD-IG), December 16, 1992, 4; various other sources.
21. Geiss, 65, 68–69.
22. Ibid., 65–66; author's notes of testimony of Geiss at Article 32 hearing for Lt. David Samples, August 18, 1993.
23. Geiss interview with DOD-IG, 64, 67–69. Geiss testimony, September 23, 1993.
24. Summarized proceedings of Article 32 hearing for Capt. Gregory J. Bonam, October 14, 1993, 39.
25. Geiss interview with DOD-IG, 69–70.
26. Ibid., 72.
27. Author's notes of testimony of James T. Kelly at board of inquiry for Capt. Frederic G. Ludwig, Jr., September 23, 1993; Geiss testimony, same date; other sources.
28. DOD-IG report on Tailhook 91, part 2, February 1993, F-29.
29. Ibid., F-37.
30. Kelly, Bonam hearing, 38; DOD-IG, part 2, F-47.
31. Geiss interview with DOD-IG, January 26, 1993, 23–24.
32. Geiss interview with DOD-IG, January 25, 1993, 66–67.
33. DOD-IG, part 2, F-23.
34. Report of Interview with Anne Merritt by DOD-IG, January 12, 1993; various other sources.
35. Kelly, Ludwig board of inquiry; Kelly, Bonam hearing, 39; Author's notes of testimony of Lt. Frank Truong at Article 32 hearing for Samples; Geiss, 74–76.
36. Truong; Geiss, 81.
37. Ibid.; Kelly, Bonam hearing, 39; Geiss, 76, 77, 80.
38. Ibid.
39. Geiss. Testimony at Bonam hearing (47) indicates the Rodgers assault was entered into the Las Vegas Hilton Hotel Security Blotter on September 7, 1991, at 11:15 p.m.
40. Kelly, 39; Geiss, 82.
41. Geiss, 86–90.
42. Kelly, 39–40.
43. Summarized proceedings of Article 32 hearing for Capt. Gregory J. Bonam, August 17, 1993, 2–3, 12.
44. Kelly, 40–41.
45. Coughlin, 4.
46. Ibid.,
47. Kelly, 41.
48. Coughlin, 5.
49. Kelly, 41.
50. Coughlin, 14–18.
51. Merritt, 5.

52. Kelly, 42.
53. DOD-IG, part 2, VI-16–17; Las Vegas Hilton Hotel Security Blotter, September 8, 1991, entries 18–19.
54. Geiss, January 26, 1993, 18–19.

Chapter 4

1. Summarized proceedings of Article 32 hearing for Capt. Gregory J. Bonam, August 17, 1993, 18, 22.
2. Interview with retired senior Navy official close to the Tailhook investigation, April 9, 1996.
3. Ibid.; Department of Defense, Office of the Inspector General (DOD-IG) report on Tailhook 91, part 1, September 1992, 16.
4. Unsworn statement read in court by Lt. Rolando Diaz at his Article 32 hearing, August 3, 1993.
5. Retired Navy official.
6. Summarized proceedings of Article 32 hearing for Capt. Gregory J. Bonam, October 14, 1993, 45.
7. Retired Navy official.
8. Ibid.
9. Coughlin, 22.
10. Retired Navy official.
11. Ibid.
12. DOD-IG, 4.
13. Transcript of taped interview with Assistant Secretary of the Navy Barbara S. Pope by DOD-IG, June 30, 1992, 15.
14. Retired Navy official.
15. Letter to members of the Tailhook Association by Capt. Frederic G. Ludwig, Jr., October 11, 1991.
16. Conversation with Gregory Vistica, *San Diego Union* reporter, August 18, 1993.
17. Interview with Vistica aired on National Public Radio's "Fresh Air" program, March 8, 1996.
18. *Congressional Record*, October 29, 1991.
19. DOD-IG, 5–6.
20. Interview with Pope, October 10, 1994.
21. DOD-IG, 7; Pope with DOD-IG, 54.
22. Pope.
23. DOD-IG, 6.
24. Retired Navy official; interview with senior Navy official close to the investigation, March 25, 1996.
25. Retired Navy official.
26. DOD-IG, 12.
27. Retired Navy official; interview with Hank Sonday, December 19, 1994. Sonday buttressed his recollections with a detailed diary he kept from the beginning of his involvement with Tailhook, in January 1992, until he left the Navy's Tailhook team in May 1993.
28. Retired Navy official; senior Navy official.
29. DOD-IG, 18.
30. Pope with DOD-IG, 17.
31. Retired Navy official.

32. Pope; Pope with author.
33. Pope with DOD-IG, 18–28; Pope with author. In an interview published in the January 1993 issue of *National Reserve Association*, Gordon said Pope never expressed dissatisfaction with the investigations until their April 1992 release.
34. Pope with author; Pope with DOD-IG, 31–38, 65–70. In an interview published in the February 1993 issue of *National Reserve Assosciation*, Williams denied that he had made any of the comments attributed to him by Pope: "I categorically deny that I ever made such statements," he said. "If I had made such statements, I should have been fired immediately; and if I made such statements to Ms. Pope and she did nothing about them, then she should be fired."
35. DOD-IG, 16.
36. Senior Navy official.
37. Sonday.
38. Ibid.
39. Ibid.; senior Navy official; retired Navy official.
40. Interview with Don Risher, June 15, 1996; Sonday.
41. Sonday.
42. U.S. Navy news release, July 9, 1992.
43. Coughlin, 19.
44. Bonam, August 17, 23.
45. Sonday.
46. Iorio.
47. Sonday.
48. Coughlin, 20; Sonday.
49. Sonday.
50. Retired Navy official.
51. Ibid.; senior Navy official.
52. Sonday.
53. Pope with author.
54. DOD-IG, 25.
55. Retired Navy official.
56. Sonday.
57. Pope.
58. Naval Inspector General Report of Investigation: Department of the Navy/Tailhook Association Relationship, April 29, 1992.
59. Sonday.
60. Risher.
61. Sonday; retired Navy official.
62. Risher.
63. Pope.
64. Risher; Sonday; senior Navy official.
65. Sonday.
66. Retired Navy official.
67. Ibid.; Sonday.
68. Ibid.
69. Sonday.
70. Retired Navy official.
71. Senior Navy official.
72. Retired Navy official.
73. Risher.
74. Ibid.

75. Transcript of taped testimony of Thomas J. Bonnar, DOD-IG, at board of inquiry for Capt. Frederic G. Ludwig, Jr., September 1993, 12.
76. Senior Navy official.
77. Interview with Lt. Mike A. Bryan, March 30, 1996.
78. Bonnar, 13–14.
79. Transcript of taped testimony of Matthew A. Walinski, DOD-IG, at Article 39(a) session for Lt. David Samples, October 19, 1993, 185.
80. Sonday.
81. Unofficial transcript of a tape-recorded briefing at El Toro Marine Corps Air Station by members of the Marine Corps Defense Service for Marine officers who'd attended Tailhook, August 1992.
82. Dan Weikel, "Advice may haunt ex-Marine defense attorney," *Los Angeles Times*, July 26, 1993.
83. Source familiar with the Marine inquiry, April 9, 1996.
84. Retired Navy official.
85. DOD-IG.
86. Sonday.

Chapter 5

1. Interview with Hank Sonday, May 16, 1995; various other sources.
2. Transcript of taped testimony of Vice Adm. J. Paul Reason at Article 39(a) session for Lt. David Samples, October 15, 1993, 16.
3. Interview with retired senior Navy official close to the Tailhook investigation, April 9, 1996.
4. Ibid.; Sonday; various other sources.
5. Mike Powell, letter to U.S. Senate, July 12, 1993.
6. Gregory Vistica, "Navy will establish convening authority for Tailhook cases," *San Diego Union-Tribune*, January 6, 1993; various other sources.
7. Report generated by the nonprofit whistleblower group Government Accountability Project, Washington, D.C., and submitted to U.S. Navy July 11, 1994.
8. Various other sources.
9. Reason, 16.
10. Reason, 73.
11. Sonday.
12. Ibid.; interview with senior Navy official close to the investigation, March 25, 1996.
13. Sonday; various other sources.
14. Sonday; senior Navy official; retired Navy official; interivew with Don Risher, June 15, 1996.
15. Sonday.
16. Ibid.; Transcript of taped testimony of Capt. Jeffry A. Williams at Article 32 hearing for Cmdr. Gregory E. Tritt, September 30, 1993, 185.
17. Williams, 184.
18. Source familiar with the Marine inquiry, April 9, 1996; various other.
19. Sonday.
20. Ibid.; retired Navy official.
21. Sonday.
22. Ibid.; senior Navy official; interview with Don Risher, June 15, 1996.
23. Transcript of taped testimony of Thomas J. Bonnar, Department of Defense In-

spector General (DOD-IG), at board of inquiry for Capt. Frederic G. Ludwig, Jr., September 1993, 12–13.

24. Sonday.
25. Retired Navy official; Sonday; testimony of Don Mancuso, DOD-IG, at Article 39(a) session for Cmdrs. Thomas R. Miller and Gregory E. Tritt, December 9, 1993; interviews with Mancuso, July 29 and August 5, 1996; testimony of Adm. Frank B. Kelso at Miller/Tritt; interview with Capt. Don Guter, July 26, 1996. This was the most difficult item to pin down in this entire text, and the legal end of it remains fuzzy. Sonday said the plan was to give the flag files to Aspin, who would hold them for the new Navy secretary. Kelso testified that the Office of the Secretary of Defense, or OSD, held the flag files. Asked if Kelso ever had possession of the files, Guter said, "Unequivocally, the answer is no." Mancuso later said that Tailhook was a Navy responsibility, not the secretary of defense's, and that per an agreement with Navy General Counsel Craig King, the flag files were turned over "technically" to the secretary of the Navy but held by the OSD. But in court, Mancuso testified that "we provided all the records to the secretary of the Navy, and it was the Navy that decided, and not us, who would handle what"; on another occasion, he testified that with the exception of one flag file (retired and then-Vice Adm. Richard Dunleavy's), "all the rest of them were provided to the secretary of the Navy's office." No one cross-examined him on the time sequence or the technicalities, and Capt. William Vest ultimately ruled that the files were delivered to Kelso and sealed for delivery to Dalton, the incoming Navy secretary. The greater issue, really, was that the prosecutions of junior officers in Norfolk and Quantico proceeded before a civilian Navy secretary could review the flag files. Political pressure made such a delay impossible.
26. Sonday; senior Navy official, Risher.
27. Williams, 217.
28. Sonday.
29. Williams, 265.
30. Sonday.
31. Author's notes of testimony of Lt. Damien J. Hansen at Article 39(a) session for Cmdr. Gregory E. Tritt, September 30, 1993, 300.
32. Senior Navy official.
33. Sonday.
34. Author's notes of testimony of Capt. Charles E. Ellis at Article 39(a) session for Cmdr. Gregory E. Tritt, September 30, 1993, 288.
35. Ibid., 286–87.
36. Interview with Hansen, February 20, 1996.
37. Ellis, 287–88.
38. Senior Navy official.
39. Ibid.; Sonday.
40. Interviews with numerous officers, January 1993–April 1996.
41. Senior Navy official; Sonday.
42. Transcript of taped testimony of Matthew A. Walinski, DOD-IG, at Article 39(a) session for Lt. David Samples, October 19, 1993, 159–60.
43. Williams, 186–87.
44. Ibid., 186.
45. Sonday.
46. Ibid.; senior Navy official.
47. Sonday.
48. Ibid.

49. Officer interviews.
50. Report of Interview with Lt.j.g. Elizabeth Warnick by DOD-IG, October 14 and 28, 1992.
51. Sonday.
52. Reason, 23.
53. Sonday.
54. William H. McMichael, "140 Navy officers face punishment for Tailhook," *Daily Press*, April 24, 1993.
55. Sonday.
56. Ibid.; retired Navy official.
57. Sonday.
58. H.G. Reza, "Navy official criticizes handling of Tailhook cases," *Los Angeles Times*, June 19, 1993.
59. Sonday; Risher.
60. Senior Navy official.
61. Atlantic Fleet Surface Force Public Affairs Office.
62. Proceedings of 23 admiral's mast hearings before Vice Adm. J. Paul Reason, Atlantic Fleet Surface Force, Norfolk, Va., May 20–June 4, 1993.
63. Ibid.; interview with Alan Bergstrom, attorney, January 12, 1996. The military attorney's name could not be tracked down.
64. Interview with Mike Powell, attorney, June 3, 1995.
65. August.
66. Powell.
67. Leaked unofficial summation of taped telephone conversations between Lt. Col. Geoffrey Lyon and Maj. Phil Seymour concerning the 19 Marine Tailhook cases, August 1992; Dan Weikel and Gebe Martinez, "Just 1 Tailhook Marine faces assault charge," *Los Angeles Times*, July 26, 1993; August.
68. Powell.
69. Ibid.
70. Source familiar with the Marine inquiry.
71. Ibid.
72. Powell.
73. Source familiar with the Marine inquiry.
74. Atlantic Fleet Surface Force Public Affairs Office.
75. USMC Col. W. Hays Parks (retired), "Tailhook," *Proceedings*, September 1994.
76. Interview with Robert Rae, attorney, March 22, 1996.
77. Senior Navy official.

Chapter 6

1. Charge sheet signed out by Atlantic Fleet Surface Force assistant force judge advocate against Lt. David Samples dated July 8, 1993; author's notes of testimony of Lt. Frank Truong at Article 32 hearing for Samples, August 18, 1993.
2. Admiral's mast hearing (redacted) for unnamed thirty-three-year-old officer before Vice Adm. J. Paul Reason, Atlantic Fleet Surface Force, Norfolk, Va., June 2, 1993.
3. Truong.
4. Ibid.
5. Ibid.; transcript of taped interview with Lt. Gregory Geiss by DOD-IG, January 25, 1993, 74–83; sworn statement of Samples to Cmdr. E.E. Irvin, June 3, 1993;

Department of Defense, Office of the Inspector General report on Tailhook 91, part 2, February 1993, F-36; Las Vegas Hilton Hotel Security Blotter, September 8, 1991, entries 8, 9, 15.

6. Essential findings and ruling on defense motion to dismiss, U.S. v. David Samples, Tidewater Judicial Circuit, U.S. Navy, October 25, 1993, 9.
7. Transcript of taped testimony of Samples at Article 39(a) session, October 20, 1993, 215–21.
8. Ibid., 221–22.
9. Essential findings, 10–11.
10. Ibid.; transcript of taped testimony of Matthew A. Walinski, DOD-IG, at Article 39(a) session for Samples, October 19, 1993, 178–81.
11. Author's notes of unsworn statement of Lt. Cole V. Cowden at his Article 32 hearing, July 15, 1993; Report of Interview with Lisa Mattiello by DOD-IG, August 25, 1992; sworn statement of Mattiello before Paul E. Leitz, notary public, July 9, 1993.
12. Mattiello interview report.
13. Charge sheet signed out by Atlantic Fleet Surface Force assistant force judge advocate against Lt. Cole V. Cowden dated June 14, 1993.
14. Report of Interview with Lt.j.g. Elizabeth Warnick by DOD-IG, October 15 and 28 and December 16–17, 1992; report of interview with Warnick by Naval Investigative Service, December 4, 1992; transcript of taped testimony of Warnick at Article 32 hearing for Cowden, July 15, 1993, 26–75.
15. DOD-IG report, October; author's notes of testimony of Lindy Billings, DOD-IG, July 15, 1993.
16. NIS report.
17. DOD-IG report, December; Billings.
18. Cowden statement.
19. Transcript of taped telephone conversation between Warnick and Cowden by DOD-IG, December 22, 1992.
20. Cowden statement.
21. Ibid.
22. Ibid.; sworn statement of Lt. Walter J. Adelmann Jr. before Lt. Cmdr. Jeffrey Good, July 4, 1993.
23. Tailhook Referral Coversheet on Lt.j.g. Elizabeth J. Warnick, February 1, 1993, DOD-IG; Cowden charge sheet.
24. Author's notes of testimony of Cowden, Capt. Jeffry Williams, Lt. Ronald Hocevar at Cowden hearing, August 27, 1993.
25. Ibid.
26. A.J. Plunkett, "Accused officer denies Tailhook assault charges," *Daily Press*, July 16, 1993; H.G. Reza, "Navy official criticizes handling of Tailhook cases," *Los Angeles Times*, June 19, 1993; interview with Good, April 11, 1996.
27. Reza; Good.
28. Transcript of taped testimony of Black and Warnick at Cowden hearing, July 15, 1993, 13–75; Mattiello statement.
29. Report of investigating officer, Article 32 hearing for Cowden, July 19, 1993.
30. Transcript of taped testimony of Cowden, September 30, 1993, 303–6; Cmdr. Rand R. Pixa, 294–97; Williams, 257–80.
31. Essentia! findings and ruling on defense motion to dismiss, U.S. v. Cowden, September 10, 1993, 5.
32. Interview with Good, August 20, 1993; Williams Article 34 advice to Vice Adm. J. Paul Reason, August 13, 1993.

33. Good and Cowden, August 30, 1993.
34. Findings, 5.
35. Author's notes of testimony of Cmdr. Christopher Remshak at Article 32 for Lt. Rolando Diaz, August 3, 1993.
36. Reports of interview with Diaz, August 5, 1992; with Lt. Andrew M. Jones, July 17, 1992.
37. Remshak.
38. Diaz; Jones; author's notes of testimony of Lt. Raymond Emmerson, Jr., August 3, 1993.
39. Remshak.
40. Sworn statement of Jones before Lt. Geoffrey M. Coan, June 28, 1993.
41. Remshak.
42. Author's notes of Remshak.
43. Remshak testimony.
44. Interview with Robert Rae, August 3, 1993.

Chapter 7

1. Charge sheet signed out by Atlantic Fleet Surface Force assistant force judge advocate against Cmdr. Gregory E. Tritt, June 14, 1993.
2. Charge sheet against Cmdr. Thomas R. Miller, June 21, 1993.
3. Interview with Cmdr. Thomas R. Miller, February 2, 1994; Transcript of taped testimony of Lt. Sean P. Cassidy at Miller Article 32, June 14, 1993, 142–43.
4. Transcript of taped testimony of Lt. Daniel F. Janssen at Miller Article 32, June 14, 1993, 36.
5. Miller charge sheet.
6. Transcript of taped testimony of Lt. John LoGuidice at Miller, June 14, 1993, 103–4; interview with Lt. James P. Hogan, April 6, 1996; transcript of taped testimony of Lt. Mark C. Nye at Article 32 hearing for Tritt, September 16, 1993, 179; Miller interview.
7. Miller.
8. Navy Report on the Fitness of Officers, Janssen, January 31, 1992.
9. Miller.
10. Tritt and Rosa Tritt at press conference at office of Robert Rae, August 19, 1993.
11. Miller.
12. Miller; interviews with Tritt, March 28, 1996; with Rosa Tritt, April 10, 1996.
13. Cassidy, 138–39.
14. Ibid.
15. Miller; Transcript of taped testimony of Miller at Article 32, September 24, 1993, 313–14.
16. Miller interview; Navy Report on the Fitness of Officers, Janssen, August 31, 1992; Transcript of taped testimony of Tritt, September 16, 1993, 217–18.
17. Miller.
18. Ibid.
19. Janssen testimony, 34–37.
20. Las Vegas Hilton Public Information Office, April 18, 1995.
21. Janssen, 37–40; LoGuidice at Article 32 for Cmdr. Gregory E. Tritt, September 17, 1993, 242–46.
22. LoGuidice at Tritt, July 7, 1993, 98–100, 104–16; Janssen at Tritt, July 7, 1993, 53–60.

23. Transcript of taped interview with Janssen by DOD-IG, February 16, 1993, 26–27.
24. Janssen at Tritt, 55.
25. Ibid.
26. Tritt testimony, 208–9.
27. Janssen at Tritt, September 17, 1993, 272, 274; Janssen interview, 28.
28. Ibid.; Transcript of taped interview with LoGuidice by DOD-IG, March 9, 1993, 45.
29. LoGuidice, 48–53; Janssen interview, 28–34; Miller.
30. LoGuidice, 52; Miller.
31. Miller.
32. LoGuidice, 53; Cassidy, 137.
33. Miller; LoGuidice, 50–52.
34. Miller.
35. Janssen interview, 32–34.
36. LoGuidice, 54–55.
37. Cassidy, 133; various other sources.
38. Miller; Janssen, 62–64.
39. Miller charge sheet; Janssen at Miller, 80.
40. Janssen at Tritt, 276–77.
41. Miller.
42. Reports of Interview with Tritt by DOD-IG, February 25, 1993; November 4, 1992.
43. Janssen at Tritt, July 7, 1993, 91–92; various other sources.
44. Janssen at Tritt, September 17, 1993, 271; July 7, 1993, 79–80.
45. LoGuidice at Tritt, July 7, 1993, 119–120; September 17, 1993, 238–39.
46. Transcript of taped testimony of Peter T. Black, DOD-IG, at Fact-Finding Board for Cmdrs. Gregory E. Peairs and Cmdr. Robert C. Yakeley, September 13, 1993, 41.
47. Miller.
48. Report of Interview with Janssen by DOD-IG, May 21, 1993.
49. Report of investigating officer, Article 32 hearing for Miller, July 20, 1993; Janssen.
50. Miller report.
51. Interview with Rae, August 25, 1993.
52. Report of investigating officer, Article 32 hearing for Tritt, July 12, 1993.

Chapter 8

1. Interview with Robert Rae, August 2, 1993; ALNAV message released by acting Navy Secretary Daniel Howard, July 2, 1992.
2. Author's notes at Article 32 for Lt. Rolando Diaz, August 3, 1993.
3. Ibid.
4. Essential findings and ruling on defense motion to dismiss, U.S. v. Cmdr. Thomas R. Miller, Cmdr. Gregory E. Tritt, and Lt. David Samples, February 7, 1994, 90–91, 109.
5. Diaz.
6. Ibid.
7. Ibid.
8. Summarized proceedings of Article 32 hearing for Capt. Gregory J. Bonam, August 17, 1993, 8.

9. Ibid.
10. Response to author's query to U.S. Navy Office of the Chief of Naval Information, August 3, 1993.
11. Interview with Don Marcari, August 12, 1993.
12. Author's notes of Article 39(a) session for Tritt, August 12, 1993, 10.
13. Interview with senior Navy official close to the investigation, March 25, 1996; interview with retired senior Navy official close to the Tailhook investigation, April 9, 1996; various other sources.
14. Ibid.
15. Court documents, U.S. v. Cmdr. Thomas R. Miller, August 13, 1993; author's notes of Tritt; interview with Rae, August 12, 1993.
16. Leaked unofficial summation of taped telephone conversations between Lt. Col. Geoffrey Lyon and Maj. Phil Seymour concerning the nineteen Marine Tailhook cases, August 1992.
17. Ibid.
18. Summarized proceedings of Article 32 hearing for Capt. Gregory J. Bonam, October 14, 1993, 2–22.
19. Ibid., 31–34.
20. Ibid., 27–29, 32.
21. Ibid., 30–34.
22. Tritt Article 39(a) session, August 18, 1993; interview with Rae, March 22, 1996.
23. Tritt.
24. Interview with Rae, August 18, 1993; interview with Hank Sonday, April 10, 1996; interview with Don Risher, June 15, 1996; response to June 3, 1996 query to Navy secretary John Dalton by Capt. Charles D. Connor, Dalton assistant, June 20, 1996.
25. Tritt.
26. Court documents, U.S. v. Diaz, August 1993; author's notes of Article 32 hearing for Samples, August 18, 1993.
27. Samples.
28. Ibid.
29. Author's notes of press conference held by Tritt and wife Rosa, August 19, 1993.
30. Author's notes of arraignment hearing for Lt. Cole V. Cowden, August 20, 1993.

Chapter 9

1. Citations awarded to Cmdr. Robert E. Stumpf and signed by Navy Secretary Lawrence Garrett, Vice Adm. Stanley R. Arthur, Rear Adm. G.N. Gee.
2. Author's notes of testimony of Cmdr. George E. Mayer, Rear Adm. William R. McGowen, Vice Adm. Robert Kihune, and others at Fact-Finding Board for Stumpf, September 2–8, 1993.
3. McGowen at Stumpf, September 3, 1993.
4. Interview with Charles W. Gittins, August 30, 1993.
5. Interview with Robert Rae, August 24, 1993.
6. Ibid.; interview with retired senior Navy official close to the Tailhook investigation, April 9, 1996.
7. Gittins.
8. Author's notes of testimony at Stumpf, September 2, 1993; U.S. Navy responses to query by Senate Armed Services Committee, August 22, 1995; Atlantic Fleet Naval Air Force directive, 1993.

9. Stumpf, September 6, 1993; interview with Stumpf, April 11, 1996.
10. Testimony at Stumpf, September 2, 1993.
11. Stumpf, September 6, 1993.
12. Ibid.
13. Ibid.; Stumpf, September 2, 1993.
14. Stumpf, September 2, 6, 8, 1993.
15. Stumpf, September 2, 1993.
16. Ibid.
17. Ibid.
18. Stumpf, September 6, 1993.
19. Stumpf, September 2, 1993.
20. Interview with Mike Powell, June 3, 1995; interview with Don Risher, June 15, 1996.
21. Stumpf, September 6, 1993; Risher.
22. Stumpf.
23. Ibid.
24. Ibid.
25. Ibid.
26. Stumpf, September 8, 1993.
27. Ibid., September 6, 1993.
28. Ibid.
29. Ibid., September 8, 1993.
30. Ibid., September 6, 1993.
31. Ibid.
32. Ibid.
33. Ibid., September 2–8, 1993.
34. Ibid., September 2, 1993.
35. Ibid., September 6, 1993.
36. Interview with Stumpf, July 27, 1996.
37. Interview with Gittins, October 15, 1993.
38. Transcript of taped testimony of Peter T. Black, DOD-IG, at Fact-Finding Board for Capt. Richard F. Braden, September 7, 1993; for Cmdrs. Gregory E. Peairs and Cmdr. Robert C. Yakeley, September 13, 1993.

Chapter 10

1. Transcript of Article 39(a) session for Cmdr. Gregory E. Tritt, August 25, 1993, 104–5.
2. Ibid., 105–14.
3. Author's notes of Article 32 hearing for Lt. Cole V. Cowden, August 27, 30, 1993.
4. Interview with Lt. Cmdr. Jeffrey Good, August 27, 1993.
5. Cowden; interviews with Alan Bergstrom, October 5, 1993, and April 19, 1994.
6. Essential findings and ruling on defense motion to dismiss, U.S. v. Cowden, September 10, 1993.
7. U.S. Navy Consolidated Disposition Authority news release, September 20, 1993.
8. William H. McMichael, "Navy dismisses Tailhook charge," *Daily Press*, September 21, 1993.
9. Investigating Officer's report, U.S. v. Lt. David Samples, September 2, 1993.
10. Interviews with Mike Powell, June 3, 1995, and April 13, 1996.

11. Source familiar with the Marine inquiry, April 9, 1996.
12. William H. McMichael, "Navy officer opts for lighter punishment in Tailhook case," *Daily Press*, September 25, 1993; interview with Robert Rae, September 30, 1993.
13. Investigating Officer's Report, U.S. v. Tritt, September 30, 1993; transcript of taped testimony, Article 39(a) session for Tritt, September 30, 1993, 230–31.
14. The Associated Press, "Parody of Tailhook scrutinized," September 24, 1993.
15. John Lancaster and Ann Devroy, "Aspin meets with Clinton, Kelso on admiral's future," *The Washington Post*, October 4, 1993; Department of Defense news release, "SecDef announces action in Tailhook flag officer cases," October 4, 1993.
16. Department of Defense news release, "Secretary of the Navy releases Tailhook decision," October 15, 1993; The Associated Press, "Tailhook scandal costs retired admiral a star; 2 others are censured," October 16, 1993.
17. David Stump, "Tony Less: On career, aircraft, Tailhook," *Soundings*, March 23, 1994.
18. William H. McMichael, "Tailhook figure cleared of blame," *Daily Press*, October 8, 1993; interview with Charles W. Gittins, October 15, 1993; interview with Gittins, March 29, 1996.
19. Ibid.; Transcript of taped Article 39(a) session for Tritt, October 14, 1993.
20. Interview with Don Marcari, October 15, 1993.
21. Letter to Lt. Cmdr. David G. Green from Cmdr. Robert P. Monahan, Atlantic Fleet Surface Force, August 16, 1993.
22. Letter to Capt. Jeffry Williams from Lt. Dawn Jordan, Naval Safety Center, October 7, 1993; interview with Jordan, October 15, 1993.
23. Monahan letter; Jordan letter; government response to motions by Cmdr. Thomas R. Miller for appropriate relief, dismissal, and mistrial, November 1, 1993.
24. Author's notes and transcript of taped Article 39(a) session for Lt. David Samples, October 15, 1993, 57–59.
25. Summarized proceedings of Article 32 hearing for Capt. Gregory J. Bonam, October 14, 1993, 34.
26. Ibid., 35–38.
27. Author's notes of testimony of Lt. Gregory Geiss at Article 32 hearing for Lt. David Samples, August 18, 1993.
28. Bonam hearing, 38–41.
29. Transcript of taped interview with Geiss by Department of Defense Inspector General (DOD-IG), January 25, 1993, 96–98.
30. Bonam, 40–41.
31. Ibid., 3–4.
32. Ibid., 41–46.
33. Las Vegas Hilton Hotel Security Blotter, September 8, 1991, entry 18.
34. Bonam hearing, 47–49.
35. Ibid., 50–51.
36. Marine Corps Combat Development Command news release, October 21, 1993.
37. William H. McMichael, "Cleared of Tailhook, flier still feels sting," *Daily Press*, October 16, 1993.
38. Kerry DeRochi, "Flier cleared in Coughlin's Tailhook case," *The Virginian-Pilot*, October 22, 1993.
39. Report of interview with Anne Merritt by DOD-IG, January 6 and 12, 1993; Memorandum for Commanding General, Quantico, Virginia, undated (summer 1993); source familiar with the Marine inquiry.

40. Memorandum of Advice, U.S. v. Miller, October 22, 1993.

41. Opinion of the Court, Samples v. Capt. William T. Vest and the U.S., U.S. Court of Military Appeals, January 11, 1994, 6–7.

42. Interview with Michael D. Kmetz, October 18, 1993.

43. Transcript of taped testimony at Article 39(a) session for Samples, October 19, 1993, 100–55, 198–215, 230–41.

44. Author's notes of Samples, October 25, 1993.

45. Ibid., October 27, 1993.

46. Interview with Rae, October 26, 1993.

47. Memorandum of Advice, U.S. v. Tritt, October 28, 1993.

48. William H. McMichael, "Flier's assault charge dropped," *Daily Press*, October 30, 1993.

49. Ibid.; interview with Miller, February 2, 1994.

50. Author's notes, Miller motion; interview with Lt. Cmdr. William C. Little; Order to Produce, U.S. v. Miller, November 4, 1993.

51. Defense Motion to Dismiss, U.S. v. Miller, November 5, 1993.

Chapter 11

1. Interview with Alan Bergstrom, October 22, 1993.

2. Author's notes of Article 39(a) session for Cmdr. Thomas R. Miller, November 8, 1993.

3. Interview with Cmdr. Steve Pietropaoli, U.S. Navy spokesman, November 8, 1993.

4. Interview with Rear Adm. James H. Finney, November 8, 1993.

5. Transcript of taped interview with Finney by agents of Department of Defense Inspector General (DOD-IG), October 2, 1992, 25–26.

6. Transcript of taped interview with Vice Adm. William C. Bowes, September 8, 1992, 15.

7. Author's notes of Miller, November 9, 1993.

8. Transcript of taped arguments, testimony at Article 39(a) session for Miller/Tritt, November 17, 1993, 375–464.

9. Ibid., November 29, 1993, 465–507; author's notes of same.

10. Author's notes, November 29, 1993.

11. Transcript of Miller/Tritt, 508–44.

12. Ibid., November 30, 1993, 548–627.

13. Report of Interview with Capt. Philip G. Howard by DOD-IG, December 8, 1992.

14. Miller/Tritt, 548–627.

15. Author's notes, November 30, 1993.

16. Ibid.

17. Miller/Tritt, 628–48; author's notes of same.

18. Ibid., December 1, 1993, 649–73.

19. Transcript of taped interview with Rear Adm. Robert J. Spane by DOD-IG, April 17, 1993.

20. Miller/Tritt, 649–73; author's notes of same.

21. Report of Interview with Daniel P. Whalen by DOD-IG, December 9, 1992.

22. Miller/Tritt, 674–709; author's notes of same.

23. Report of Interview with Lt. Ellen E. Moore by DOD-IG, September 15, 1992.

24. Miller/Tritt, December 2, 1993, 747–71.

25. Ibid., December 6, 1993, 851–74.

26. Reports of Interview with Cmdr. Kathleen Ramsey, Cmdr. Richard Martin, Robert Nordgren, Cmdr. David Cronk, Lt. Brian Lawler, Lt. John Wood, Lt. Jack Moriarty, Lt. James Quinn, Cmdr. John Hoefel, 1st Lt. Adam Tharp, Lt.j.g. Mike King, Jill Cooke, Lt. Cmdr. Larry Rice, Cmdr. Michael Sturm, Cmdr. Charles Nesby, Ray Powell, Ronald Rives, Lt. Joe Fordham, Lt. Cmdr. Richard Scudder, Eugene "Mule" Holmberg, Robert Lawson by DOD-IG and Naval Investigative Service, various dates.
27. Author's notes of Miller/Tritt, December 2, 6, 1993.
28. Ibid., December 13, 1993.
29. Ibid.
30. Ibid., December 14, 1993.
31. Report of Interview with Lt. Cmdr. Paul A. Larocque by DOD-IG, September 22, 1992; with Karye Y. Larocque, September 23, 1992.
32. Joe Taylor, "Navy's top brass watched raucous behavior at Tailhook," The Associated Press, December 9, 1993; Miller/Tritt, December 9, 1993, 933–63.
33. Author's notes of Miller/Tritt, December 14, 1993.
34. Joe Taylor, title unknown, The Associated Press, December 14, 1993.
35. Interviews with Rae, December 15 and 16, 1993.
36. Miller/Tritt, December 17, 1993, 1274–97.
37. See chapter 5, note 25.
38. Ibid., 1298–1337.
39. Miller/Tritt, 1298–1337.
40. Memorandum for trial counsel from John H. Dalton, December 21, 1993.
41. Interview with senior Navy official close to the investigation, March 25, 1996; with retired senior Navy official, April 9, 1996.

Chapter 12

1. Interview with Stanley R. Arthur, April 12, 1996.
2. Ibid.
3. Opinion of the Court, Samples v. Capt. William T. Vest and the U.S., U.S. Court of Military Appeals, January 11, 1994.
4. William H. McMichael, "New Tailhook trial ordered for Navy flier," *Daily Press*, January 12, 1994.
5. Opinion.
6. Various defense attorneys.
7. Author's notes of Article 39(a) session for Cmdr. Thomas R. Miller, Cmdr. Gregory E. Tritt and Lt. David Samples, January 28, 1994.
8. Interview with Don Marcari, January 28, 1994.
9. Author's notes, February 8, 1994.
10. See chapter 5, note 25.
11. Essential findings and ruling on defense motion to dismiss, U.S. v. Miller, Tritt and Samples, February 7, 1994 (presented on the 8th), 1–111.
12. Interview with Navy spokesman Cmdr. Steve Pietropaoli, February 8, 1994.
13. John Hall, Media General News Service, "Navy's investigations under fire," *Richmond Times-Dispatch*, February 10, 1994.
14. Susanne M. Schafer, "Former Navy secretary puzzles over Tailhook ruling," The Associated Press, February 10, 1994.
15. Essential findings, Miller/Tritt/Samples.

16. Interview with senior Navy official familiar with the Tailhook investigation, March 25, 1996.
17. Essential findings.
18. News releases, U.S. Navy Office of the Chief of Naval Information, February 11, 1994.
19. "Remaining Tailhook case is dismissed," *The Washington Post*, February 10, 1994; leaked unofficial summation of taped telephone conversations between Lt. Col. Geoffrey Lyon and Maj. Phil Seymour concerning the 19 Marine Tailhook cases, August 1992; interview with source familiar with the Marine inquiry, April 9, 1996.
20. Author's notes of February 11, 1994.
21. Interview with Cmdr. John Tull, Atlantic Fleet Surface Force, February 11, 1994.
22. Author's notes.
23. Transcript of taped testimony, Article 39(a) session for Lt. David Samples, October 15, 1993.
24. Senior Navy official.

Chapter 13

1. Various wire service reports, February 11 and 15, 1994.
2. *The Washington Post*, "Clinton assails GOP crime record," reprinted in the *Daily Press*, April 3, 1996.
3. Various wire service reports, February 15, 1994.
4. Ibid.
5. Press release from office of Sen. John Warner, R-Va., February 15, 1994.
6. Transcript of "Mac Neil/Lehrer Newshour," Show no. 4864, February 15, 1994.
7. Essential findings and ruling on defense motion to dismiss, U.S. v. Miller, Tritt and Samples, February 7, 1994 (presented on the 8th), 1–111.
8. William H. McMichael, "A New Ike returns," *Daily Press*, April 14, 1995.
9. Eric Schmitt, "Military women say complaints of sex harassment go unheeded," *The New York Times*, March 10, 1994.
10. John Diamond, "Admiral receives honorary retirement," The Associated Press, September 21, 1994.
11. Report generated by the nonprofit whistleblower group Government Accountability Project, Washington, D.C., and submitted to U.S. Navy July 11, 1994.
12. Peter J. Boyer, "Admiral Boorda's War," *The New Yorker*, Sept. 16, 1996.
13. Remarks of Sen. Daniel K. Inouye, D-Hawaii, June 28, 1994; Diamond.
14. Editorial, "Two Stars Are Plenty," *The New York Times*, April 14, 1994.
15. William H. McMichael, "Tailhook judge to retire, ending 35–year Navy career," *Daily Press*, May 4, 1994.
16. Michelle DeArmond, "Tailhook whistle-blower's award reaches $6.7 million," The Associated Press, November 1, 1994; various other news reports.
17. Interview with attorney familiar with the Tailhook settlements, April 11, 1996.
18. Interview with attorney knowledgable of the Senate Armed Services Committee's (SASC) handling of military nominees, April 11, 1996.
19. Statement from office of Navy Secretary John H. Dalton, August 29, 1995; interview with Charles W. Gittins, June 5, 1995.
20. Dalton statement.
21. Letter from Senators Sam Nunn, D-Ga., and Strom Thurmond, R-S.C., to Dalton, June 30, 1994.

22. Letters from Dalton to Nunn and Thurmond, August 22, 1994.
23. Gittins.
24. Interview with retired senior Navy official familiar with the Tailhook investigation, August 28, 1995; with senior Navy official, August 31, 1995.
25. Interview with source close to Senate Armed Services Committee, March 13, 1996.
26. Attorney, April 11, 1996.
27. Letter from R.J. Natter to Charlie Abell, March 29, 1995; Responses to Specific Questions from Naval Bureau of Personnel via Capt. Fred Becker to Abell, undated.
28. Retired senior Navy official, August 28, 1995.
29. Interview with Cmdr. Robert E. Stumpf, March 12, 1996.
30. Interview with Chris Cimko, Senate Armed Services Committee spokeswoman, August 28, 1995.
31. Interview with Capt. Bill Harlow, August 29, 1995.
32. Gittins.
33. Query response from U.S. Navy office of Chief of Naval Information, August 29, 1995.
34. Letter from Dalton to Thurmond, August 30, 1995; interview with Mike Powell, August 29, 1995.
35. Transcript of taped interview with Lt. Mike A. Bryan by DOD-IG, January 22, 1993; interview with Bryan, March 30, 1996.
36. Review of Naval Record of Lt. Cmdr. John W. Marshall, Board for Correction of Naval Records, September 28, 1995; interview with Alan Bergstrom, January 12, 1996.
37. Interview with Capt. Jerry "Popeye" Doyle, July 24, 1995.
38. Interview with source familiar with the Marine inquiry, August 30, 1995.
39. Bergstrom.
40. Robert J. Caldwell, "Another Tailhook atrocity," *The San Diego Union-Tribune*, January 1996.
41. Attorney knowledgable of SASC handling of military nominees, April 11, 1996.
42. Statement by Thurmond on Senate floor, March 13, 1996.
43. Gittins.
44. Stumpf, January 31, 1996.
45. Gittins, January 31, 1996.
46. Stumpf.
47. Bryan interview.
48. Attorney.
49. Notes of SASC hearing by Bob Kemper, *Daily Press*, March 12, 1996.
50. Stumpf, March 12, 1996.
51. Kemper.
52. Stumpf.
53. Thurmond.
54. Gittins.
55. Thurmond.
56. Statement by Nunn at meeting of SASC, June 26, 1992.
57. Attorney.
58. Retired senior Navy official, August 28, 1995.
59. Harlow.
60. Rowan Scarborough, "Navy leaked Stumpf letter," *The Washington Times*, March 27, 1996.

61. Interview with Stanley R. Arthur, April 12, 1996.
62. Gittins; Stumpf; retired senior Navy official; attorney. Punaro did not respond to a detailed August 7, 1996 query on his interest in Stumpf's case, whether he had knowledge of how the Armed Services Committee obtained the Letter of Caution Stanley Arthur gave Stumpf, and on his general attitude toward the Navy. Arnold Punaro's response to author's query, December 1996.
63. Gittins, March 16, 1996.
64. Various news accounts.
65. Gittins.
66. Letter to SASC from Stumpf, March 22, 1996; Letter to Dalton from Thurmond, March 1996. At this point, the Navy had apparently had enough of Tailhook queries from reporters—this one, at least. A March 29, 1996 query by the author containing questions about the Tailhook certification process, how many officers were on "the list," and the particular information the Navy was forwarding to the SASC on officers whose files had been flagged was never answered, despite a subsequent phone call, resending the faxed query, making telephone confirmation that it was received, and an additional follow-up call. Capt. Charles D. Connor took the other tack. In response to a June 1996 query about Navy Secretary John Dalton's telephone communications with Vice Adm. J. Paul Reason in May 1993, Connor, Dalton's special assistant for public affairs, sent a cordial, detailed reply within two weeks.
67. Interview with Stumpf, April 20, 1996.
68. Dale Eisman, "Stumpf decides to retire, giving up promotion battle," *The Virginian-Pilot*, July 13, 1996.
69. Interview with Stumpf, July 27, 1996.
70. Various sources, including individuals named, attorneys, and U.S. Navy.

Chapter 14

1. Transcript of taped interview with Lt. Gregory J. Geiss by Department of Defense, Office of the Inspector General (DOD-IG), January 26, 1993, 176.
2. DOD-IG report on Tailhook 91, Part 2, February 1993, X-3, 4 (see figure 16).
3. Atlantic Fleet Surface Force; Marine Corps Combast Development Command.
4. Dana Priest, "Burden eased for Tailhook officers," *The Washington Post*, October 1, 1996; Rick Maze, "Off the (Tail)hook?" *Navy Times*, October 14, 1996.
5. "Ex-Marine's spy sentence reduced 5 years by judge," The Associated Press, October 30, 1993; various other sources.
6. Eric Schmitt, "Iowa case sparks criticism against Navy probers," *The New York Times*, June 11, 1990; A.J. Plunkett, "Navy apologizes to family, says cause unknown," *Daily Press*, October 18, 1991.
7. Interview with senior Navy official familiar with the Tailhook investigation, March 25, 1996.
8. Ibid.
9. Interview with Don Marcari, February 8, 1994.
10. Tom Hays, "Investigators seek to question officers in 'Tailhook II'," The Associated Press, May 19, 1995.
11. Dana Priest, "Navy admiral punished in adultery case," *The Washington Post*, December 9, 1995; various other sources.
12. *The Washington Post*.
13. David Chernicky, "Woman's body found in NN park," *Daily Press*, June 28, 1995.

14. "Rape case alters Japanese-U.S. relations," The Associated Press, November 7, 1995.
15. Bradley Graham and John F. Harris, "Admiral retires after rape remark," *The Washington Post*, November 18, 1995.
16. William H. McMichael, "Navy's most senior fliers recall demands of the sky," *Daily Press*, February 29, 1996.
17. William H. McMichael, "Tailhook looms over farewell," *Daily Press*, March 16, 1996; author's notes of same.
18. Hearst Newspapers, "Former Navy Secretary asks leaders to defend their 'military culture,'" July 13, 1996.
19. Pacific Fleet Naval Air Force investigation into October 25, 1994, F-14 crash that killed Lt. Kara Hultgreen, February 24, 1995; *Los Angeles Times*, "New Navy report blames errors on woman pilot in fatal crash, March 22, 1995.
20. William H. McMichael, "A new Ike returns," *Daily Press*, April 14, 1995.

Index